A HISTORY AND ARCHAEOLOGY OF TAMESIDE

TAMESIDE
1700-1930

Michael Nevell

1993

TAMESIDE METROPOLITAN BOROUGH COUNCIL

A History and Archaeology of Tameside

Tameside 1700-1930

ISBN 1 871324 08 4

Published by
Tameside Metropolitan Borough Council

with
The Greater Manchester Archaeological Unit

Printed by
Bemrose-Shafron Printers Ltd
Chester

© Tameside Metropolitan Borough Council 1993

Preface

The Metropolitan Borough of Tameside was created in 1974 and brought together the nine towns of Ashton, Audenshaw, Denton, Droylsden, Dukinfield, Hyde, Longdendale, Mossley and Stalybridge. Since that time there has been no attempt to write a full-scale history of the area. This Borough has a rich and interesting past, and I felt that this should be documented so that we, and future generations, could increase our knowledge and understanding of our heritage.

The previous books in the series covered the period prior to 1066 (vol. 1) and 1066 to 1700 (vol. 2). This third volume brings the story of Tameside up to 1930 and describes in detail the major industries which contributed to the wealth of the country during the nineteenth century.

These three volumes, together with a projected fourth volume covering the major personalities who helped to shape the Borough's history, form an essential reference source on the area.

It is appropriate that this book should be published at this time with Tameside on the brink of a new and exciting period in its history, with major opportunities for economic regeneration and industrial development. Improved transport links will make this area more accessible to a greater number of people and these volumes will provide an important source of information for tourism initiatives in the Borough.

Councillor S. Roy Oldham
C.Eng. M.I. Mech.E
Leader of the Council

Acknowledgments

In the face of rapid change in social and economic affairs, perspectives created by our knowledge and understanding of the past can introduce balance and stability. The recent reorganization of local administrative groupings in Greater Manchester reflects and continues a process of organic change which has taken place over the centuries. The possibility of translating these theoretical historic values into practical benefits for the community arose in the course of a meeting between the leader of the Council, Councillor Roy Oldham, the Director of the Greater Manchester Archaeological Unit, Phil Mayes, the Director of Planning, Mike Eveson, through whose good offices the meeting was arranged, and Local Studies Librarian Alice Lock. Councillor Oldham pursued his belief in the value of the work and a publication programme was designed to cover the History of Tameside up to 1930 in three volumes. The responsibility for monitoring the progress of the commission for Tameside fell to Barry Delve, Assistant Director of Leisure Services (Libraries and Heritage). His support and that of the staff of the Local Studies Library at Stalybridge are gratefully acknowledged.

Many individuals kindly assisted in the research and writing of this third volume of *A History and Archaeology of Tameside*. Norman Bamford provided information on the collieries of Tameside. David Cordingley once more allowed access to the Stamford estate archives in Ashton-under-Lyne. Denton Local History Society gave access to its archives. Dr Douglas Farnie provided help with Chapter 3 and with other aspects of this volume. Clare Hartwell of the Victorian Society made useful comments on the development of Ashton-under-Lyne. I must especially thank Ian Haynes for allowing me to see a typescript of his forthcoming book on the cotton industry in Dukinfield, and his notes on the cotton industry in Mossley. John Hodgson of the John Rylands University Library of Manchester was good enough to hunt for various estate surveys in the Dunham Massey archives. Bill Johnson furnished information on the water supply of Tameside. Frank Kelsall of English Heritage provided advice on the development of Ashton-under-Lyne. Carol O'Mahony of the Portland Basin Museum allowed access to its archive. David Morris gave a great deal of help with the Listed Buildings of Tameside, as well as many ideas on the layout of Georgian and Regency Ashton-under-Lyne. Joyce Powell once more allowed extensive use of her personal archive. Alan Rose provided comments on some of the most notable religious buildings in Tameside. Their advice, help and suggestions have greatly enhanced the authority and scope of this volume. Certain private individuals and landowners gave access to specific sites. Mr and Mrs Shepherd allowed access to the Hodge Print Works site. Mr Eric Davenport of Cannon Ltd, Stockport, kindly took the author on a tour of the Wilsons' hat factory site. The owners and staff of Fizz Ltd allowed access to nos 25-7 Wellington Street in Ashton. Derek Pierce assisted the author during this building survey work. Thanks are also due to Alice Lock, Tameside Local Studies Librarian, and the staff of the Cheshire and Lancashire record offices for their tireless help and assistance over the last three years. Many colleagues at the Greater Manchester Archaeological Unit have also been involved in the production of this third volume. Anthony Mahon helped in gathering information on the textile mills of Tameside for Appendix 1. Edna Curry provided material on the public parks of Tameside, whilst Helen Boyd gave her usual care and attention to the production of the maps and plans. Judith Kent of the John Rylands University Library of Manchester assisted with the proof-reading. Catherine Nevell helped in compiling the index. If I have missed any persons from this long list, my apologies. A work such as this necessarily rests on the goodwill of many individuals. Finally, I must thank Dr Peter Arrowsmith who edited this volume with great thoroughness, carrying through substantial revisions. The success of the *History and Archaeology of Tameside* series is in large measure due to his work.

Michael Nevell
Greater Manchester Archaeological Unit

Contents

Chapter 1: The Sources

1.1	**Facing the Past**	1
1.2	**Documentary Evidence**	1
	National and local government records	2
	Ecclesiastical records	2
	Business, estate and family records	3
	Trade directories	4
1.3	**Map Evidence**	4
1.4	**Photographic Evidence**	6
1.5	**Industrial Archaeology**	6
1.6	**Contemporary and Secondary Sources**	7
	Local accounts	7
	Modern studies	7

Chapter 2: An Industrial Society

2.1	**Introduction**	8
2.2	**The Demography of Tameside 1700-1930**	8
	Population growth 1700-1800	8
	The census and population growth 1801-1931	9
	The boom years 1801-61	11
	The slow down in growth 1861-1931	13
2.3	**Local Government**	13
	The spread of local government	13
	The local public services	17
2.4	**Trade Unionism and Factory Conditions**	18
	Early combinations and the cotton industry	18
	The Chartist movement in Tameside	19
	The new factory system and working conditions	21
2.5	**The Rise and Fall of Industrial Paternalism**	22
2.6	**Leisure and the Working Class**	24
	Paternalism and leisure	24
	Public houses	25
	Leisure and the cotton industry in the early twentieth century	25
2.7	**Rural Society and the Industrial Revolution**	26

Chapter 3: The Textile Industry

3.1	**Introduction**	28
3.2	**Outline History**	28
	The rural textile industry in the eighteenth century	28
	The number of sites	28
	Innovators and factory pioneers 1771-1853	30
	The rise of specialization 1853-1901	32
	Boom and bust 1901-30	33

3.3	**The Development of the Main Centres**	35
	Ashton-under-Lyne (including Audenshaw)	35
	Droylsden	39
	Dukinfield	40
	Hyde (including Denton)	43
	Longdendale	45
	Mossley	48
	Stalybridge	53
3.4	**Selected Textile Building Complexes**	57
	Hodge Print Works, Broadbottom, *c* 1763-1913	57
	Wagstaffe's factories, Mottram, 1786 - *c* 1813	60
	Broad Mills (Broadbottom Mills), 1801/2 - *c* 1938	61
	Brunswick Mill, Mossley, *c* 1890-1990	63
	Cavendish Mill, Ashton-under-Lyne, 1884-1934	63
	Premier Mill, Stalybridge, 1906-82	64

Chapter 4: Hatting

4.1	**Introduction**	66
4.2	**The Felt Hatting Process**	66
	Hand production	66
	Technical improvements	69
4.3	**The Development of the Felt and Silk Hatting Industries**	70
	Early history	70
	Depression	73
	Revival in the late nineteenth century	74
4.4	**Straw Hat Making in Tameside**	76
4.5	**The Main Hatting Firms**	76
	Joseph Howe & Sons, Annan Street, Denton	76
	J Moores & Sons, Heaton Street, Denton	76
	Joseph Wilson & Sons Ltd, Wilton St, Denton	77
	James Higinbotham & Son, Mount Street, Hyde	79

Chapter 5: Agriculture

5.1	**Introduction**	80
5.2	**Farming before 1750**	80
5.3	**Farming 1750-1873**	83
	Cattle	84
	Sheep	85
	Arable farming	86
	Market gardening and Ashton Moss	86
	Enclosure	86
	The mini-rebuilding *c* 1750 - *c* 1873	87
5.4	**Farming 1873-1930**	88
5.5	**Farms, Tenants and Rents**	89
	Size of farms	89
	Leases and rents	91

5.6 The Stamford and Tollemache Estates   92
     The Stamford estate   92
     The Tollemache estate   93

Chapter 6: Coal Mining

6.1 Introduction   96

6.2 The Development of the Industry   96
     The Lancashire coalfield   96
     Technological developments   96
     Transportation   98
     Output and colliery numbers 1700-1850   99
     Rationalization and decline 1850-1930   101

6.3 The Collieries of Tameside   101
     Ashton and Audenshaw   101
     Denton and Haughton   102
     Dukinfield, Newton and Hyde   104
     Mottram   105

Chapter 7: Secondary Industries

7.1 Introduction   108

7.2 Ironworking and Engineering   108

7.3 Building Trade   111
     Raw materials   111

7.4 The Retail Trade   113
     The growth of the retail trade   113
     Co-operatives   114
     Joseph Booth's grocer's shop, Broadbottom   115

Chapter 8: The Infrastructure

8.1 Introduction   118

8.2 Transport I: Turnpikes   118

8.3 Transport II: Canals   121
     National background   121
     The building of the canal system in Tameside   122
     The Tameside canals and railway competition   123
     The surviving canal fabric   124

8.4 Transport III: Railways   126
     The railways of Tameside   126
     The impact of the railways   128

8.5 Transport IV: Buses and Tramways   130

8.6 Water Supply   131

8.7 The Gas Industry   132

8.8 Electricity   134

Chapter 9: Urban Communities

9.1	**Introduction**	136
9.2	**The New Urban Landscape**	136
	Workers' housing	137
	Weavers' cottages	140
	Early town houses	140
	Manufacturers' houses	141
	Community and public buildings	142
	Public parks	145
	Urban corn-mills	145
9.3	**Ashton**	146
	Outline development	146
	The design of the Georgian and Regency town	147
	The later development of Ashton	149
	Oxford Mills community	151
	Park Bridge ironworking community	152
9.4	**Audenshaw**	152
	Audenshaw village	152
	Hooley Hill	152
9.5	**Denton**	153
	Dane Bank hatting community	153
9.6	**Droylsden**	154
	Fairfield Moravian settlement	155
9.7	**Dukinfield**	156
	The eighteenth-century township	156
	Dukinfield Circus	156
	Nineteenth-century Dukinfield	156
9.8	**Hyde**	157
	Gee Cross	157
	Hyde	158
9.9	**Longdendale**	161
	Mottram	161
	Hollingworth	162
	Broadbottom	163
9.10	**Mossley**	163
9.11	**Stalybridge**	166

Chapter 10: Conclusion   168

Appendix 1: The Textile Sites of Tameside   171

Appendix 2: The Earl of Stamford Records in the Cordingley Archives, Ashton-under-Lyne: Part 2, the Maps   180

Glossary   181

Sources   184

Index   194

List of Figures

Fig 2.1	Aggregative analysis of Ashton parish registers in the eighteenth century	10
Fig 2.2	Parishes and townships in Tameside in 1800	14
Fig 2.3	Local government in Tameside in 1930 showing municipal boroughs, urban districts and civil parishes	15
Fig 3.1	The mills of Ashton and Audenshaw	34
Fig 3.2	The mills of Droylsden	38
Fig 3.3	The mills of Dukinfield	41
Fig 3.4	The mills of Hyde and Denton	42
Fig 3.5	The mills of Longdendale	47
Fig 3.6	The mills of Mossley	49
Fig 3.7	Weavers' cottages – no 18 Carhill Road, Mossley, and nos 1 and 2 Higher Croft, Stalybridge	51
Fig 3.8	Brunswick Mill, Mossley	52
Fig 3.9	The mills of Stalybridge	54
Fig 3.10	Premier Mill, Stalybridge	56
Fig 3.11	Plan of Hodge Print Works, Broadbottom, in 1841	59
Fig 3.12	Wagstaffe's Factory, Mottram	61
Fig 3.13	Broad Mills, Broadbottom, in about 1900	62
Fig 3.14	Ground-floor plan and elevation of Cavendish Mill, Ashton-under-Lyne	65
Fig 4.1	Distribution of hat shops in Hyde and Gee Cross in 1857	72
Fig 4.2	Surviving hat factories in Denton	75
Fig 4.3	Phased plan of J Moores & Sons' factory	77
Fig 4.4	Phased plan of J Wilson and Sons' factory	79
Fig 5.1	Distribution of farmsteads in Tameside in 1700	82
Fig 5.2	Distribution of mid-nineteenth-century farmsteads in Tameside	84
Fig 5.3	Roe Cross Farm, no 49 Old Road, Mottram	87
Fig 5.4	Hollingworth Hall Farm in the early twentieth century	88
Fig 5.5	Hollingworth Old Hall and Thorncliffe estates in 1890	90
Fig 5.6	Farmholdings on the Tatton estate in Werneth township in 1857	91
Fig 5.7	The Stamford estate in Tameside in the early nineteenth century	92
Fig 5.8	Tollemache estate holdings in Mottram in 1919	94
Fig 6.1	Collieries in Tameside	100
Fig 6.2	Plan of Mottram showing collieries and coal seams	106
Fig 7.1	Distribution of quarries and brick works in mid-nineteenth-century Tameside	111
Fig 7.2	Plan of John Hall & Son (Dukinfield) Ltd, tile and brick makers	112
Fig 8.1	The turnpikes of Tameside	120
Fig 8.2	The canals of Tameside	123
Fig 8.3	Portland Basin, Ashton-under-Lyne	124
Fig 8.4	The Ashton Canal Warehouse	125
Fig 8.5	The late nineteenth-century railway network of Tameside	126
Fig 8.6	Britannia Mill and the L&NWR through Mossley	129
Fig 8.7	The reservoirs of Tameside	131
Fig 8.8	Plan of Ashton gas works, 1822	133
Fig 9.1	Urban areas in Tameside in 1700	138
Fig 9.2	Urban areas in Tameside in 1841-2	139
Fig 9.3	Urban areas in Tameside in 1913	141
Fig 9.4	Plan and internal elevations of Ashton baths	143
Fig 9.5	The Stalybridge corn-mill	146

Fig 9.6	The Regency planned town of Ashton as envisaged in the early nineteenth century	149
Fig 9.7	Third-storey plan, as existing, of the loomshop in Wellington Street, Ashton	150
Fig 9.8	Plan of the Oxford Mills community	151
Fig 9.9	Plan of the Dane Bank hatting community	154
Fig 9.10	Plan of nos 32, 31C and 31B Fairfield Square	155
Fig 9.11	Plan and elevation of Harewood Lodge, Broadbottom	164

Figs 3.7, 3.8, 3.14, 5.3, 9.4, 9.10 and 9.11 are reproduced with kind permission from plans and elevations held by David Morris, Planning Officer (Conservation) for Tameside MBC.

Figs 2.2, 2.3, 3.1, 3.2, 3.3, 3.4, 3.5, 3.6, 3.9, 4.1, 4.2, 6.1, 7.1, 8.1, 8.2, 8.5, 8.7, 9.1, 9.2 and 9.3 use as their base map the Ordnance Survey 1in to 1 mile Third Edition (large sheet series) Sheet 36, published in 1913. Figs 5.5, 5.6, 5.8 and 6.2 use as their base maps the Ordnance Survey 6in to 1 mile (county quarter sheet series) Cheshire Sheet XI, Editions of 1910 and 1911, and Cheshire Sheet III SE, Edition of 1911. The base map of Fig 8.3 is the Ordnance Survey 1:2500 series Lancashire Sheet CV.6, Revision of 1933.

List of Plates

Plate 1.1	Hooley Hill in 1923	3
Plate 1.2	Sketch plan of Ashton town in the period 1799-1803	5
Plate 2.1	Cotton operatives at Cedar Mill, Ashton	9
Plate 2.2	Ashton Old Court House in the 1880s	16
Plate 2.3	Ashton baths	23
Plate 3.1	Broad Mills, Broadbottom	29
Plate 3.2	Cavendish Mill, Ashton	37
Plate 3.3	Dry Mill, Mottram	60
Plate 4.1	Mechanized hat body making in Denton	67
Plate 4.2	J Moores & Sons' factory, Denton	68
Plate 4.3	J Wilson & Sons' factory, Wilton Street, Denton	78
Plate 5.1	Hollingworth Hall farmhouse	81
Plate 6.1	Hand digging for coal near the Hague, Mottram	97
Plate 6.2	Ashton Moss Colliery	103
Plate 7.1	Park Bridge ironworks	109
Plate 7.2	Joseph Booth's grocer's shop and Robert Booth's butcher's shop, Broadbottom	117
Plate 8.1	Portland Basin, Ashton-under-Lyne	119
Plate 8.2	Broadbottom viaduct	128
Plate 9.1	Dukinfield Circus	137
Plate 9.2	Dukinfield town hall	144
Plate 9.3	Old Square, Ashton	148
Plate 9.4	Loomshop in Wellington Street, Ashton	150
Plate 9.5	Housing in Hyde town centre	160
Plate 9.6	Weavers' cottages, Summerbottom in Broadbottom	162
Plate 10.1	Georgian shop front, Stamford Street, Ashton	169

Plates 1.1, 2.1, 2.2, 4.1, 6.2, 7.1, 9.1, 9.2 and 9.3 are reproduced by kind permission of Tameside Local Studies Library; Plates 2.3, 3.2, 4.2, 4.3, 8.1 and 9.5 by kind permission of David Morris, Planning Officer (Conservation) for Tameside MBC; Plates 3.1, 3.3, 6.1, 8.2 and 9.6 by kind permission of Mrs Joyce Powell; and Plate 1.2 by kind permission of the Reverend D W Hirst, Rector of St Michael's Parish Church, Ashton-under-Lyne.

Chapter 1

The Sources

'To study something of great age until one grows familiar with it and almost to live in its time, is not merely to satisfy a curiosity or to establish aimless truths: it is rather to fulfil a function whose appetite has always rendered History a necessity. By the recovery of the Past, stuff and being are added to us; our lives which, lived in the present only, are a film or surface, take on body – are lifted into one dimension more. The soul is fed.'

(H Belloc, *The Old Road*, 1910, 9)

1.1 Facing the Past

The rate of change in the society and the landscape of Britain has increased immeasurably during the last 300 years. The catalyst for this change was the Industrial Revolution which in the late eighteenth and early nineteenth centuries, through increased mechanization, innovations in technology and improvements in transport, shifted the basis of our society from agriculture to the manufacture of goods. At the forefront of this revolution were the textile-producing towns of south-east Lancashire and north-east Cheshire, centred on the great 'cottonopolis' of Manchester. Modern perceptions of the Industrial Revolution in the North-West are often dominated by Manchester, and indeed its importance should not be denied. Long before the Industrial Revolution it had been the largest town in its region and in the late eighteenth century it embarked on a process of rapid population growth and expansion which by the early decades of the nineteenth century had transformed it into arguably the world's first industrial city.

At the same time the role of the surrounding towns was also of great significance. In areas such as Tameside textiles were already an important element in the local economy before the Industrial Revolution, and Manchester's own growth rested as much upon its role as a commercial centre for this local industry as upon its own textile output. Indeed, it was in areas such as Tameside that the earliest textile mills were established in the region, powered by fast flowing streams; Manchester, which lacked this natural advantage, had to await the introduction of steam power in the 1780s before a comparable power source was available. Furthermore, from the mid-nineteenth century the success of the neighbouring industrial towns meant that Manchester's own textile industry decreased in importance as its commercial role grew, and such towns increasingly took on the mantle of the chief textile manufacturing centres of the North-West.

The effect of the new textile industry on the population and landscape of Tameside was profound, since it encouraged the concentration of large numbers of people in burgeoning manufacturing towns, generated new industries such as engineering, fostered old ones such as coal mining and helped the creation of much of the transport infrastructure of the Borough.

This third volume of *A History and Archaeology of Tameside*, covering the period 1700-1930, therefore takes as its dominant themes the industrialization and accompanying urbanization of the Borough. The work is neither a narrative history nor a social commentary nor a narrow economic study. Rather it uses historical and archaeological landscape techniques to investigate the development of the manmade environment in a period of rapid social and economic change.

1.2 Documentary Evidence

A wealth of documentary evidence exists for the period 1700-1930. Ranging from personal letters and diaries to Parliamentary reports, the breadth of the material is daunting. Inevitably any study of this period has to be selective as to the material which it uses, for it often seems that the amount of surviving information increases exponentially the closer one comes to the present. In this study a variety of sources have been used to highlight the development of the environment of Tameside and the way in which this affected the local population. These include national

Chapter 1 The Sources

and local government records, ecclesiastical documents, business records and family and estate papers. Often these sources provide information for more than one topic.

National and local government records

Of the national and local government records held in the county record offices of Cheshire, Greater Manchester and Lancashire and in other local collections, either in the original or in copies, use has been made of a number of categories of material.

Land tax returns for the Cheshire part of Tameside have been extensively employed in this study to reconstruct landholding patterns and the spread of early industry. These documents relate to a tax collected by county authorities, between *c* 1692 and 1832. From 1780 the returns were used to show the entitlement to vote in Parliamentary elections, which in the period 1780-1832 was based upon ownership of freehold land worth 40s per annum. (In practice prior to the Reform Bill of 1832 less than 5% of the total population of England and Wales was entitled to vote.) The land tax itself was assessed at the rate of 4s to the pound and the returns, divided by borough and township, listed all freeholders (Cootes 1982, 196; Riden 1987, 62-3). The quality and quantity of additional information within the returns vary with time and place. Until the Land Tax Commissioners Act of 1797-8 the clerk of the peace was the recipient of land tax returns for the county, but from 1798 its collection was the responsibility of commissioners appointed for each hundred (Williams 1991, 63). Within Tameside this administrative change had the effect of improving the quality and scope of the evidence included. Before this date only the name of the freeholder and the amount owed was usually included, although occasionally details of occupation were mentioned. After this date both the landowners and land occupiers were listed, along with the amount of tax paid. Unfortunately, the amount of rent paid, the number of tenants in occupation and the parcel of land on which the tax was assessed were not always included, this being particularly the case in the period 1812-25.

Acts passed and reports commissioned by Parliament in the eighteenth and nineteenth centuries have also been used in this study. Most of the acts relate to the granting of permission to build and manage turnpikes, canals, railways, reservoirs or gas works and copies of many of the relevant documents can be found in the Tameside Local Studies Library in Stalybridge. Various Parliamentary papers have proved useful in relation to the history of specific industrial sites and the working conditions of their employees. In particular the Stanway returns of 1833, published as an appendix to the Supplementary Report of the Factory Commissioners Part 1 (PP 1834 xix), provide valuable evidence for the textile industry in the Borough.

Unfortunately, one of the major sources of information relating to farming and domestic-based industries in the post-medieval period, the practice of compiling inventories, declined sharply after 1750. Nevertheless, wills and inventories, where they exist, are a useful tool in the assessment of the origins and growth of the Industrial Revolution in Tameside. This approach is exemplified by Smith's doctoral thesis in which such evidence was used to assess the origins of the hatting industry in the North-West (Smith 1980).

Local government records have also been used in this study, especially those relating to the development of public utilities such as water, gas and electricity. Again, a large proportion of this material can be found in the Tameside Local Studies Library in Stalybridge. Much remains to be gleaned from the minutes and correspondence of the various local boards in nineteenth-century Tameside, the precursors of the later municipal boroughs and urban district councils, as regards the attitude of local government to the problems of rapid industrialization and urbanization. One group of local government documents which highlights the spread of urban development, industry and the retail trade comprises the local rate books, which at their best detail landownership and occupancy property by property, giving the value of the property and the occupations of the residents. Similarly, the census returns from 1841 onwards provide details of individual households, including places of birth and occupations and occasionally such additional information as the number of people in an individual's employment or the size of his landholding. However, the analysis of both categories of material as regards the development of Tameside society in the nineteenth century is still in its infancy, and the volume of material is such that for the present survey these sources have been used only in selective cases.

Ecclesiastical records

Parish registers survive both for the Anglican parish churches in the Borough, St Michael's, in Mottram-in-Longdendale, and St Michael's, in Ashton-under-Lyne, and for many of the non-conformist chapels. As regards the historical value of the Anglican parish registers, the strength of the non-conformist movement in both parishes in the late eighteenth and nineteenth centuries has undoubtedly led to under-registration (although until 1840 all births were required by law to be registered at an Anglican church or chapel). As a result, their use for the analysis of

Plate 1.1 Hooley Hill, Audenshaw, in 1923.
This early aerial view shows the core of the nineteenth-century town, looking south towards Denton, with its linear development of terraced housing and hat factories. Much of this area was demolished in the mid-twentieth century.

population and the distribution of trades and professions is problematical from the late eighteenth century onwards. The value of the Mottram parish registers is further degraded by the virtual absence of any reference to the trades or professions of the parishioners in the eighteenth century (CRO MF41/1-9). This is in contrast to the Ashton registers, which can be tentatively used to assess the relative importance of various trades in the early industrial era (Brierley 1928).

Business, estate and family records

Business records for the Borough, held in the Tameside Local Studies Library and other collections, relate chiefly to textile firms but records also survive relating to engineering firms, including the Park Bridge ironworks, and mining companies, including Ashton Moss and Denton collieries (TLSL DDL, DD 60, DD 83).

Estate and family records provide an extensive source of material and can be divided into two categories. The first are those papers concerned with older family estates in Tameside, such as the Stamford, Tatton and Tollemache estates. These contain details of estate management, farming practice and industrial development invaluable to the landscape study of the Borough and have been widely used for the present work. The second group of documents relates to those industrial families and political figures who rose to prominence in the nineteenth century. These reflect the aims and aspirations of the individuals involved in their compilation and are among the most personal evidence surviving from this period; however, much of this material is peripheral to the present work and has been used only sparingly.

Chapter 1 The Sources

Trade directories

Trade directories are lists of names and addresses in specific localities, usually divided by township or parish, published from the mid-eighteenth century until the 1930s. They provide information on the nobility, gentry, trade, public buildings and services of a particular area. They are useful as both a general guide to the scope of society within a given area in a particular period, and as a catalogue of specific concerns. The earliest volumes to include material relating to Tameside begin in the 1780s and are thus an important aid to the study of the first phase of industrialization. Nevertheless, there are specific problems inherent in this source which need to be borne in mind.

The entries themselves tended to vary throughout the life of the directories, the most detailed entries often being those from the mid- to late nineteenth century. As private ventures the publishers of each directory solicited the commercial concerns of the chosen area for business, with the result that the directories represent an unknown percentage of the individuals and occupations in a given area. The value of the evidence of each entry needs to be carefully weighed. If a specific address is not given for an industrial activity then the entry may be referring to the home address of the owner. Indeed some entries are so vague that it is difficult to tell in which township the individual or business in question was located.

As well as general directories use has been made of a more specific publication, Worrall's *Cotton Spinners' and Manufacturers' Directory*, in 1931 renamed *The Lancashire Textile Industry*. First published in 1882 and then annually from 1884 until 1970, this contains valuable information regarding both the cotton and woollen industries in Tameside and includes the textile districts of Broadbottom, Dukinfield, Hollingworth, Hyde, Mottram and Stalybridge in Cheshire, as well as Ashton, Denton, Droylsden and Mossley in Lancashire. Farnie has reviewed the reliability and the drawbacks of these directories as a source for the decline of the textile industry in the North-West. Each volume includes details of the spindleage, looms, products and names of every firm in each cotton district of the Lancashire textile region, making possible a continuous census of these firms and districts over an 88 year period. The shortcomings of this source lie in the omission of such details as the consumption of raw cotton or coal, the power supply, the number of employees and the distinction between ring spindles and mule spindles. However, even with these failings, Farnie concluded that 'the directories remain an indispensable and authoritative source for any student of history' (Farnie 1990a, 32-3).

1.3 Map Evidence

The map base for the period 1700-1930 is particularly extensive for Tameside, although the researcher has to be aware of the aims of the cartographer and the context of the survey (Porter 1990, 21-31). The 1in and 6in to 1 mile Ordnance Survey maps of the period 1841-1930 contain a wealth of information as regards the development of the urban and rural landscapes of the Borough, including highly localized information concerning agriculture, industry and the communications network. The larger 1:2500 scale maps and the 50in to 1 mile survey of Ashton in 1850, which also includes parts of Stalybridge and Dukinfield, can be used to assess the development of specific buildings, since they often show internal partitions and sometimes even label rooms. Extensive as this evidence is, the researcher has to be aware that the time lag between the survey and publication of these maps could be great. The First Edition 6in survey of Cheshire, for instance, was undertaken in 1870-2, but not published until 1880-2. Furthermore, later editions did not always fully revise the whole sheet.

Prior to the publication of the first Ordnance Survey maps covering Tameside, there is a large body of estate and parish maps from the eighteenth and early nineteenth centuries. The earliest and largest group are those of the Stamford estate, covering the period from 1765 onwards. This collection is now divided between the Tameside Local Studies Library and the archive of Cordingleys in Ashton, the stewards of the residue of the Stamford estate in Tameside. A list of the maps held by Cordingleys is given in Appendix 2.

The Stamford estate owned more than half of the total area of the Borough during the eighteenth and nineteenth centuries and the maps include land in Audenshaw, Ashton, Hattersley, Mossley and Stalybridge. Of particular value is a series of large-scale plans spanning the years 1787-1832 and relating to the layout of the Georgian and Regency planned town of Ashton (ESRCA 14, 16-23). Most of the maps and plans were produced to illustrate a proposed or recently completed development for housing, industrial or agricultural needs, and the amount of detail varies depending on the purpose for which the survey was made and the scale at which it was taken. In general their quality is very high, and details given include the name and the date of the survey, field-names, road details including widths, the names and alignments of turnpikes, sometimes the names of lessees and their rent, and plans of farm and urban buildings. The largest plans, of Ashton parish and Hattersley (ESRCA 15; TLSL DDS 838), were accompanied by a separate schedule giving details of tenancies, but in the case of the Ashton estate plan of 1765 this has not survived.

Chapter 1 The Sources

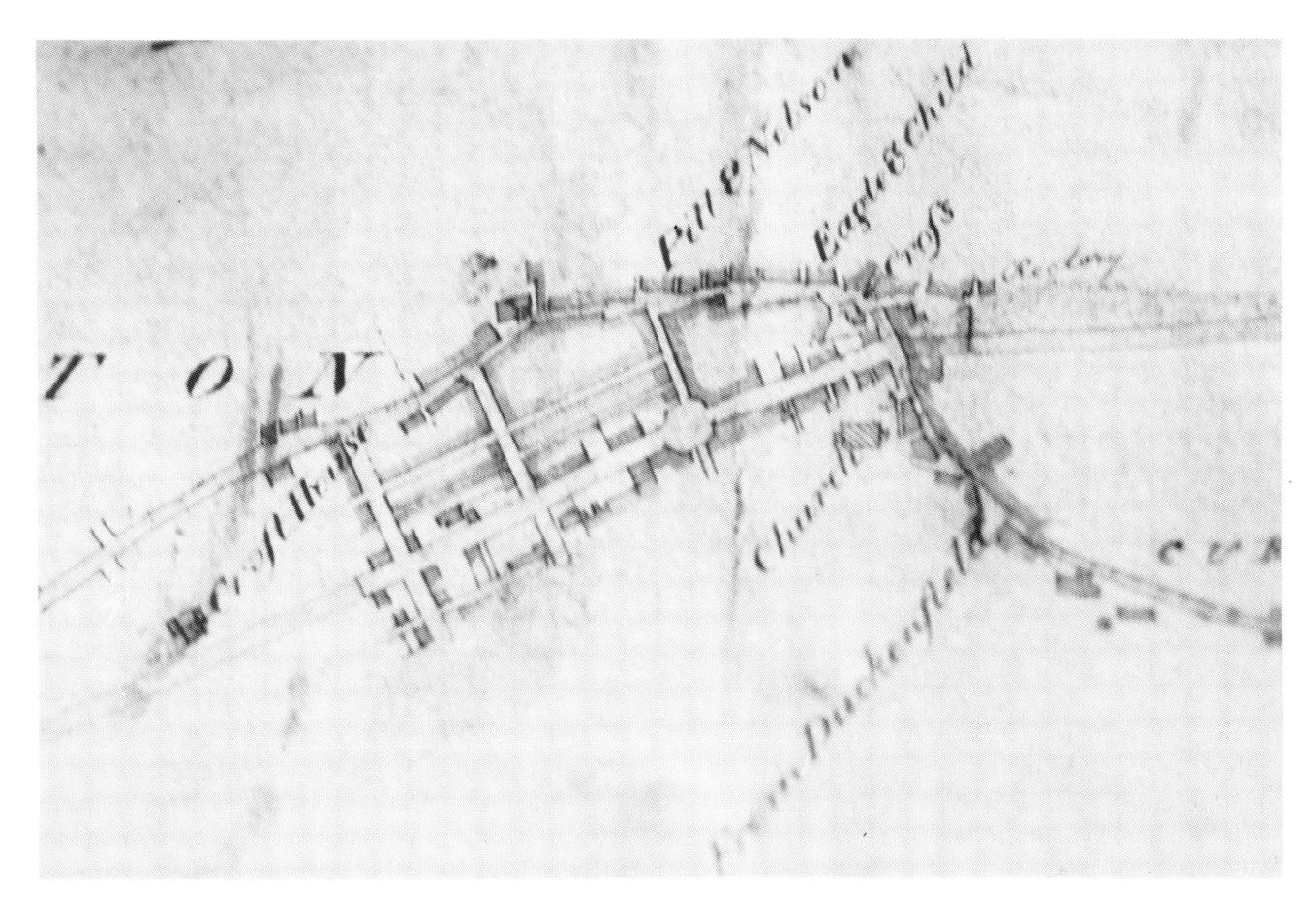

Plate 1.2 Sketch plan of Ashton town in the period 1799-1803.
Map evidence forms an important aspect of any landscape assessment, although the details shown may be selective. This sketch of Ashton is part of a much larger plan, drawn to show improvements to the Salters Brook Turnpike Trust and now held at St Michael's Parish Church, Ashton-under-Lyne. The fronts of the buildings along Old Street and Scotland Street are shown in detail and the two inns where the coaches stopped are named, but the rest of the town is depicted in sketch fashion. The plan is undated, although internal evidence, such as the presence of the Huddersfield Canal and the absence of Delamere Street Mill on the corner of Old Street and Delamere Street, indicates that it was drawn in the years 1799-1803. It is the only known plan of Ashton to show the development of the Georgian town between 1787 and *c* 1819.

Two large-scale surveys of Cheshire and Lancashire were undertaken in the late eighteenth century, and these have been useful in identifying historic town cores and the spread of early industries. The earliest of these is Burdett's map of Cheshire, surveyed during the years 1772-4 and published in 1777. It incorporated some of the latest ideas in county surveying, using a scientific framework of triangulation as the base for the survey, while the large scale of 1in to 1 mile enabled a series of conventional symbols to be used to distinguish town sizes and types of local industry. Harley and Laxton have assessed the reliability of Burdett's portrait of the Cheshire landscape of this period and concluded that although the map does have certain limitations, especially in comparison with other county maps of the period, 'it can provide valuable information about the landscape and economic geography of 18th-century Cheshire' (Harley & Laxton 1974, 18).

In particular the map provides the first county-wide cartographic evidence for much of the rural settlement of the area, the road system and the early development of the canal system. In north-east Cheshire, for example, it indicates the scattered nature of rural settlement, the only substantial settlements shown being Mottram and Tintwistle. However, the representations are generalized and comparison with contemporary estate plans indicates that not every isolated farmstead was included. No field boundaries are shown and there is unsatisfactory depiction of woodland and a lack of differentiation between common, heath and wastelands. Its depiction of industry is patchy, with only water-powered mills and coal pits receiving detailed attention, and as far as Tameside is concerned the sites shown are almost certainly under-representative (*ibid*, 20-33). Many of the same problems of interpretation surround Yates's map of Lancashire, surveyed in 1775-80 and published in

1786 (Harley 1968, 11-12). However, Yates's survey appears to provide more comprehensive coverage than Burdett's, especially in its record of industry and in the several categories of rural land use which are included (*ibid*, 16-19).

Similar restrictions need to be borne in mind when assessing the 1in to 1 mile county surveys of Lancashire and Cheshire by Greenwood in 1818-19 and of Cheshire by Teesdale in 1828-9 and Bryant in 1829-31, although these do provide a valuable insight into the landscape of Tameside in the early nineteenth century.

Among the more specific nineteenth-century maps and plans are those relating to public utilities, such as water and gas, or to communications, such as proposed turnpike, canal and railway alignments. Many of these were 'deposited' plans, that is they were the basis for the authorizing of legislation and were thus deposited in the local quarter sessions and in the House of Lords records office. Although confined to specific lines or small areas, they often contain details of the immediate landscape and properties through which they passed. In Tameside these maps have provided useful material relating to the urban spread of Ashton in the 1790s and 1800s (Plate 1.2), Broadbottom in the 1810s and 1825s, Hyde in 1832, Mossley and Stalybridge in 1826, and Mottram and Hollingworth in the period 1800-32 (CRO QDP 39, 67 B2/5, 67 1/2, 110; Powell Collection). Furthermore, the local government reforms of the 1830s led to a number of surveys of those towns requesting borough status, and plans of these including Ashton and the surrounding parish can be found in the report of the Municipal Corporation Boundaries Commission (Dawson 1837). Tithe maps should also be classed within this group. Produced as a result of the Tithe Commutation Act of 1836, each tithe map usually shows all or part of a single township and was accompanied by a schedule, or apportionment. Not only are the maps themselves of a high cartographic standard but also the schedules list the owners of individual landholdings, their occupants, the size of fields, usually with their field-names, their agricultural usage and their value. Tithe maps, variously dated to between 1839 and 1849, were drawn for all of the townships of Tameside with two exceptions: Ashton township and parish, for which a comparable map was already available in the form of the 1765 Stamford survey, and the Quickmere division of Saddleworth township and parish for which a map was also already in existence, dating from 1822 (Barnes *et al* 1983).

1.4 Photographic Evidence

From the mid-nineteenth century onwards much photographic material is available relating to the social and economic history of Tameside, and selections of the archive now held in the Tameside Local Studies Library and in private collections have been published over the last two decades for many of the former nine towns which make up the modern Borough (J Powell 1977; Lock 1981a; 1981b; 1982; 1983; Wilkins-Jones 1979). For the student of landscape history these records contain much detail of the urban and rural landscape which has now gone (Plate 1.1). In particular, photographs of prominent public buildings, industrial sites and streets long since demolished help to flesh out the written record of the growth of the nine towns.

By applying rectified photographic techniques to such old photographs, it has been possible to reconstruct for the present study particular elevations of lost buildings in Tameside, where those buildings were unique or among the best of their type. This technique was used in the reconstruction of the elevations of Wagstaffe's Factory in Mottram, the Ashton Canal Warehouse in Ashton (now much reduced after a fire in 1972) and Stalybridge Corn Mill (Figs 3.12, 8.4 & 9.5). While such a technique cannot provide a wholly accurate record of the site, it nevertheless furnishes an elevation which may be used in comparison with other standing buildings elsewhere in the region and so help to place these lost structures in their appropriate typological contexts.

1.5 Industrial Archaeology

The term industrial archaeology is applied to the study, through physical remains, of the course of the industrialization of society and its impact on technology and people. The discipline was only recognized as a separate study in the mid-twentieth century and involves the detailed examination of industrial monuments in situ through excavation or building survey, or both. Categories of such monuments include cotton factories, corn-mills, collieries, communications systems, such as canals, railways and roads, and domestic housing. Contemporary machinery and equipment are also recorded in detail. The discipline also extends to more traditional methods of historical archaeology, including the study of documentary sources, economic history and geography. This approach is exemplified by the recent *Cotton Mills of Greater Manchester*, by Williams with Farnie (1992).

In the North-West pioneering research in this field was undertaken by Owen Ashmore in the 1960s and 1970s. His study of industrial Lancashire, published in 1969, laid the framework for the understanding of many of the classic industrial monuments of the period 1770-1914, cotton mills, collieries and canals.

The culmination of his work was the publication in 1982 of *The Industrial Archaeology of North-West England*. This is a gazetteer of the surviving major categories of industrial sites in each district of the North-West, encompassing factories, transport systems and industrial housing. While not comprehensive it does provide a useful guide to the major industries of each town in the region. Ashmore's separate study of industrial Ashton was the first case history of its type for Tameside (Ashmore 1974). More recently there have been various overviews of the cotton industry in the Borough (Haynes 1987, 1990, forthcoming; Williams with Farnie 1992) as well as a study of the hatting industry in Denton (Holding 1986). Interest in the industrial archaeology of the Borough has also been furthered by a series of restoration works beginning with the renovation and partial re-opening of the Ashton, Huddersfield and Peak Forest canals from the 1960s onwards. This was followed in the 1980s by the restoration of the Ashton Canal Warehouse of 1834 and its conversion into the Portland Basin Museum, and in the 1980s by excavation and conservation at two sites in Broadbottom – the bleaching baths at Hodge Print Works and the cotton-spinning and weaving complex at Broad Mills.

1.6 Contemporary and Secondary Sources

In addition to the sources discussed above extensive use has been made of contemporary accounts and secondary sources. The first of these includes descriptions of living conditions in Ashton by Engels in 1844 and Reach in 1849 (Aspin 1972), while the second comprises material such as the town histories of Hyde and Denton by Thomas Middleton (1932; 1936) and unpublished dissertations on specific aspects of industrialization in the Borough, be they M Powell's study of education in mid-nineteenth-century Hollingworth (1977) or Eckersley's study of the growth of the cotton industry in Mossley and the role played by the mill-owning Mayall brothers (1991). Regional and national studies have been used as a framework for this study but the detailed case histories have been provided by these local studies.

Local accounts

There are a number of contemporary local accounts of the life and topography of the Tameside area. The earliest of these is Aikin's study of the Manchester region, in which Ashton and Mottram parishes each warrant large sections (Aikin 1795). James Butterworth published two volumes of topographical and historical notes on Ashton, Dukinfield, Mottram and Stalybridge in 1823 and 1827, whilst his son Edwin published a fuller account of Ashton in 1842. These were followed by Booker's history of Denton chapelry in 1855, Higson's history of Droylsden in 1859, Chadwick's *Reminiscences of Mottram* around 1870 and finally Glover's history of Ashton, published in 1884. These Victorian studies are perhaps of most use for the contemporary material which they contain, their topographical surveys and their biographical notes, for most of their history is unreferenced and concerned with the development of landownership rather than the progress of the industries of the eighteenth and nineteenth centuries. By the time the second wave of local histories was published in the early twentieth century interest had shifted towards the development of the township; although studies such as Hill's *Bygone Stalybridge* (1907), Hickey's *Dukinfield Past and Present* (1926) and Middleton's *History of Hyde and its neighbourhood* (1932) still contain biographical and topographical sketches, much space is devoted to the development of local government and local industries. Much of this history was still unreferenced, although a growing awareness of the value of historical documents is shown by the length of quotations printed from diaries, directories and ancient deeds found in all these later works.

Modern studies

The modern study of the eighteenth, nineteenth and twentieth centuries in the Tameside area began with Kenworthy's analyses of the industrial development of Mossley and Ashton (1928; 1929). His work recognizes the need to place the development of the local industries in their historical, physical and social contexts, although he did not attempt to assess the surviving physical remains of the Industrial Revolution. Both studies remain unpublished but copies are held in the Tameside Local Studies Library. This pioneering work was not taken up again until after the Second World War with studies of the Plug Riots of 1842 by Rose (1957) and the life of Joseph Rayner Stephens by Ward (1958) marking the restart of such research. Since then many studies have been published on the political, economic and social aspects of industrialization, particularly for the nineteenth century, with subjects ranging from Chartism and the Murphy Riots, to the cotton famine and the growth of the Methodist movement.

Without this previous research it would have been much harder to assess the development and impact of industrialization in Tameside, while the landscape survey of the period 1700-1930, an approach which underlies all three volumes of *A History and Archaeology of Tameside*, would have relied unduly on the surviving physical evidence of this era.

Chapter 2

An Industrial Society

'No branch of the cotton trade has been so uniformly successful as the spinning, and it is to this circumstance principally that Stayley Bridge owes its wealth and numbers, since it is a principle in political economy almost unerring as the descent of water in physics, that population follows prosperous trade, and hence the inhabitants of this place have, within the last 70 years, increased from 140 to 12,000 souls.'

(Baines 1825, 556)

2.1 Introduction

This chapter assesses the impact of industrialization on the political and social composition of Tameside, providing a framework for the subsequent chapters of this study. It begins with an analysis of the interplay between the progress of industrialization and population growth in Tameside throughout the period under study, before going on to summarize the changes brought about in local government by the rapid urbanization of the Borough. There then follow three sections dealing with different aspects of the social effects of industrialization, concentrating on the social cost of factory conditions and the consequent rise in trade union organizations; the rise and fall of industrial paternalism; and the changes brought about in people's leisure pursuits by the demands imposed upon them by the factory system. The final section of this chapter deals with the impact of the new textile industry in the late eighteenth and early nineteenth centuries on those members of Tameside society who remained attached to their rural roots.

2.2 The Demography of Tameside 1700-1930

Population growth 1700-1800

Aggregative analysis of the parish registers for Ashton and Mottram suggests that during the seventeenth century the population of Tameside remained static, with growth in the early part of the century being offset by the excess number of deaths over births in the latter part (Nevell 1991, 103-4). However, analysis of the Ashton registers for the eighteenth century by Moore indicates that from 1731 births were consistently above deaths (except for 1794 when they met), the average fertility rate being between 4 and 4.5 children per couple (Moore 1971, 11-13; Fig 2.1). This increase is reflected in the rise in the population of Ashton town. In the mid-seventeenth century this had been about 550, but according to an enumeration carried out in 1775 the population of the town had reached 2859, a five-fold increase (Nevell 1991, 103; Aikin 1795, 228).

During the last quarter of the eighteenth century the rate of growth was to increase dramatically. Unfortunately the first national census, in 1801, does not provide an accurate figure for Ashton town, as this was grouped in the returns with the Knott Lanes division, the total for the two being 7855. However, Edwin Butterworth later estimated from that combined total that the figure for Ashton town in 1801 was 6500 (Butterworth 1842, 94). If this figure is accurate, comparison with the 1775 figure of 2859 provides a population growth of 127% in the period 1775-1801.

A comparable aggregative analysis of the parish registers of Mottram has not been carried out for the eighteenth century. However, in 1795 Aikin noted 'a gradual increase of population of this parish' and cited in support the total number of marriages, baptisms and burials for each fifth year between 1745 and 1785 inclusive, and then for each year from 1786 to 1794 (Aikin 1795, 463). In each of the years given, apart from 1750 and 1794, baptisms outnumbered deaths. The figures for the period 1745-75 suggest a period of overall steady growth, with births exceeding deaths by an average of about 27 per annum. However, from about 1780 the population saw a sharp increase, with the numbers of births exceeding deaths by 100 in both 1780 and 1785, and by an annual average of 80 in 1786-94. In Mottram township the effect of this eighteenth-century growth was that at the time of the

Plate 2.1 Cotton operatives at Cedar Mill, Ashton, immediately before the First World War.
By the early twentieth century women formed the majority of the cotton workforce in Tameside. The 1911 census records 11,455 workers in the cotton industry of Ashton municipal borough, of whom 7001 were women and 4454 were men.

census in 1801 the population was 948 compared with approximately 237 in 1664 (Nevell 1991, 102; Table 2.1). Elsewhere in the Cheshire half of the Borough, Booth has used the registers of Hyde chapel from 1750 onwards to suggest that the population of the Hyde area remained stable until the last two decades of the eighteenth century, when it increased by two and a half times (Booth 1987, 26).

In the mid-seventeenth century Ashton town and the village of Mottram were the only settlements of any notable size in Tameside (Nevell 1991, 98-103). That both should have seen renewed growth from the mid-eighteenth century probably reflects not only their continuing primacy but also their role as centres of the burgeoning domestic-based textile industry (see Chapter 3). More importantly for the expansion of these settlements, the rapid acceleration in the growth rate of their populations from the period 1775-80 coincided with the arrival of the first cotton factories in the vicinity of these towns. There can be little doubt that the factory system, which relied on a concentration of the workforce, was a key factor in this stimulation. Although the existence of an experienced textile labour force enabled the early factories to be established in these areas, the factories in turn appear to have attracted an influx of new workers on a scale previously unseen. A similar process may be seen at work in other, previously rural, areas such as Hyde. The fact that the population remained stable until the early 1780s in the Hyde area may be attributable to the lack of an urban core. Although weaver-farmers are known from the Gee Cross area, agriculture was still the dominant economic activity (Bann 1976, 14-16). It was only with the introduction of the factory system in Hyde during the early 1780s, with its concentration of people in the new factory colony of Red Pump Street, that a focus was provided for the subsequent rapid population growth of this area (Booth 1987, 26-7).

The census and population growth 1801-1931

The population figures for the Tameside area during the period 1801-1931 are laid out in Table 2.1. These figures are derived from the census returns, the first nationwide census being taken in 1801. This information covers an era of both rapid population growth and

Chapter 2 An Industrial Society

extensive changes in local government, and consequently the figures require a note of explanation.

In the earliest censuses the population counts were taken by township, parish and borough. In the case of Tameside some of these enumeration areas had boundaries which extended beyond the modern Borough. The extreme instances were the townships of Tintwistle, of which only the division of Micklehurst lay within Tameside, and the parish and township of Saddleworth, of which only part of the division of Quickmere lay within the modern Borough. The figures for both townships have accordingly been omitted from Table 2.1. In the case of the township of Werneth and the Audenshaw and Knott Lanes divisions of Ashton parish the proportion of the population living within Tameside was somewhat greater and the census figures have been included in Table 2.1, although these still include a number of individuals living outside the Borough.

The development of local government during the second quarter of the nineteenth century saw the establishment of two new forms of administration – local boards and municipal boroughs. In Tameside these usually encompassed the same areas as the old townships but there were three exceptions. Firstly, the local board of Stalybridge, created in 1828, encompassed the south-western parts of Stayley township, eastern Dukinfield and south-eastern Hartshead. However, the censuses did not consistently include a separate entry for Stalybridge until after the local board had been created a municipal borough in 1857: hence the fall of 11,394 witnessed in Dukinfield's population between 1851 and 1861. Secondly, Hurst local board was created in 1861 out of part of the Hartshead division of Ashton parish. Thirdly, Mossley local board was created in 1864 out of the remaining part of the Hartshead division, the Micklehurst division of Tintwistle township and part of the Quickmere division of Saddleworth parish.

Between 1847 and 1899 five municipal boroughs were created in Tameside. The first, Ashton, initially encompassed that area formally known as the town

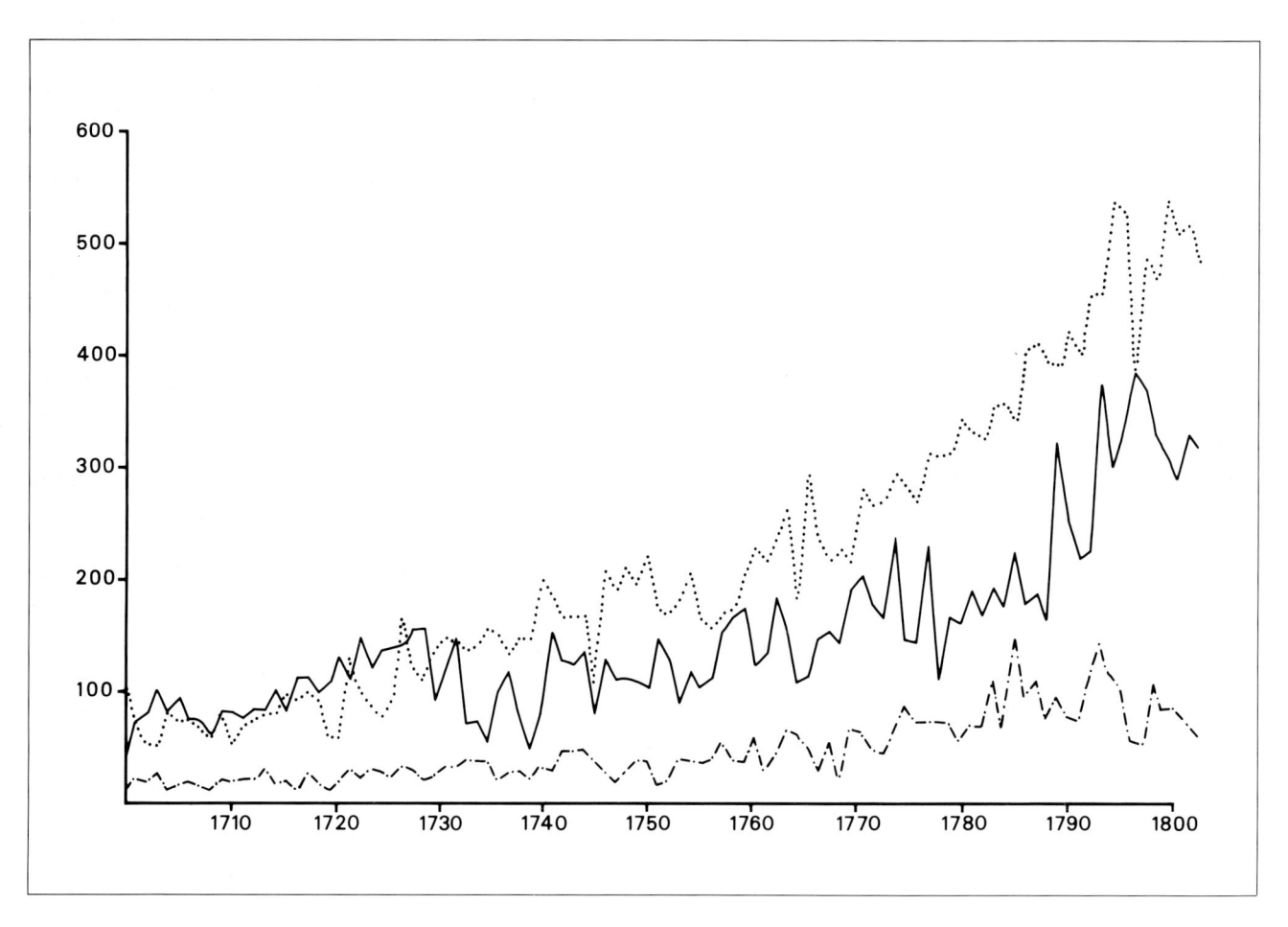

Fig 2.1 Aggregative analysis of Ashton parish registers in the eighteenth century (after Moore 1971, Graph 3).
Key: —·—·— marriages ·············· births ——————— deaths.
Ashton parish experienced steady population growth from 1731 onwards with baptisms consistently outstripping deaths. The exception is the year 1794, a crisis year of high mortality.

division of Ashton parish, but with the abolition of Hurst UDC in 1927 most of this area was transferred to Ashton borough. As already noted, Stalybridge municipal borough was created in 1857 out of the local board. In the late nineteenth century the area of the borough was extended to encompass the whole of Stayley township, which partially accounts for the leap of 10,399 seen in the borough's population between 1881 and 1891. Hyde municipal borough was created in 1881 out of the townships of Hyde, Newton and Godley and the northern part of Werneth. Although the census continued to give population figures for these townships until local government reorganization in 1936, only the figures for the borough of Hyde have been included in Table 2.1. Mossley and Dukinfield municipal boroughs were created in 1885 and 1899 from the respective local boards.

There was further reorganization of local government in the 1890s, when local boards and townships were replaced by urban district councils, rural district councils and civil parishes. The new urban district councils (UDCs) in Tameside were Audenshaw (part of the Littlemoss area of that division being given to Ashton borough), Denton (which included Haughton), Droylsden, Hollingworth, Hurst and Mottram. Limehurst rural district council was mostly comprised of those parts of Ashton parish now in Oldham Metropolitan Borough, with only part of Littlemoss and Alt Edge now lying in Tameside. The civil parishes of Tameside were the former townships of Hattersley and Matley. Minor reorganization in 1936 abolished these civil parishes, dividing them between the boroughs of Dukinfield, Hyde, Stalybridge and the new urban district council of Longdendale created from the merger of Hollingworth and Mottram.

Explanations for some of the fluctuations in the population of individual areas can be found in the footnotes of the summary census reports. Thus the increase in the population of Hattersley of 133 between 1831 and 1841 was accounted for by the presence of railway navvies constructing the new line between Manchester and Sheffield, whilst the near doubling of the population of Droylsden in the period 1841-61 was explained by the rapid growth of the cotton industry in that township. In contrast, the decline in the populations of Ashton, Dukinfield, Mottram, Newton, Stalybridge and Werneth during the decade 1861-71 was attributed to the decline in the cotton industry. However, the rise in population seen in Denton and Haughton in 1861-71 was stated to be a result of the flourishing felt hat trade.

The boom years 1801-61

The inter-relationship between population growth and the factory-based textile industry in Tameside in the late eighteenth century, noted above, was to continue throughout the life of this industry. During the period 1801-61 the cotton industry in Tameside rapidly expanded, reaching a peak in terms of the size of the workforce, although not in terms of the volume of cotton goods produced (see Chapter 3). This period saw the highest rate of population expansion in the Borough's history, with the population of the townships listed in Table 2.1 rising from 28,565 in 1801 to 153,618 in 1861, an increase of 437%, compared to the national population growth in the United Kingdom during this period of 105% (Cootes 1982, 179). Population growth in Tameside was thus more than four times the national average but this development was not uniform. Two townships, the rural districts of Hattersley and Matley, recorded a decrease in population, while Hyde recorded a population growth of 1191% in this period.

Ashton town witnessed an overall increase of around 28,400, or 437%, in the period 1801-61. The years 1801-21 saw an average yearly increase of about 136, whereas the following two decades saw an average annual rise of 673, and the years 1841-51 of 711, this figure falling to 510 in the years 1851-61. This varied growth pattern is characteristic of the development of a number of other townships and divisions during this era, in particular Audenshaw, Dukinfield, Hartshead, Hyde, Newton and Stayley.

Contemporary accounts indicate that much of this new population was accounted for by immigration from the surrounding countryside and from Ireland (Walton 1987, 183-5). Powell has studied the census enumeration schedules from Mottram and Hollingworth for the period 1841-71 and concluded that by 1871 in those areas, which had only small urban cores, 5% of the population were immigrants from Ireland (M Powell 1977, 21, 37). In the heartlands of the cotton industry in Tameside this figure was higher, with Irish immigrants accounting for 7% of the population of Ashton in the 1851 census (Walton 1987, 252).

In Ashton parish Moore has shown that the birth rate during the period 1801-41 increased by 50% over its eighteenth-century average to around 6.7 children per couple in 1831, even when allowance is made for a degree of under-registration in the parish records of this period (Moore 1971, 22). However, the excess number of births over deaths in the parish registers only accounts for approximately half of the increase in population during the period 1801-41. The remainder must, therefore, be accounted for by immigration from outside the parish.

Chapter 2 An Industrial Society

Assessment Division	1801	1811	1821	1831	1841	1851	1861	1871	1881	1891	1901	1911	1921	1931
Ashton Town	{7855	{9574	9222	{16883	22678				see Ashton-under-Lyne MB					
Knott Lanes div			3827		5521	6044	7312		divided between Hurst, Limehurst and Mossley LBs					
Ashton-under-Lyne MB			created 1847			29790	34886	31984	36399	40486	43890	45172	51409	51573
Audenshaw div/UDC	2275	2772	3781	4891	5374	5427	6327	7024	7308	7958	7216	7977	7876	8460
Denton tns/LB	1362	1594	2012	2792	3440	3147	3335	5117	7660	8666	see Denton UDC			
Denton UDC					created 1894						14934	16877	17620	17383
Droylsden tns/LB/UDC	1552	2201	2855	2996	4933	6280	8798	8973	8679	9482	11087	13259	13878	13277
Dukinfield tns/LB/MB	1737	3053	5096	14681	22394	26418	15024	14085	16942	17385	18929	19422	19509	19309
Godley tns	270	451	514	636	1399	1353	1185	1222			see Hyde MB			
Hartshead div	5502	6706	9137	11823	12731	18885	19245		divided between Hurst, Limehurst and Mossley LBs					
Hattersley tns/CP	455	473	563	477	610	497	400	276	263	286	287	256	268	280
Haughton tns/LB	1139	1526	2084	2914	3319	3042	3371	4276	5051	5327	see Denton UDC			
Hollingworth tns/LB/UDC	910	1089	1393	1760	2012	2347	2155	2280	2658	2895	2447	2580	2466	2299
Hurst LB/UDC				created 1861				2916	6384	6772	7145	7858	8074	see AuL
Hyde tns/LB	1063	1806	3355	7144	10170	11569	13722	14223			see Hyde MB			
Hyde MB					created 1881				28630	30670	32766	33437	33424	32066
Matley tns/CP	285	311	324	262	251	252	231	207	205	174	196	289	273	348
Mossley LB/MB				created 1864				10578	13850	14162	13452	13205	12703	12041
Mottram-i-L tns/LB/UDC	948	1446	1944	2144	3247	3199	3406	2590	2913	3270	3128	3049	2883	2636
Newton tns/LB	1005	1445	2159	5997	7501	7481	6440	6295			see Hyde MB			
Stalybridge MB				created 1857			18130	15323	16384	26783	27673	26513	25216	24823
Stayley tns	1055	1104	1609	2440	3905	4579	6187	5788	3651		see Stalybridge MB			
Werneth tns	1152	1304	1804	3462	3904	3635	3464	3402			see Hyde MB			

Table 2.1 The population of Tameside by township (tns), civil parish (CP), local board (LB), urban district council (UDC) and municipal borough (MB), 1801-1931. Sources: Farrer & Brownbill 1908, 342-4 and Harris 1979, 214-37, with emendations from the census returns of 1871, 1891, 1901, 1911, 1921 and 1931 (HMSO).

The slow down in growth 1861-1931

The cotton famine of 1861-5 caused the arresting, and in some cases the decline, of the population in certain townships within Tameside. Those boroughs and townships which witnessed population decline between 1861 and 1871 were Ashton, Dukinfield, Hattersley, Matley, Mottram, Newton, Stalybridge, Stayley and Werneth. Among the industrial towns of the Borough Stalybridge, which was heavily dependent on cotton, was affected particularly badly, with a population decrease of 15.5%, compared to 8.3% in Ashton and 6.25% in Dukinfield. The greatest decreases, however, were in Mottram, by 24%, and neighbouring Hattersley, by 31%; this was probably, in part, the result of the virtual collapse of the cotton industry in Broadbottom which had previously been a major employer in this locality.

When population growth resumed in the decades after 1871, in most areas the rate of annual increase was considerably lower than that for the preceding 60 years, the population of the component districts of the Borough rising only 19.2% in the 40 years 1861-1901, to 183,150, at an average annual increase of 738. This was a third of the national increase of 60% during the same period (Cootes 1982, 179). The highest growth was experienced by Denton and Haughton, which rose from 6706 in 1861 to 14,934 in 1901, an increase of 123%, reflecting the continuing strength of the hatting industry in these townships, and Denton in particular.

While the cotton industry in Tameside reached its peak production level in the decade 1911-21, the population of the districts of the Borough remained fairly static, at 183,150 in 1901 and 184,495 in 1931 (Table 2.1). A number of areas saw significant population decline during the years 1901-31 as their cotton industries collapsed, notably Mossley (whose population was in decline from 1891) and Stalybridge (whose population peaked at 27,673 in 1901 and fell back to 24,823 in 1931). Only Ashton, Audenshaw, Denton, Droylsden, Dukinfield and Matley saw increases in population during the years 1901-31. This period of stagnation in Tameside is in sharp contrast to national developments, the population of the United Kingdom growing by 20.4% in the period 1901-31 to reach 46 million (Cootes 1982, 352).

2.3 Local Government

The spread of local government

In the early eighteenth century the chief organs of local government in Tameside, as in most other parts of the country, were the manor, parish and county, the majority of people's lives still being centred on the village or farmstead (Fig 2.2). The rapid growth in the population of industrial Britain during the late eighteenth and nineteenth centuries put a severe strain on the traditional forms of local government as parish and manorial courts struggled to cope with populations which in some cases were larger than in neighbouring long-established boroughs. In the new industrial towns these stresses were manifested in appalling living conditions, overcrowding, a high birth rate and political agitation for democratic reform. Perhaps the most famous example of this was Manchester, which long before its incorporation in 1838 had been called the largest village in England because of its poor local government (Walton 1987, 134).

In Tameside much of the local government was conducted by the manorial courts until the mid-nineteenth century, with records from Hattersley and Mottram surviving until this period, while the Ashton court leet was still functioning at the beginning of the twentieth century (Bowman 1960, 580-3; CRO DTW 2477/F/12; GMCRO M95). The most hard-pressed manorial court and parish vestry were in Ashton, the only significant urban area in the Borough during the eighteenth century (Plate 2.2). Here the court leet met twice a year and appointed local officials such as constables, whose duties included not only the maintenance of order but also the collection of rates and taxes (Bowman 1960, 608-14). Ordinary townsfolk could also participate in local affairs through vestry meetings. Here people could discuss local issues and every year vestry officers, such as overseers of the poor, surveyors of highways and churchwardens, were nominated to deal with parish affairs. Resolutions could also be made at vestry meetings, and although they were not always acted upon by the court leet they did show public feeling in local matters (Richardson 1986, 34).

The new stresses in local government were not, of course, confined to Tameside, or the North-West, but were a national consequence of the impact of industrialization and they resulted in many representations to Parliament for proper self-government (Cootes 1982, 116-17). Nationally, this pressure led to the Reform Bill of 1832, which introduced limited changes to Parliamentary elections by abolishing rotten boroughs and re-allocating 143 seats to the new industrial towns, the counties, Ireland and Scotland. The qualifications for voting were also relaxed slightly, although a property qualification was still in force. The result was that in boroughs proprietors with annual incomes of £10 or more and tenants paying rent of £10 or more a year could vote, while in the counties those with land valued at £10 or more a year had the vote. In the North-West the beneficiaries of this redistribution of seats were the cotton towns, Ashton-

Chapter 2 An Industrial Society

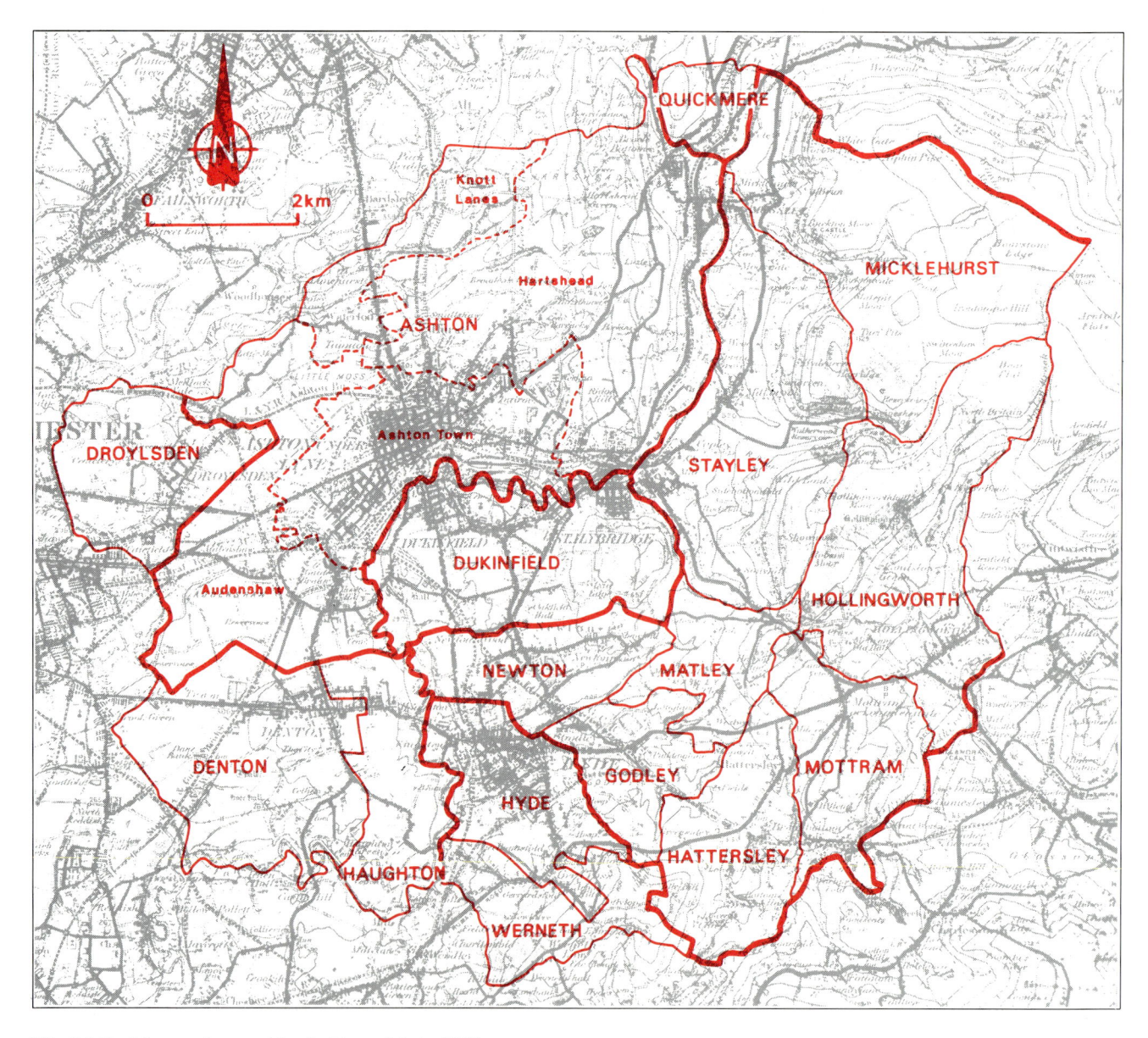

Fig 2.2 Parishes and townships in Tameside in 1800.
Key: ▬▬▬ = parish boundary; ─── = township boundary.
Until the early nineteenth century the key units of government in Tameside were the local manorial court and the local parish. In the Lancashire part of the Borough, Droylsden, Denton and Haughton were in Manchester parish; Ashton was both a township and a parish and contained four divisions, Ashton town, Audenshaw, Knott Lanes and Hartshead. Quickmere division was in Saddleworth township and parish, in the West Riding of Yorkshire. In the Cheshire part of Tameside, Dukinfield, Hyde and Werneth were in Stockport parish and the remaining townships in Mottram parish.

under-Lyne being given one seat, as was Bury, Rochdale and Salford, while Bolton, Manchester, Oldham and Stockport each received two seats (*ibid*, 117-18). The area of the new Parliamentary borough of Ashton-under-Lyne was, however, only that of the town division of the old parish, and the total electorate was merely 422, all male, out of a town population estimated by Butterworth to be 14,670 in 1831 (Butterworth 1842, 95). This represents slightly less than 3% of the population of Ashton, whilst nationally 7% of the population had the right to vote (Cootes 1982, 196). Despite two further Parliamentary reforms, in 1867 and 1884, it was not until the Reform Act of 1918, when women were first enfranchised, that more than half of the population could vote (*ibid*, 238). Of more immediate impact for Tameside was the Redistribution Bill of 1885 which widened the Parliamentary constituency of Ashton to include most of the old parish and created a new constituency of Hyde, covering all of the Cheshire side of Tameside (Bowman 1960, 642; Harris 1979, 139).

The reform of Parliament was also matched by the beginnings of reform in local government. At first these reforms were achieved through individual

Chapter 2 An Industrial Society

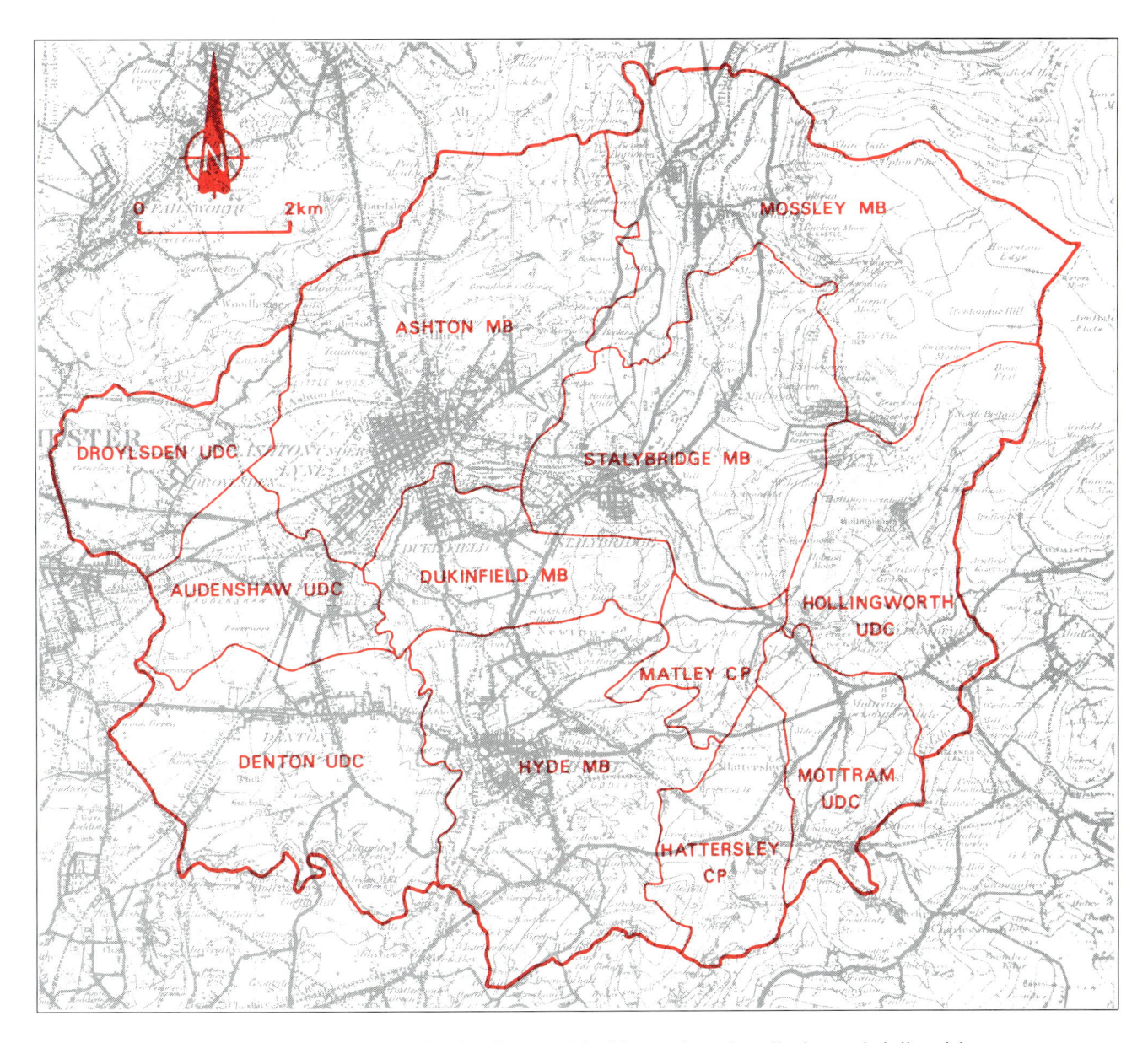

Fig 2.3 Local government in Tameside in 1930 showing municipal boroughs, urban districts and civil parishes.
The growth of the new industrial towns of Tameside during the nineteenth century led to major changes in the way in which the people of the Borough were governed. By the early twentieth century local government was carried out by three types of authority – the municipal borough (MB), the urban district council (UDC) and the civil parish (CP).

improvement acts. In 1827 an act was passed giving Ashton town a self-governing board, independent of the manor, parish and county, and responsible for its own lighting, cleansing and appointment of petty constables. These powers were vested in town commissioners, who were usually substantial ratepayers, elected by other ratepayers. Their powers included the regulation of Ashton's market, and the right to purchase land for a new market place; the paving of town streets and passages, and the numbering of houses and naming of streets; the appointing and paying of deputy and assistant constables of the town; the building of sewers; the provision of a fire service; the impounding of stray animals; and the purchase of any properties in the town necessary for the place's improvement (Bowman 1960, 633-5). Stalybridge received such a governing body in 1828, 21 town commissioners being elected (March 1957, 77).

However, the powers of such bodies were limited. In particular there was very little control over public health, and Parliament was soon forced to pass a series of acts reforming local government to cope with the problems of rapid urban growth. The most radical of these was the Municipal Corporations Act of 1835. This provided a new form of local government for the industrial urban areas of the country, by allowing the creation of new boroughs, with councillors being elected every three years and aldermen every six. Ultimately this act led to the creation of five municipal boroughs in the later area of Tameside; Ashton in

Chapter 2 An Industrial Society

Plate 2.2 Ashton Old Court House in the 1880s.
Now the site of St Michael's Square, the court house was a seventeenth-century building which originally functioned as the Market House. From 1831, when the new market opened, this building was used for the twice yearly meetings of the court leet, hence the later name of the structure. It remained in use until its demolition in 1889.

1847, Stalybridge in 1857, Hyde in 1881, Mossley in 1885 and Dukinfield in 1899.

The Municipal Corporations Act of 1835 was designed to deal only with those urban areas of the country where there was a high concentration of population. In Tameside there were many areas which had an urban core but did not warrant immediate municipalization. For such areas other acts were passed in the 1830s and 1840s which enabled local boards to be set up to deal with the specific problems of urbanization, such as poor relief, highways and public sanitation (Harris 1979, 75). The Poor Law Amendment Act of 1834 established poor law unions and set down the rules for the election of poor law 'guardians', or administrators. The Ashton-under-Lyne poor law union was created in 1837, and encompassed not only the parish of Ashton but also the Lancashire townships of Denton, Droylsden and Haughton, and the Cheshire townships of Dukinfield, Godley, Hattersley, Hollingworth, Matley, Mottram, Newton, Stalybridge and Tintwistle. Ashton parish elected five guardians, Dukinfield two guardians and the other townships one each (Bowman 1960, 524). The Highways Act of 1835 allowed the unification of parishes into highway district authorities and the levying of a rate to pay for a surveyor and labour. As a result, in 1836 highway boards were set up for Hyde and Dukinfield (Middleton 1932, 260). The Public Health Act of 1848 allowed the boroughs to act as local health boards and for other local health boards to be created. Although Ashton and Stalybridge boroughs took on these powers almost immediately, boards of health were not established elsewhere in Tameside until later (Bowman 1960, 334; March 1957, 87).

Despite the many acts passed in the mid-nineteenth century encouraging elected local boards, the development of local government in Tameside was slow. It was not until after the Local Government Act of 1857 had simplified the procedure for establishing local boards that they spread throughout Tameside. Thus boards of health were established in Denton and Dukinfield in 1857, in Droylsden in 1858, in Hurst in 1861, in Hyde in 1863, in Mossley in 1864, in Hollingworth in 1871, in Newton in 1872, in Mottram in 1873, in Audenshaw in 1874 and in Haughton in 1877 (Parry 1908, 1-2; Middleton 1932, 262-3; Middleton 1936, 31-2; Speake & Witty 1953, 196; Harris 1979, 77).

Following the examples of Ashton and Stalybridge, other urban areas which saw rapid growth in the mid- to late nineteenth century achieved municipal borough status by the end of the century; Hyde in 1881, Mossley in 1885 and the last, Dukinfield, in 1899 (Eckersley 1991, 76; Pavasovic 1984, 45; Middleton 1932, 265). By that time further reorganization had been ordered by the local government acts of 1888 and 1894. The first of these created the county councils and transferred to them the administrative functions of the quarter sessions, while the 1894 act established urban and rural district councils and civil parishes (Richardson 1986, 32). The local boards of health in Audenshaw, Denton, Droylsden, Hollingworth, Hurst and Mottram consequently became new urban district councils, while new civil parishes were created for Hattersley and Matley (Fig 2.3). Minor local government reorganization in 1936 divided these civil parishes between the boroughs of Dukinfield, Hyde and Stalybridge and the newly created Longdendale UDC, establishing the pattern of local authorities in the area of the later Borough until the Local Government Reorganization Act of 1972 established the metropolitan borough of Tameside (Harris 1979, 220). When Tameside came into being in 1974 it replaced nine local authorities, of which five were municipal boroughs – Ashton, Dukinfield, Hyde, Mossley and Stalybridge – and four were urban district councils – Audenshaw, Denton, Droylsden and Longdendale.

The local public services

By the early twentieth century local authorities were providing a range of services encompassing sanitation, policing and highway maintenance. Some local authorities were also providing services such as water, gas, electricity, trams, buses, libraries, museums, parks, cemeteries and, in some cases, municipal entertainments. These responsibilities were acquired gradually in answer to a succession of differing needs and demands throughout the nineteenth century.

Long before its creation as a local board in 1827, Ashton town had its own constables, appointed by the court leet whose origins can be traced to the seventeenth century. When the local board was created a municipal borough in 1847 the policing powers of the town commissioners were transferred to a watch committee. At first there was a permanent police force of twelve men under a chief constable but by the end of the century the corporation employed more than 60 constables (Bowman 1960, 613). A police force was established by the new municipal borough of Stalybridge in 1857, the permanent force consisting of a chief constable, two inspectors and eight constables (March 1957, 128). The duties of the police varied as the town councils gained responsibilities. As well as protection of life and property and the prevention of crime, the police at various times had to deal with fires, food purity, weights and measures, sanitation and explosions (March 1957, 130-3).

From the 1840s many local authorities were empowered to take over private gas and water companies. In 1856 Ashton Corporation purchased the Ashton Waterworks Company (Bowman 1960, 336). Dukinfield and Denton local boards took over the Dukinfield Gas Company in 1877 (Pavasovic 1984, 45). In 1885 Stalybridge and Mossley corporations bought the Stalybridge Gas Light Company, each taking the gas works situated in its borough (March 1957, 105).

The Tramways Act of 1870 allowed local authorities to run their own horse-driven trams, although initially local authorities leased their tramways to private companies (Hyde 1978, 7). In Tameside the first horse-driven tramway opened in 1881, between Stalybridge, Ashton and Audenshaw, and was run by the Manchester Carriage & Tramways Company. It was not until 1898 that tramways in Tameside were actually run by a local authority. These were the routes of the Manchester Carriage & Tramways Company through Denton, which had been bought by Denton UDC. In 1900 Ashton MB began to build its own tramway system, whilst the founding in 1901 of the Stalybridge, Hyde, Mossley and Dukinfield Tramways and Electricity Board, known as the SHMD, marked the beginning of involvement by the Tameside local authorities in the new electric tramways (Hyde 1980, 31-2). By 1921 all of the tramway routes through Tameside were run by local authorities and all had been converted to electricity (Hyde 1978, 43). The SHMD was also responsible for the domestic and industrial supply of electricity to its component districts until its demise in 1967 (Aldcroft 1974, 184).

In the 1920s the greater efficiency and flexibility of the motor-bus persuaded the Tameside local authorities to begin converting their tramway systems, Ashton Corporation and the SHMD introducing their first motor-bus services in 1925 (Hyde 1978, 48).

Various committees were set up by the Tameside town councils to provide other services. Acts of Parliament enabled councils to expand their public services to include free libraries, public baths and recreational grounds (Plate 2.3). The Public Libraries Act of 1850 allowed towns with a population of more than 10,000 to provide free libraries (Richardson 1986, 167). Ashton borough chose to adopt the act in 1880 and opened a library in the town hall in 1882 (Bowman 1960, 555). Stalybridge set up a library committee in 1886, and opened a library in its town hall in 1889, this being transferred to the Astley Cheetham Public Library in 1901. Hyde followed in 1893 (Preece 1989, 108-10). Libraries had existed in towns long before this, usually associated with churches and schools or established by influential members of the community, such as the philanthropic mill-owners Hugh Mason, who set up a library in the Oxford Mills institute, and Samuel Robinson, who established Dukinfield library in 1833 (Ashmore & Bolton 1975, 42; Pavasovic 1984, 46).

The first public park to be opened in Tameside was Stamford Park in 1873. This was initially run by Ashton Corporation but in 1891 a joint committee was formed by Ashton and Stalybridge boroughs to manage and enlarge the park (Bowman 1960, 340). The success of this venture encouraged other local authorities to found public open spaces. Dukinfield Park was opened in 1902 by the new Dukinfield borough, Hyde Park was opened in 1904 by Hyde borough and Cheetham Park in 1931 by the borough of Stalybridge (Pavasovic 1984, 45; March 1957, 68).

The Artisans and Labourers Dwelling Improvement Act of 1875 and the Housing Act of 1890 granted further responsibilities to local authorities, the first giving the right to buy, condemn or improve slum property, and the second the right to build houses which could be rented to working men and their families. However, the first local authority housing in Tameside was not constructed until the 1920s, when both Dukinfield and Stalybridge embarked on a programme of house building (Pavasovic 1984, 47; March 1957, 85).

2.4 Trade Unionism and Factory Conditions

Early combinations and the cotton industry

Before the Industrial Revolution there were no trade unions in Britain, although there were the associations or trade clubs for such skilled workers as bootmakers, hatters, printers and woolcombers. In Tameside the only significant body of this kind was the Hatters' Association, a trade club which developed in the late eighteenth century as part of an increasing national trend towards the organization of the manufacturing workforce. The growth of trade clubs into trade unions was achieved by combining a group of clubs into a regional or national organization. In 1790 the hatting clubs, including the Hatters' Association, formed the Hatters' Society of Great Britain and Ireland, also known as the Fair Trade Union (Holding 1986, 85).

The hat-making industry employed only a small percentage of the population and, even in its most important areas like Tameside, the influence of the union was limited to affecting working conditions in its own industry. Nevertheless, the perceived threat posed by such clubs in the era of the Napoleonic Wars led to the passing of the Combination Acts in 1799 and 1800. These barred workers from meeting to plan joint action for higher wages or shorter working hours, either by negotiating with employers or by threatening them (Cootes 1982, 127). Such laws failed to prevent the new combination unions from growing, especially as the textile workforce became increasingly organized in the early nineteenth century (Walton 1987, 143-4).

Although wages in the cotton industry fluctuated according to the state of trade, they were generally better than those offered by other trades such as hatting, coal mining or agriculture. Nevertheless wages varied from mill to mill, and although operatives often won advances in wages during good years these were wiped out by the employers who cut wages during times of poor trade – as can be seen from a survey of the income of Dukinfield textile workers in 1841 (Mackenzie 1965, 124-5). The frequent depressions in the cotton trade during the first half of the nineteenth century saw periods of high prices and low wages (*ibid*, 126-7). There were strikes against these conditions but employers often responded by bringing in workers from other textile-producing towns and areas (Cootes 1982, 125-30; Hall 1991, 110-11).

Of the two main types of cotton worker, handloom weavers found it difficult to organize themselves, since they were dispersed in small workshops across the countryside rather than concentrated in large factories. In 1808 and 1818-19 there were strikes by handloom weavers in Ashton, Hyde and Stalybridge, wanting a minimum wage (Walton 1987, 143-4, 154-5; Cotton 1977, 80). Unlike the weavers, the spinners had tended to join together in unions as soon as the trade became factory-based, often through Friendly Societies. One of the earliest unions in the North-West was the General Union, established in 1810 by the uniting of some of these smaller societies. In the same year this new union organized a strike to raise wages in the whole of the Lancashire textile region to Manchester levels. Spinners still working raised £1500 a week to support the strike, which began in Stalybridge and Preston. The employers responded by locking out the whole district, with the result that in the Tameside area 10,000 people were out of work for four months (Cootes 1982, 127; Cotton 1977, 81-2).

The repeal of the combination laws in 1824, largely due to the campaigning of Francis Place, gave greater strength to the spinning associations by allowing unions the legal right to strike on matters of hours and wages (Cootes 1982, 127). Unfortunately in the following year a new repressive act was passed which led to a further burst of strike activity. When the mill-owners attempted to reduce wages in 1828-9, there was a widespread strike in the Tameside area, Stockport and Manchester. However, the mill-owners were successful in draining the union's funds and defeated the operatives (Cotton 1977, 147-50). As a result, a more extensive organization was formed in 1829, the Grand General Union of Cotton Spinners of the United Kingdom (Cootes 1982, 127-8). Under this new union groups of mills in the Lancashire textile district took it in turn to strike, supported by those in work elsewhere. In response employers formed themselves into larger organizations. In November 1830 the employers in Ashton, Dukinfield and Stalybridge signed an agreement to reduce wages. The operatives refused to accept this and 23,000 workers were locked out, many until March 1831, thereby depleting the Grand General Union's funds and ultimately leading to the collapse not only of the strike but also of the union itself (Cotton 1977, 215-31).

The Chartist movement in Tameside

The collapse of the Grand General Union and the failure of the Reform Bill of 1832 to give the majority of the working population the vote led to an upsurge in union membership and continued agitation for reform. In 1836 a group of skilled tradesmen and shopkeepers, under the leadership of William Lovett, founded the London Working Men's Association, which drew up a charter for equal political rights. The People's Charter was a petition for reform in six areas; adult male suffrage, annual Parliaments, votes by ballot, equal electoral districts, abolition of the property qualification for MPs and payment for MPs. The petition was presented to Parliament three times, in 1839, 1842 and 1848, and each time rejected, although all the reforms except annual Parliaments eventually became law. There was no call in the petition for women to have the vote, although women made a major contribution to the Chartist movement, and many local Chartists demanded female enfranchisement. According to a report in the *Northern Star* on 2nd February 1839, Chartist women in Ashton were

> 'determined that no man shall ever enjoy our hands, our hearts or share our beds, that will not stand forward as the advocate of the rights of man and the determined enemy of the damnable new poor law...we do not despair of yet seeing intelligence the necessary qualification for voting, and then sisters, we shall be placed in our proper position in society, and enjoy the elective franchise' (Taylor 1992, 147).

Women were mostly concerned with issues which affected them directly, such as low wage levels, long working hours, child labour and factory conditions. A further cause of discontent was the poor law of 1834. This concentrated those in need of relief, the unemployed, homeless, sick and old, in large workhouses which were frequently overcrowded and unsanitary. The workhouses also segregated men, women and children, which meant that in times of bad trade in the textile industry, when workers were forced to seek relief, families could be separated. In the early years women played an active part in the Chartist movement but after 1842, as a result of the Parliamentary rejection of the Charter and an improvement in economic conditions, many channelled their reforming activities through institutions such as chapel or Sunday School societies (*ibid*, 143-4, 187-8).

The Chartist movement in the North-West was strongest in the cotton towns around Manchester, where it drew support from among weavers, factory workers and the unemployed (Walton 1987, 161-4). Prominent Chartists in Tameside included Richard Oastler, Dr Paul Murray McDouall and Joseph Rayner Stephens. Stephens was born in Edinburgh in March 1805, the son of a Methodist minister, and as a young man he himself became one of the first Methodist missionaries to Sweden. On his return to England in 1832 he was appointed to the Ashton-under-Lyne circuit and it was here that he became interested in the living and working conditions of the poor. Two important influences on Stephens during the 1830s were Charles Hindley, later the MP for Ashton, and Richard Oastler, an evangelical Anglican; both applied the message of the Bible and the fervour of their religion to improve social conditions (Spence 1989, 35-7).

In 1834 Stephens was forced to resign from the Methodist ministry because of his views. Stirred by the iniquities of the new poor law he began a campaign for social justice and by 1836 was advocating factory reform (*ibid*, 37-8). He quickly became known as a great orator and Tory radical who championed the disadvantaged of the manufacturing towns. Although he became associated with the People's Charter, Stephens's main concerns were the anti-poor law campaign and factory legislation. He supported the Charter because he believed it to be a symbol of the rights of the poor as human beings;

> 'I don't care about your Charter; it may be all very right, it may be all very good; you have a right to get it, mind you, and I will stand by you in it; but I don't care about it...You have a right, every working man amongst you has the right, to as much for your labour as will keep you and your families' (TLSL MF 83 Sermon given at Ashton, 26th May 1839).

In a number of speeches he appears to have advocated the use of violence to achieve reform, a policy which was taken up by the northern Chartists (Spence 1989, 39; Ward 1958, 104). The authorities were alarmed at his effect and in December 1838 Stephens became the first prominent Chartist to be arrested, three weeks after he addressed a meeting at Hyde at which, it was said, guns were displayed and the crowd incited to burn down a local mill (Ward 1958, 105-6; Middleton 1932, 101-2). The charges laid against him were 'seditious behaviour endeavouring to inflame and excite people to riot and break the peace' (Spence 1989, 41).

At his trial, in August 1839, he made a six and a half hour speech in his defence but was sentenced to eighteen months' imprisonment. Even in prison he carried on his work by writing and editing *Stephens' Monthly Magazine*. After his release he was much less politically active, and critics accused him of being afraid of being sent back to prison. However, in the 1840s the introduction of new factory legislation and the beginnings of a period of prosperity in the cotton industry, which preceded the cotton famine, meant that there were less opportunities for radical social reform (*ibid*, 41-2).

Dr McDouall was another leading Chartist who was arrested for seditious language. He spoke at a meeting in Hyde along with John Bradley, a clogger and a leader of the Hyde Chartists. They were both arrested and at the trial it was claimed that McDouall

> 'advised them all to get armed. Those who could not purchase a gun, pistol or a pike, must get lucifer matches, which were very cheap' (Middleton 1932, 108).

Because of the increasingly successful working-class agitation the government responded by building barracks in many of the northern manufacturing towns, so that troops would be on hand to quell disturbances. Under General Sir Charles Napier the whole of the north of England was garrisoned. In 1841-2 barracks were built on Mossley Road, immediately north of Ashton; these later became the home of the Manchester Regiment (Bowman 1960, 277).

Following a wave of arrests of Chartist leaders in 1840, the local movements went into a temporary decline and had to rebuild (Taylor 1992, 14). This was achieved fairly quickly, demonstrating the level of popular support. By 1842, when the movement was at its peak in the North-West, there were about 60 Chartist associations in Lancashire and Cheshire, with over 300,000 signatures on the 1842 petition, accounting for more than 25% of the local population (Walton 1987, 162). Ashton had over 14,000 signatures out of

Grade	Weekly wage	
	s	d
Dressers	27	0
Overlookers	26	0
Engineers	25	0
Spinners	22	6
Warehousemen	15	0
Misters	14	0
Weavers	10	0
Cardroom hands	9	0
Winders	8	6
Warpers	8	6
Reelers	8	6
Big piecers	8	6
Little piecers	4	6

Table 2.2 Average mill operative wages in Ashton in 1843. Source: Coulthart 1844, 31.

a population of about 22,000 whilst Stalybridge had 10,000 out of a population which, according to Butterworth, numbered about 21,000 (Hall 1991, 183; Butterworth 1842, 148). Nationally there were over three million signatures (Cootes 1982, 131). The rejection of the petition in May 1842 led to the disturbances in the industrial heartlands of the country known as the Plug Riots (Rose 1957, 75-6). These were quickly quelled and it was not until 1848 that the movement was able to mount its last campaign, with the presentation of a third petition, which was also rejected by Parliament (Cootes 1982, 132).

In the second half of the nineteenth century there were fewer popular demonstrations. Although rioting still occasionally occurred in areas such as Manchester and Blackburn in the latter half of the nineteenth century, the last popular demonstrations in Tameside were associated with the Murphy Riots of 1867 (Walton 1987, 252). It is not entirely clear why popular unrest should have declined amongst the working classes during the mid-nineteenth century but Walton has argued that there were a number of factors, both economic and social. During the mid-nineteenth century the working class split between the skilled, supervisory and the rest. There were also economic divisions between workers from different industries who were interested in lobbying only for reforms in their own areas. Further divisions were exposed by the mass Irish immigration of the 1840s and 1850s which set worker against worker. At the same time there was a strengthening of the forces of law and order with the establishment of many new police forces. Walton has thus concluded that in the late nineteenth century the forces keeping the working classes apart were far greater than those which might force them together into collective action (*ibid*, 251-4, 264-5).

The new factory system and working conditions

The coming of the factories introduced a regime of work radically different to the domestic-based textile industry of the early and mid-eighteenth century. Prior to 1770 families worked at home individually, or in small community groups, in control of their own hours and conditions (Fitton 1965, 2). In contrast the new factory-based textile industry which established itself in Tameside from the 1770s imposed a harsh discipline on people's lives and broke up the family work unit. The hours were long – during the 1820s Ashton mills worked a fourteen hour day from 5am to 7pm – so that home became merely a place to sleep (Kenworthy 1929, 53-5). Within the mills there was quite a strict gender division; spinners were nearly always men on the grounds that spinning was a highly skilled job, while weaving by powerloom was seen as less skilled and was thus normally undertaken by women (Cotton 1977, 14-23). Each spinner employed a big piecer and a little piecer to mend broken threads as well as a scavenger to clean around the machinery. These jobs were filled by the spinner's children whenever possible. Before the advent of the factory system spinning had been a female occupation, while handloom weaving had been generally undertaken by men (Fleischmann 1973, 199-201). However, by the early twentieth century women had become the mainstay of the cotton workforce in Tameside. The 1911 census records that 11,455, or 40% of the workforce in the municipal borough of Ashton, worked in the cotton industry. Of these 7001 were women and only 4454 were men (Plate 2.1).

Children were an essential part of the mill economy. By the late eighteenth century mill-owners had learnt that children could operate certain machinery as well as an adult but could be paid considerably less. According to Aikin, during the 1790s children in the cotton mills of Dukinfield were treated especially badly, leading him to comment that the industry had

> 'debilitated the constitutions and retarded the growth of many, and made an alarming increase in the mortality. This effect is greatly to be attributed to the pernicious custom, so properly reprobated by Dr Percival and other physicians, of making the children in the mills work night and day, one set getting out of bed when another goes into the same' (Aikin 1795, 456).

Such practices led to demands for factory legislation, initially to improve the working conditions of children. However, progress was very slow. The first factory legislation, the Health and Morals of Apprentices Act, was passed in 1802. This prohibited night work for child apprentices and limited day work to twelve hours. This first act was largely ineffective, and by 1815 its sponsor, Sir Robert Peel, considered a further bill; in the spring of 1816 Peel began to gather evidence from operatives, some of whom attested to children in Ashton working up to fourteen hours a day. With the support of medical evidence from surgeons, the aid of Anglican clergymen and local petitions which included the names of other local worthies, the first true Factory Act was passed in 1819 (Ward 1966, 187-8). Of equal importance was the pattern which this support set for future campaigns. The new bill limited child labour to 72 hours per week, with a minimum age of nine years. The success of this first bill prompted the establishment of various factory reform groups throughout the North-West from the 1820s onwards. In Tameside the first such group was established in Ashton in 1831, followed by groups in Dukinfield in 1833, Stalybridge in 1835 and Hyde in 1844 (*ibid*, 206). An early success for the factory reform movement was Althorpe's Factory Act of 1833, which reduced the time children between the ages of nine and thirteen years could work to ten hours per day, and stipulated that each child had to be given two hours of schooling each day.

In order to monitor the implementation of this new law the first factory inspectors were appointed. Despite these new inspectors the law was still open to evasion and abuse. Children's ages could be falsified by either their parents or their doctor. In Stalybridge in 1838 out of 112 children who had been certified as being over thirteen years of age, 75 were found to be much younger (Kenworthy 1929, 55). Another tactic used by the employers to circumvent the new laws was to introduce shift working for children, with the child working several short shifts during the day, perhaps totalling as much as eighteen hours (Fleischmann 1973, 231-3).

In 1844 an act was introduced allowing children to work half a day if the next day was spent in school. This was followed in 1847 by Fielden's Act which fixed the working day at ten hours for women and all young persons under eighteen years of age. However, there were still many loopholes in the law which mill-owners were quick to exploit. In 1849 mills in Ashton, Mossley and Lees were still running twelve to sixteen hours a day (Kenworthy 1929, 55-6). Female workers went on strike against these conditions as public agitation grew against local employers. Fielden's Act was hastily redrafted in 1850 in an attempt to prevent these

Chapter 2 An Industrial Society

abuses, but as late as 1853, when another factory act was passed stating that children could only be employed between 6am and 6pm, with one and a half hours for meals, John Mayall of Mossley was fined a total of £12 11s for allowing between 40 and 50 'young persons and females' to work more than the legally permitted hours. Other cotton masters in Mossley were also fined for similar offences in that year (Eckersley 1991, 17-18).

By the late 1840s wages and working conditions were much improved, as can be seen from Angus Reach's tour of 1849. He visited two mills in Ashton, the Bankfield Mill of John Redfern & Sons, and the Oxford Mills of Hugh Mason. He was offered no specific details as to the wages of the operatives at Bankfield Mill but Hugh Mason provided a list of weekly wages for each type of employee who worked twelve hours a day. Spinners earned 42s a week, while the average of all employees, both skilled and unskilled, was 22s 5d per week, although Reach noted 'that piecers are not included in the calculation' (Aspin 1972, 77). For comparison, the typical scale of wages for Ashton mill operatives in 1843 can be seen in Table 2.2. A widespread system of fines, stoppages and payments in kind, or truck, meant that workers were often paid less than they were owed, despite the passing of the Truck Act in 1831 which aimed to stop the practice. Dr McDouall in 1838 angrily denounced the great mill-owning Ashton family of Hyde:

'Mr Ashton has always a book very neatly balanced, showing a certain number of men to have received so much money. Now that money Mr Ashton knows never was paid, because he deducts his charges, as a landlord, for house, coal, water, and 2d per week for a Sunday School, besides other drawbacks in fines etc' (Middleton 1932, 94).

Factory conditions continued to improve in the second half of the nineteenth century, as further legislation was passed. The minimum working age of children was raised to ten in 1875, eleven in 1891, twelve in 1901 and fourteen in 1920 (Richardson 1986, 232).

However, cotton factories remained hazardous work places. Spinning required a high humidity so that mills were poorly ventilated and had high temperatures – often up to 100 degrees fahrenheit for spinning the finest cottons – conditions which made operatives susceptible to the cold. The carding room was particularly unhealthy because of the air-borne fibres which could cause severe bronchial illnesses (byssinosis), as well as stomach and eye complaints. As late as 1872 the cardroom and blowing hands in John Mayall's mills asked for an advance of 15% of their wages,

'on the grounds that the work they undertook often led to attacks of asthma, consumption, and other respiratory diseases due to the inhalation of dust' (Eckersley 1991, 22).

The Factory Act of 1867 required the installation of fans to extract dust and gases from industrial premises, and of proper sanitary facilities, but efficient air extractors and filters were not made widespread until the end of the century (Richardson 1986, 232).

Accidents were a regular feature of factory life. One of the most frequent was being caught in the textile machinery itself. In 1864 an eighteen-year old was caught in a revolving shaft at one of George Mayall's mills in Mossley and had his foot torn off, being 'quite dead by the time the machinery stopped' (*Ashton Reporter* 13/12/1864). An indication of the poor provision for health and safety needs in the nineteenth-century cotton mills of Tameside is given by the case of Jane Schofield, a nineteen-year old girl who injured her hand in one of the machines in George Mayall's mills in 1865. There were no medical provisions in the mill, and by the time the girl was taken to the doctor tetanus had set in and she died soon after. At the inquest the coroner commented that it was unfortunate that the girl had to be taken to the doctor, rather than the doctor brought to the injured (*Ashton Reporter* 23/9/1865). It was not until 1894 that the Operative Spinners Association set up its own hospital fund, through a levy of its members, with monies being donated to Ashton and District Infirmary, the Manchester Eye Hospital and the Manchester Infirmary (Eckersley 1991, 22-3).

2.5 The Rise and Fall of Industrial Paternalism

Paternalism was a significant feature of the evolution of North-West industrial society in the nineteenth century, in that it represented a fundamental change in the attitude of employers to their employees. In the early nineteenth century many employers were concerned solely with profit, and saw their workforce as merely another commodity, alongside raw materials or machinery. Employees were expected to work long hours with little rest and few holidays, thus maximizing the monetary returns of the employer (Fitton 1965, 24-5). By the mid-nineteenth century some employers had begun to view their workers in more benevolent terms, and saw themselves as the head of a large family (Walton 1987, 133).

This paternal attitude manifested itself in a number of ways. Mill-owners took the operatives on day trips to the country or seaside or provided dinner and tea parties at the mill, built houses in communities around the mill and provided recreational facilities. During

Plate 2.3 Ashton baths.
The baths were built in 1870-1 for Ashton borough with money donated by the mill-owner Hugh Mason. The external facade is Italian Romanesque in style. The building is an early example of municipal swimming baths and is exceptional in its forceful architecture.

the cotton famine of 1861-5 John Whittaker, the owner of Hurst Mills, spent over £7000 on providing for his employees and donated money to the Ashton and District Infirmary (Eckersley 1991, 99-100). This change in attitude was epitomized by Hugh Mason, one of a number of wealthy mill-owners in Tameside whose new sense of social responsibility extended to other, public works (Plate 2.3). Mason opposed trade unions and factory legislation and was a strong supporter of the prevalent ideology that everybody should look after their own interests. However, by the 1850s he regarded himself as a 'father' creating an estate of 'happily housed workers'. He held his position as employer to be 'far more sacred than that of a mere capitalist' (Ashmore & Bolton 1975, 38-9, 45).

This benevolence was not given freely. In return employers expected a disciplined workforce which obeyed factory rules, lived in model housing, was punctual, worked hard and conformed to the moral standards of the mill-owner (Walton 1987, 247-8). Arthur Mayall, of the great mill-owning family of Mossley, noted in his works' diary that workers who were also his tenants should not sublet their premises;

> 'we have plenty of minders at Britannia [Mill]...living under us and no one else working for us should engage others with families in their place' (Eckersley 1991, 103).

Hugh Mason expected his operatives to be clean, regular attenders at church, with children in Sunday School, to abstain from 'drink in any quantity or colour, gambling, racing, trotting,...the theatre, and even tobacco', even though Mason himself drank occasionally (Walton 1987, 247). He also frowned upon working wives, thus upholding the concept of paternalism in the homes of his workers (Ashmore & Bolton 1975, 39).

When this relationship broke down so-called paternalistic employers were prepared to take drastic action. During a strike in 1867, and on other occasions, the Mayall family considered breaking the protest by ejecting the mainly union strikers and their families from the workers' housing which the family owned (Eckersley 1991, 103). As for the rest of the operatives Samuel Mayall suggested in his works' diary that they should be laid off

> 'as they will be spoiled having wages paid and not working' (*ibid*, 105).

On the other hand, the success of paternalism could be reflected in the operatives' expressions of warmth and gratitude. In 1860 John Whittaker's operatives presented him with an inkstand, in recognition of

> 'those acts and principles which have endeared you to every person from the highest to the humblest' (Parry 1908, 146).

The golden age of paternalism in Tameside was between the years 1825 and 1875. In the last quarter of the nineteenth century changes in society led to its decline in importance. Industrial paternalism in Tameside was concentrated in the textile industry and by the end of the nineteenth century two trends were working against it: the stagnation, and in some areas the decline, of the textile workforce which began to emerge in this period, and the growth of large multiple-factory textile firms, which increasingly supplanted the family firm with the impersonal public limited company (Farnie & Yonekawa 1988, 178-9). Not only were the cotton firms becoming larger, but so too were people's lives and experiences. Urban development expanded and swamped the small factory colonies of early and mid-nineteenth-century Tameside, such as the Oxford Mills community in Ashton and Flowery Field in Hyde. Paternalistic mill-owners found it increasingly difficult to keep control of their operatives in towns where a growing percentage of the workforce and the electorate were not directly dependent on the textile industry for their livelihood. In Ashton the proportion of the workforce employed in the textile industry fell from 73% in the late 1830s and early 1840s to only 40% in the 1911 census (Cordingley 1986, 25; Moore 1971, 62; Shortland 1966, 27). Developments in transport separated home and workplace. Religion was also a declining influence. Where religion and work had overlapped it had been important in cementing paternal authority, as can be seen in the case of Hugh Mason. At the same time the rise of socialism and the resurgence of trade unions in the 1880s played a major role in the disintegration of the old paternal order (Walton 1987, 247-50). By the 1920s paternalism in the cotton industry was largely confined to the labour needs of the management and industrial relations (Jones 1987, 47). In other words, paternalism, where it survived into the early twentieth century, was transformed into organized industrial welfare.

2.6 Leisure and the Working Class

Prior to the Industrial Revolution people's lives were largely governed by the rhythms of the agricultural cycle. Of necessity this meant that working hours were flexible, with contrasting periods of intense activity during harvest time and relative quiet during the winter months (Jones 1987, 33). Pastimes such as drinking, horse-racing, cock-fighting and wakes were particularly popular in the pre-industrial agrarian society of the North-West (Walton 1987, 98-9). The factory system changed this, with the place of work and number of hours now being dictated by the mill-owner for an increasingly large proportion of the workforce. In the early nineteenth century this meant working over twelve hours a day, six days a week (Jones 1987, 33). Some employers were even loath to give Sundays off, as they would lose money and believed that such 'idleness' would lead the operatives into mischief. The new industrial workforce was unused to this new regimentation and some mill-owners found it necessary to lock their employees in, leading to allusions by local poets to mills as a Bastille or prison (Preece 1989, 104).

Paternalism and leisure

By the mid-nineteenth century two developments had increased people's opportunities for leisure. Firstly, there was the reduction in working hours brought about by the factory acts. Secondly, as noted above, employers adopted a different concept of their position in society, and this changed their attitude to their employees. Rather than being concerned solely with maximizing profits they now assumed a more paternal approach. As a result employers not only gave more time off work but also organized outings and provided leisure facilities.

Robert Platt, a Stalybridge mill-owner, ran annual outings to his estate at Handforth in Cheshire. The day was spent in sports competitions, eating and drinking. At one such outing, in 1856, 900 employees consumed 300lb of beef, 160lb of ham, 250lb of assorted meats, 600lb of potatoes, 300lb of plum pudding, 100lb of rice and 144 gallons of ale. Mill workers in Mossley were treated to trips to Liverpool, Blackpool and Belle Vue in Manchester, while in 1860 the *Ashton Standard* reported that 'scarcely a week passes but we chronicle a treat to the work people in some part of the district' (Eckersley 1991, 103-4).

Hugh Mason not only spent large sums of money on trips but by 1870 had provided a library, reading, lecture and smoking rooms, baths and a gymnasium for his operatives in the Oxford Mills community in Ashton (Ashmore & Bolton 1975, 40). As late as the 1920s the largest, most integrated, of the textile companies of the North-West were still able to promote a wide range of social events and leisure activities, although by the early twentieth century their organization had been absorbed into the company structure. Thus at Ashton Brothers in Hyde the responsibility for planning and regulating the recreation activities of the company was undertaken by the Labour and Welfare manager, a Mr H Clark. These activities included a sports club and gymnastic and theatrical performances (Jones 1987, 47-8).

Public houses

Even during the late nineteenth and early twentieth centuries, when new sources of recreation were available, the most popular pastime venue for the working classes was the public house (Walton 1987, 317). Public houses were more than merely drinking establishments. In the newly industrialized towns of the nineteenth century they were host to a variety of specialized organizations as disparate as discussion groups and choral societies (*ibid*, 181-2). A number of sectors of Victorian society, such as the Evangelical wing of the Church of England, strongly disapproved of public houses, and rival pursuits such as free libraries, day trips and Sunday School teas were promoted in the mid-nineteenth century in an attempt to 'improve' the working classes (*ibid*, 189-90). A variety of such events are listed in the *Ashton Reporter* for 1855 (Gow 1974, 76-8). Such disapproval was not new. Attempts to suppress alehouses had reached their peak in the North-West during the interregnum in the 1640s and 1650s, and although this ultimately failed disapproval of alehouses continued to be expressed by the upper reaches of society during the eighteenth century; the Second Gin Act of 1736, for instance, aimed to reduce the consumption of gin and the social disorder which it caused (Richardson 1986, 228; Walton 1987, 56-7, 97-9).

The growth in the number of public houses in the rapidly industrializing towns of northern England is perhaps best illustrated in Tameside by the experience of Ashton-under-Lyne. In 1718 thirteen innkeepers and alehouses are recorded in the town. By the 1770s this number had more than doubled to 32, while the population of the town was reckoned by Aikin to be 2859 in 1775, giving a ratio of one public house to every 89 inhabitants (Magee 1989, 2; Aikin 1795, 228). During the nineteenth century there were three main types of retail outlet selling alcohol; alehouses in which beer and ale were brewed and sold on the premises, taverns in which wine could be sold, and inns which provided food and lodging as well as alcohol. By the early nineteenth century nearly all the establishments in Ashton were inns and alehouses, but by 1900 inns dominated the numbers. In 1830 the number of public houses in Ashton had risen to 52 and the ratio to approximately 1 to 250. The growth in drinking establishments was encouraged by the Beerhouse Act of 1830; this aimed to popularize beer at the expense of spirits by allowing a householder on the rates to retail beer and cider from his own house for a payment of two guineas (Richardson 1986, 228). By 1860 the number of public houses in Ashton town had increased to 166, and the ratio had changed to 1 to 210. In 1900 this figure stood at 209, and the ratio had not changed. However, the Compensation Act of 1904, which set up a fund to compensate owners and licensees in the event of a house being lost, and allowed houses to be closed simply because they were no longer necessary, brought about a reduction in numbers. By 1930 there were 173 left in Ashton town (Magee 1989, 3).

The oldest public houses still on their original sites in Ashton are the Pitt and Nelson on Old Street, which dates back to at least 1749, and the Wheatsheaf in Old Square, where an inn is first recorded in 1784 (*ibid*, 46, 67). Both structures were largely rebuilt during the nineteenth century. The oldest public house in Ashton which still retains much of its original external appearance is the Stamford Arms on Stamford Street, licensed in 1796 (*ibid*, 56).

Leisure and the cotton industry in the early twentieth century

The growth in the average earnings of cotton operatives in the textile industry during the first two decades of the twentieth century allowed the development of new leisure pursuits and the expansion of others among the working classes (Jones 1987, 42). These included cinemas – by 1924 there were five cinemas in Ashton and five in Hyde – and seaside holidays (*ibid*, 37). The corollary to this relationship was that any downturn in the cotton industry might also reduce the money available for such pursuits. In Ashton holiday savings reached a peak in the year 1920 at around £100,000, but during the slump in the cotton-spinning industry in the following year they fell to around £50,000 and by the time of the great depression of

Chapter 2 An Industrial Society

1929-31 were only averaging £75,000. In the weaving centre of Hyde the figures for holiday savings peaked in 1925 at around £54,500, falling to £40,384 in 1930 (S G Jones 1989, 135).

2.7 Rural Society and the Industrial Revolution

By the eighteenth century rural society in the North-West was largely arranged on a pyramidal basis which had its origins in the medieval period (Mingay 1989, 545-8). At the top were the great landowners who had more than 3000 acres. In Tameside there were three such families during the eighteenth and nineteenth centuries, the Stamfords, Egertons and Tollemaches. Below them were the gentry – who individually held estates between 300 and 3000 acres in this period and in Tameside included old landed families such as the Dukinfields, Hollingworths and Hydes and their heirs. At the bottom were tenant farmers and landless labourers.

However, from the later eighteenth century this pattern was increasingly upset by wealthy manufacturers who wished to invest their new wealth in land. In Tameside the growing influence of such men on rural society is reflected in the land tax returns for the Cheshire townships of the Borough in the period 1780-1830 (Table 2.3). These show a clear distinction in landownership between those townships where there was an increase in the number of mills, mines, workshops, shops and houses without attached farmland, and those which remained substantially rural down to 1830. In Hollingworth, Hyde, Mottram and Newton the number of proprietors more than doubled between 1780 and 1810, while in Dukinfield there was a more than six-fold increase during the period 1820-30.

Often the new proprietors were the rising mill-owners of these townships. In 1830 the greater part of the township of Newton was held by four landowners, Lord Astley and the mill-owners George Goodier, Joseph Lees and the Ashton family. In contrast in 1790 Francis Dukinfield Astley had been the major landowner (CRO QDV2/313). A similar pattern can be seen in the township of Stayley where in 1780 the major landowner was the earl of Stamford; by 1820 he had been joined by 22 other significant landholders, many of them wealthy mill-owners, such as Joseph Harrop and Abel Hyde (CRO QDV2/393).

Not all of the industrializing townships, however, saw changes in landownership on this scale. Mottram was one of the early centres of the cotton industry in Tameside during the late eighteenth century, yet throughout the period 1780-1830 virtually the whole of the township was owned by the Tollemache family, only the bishop of Chester and the earl of Stamford

Year	Dukinfield P	Dukinfield T	Dukinfield O	Godley P	Godley T	Godley O	Hattersley P	Hattersley T	Hattersley O
1780	30	41	28	–	–	–	22	22	19
1790	21	46	26	25	25	6	39	40	12
1800	15	157	24	18	23	12	33	36	15
1810	20	195+	38	21	27	13	22	24	9
1820	29	103+	56	22	30	11	27	31	10
1830	202	342+	58	20	27	13	31	42	7

Year	Hollingworth P	Hollingworth T	Hollingworth O	Hyde P	Hyde T	Hyde O	Matley P	Matley T	Matley O
1780	16	17	5	25	45	11	12	14	7
1790	43	53+	0	19	42	20	15	22	8
1800	29	62+	21	27	51	18	17	26	6
1810	35	61+	11	60	100+	16	20	46	7
1820	26	67+	8	58	102+	18	14	57	13
1830	22	68+	23	53	114+	14	17	54	15

Year	Mottram P	Mottram T	Mottram O	Newton P	Newton T	Newton O	Stayley P	Stayley T	Stayley O
1780	16	56	7	–	–	–	87	29	39
1790	32	68+	10	19	27	–	97	40	45
1800	33	78+	24	12	69	–	94	45	44
1810	43	73+	14	50	52	21	100	63	41
1820	45	73+	19	44	94+	18	96	71+	41
1830	57	83+	29	65	184+	20	–	–	–

Table 2.3 Land tenure in the Cheshire part of Tameside by township, 1780-1830.
Key: P = proprietor; T = tenant; O = owner-occupier.
Source: land tax returns, CRO.

holding other significant blocks of land. Even though by 1841 the Hillend estate and Hague Farm had been sold to Lord Dysart and the local mill-owner Samuel Marsland, Lord Tollemache still held over half of the land in the township (CRO DTW 2477/B/10; Powell Collection). The reason why other major landowners did not emerge in Mottram is not entirely clear, but may reflect the relatively small number of large, successful textile sites established in the locality in the late eighteenth and early nineteenth centuries.

There was also a marked increase in tenants in the industrializing townships; indeed in Dukinfield, Hollingworth, Hyde and Stayley tenants were so numerous from 1800 onwards that they were no longer counted individually in the land tax returns but were referred to under the heading of 'sundry tenants' (CRO QDV2/ 148, 217, 231, 393).

Those Cheshire townships which remained largely rural in the period 1780-1830, such as Godley, Hattersley and Matley, by contrast show little fragmentation of landownership. However, one of the consequences of industrialization was substantial emigration from the countryside into the burgeoning industrial towns of Tameside, which were also swollen by immigrants from further afield, particularly from Ireland during the 1840s as a result of the potato famine (M Powell 1977, 23-4). This movement from the rural landscape to the new industrial towns may have been the cause of the drop in the population of the townships of Hattersley and Matley in the 1820s (Table 2.1), and of the static number of tenants in the Godley land tax returns for the period 1790-1830. In the words of Garnett, industrialization

> 'created a market for Labour and skill far beyond anything the farmer could offer, and the consequence has been that all who were anxious to 'get on' in the world...have been drawn into the great vortex of trade, and now people the large towns of Liverpool, Manchester, Bolton, etc' (Garnett 1849, 2).

Indeed Garnett went on to estimate that in the 1841 census only 416,763 of the 1,667,054 population of Lancashire, or 25%, were still involved in agriculture (*ibid*, 7).

Chapter 3

The Textile Industry

'Ashton...is well supplied with water, except about two months in the summer, when the inhabitants are obliged to fetch their soft water in carts from the Tame. This river abounds with trout. It is also of the highest utility to the machinery of the woollen and cotton factories of the neighbourhood; it being reckoned that within the space of ten miles from Ashton there are near 100 mills upon this stream and its tributary branches.'

(Aikin 1795, 227)

3.1 Introduction

The principal industry of Tameside from the late eighteenth to the mid-twentieth century was the production of textiles. It was this venture which introduced the factory system into the Borough, was responsible for the hundreds of mills characteristic of the area and directly led to the growth of a large urban population. The flowering of all other industries surveyed in this work sprang from the consequences of cotton's success. Even agriculture had to adjust to the increasing demands of a rapidly growing population, the result of the rise of the textile trade. The following discussion begins with a general outline of the development of the industry in the Borough, followed by a review of its progress in the seven major centres. Finally, six individual mill sites are examined, illustrating the major changes in the industry from the late eighteenth to the early twentieth century.

3.2 Outline History

The rural textile industry in the eighteenth century

Before the advent of factory-based production in the last quarter of the eighteenth century and with it the over-riding importance of cotton, the textile industry in Tameside was a domestic occupation. This early industry in the Borough was divided into two textile zones. In the upland parts, along the Longdendale valley and in the upper Tame valley at Stalybridge and Mossley, woollen spinning and weaving were the usual forms; both areas had a long history of textile production and took part in the expansion of the woollen trade during the eighteenth century.

In the lowland parts of Tameside the development of the textile industry during the eighteenth century was different, in that it was based on linen and fustian production. The focal point of this activity was Ashton-under-Lyne, which had a strong domestic-based textile industry in the seventeenth century (Nevell 1991, 89-91). Besides Ashton there were two further lowland areas which had well-established textile industries prior to the late eighteenth century: Droylsden, where the handloom weaving and bleaching of linen were extensive; and Hyde, where by the mid-eighteenth century a number of tenant farmers had turned to linen and fustian production as a secondary source of income (Speake & Witty 1953, 85-7; Bann 1976, 15).

Perhaps not surprisingly, when the factory-based cotton industry established itself in Tameside in the last quarter of the eighteenth century its distribution was centred upon the lowland zone. However, its influence even at this early date extended to the areas of Longdendale and Stalybridge where it replaced woollen production as the dominant textile industry. The last bastion of woollen manufacture in Tameside was Mossley, although by the 1830s this local industry had itself been eclipsed by cotton.

The number of sites

The present survey has identified 274 textile sites from the period *c* 1763-1930. These range from late eighteenth-century water-powered woollen mills, for scribbling and fulling, through water- and later steam-powered cotton factories, to the huge new mills of the late nineteenth and early twentieth centuries. Summary details of all of these sites, including their date

Plate 3.1 Broad Mills, Broadbottom.
Originally known as Broadbottom Mills, this mill complex was founded by William and George Sidebottom in the early 1800s for cotton spinning, weaving being added around 1834. It is a multi-period site, showing the transition from water power in the early nineteenth century to the later use of steam power. This view shows, centre right, the multi-storey Old Mill, built in two phases, in 1802 and 1814, and powered by a leat which discharged into the River Etherow through an arched outfall at the near end of the building. The two tall chimneys in the centre background flank a spinning mill added to the site in 1824, the right-hand of these chimneys marking the position of the boiler house and engine house built against the gable of this mill in the early 1830s. Broad Mills were demolished following fire damage in the late 1940s, but much of the site has recently been cleared and landscaped and the remains of the mill buildings consolidated.

ranges and the branches of the industry which each carried out, are given in Appendix 1. For convenience these sites have been divided into districts which largely correspond with the pre-1974 local government divisions of Tameside; it should be noted that Audenshaw is here included within the Ashton area and Denton within the Hyde area, the industries of both Audenshaw and Denton being offshoots of the two larger cotton towns.

The total numbers of sites in each district in the textile industry as a whole and in each of its main branches are summarized in Tables 3.1 and 3.3-3.7, with the total number of new sites per decade being given in Table 3.2. In some instances the date at which a site opened or closed could not be established to a precise year or even to a particular decade; the inclusion of the latter cases within the tables is based upon the first and last dates at which the site is known to have been in operation.

It should also be noted that in Tables 3.1 and 3.3-3.7 the given totals more often than not exceed the maximum number of mills known to have been working within any single year in that decade. There are two exceptions. The first involves the early decades of the industry and its various branches, before the first closures – prior to the 1790s in cotton spinning, for example; the second exception involves those decades when the opening of new sites had finally ceased – after the 1900s in the case of cotton spinning – in which cases the figures given are for the number of working mills at the start of the decade.

Chapter 3 The Textile Industry

Decade	AuL	Dr	Du	Hy	Long	Mos	St	Total
1760-9					1	1		2
1770-9	3				1	5	2	11
1780-9	5	2		4	5	6	3	25
1790-9	16	5	3	10	11	14	10	69
1800-9	24	5	5	14	12	16	19	95
1810-9	24	3	8	19	12	18	22	106
1820-9	38	2	10	21	10	21	28	130
1830-9	41	5	12	23	8	22	30	141
1840-9	42	6	12	23	8	27	30	148
1850-9	49	9	15	25	10	31	34	173
1860-9	**56**	12	18	29	**13**	36	**35**	199
1870-9	51	13	**20**	**31**	12	**38**	35	**200**
1880-9	49	13	20	30	11	36	29	188
1890-9	43	13	18	23	10	37	26	170
1900-9	41	**14**	17	22	10	35	28	167
1910-9	38	13	17	21	9	34	25	157
1920-9	35	12	16	20	6	34	25	148
1930-9	32	10	16	18	6	33	23	138

Table 3.1 Working textile sites (**not** firms) per decade in Tameside, 1760-1939.
Sources: see individual entries in Appendix 1.
(The term site here and in Table 3.2 refers to purpose-built mills or converted buildings used for cotton production, wool production or finishing. Emboldened numbers here and in Tables 3.2-3.7 indicate the peak number of sites recorded in a single decade. *Key:* AuL – Ashton-under-Lyne; Dr – Droylsden; Du – Dukinfield; Hy – Hyde; Long – Longdendale; Mos – Mossley; St – Stalybridge.)

Decade	AuL	Dr	Du	Hy	Long	Mos	St	Total
1760-9					1	1		2
1770-9	3					4	2	9
1780-9	3	2		4	4	1	1	15
1790-9	11	**3**	**3**	**6**	**6**	**8**	7	**44**
1800-9	8	2	2	4	1	2	**9**	28
1810-9	3		3	5		3	4	18
1820-9	**13**		2	3		3	9	30
1830-9	5	3	2	4		3	4	21
1840-9	4	1	2	1		5		13
1850-9	9	3	3	3	2	4	4	28
1860-9	8	3	3	5	3	5	2	29
1870-9	2	1	2	2		2		9
1880-9	3		2			1	2	8
1890-9	4		1		1	1	1	8
1900-9	4	1	1	2		1	3	12
Total	80	19	26	39	18	44	48	274

Table 3.2 Textile sites (**not** firms) established in Tameside, 1760-1909.
Sources: see individual entries in Appendix 1.

Innovators and factory pioneers 1771-1853

The opening of Richard Arkwright's first water-powered cotton-spinning mill in 1771 at Cromford, in Derbyshire, arguably marked the beginning of the factory system in the textile industry (Williams with Farnie 1992, 13). Such novel manufactories required large concentrations of operatives working in multi-storey purpose-built blocks. In towns and rural areas where the largest building had been the parish church or local manor house, the new mills formed the focal point of the landscape, expressing the new industrial system's economic and social dominance.

Such a revolution in the process of textile manufacture was made possible by a series of inventions from 1764 which transformed the preparation and spinning of cotton and, later, wool. The first of these was James Hargreaves's spinning jenny in 1764. Next was the water frame, which was patented by Arkwright in 1769 and was the first spinning machine to be used in the new cotton mills. In 1775 Arkwright also developed a continuous carding machine. The mule spinning machine was designed by Samuel Crompton in 1779, although it was not made fully automatic until the introduction of the self-acting mule by Richard Roberts in 1830. Around 1800 a larger, faster water frame, the throstle, was introduced. A cost-effective powerloom was only introduced into the cotton industry in 1822, when Roberts patented his cast-iron frame powerloom. The woollen industry had to await the arrival of a powerloom in the 1830s and a fully automatic combing process in 1853, before it too was fully mechanized (Benson 1983).

The finishing processes were transformed in the late eighteenth and early nineteenth centuries by the introduction of chemicals and mechanization. In the bleaching industry these innovations included the use of sulphuric acid for souring, the manufacture of bleaching powder (resulting from the discovery of chlorine in 1774) and the gradual replacement of plant alkalis with caustic soda (Ashmore 1969, 61). These developments in the bleaching industry were coupled with the use of first water-powered and later steam-powered printing, a cylinder printing machine being patented by Thomas Bell in 1783 (Benson 1983, 18). Later, steam power was applied to many of the other finishing processes such as washing, squeezing, singeing and drying. In Tameside finishing sites were relatively few (Table 3.7), perhaps because the type of site which was required, with plentiful supplies of clean water, had already been taken by the first generation of spinning factories. Consequently a number of the finishing sites in the Borough, such as Hodge and Buckton Vale print works, were on the site of earlier spinning mills (Appendix 1, nos 169 and 226).

Decade	AuL	Dr	Du	Hy	Long	Mos	St	Total
1770-9	1						1	2
1780-9	5	1		4	4		2	16
1790-9	16	4	3	10	9	2	6	50
1800-9	24	2	4	13	10	5	16	74
1810-9	23		7	17	9	8	25	89
1820-9	31		8	16	8	10	24	97
1830-9	30		7	7	5	13	20	82
1840-9	29		6	7	5	18	20	85
1850-9	29		8	7	7	19	21	91
1860-9	31	1	9	11	7	21	21	101
1870-9	26	3	10	13	6	24	20	102
1880-9	25	3	11	12	5	23	16	95
1890-9	25	3	13	11	4	23	13	92
1900-9	25	4	12	10	4	21	13	89
1910-9	22	3	12	9	3	21	12	82
1920-9	21	3	11	9	2	21	12	79
1930-9	18	3	11	8	2	20	11	73

Table 3.3 The distribution of working cotton-spinning, doubling and waste mills in Tameside per decade. Sources: see Appendix 1.

Steam power, in the form of the Boulton and Watt beam engine, was first introduced into a mill as an additional power source to water in 1785. In Tameside it was not until 1790-3 that the first such engine was installed, in the mill at Stalybridge known as the Old Soot Poke, and not until around 1800 that they became

Decade	AuL	Dr	Du	Hy	Long	Mos	St	Total
1760-9					1	1		2
1770-9					1	4	1	6
1780-9					1	4	1	6
1790-9					1	11	4	16
1800-9			1		1	12	5	19
1810-9			1		1	11	4	17
1820-9			1			11	4	16
1830-9			1			10	2	13
1840-9						11	2	13
1850-9						11	1	12
1860-9						11	2	13
1870-9						11	2	13
1880-9						8	1	9
1890-9						9	2	11
1900-9						7	2	9
1910-9						6	2	8
1920-9						6	2	8
1930-9						11	2	13

Table 3.4 The distribution of working woollen mills in Tameside per decade. Sources: see Appendix 1.

popular (Haynes 1990, 16). After this date those towns nearest coal-bearing deposits saw the greatest growth in the textile industry. The introduction of the steam engine also encouraged the building of many mills beside the new canals, which provided not only a ready means of transport but also a supply of water for the steam condensers. From the 1800s most new mills were built using steam as the sole source of power, the first purpose-built steam-powered cotton factory in Tameside probably being Water Street Mill in Stalybridge, erected in 1797 (*ibid*, 21). Nevertheless, water power remained an important adjunct until the middle of the nineteenth century.

In Tameside, as elsewhere in the North-West, the movement from a domestic- to a factory-based and increasingly mechanized industry required new forms of accommodation, giving rise to the building of multi-storey water- and steam-powered mills. Williams's recent study of cotton mills in Greater Manchester has provided a framework for the technological and stylistic development of the region's mills, and makes any detailed discussion here superfluous (Williams with Farnie 1992). In the initial pioneering phase of industrial expansion, during the 1780s and 1790s, the early factories were frequently housed in converted barns or purpose-built sheds. In Tameside two such early factories have been identified, both in Mottram (Fig 3.12; Plate 3.3).

By 1795 Aikin could state that there were nearly 100 cotton mills along the River Tame and its tributaries (Aikin 1795, 227). It is now possible to at least partially confirm this assertion, for the present study has identified 69 textile sites in Tameside during the 1790s (Table 3.1). In this early period the main cotton mill concentrations were in Ashton, Hyde, Longdendale and Stalybridge, whilst most of the woollen mills were located in Mossley (Tables 3.3 and 3.4).

The growth in the size of mills during the early nineteenth century was slow, despite the dramatic leap in the country's cotton production. The average size of the Lancashire spinning mill in Samuel Crompton's survey of 1811 was 8161 spindles; by 1850 this had risen only to 11,818 (Farnie 1979, 215). Most of the new mills of the early nineteenth century were built by single-unit firms or private individuals and many were in multiple occupancy (Williams with Farnie 1992, 50-1). It has been estimated that in Lancashire in 1841 the average cotton firm employed between 100 and 200 people on a single site, while only 85 firms employed more than 500 people and only 25 employed more than 1000 (Walton 1987, 108).

The advent of the powerloom in the 1820s, coupled with a mill-building boom in 1823-5, marked a shift in the Lancashire cotton industry towards combined firms, carrying out both spinning and weaving. Power-

Chapter 3 The Textile Industry

looms were first installed in a Tameside spinning mill at Newton Moor Mills in Hyde by the Ashton brothers around 1810 (PP 1834 xx, D1, 55 no 40). By the 1820s Hyde was the leading centre of powerloom weaving in the Borough with twelve combined mills, although the growth of combined mills in Ashton had matched that in Hyde by the 1840s (Table 3.5). By 1833 there were 14,000 powerlooms in Ashton, Stalybridge, Hyde and Dukinfield and handloom weaving had virtually disappeared (Haynes forthcoming; Walton 1987, 109). Combined mills reached their peak nationally in the 1850s when they contained 52% of all spindles and 82% of all looms in the country (Farnie 1979, 317). In Tameside they accounted for 37.6% of all working textile sites recorded in the Borough during this period, although their greatest number was not reached until the 1870s when 74 are recorded (Table 3.5).

The rise of specialization 1853-1901

This period saw the impetus for growth in the industry move away from improvements in machinery towards economic change. The arrival of the railways in Tameside during the 1840s gave the local industry better access to raw materials and coal supplies, and its goods easier access to markets at home and abroad. Many mills were located close to the railways and some were even linked by their own sidings.

The development of British textile machinery slowed considerably during this period. John Thorpe's ring spindle was developed in America in 1828 (Benson 1983, 20-1), but was slow to become popular in Britain and it was not until the 1880s that ring spindles began to be installed in Tameside mills (Haynes 1987, 5). In 1894 the first Northrop loom was installed in America (Benson 1983, 26). This was the first system to replace the weft automatically without stopping and its greater efficiency was quickly realized in the weaving concerns of the Hyde area, where firms were installing them in their mills by the early 1900s. Both inventions were of great significance in that they provided new machines capable of further technical development, unlike the spinning mule which by the end of the nineteenth century had reached its maximum potential.

A short-lived boom after the cotton famine of 1861-5 marked the end of expansion in most of the textile towns of Tameside, at least in terms of the number of working textile sites which appear to have peaked in 1869-70 at approximately 190 (Appendix 1). Nationally the depressions of 1877-9, 1884-5 and 1891-3 marked the permanent loss of some overseas markets and accentuated a growing tendency in the industry towards specialization in either weaving or spinning (Farnie 1979, 171-2, 187-8). In Lancashire the north-

Decade	AuL	Dr	Du	Hy	Long	Mos	St	Total
1800-9				1				1
1810-9	1			3		1		5
1820-9	9		2	12		1	4	28
1830-9	12	2	5	15	1	1	9	45
1840-9	15	3	5	15	1	1	9	49
1850-9	23	4	7	16	2	2	11	65
1860-9	**24**	5	7	17	**3**	**4**	**12**	72
1870-9	24	5	**8**	**18**	3	4	12	**74**
1880-9	21	5	6	17	3	4	11	67
1890-9	17	5	3	11	3	4	11	54
1900-9	14	**6**	2	11	3	4	12	52
1910-9	13	6	2	11	3	4	10	49
1920-9	13	6	2	11	3	4	10	49
1930-9	12	4	2	10	3	4	10	45

Table 3.5 The distribution of working combined cotton mills in Tameside per decade.
Sources: see Appendix 1.

east of the county concentrated on weaving and the south-east on spinning. Specialist weaving had never been a significant element of the Tameside textile industry. The first weaving mill had been built in the 1830s, at Edge Lane in Droylsden (Appendix 1, no 81). In the 1880s there were still only nine weaving mills, accounting for only 4.8% of all textile sites in the Borough (Table 3.6).

Although the combined mill-building boom of the 1820s and 1830s had led to a drop in the number of working specialist spinning mills, these had remained in the majority in all townships except Droylsden (a township dominated by combined mills and weaving mills) and Hyde (where 65% of all textile sites in the 1830s were combined mills) (Tables 3.3 and 3.5). Nevertheless, the proportion of specialist spinning

Decade	AuL	Dr	Du	Hy	Long	Mos	St	Total
1830-9		1	1					2
1840-9		1						1
1850-9	1	**2**		1		**1**		5
1860-9	2	2	1	1		1		7
1870-9	2	2	**2**	1		1		8
1880-9	**3**	1	2	1		1	**1**	**9**
1890-9	2	1	2	1		1		7
1900-9	1	1	2	**2**		1		7
1910-9	1	1	2	2		1		7
1920-9	2	1	2	2		1	1	9
1930-9	2	1	2	2		1	1	9

Table 3.6 The distribution of working cotton-weaving mills in Tameside per decade.
Sources: see Appendix 1.

Decade	AuL	Dr	Du	Hy	Long	Mos	St	Total
1770-9	2							2
1780-9	2	1						3
1790-9	1	1			1			3
1800-9	1	2			2	1		6
1810-9	1	2		1	2	1		7
1820-9	1	2	1	1	2	2		9
1830-9	1	2	1	1	2	1		8
1840-9	1	2	1	1	2	1	1	9
1850-9	1	3	1	2	2	1	1	11
1860-9	1	4	1	2	3	1	1	13
1870-9	1	4	1	2	3	1	1	13
1880-9	1	4	1	2	3	1	1	13
1890-9	1	4	1	2	3	1	1	13
1900-9	1	4	1	2	3	1	1	13
1910-9	1	4	1	2	3	1	1	13
1920-9	1	3	1	2	1	1	1	10
1930-9	1	3		2	1	1		8

Table 3.7 The distribution of working finishing works in Tameside per decade.
Sources: see Appendix 1.

mills in the Borough fell from 75% of all textile sites in the 1820s to 51% in the 1860s. In the 1890s, however, this figure was perceptibly on the rise, at 54%. By contrast combined mills, which in the 1880s still accounted for 36% of all textile sites, had dropped to 32% by the following decade. Hyde in particular saw a great retreat from the combined mill, from seventeen sites in the 1880s to eleven in the 1890s, a fall of 35%.

After the peak in the 1870s the total number of working mills per decade fell steadily to the end of the century (Table 3.1). Similarly in each of the last three decades of the century the number of new mill sites established was less than a third of the number established in the 1850s or 1860s (Table 3.2). At the same time, however, the number of spindles and looms continued to rise, although the rate of expansion in Tameside was far lower than that experienced nationally (Haynes 1990, 11). Nationally, the average size of a mill increased by 227% between 1850 and 1890, from 11,818 to 38,618 spindles, but these figures mask a shift towards very much larger spinning mills, firstly of around 50,000 spindles in the 1870s, then of around 100,000 spindles in the 1890s (Farnie 1979, 215). This expansion was led by the joint-stock limited liability companies, the only ones with sufficient capital to invest in the expensive, huge new mills.

There was also a corresponding growth in the late nineteenth century in the size of firms. This was expressed not just in terms of these new 'super' mills, but also in the growth of the multiple-unit firm. In Tameside the main centres of these large firms were Ashton and Mossley. In Ashton the syndicate of Messrs Barlow, Marland, Coop, Newton, Pollitt and Pownall built seven mills between 1891 and 1905 adding a total of 550,710 spindles to the town's spinning capacity (Haynes 1987, 48-53). Perhaps the most significant of these large firms in the late nineteenth century was that of John Mayall & Co in Mossley. Founded in 1846, from 1857 to 1891 this was the largest spinning company in the world and in the mid-1890s had a spindleage of 444,000 in seven mills (Farnie & Yonekawa 1988, 173; Williams with Farnie 1992, 27).

Boom and bust 1901-30

The Edwardian period marked the Indian summer of the cotton industry, not only in Tameside, but across the country. There was a mill-building boom in Lancashire during the period 1900-10 which saw capacity increase even further, despite the continuing loss of overseas markets (Williams with Farnie 1992, 14). The degree to which the textile areas of Tameside took part in this Edwardian mill-building boom varied. Droylsden, Dukinfield and Mossley each saw only one new site established in this period, and Longdendale none; Ashton, Hyde and Stalybridge witnessed the greatest activity (Table 3.2). In Ashton the last of the Ashton syndicate mills were built in the 1900s. In Stalybridge the Premier, Victor and Ray mills were all built by the same syndicate between 1903 and 1907 and formally united as one firm in 1911 (Haynes 1990, 38-9). Of particular note was the first completely electrically powered mill to be built in Tameside, Premier Mill, erected in 1906; this mill was also remarkable in its unusual shed design for a combined mill and for its use of only ring spindles (Fig 3.10). The textile industry in Hyde was particularly strong during this period as the town increasingly specialized in weaving on Northrop looms. As a consequence the number of looms in Hyde mills increased by 50% between 1904 and 1921 (Williams with Farnie 1992, 29).

The end of the First World War was followed by the boom of 1919-20, engendered by the great demand for Lancashire goods in countries which had been cut off from Britain during the war and by an attempt to catch up with domestic demand (*ibid*, 14). This boom proved inflationary and did not lead to any significant increase in capacity. Although national output was to peak in 1926, exports in the boom period did not reach pre-war levels and many companies were refloated at vastly inflated prices (*ibid*, 16-17). Depression set in during 1921, with over-capitalization leading to a financial crisis as it became apparent that Lancashire's traditional export areas in China, Egypt and India were permanently lost to their native industries (Walton

Chapter 3 The Textile Industry

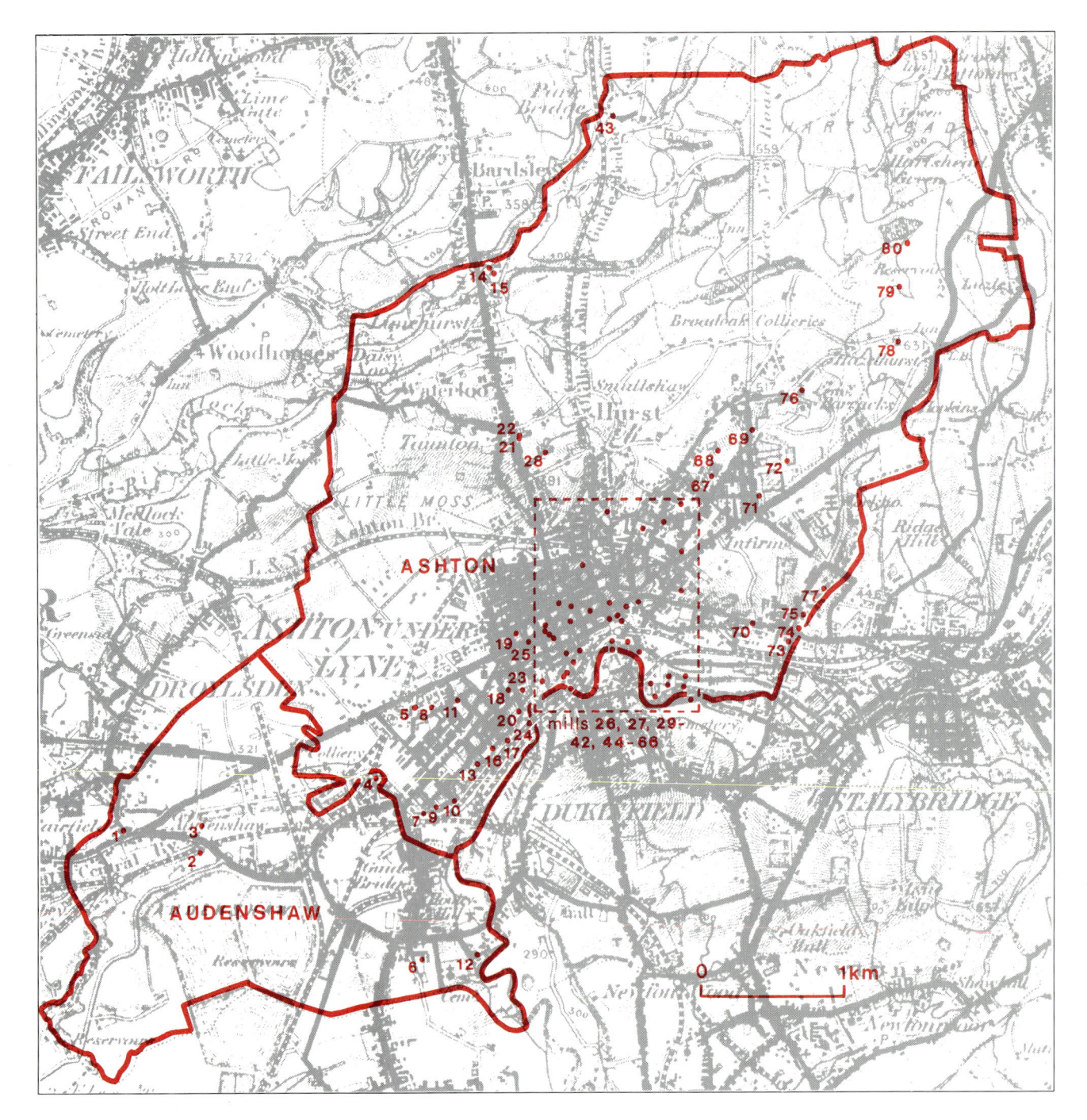

Fig 3.1 The mills of Ashton and Audenshaw.
Key: 1 Moss Brook Mill; 2 Dean Head Mill; 3 Slate Lane Mills; 4 Guide Bridge Mills; 5 Fern Mill; 6 Braganza Mill; 7 Guide Mills; 8 Ryecroft Mills; 9 Duncan Street Mills; 10 Birch Mill; 11 Ryecroft Mills; 12 Shepley Mills; 13 Oxford Mills; 14 Bardsley Vale Mill; 15 Bardsley Mills; 16 Grosvenor Mill; 17 West Mill; 18 Junction Mills; 19 Portland Mills; 20 Walk Mill; 21 Wilshaw Mill; 22 Rock Mill; 23 Tudor Mill; 24 Bridge End Mills; 25 Egret Mill; 26 Bank Mills; 27 Flash Hall Mills; 28 Atlas Mill; 29 Cross Street Mill; 30 Old Street Mill; 31 Good Hope Mill; 32 Stanley Mill; 33 Bankfield Mill; 34 Cavendish Mill; 35 Cavendish Street Mill; 36 Gas Street Mill; 37 Ashton Old Mill; 38 Croft Mill; 39 Albion Mill; 40 Charlestown Mill; 41 Wharf Mill; 42 Delamere Street Mill; 43 Park Bridge Mill; 44 Lees Street Mill; 45 Kenworthy's Mill; 46 Foundry Street Mill; 47 Gladstone Mill; 48 Brassey's Mill; 49 Oldham's Mill; 50 Grey Street Mill; 51 Knowles' Mill; 52 Wood and Harrop's Mill; 53 James Ogden's Mill; 54 Bridge End Mill; 55 Hurst Mount Mill; 56 Minerva Mill; 57 Texas Mill; 58 Hurst Brook Mill; 59 Sharp's Shrubbies; 60 Ralph Ogden's Mill; 61 Bengal Mill; 62 Waterside Mills; 63 Harper Mills; 64 Leigh/Tame Valley Thread Mill; 65 Wellington Mills; 66 Whitelands Mills; 67 Curzon/Alger Mill; 68 Cedar Mill; 69 Hurst Mills; 70 Currier Slacks Mill; 71 Carrs/Whittaker's Mill; 72 Carrs/Stamford Commercial Mill; 73 Cockbrook Mill; 74 Throstle Nest Mill; 75 Higham Fold Mill; 76 Gibraltar Mill; 77 Park Hall Mill; 78 Hazelhurst Mill; 79 Mellor's Mill; 80 Tongue Bottom.

1987, 328). The situation was worsened by the deep world depression of 1929-32 which saw world cotton production drop (Farnie & Yonekawa 1988, 179).

These crises affected the whole of the cotton industry, but according to Farnie the spinning capacity of Tameside declined more rapidly than any other sector of the Lancashire cotton industry (Williams with Farnie 1992, 29). In Mossley the collapse of the cotton industry during the late 1920s and early 1930s was partly offset by a move back to woollen production. The number of woollen mills in the town actually rose in the 1930s for the first time in more than 100 years, as the woollen industry assumed primacy over the cotton industry for the first time since the 1820s.

3.3 The Development of the Main Centres

Ashton-under-Lyne (including Audenshaw)

The borough of Ashton-under-Lyne was the leading textile centre in Tameside and one of the leading cotton-spinning areas in the Lancashire textile region. During the last quarter of the eighteenth century the beginnings of the factory system were introduced to the area in the form of hand-, horse- or water-powered cotton-spinning mills. With the introduction of steam power around 1800 Ashton entered 60 years of rapid expansion which saw the population of the town increase more than five-fold and the number of textile sites more than double (Tables 2.1 and 3.1). By the time the cotton famine of 1861-5 arrested the town's growth the industry was dominated by medium-sized family or privately owned spinning and combined firms. The cotton famine marked the end of this period of rapid expansion, with the greatest number of operatives, firms and mills being reached in the 1860s. During the next 60 years the industry remained generally stable and while the number of firms and mills slowly declined, the number of spindles used in the local mills continued to rise. During the late nineteenth century the joint-stock companies became popular in the Ashton area and were responsible for building the largest spinning mills in the town, at around 85,000 spindles. Ashton could not escape the effects of the permanent loss of overseas markets in the 1920s. Although most mills in the Ashton area remained in production, the collapse of the industry was only postponed by a decade, with more than half of the area's mills and firms closing in the 1930s.

The present survey has recorded 80 textile sites established in the modern districts of Ashton and Audenshaw in the period 1773-1905 (Appendix 1; Fig 3.1). These included 59 spinning and doubling mills, fifteen combined mills, three weaving mills, two print works and one silk mill, although between 1824 and 1896 thirteen spinning mills became combined.

Haynes's recent work on the rise and fall of the cotton industry in Ashton provides the most detailed study of the industry in this area, although Ashmore's brief discussion remains very useful (Haynes 1987; Ashmore 1974). Much of what follows is of necessity taken from Haynes's work, although the emphasis of the present survey differs.

Analysis of the Ashton parish registers for the first decade of the eighteenth century indicates that of the 57.5% of entries which recorded occupations 33.2% named textiles as the primary occupation. The dominant textile occupation was weaving, probably of fustian fabrics, accounting for 19.7% of the total occupation entries, with clothiers accounting for 5.5% (Brierley 1928). By the middle of the eighteenth century this industry was based on the putting-out system, with Manchester check merchants using Ashton weavers to supply their cloth (Ashmore 1974, 87; Baines 1836, 551). In 1795 Aikin stated that

> 'The people of Ashton and the neighbourhood about sixty years ago were almost wholly employed in spinning cotton wefts for check-makers or twist to make fustian warps. They likewise furnished single cotton harder thrown to make warps for flight goods' (Aikin 1795, 233).

From about 1760 houses with loomshops were built or converted in increasing numbers (Ashmore 1974, 87-8). In Ashton town itself the earliest surviving loomshop is situated on Wellington Street and was built as part of the Georgian planned town in the period 1787-1803 (Plate 9.4; Fig 9.7). However, the whole parish took part in the domestic-based industry, and according to the eighteenth-century parish registers there were significant numbers of textile workers in the Hartshead/Hurst and Littlemoss areas. At the junction of Old Road and Gorsey Lane in Hazelhurst is a three-storey stone-built house, the upper floor of which has been identified as a probable loomshop (Ashmore 1974, 87), and there are two other such buildings on the road from Hartshead to Mossley (SD 964 026, SD 967 022). In Littlemoss a row of brick cottages, New Row (SJ 917 999), with the datestone 1787, is the last remnant of an extensive weaving community which according to the parish registers was established here by the 1720s (Brierley 1928). In 1823 Butterworth described New Row as

> 'a group of neat brick-built cottages...which gives a rural charm to the habitations of the laborious and industrious artisans most of whom are employed in forming that delicate fabric called muslin' (Butterworth 1823, 80).

Chapter 3 The Textile Industry

Throughout Ashton's life as a major cotton centre spinning was always dominant, although weaving continued to form a significant minority sector. The first cotton-spinning mills to be erected in the Ashton area were water-, hand- or horse-powered. A favoured location in the period 1773-1800 was along the fast flowing Hurst and Cock brooks, in the hilly north-eastern part of the township. The earliest known spinning mill in the Ashton area was Throstle Nest Mill, a water-powered mill on Cock Brook, in operation by 1779 and probably then owned by a small group of local fustian manufacturers (Ashmore 1974, 88; Haynes 1987, 1, 10). However, the two earliest known textile sites in the township were on the River Tame. Part of the old manorial corn-mill in Ashton town was converted for use as a print works by Surries and Whitaker in 1773 (Graham 1846, 343). This was followed around 1777 by the establishment of the Shepley print works by Thomas Phillips and John Nash at Shepley Hall (*ibid*, 424).

By 1803 there were seven mule spinning factories in Ashton town (Haynes 1987, 2). The earliest of these was probably the premises belonging to John Wood and John Harrop in Stamford Street, described as a factory as early as 1793. It was also probably the first mill in the Ashton area to have a steam engine installed, Wood and Harrop ordering a 12hp Boulton and Watt engine in 1799 (*ibid*, 13). Conversely, the last water-powered mill to be erected in the Ashton area was at Park Hall in about 1805. Built by John and Edward Chadwick, it was the fourth water-powered mill to be erected on Cock Brook (*ibid*, 19).

By the end of 1805 a total of 25 textile sites had been established in the Ashton area, although by that same date one of these had already closed. All bar Shepley Hall print works were cotton-spinning factories. Seven were in Ashton town and a further four could be found in the vicinity of Hurst Brook. Most were owned by separate individuals and only three were in multiple tenancy (Appendix 1; Haynes 1987, 9-19).

No new mills were built in the Ashton area until 1815. When building resumed in that year, with the erection of Croft Mill, the nature and gravity of the industry had shifted decisively. From now on all new mills were steam-driven and Ashton town centre, with the Ashton Canal providing the mills with both water and coal, was the favoured location. Sixteen mills were built in the town during the period 1815-29 (*ibid*, 22-3).

The number of mule spindles in Ashton town was already 95,880 by 1811, although Haynes believes that this may have been lower than during the mill-building boom in the Lancashire textile industry in 1801-3 (*ibid*, 3). Powerloom weaving was introduced around 1818, by which time there were 300 looms in the town, possibly at Flash Hall Mills, which was also the earliest mill in Ashton to be lit by gas (*ibid*, 3, 24). In the 1820s the number of powerlooms in the town increased rapidly; by 1835 there were 4000 looms and by 1843 as many as 6738. This rise was achieved by the conversion of many spinning mills to combined operations – the first purpose-built combined mill, Whittaker's Mill, was not erected in the Ashton area until 1847 (*ibid*, 39). As a consequence of the rise of the powerloom, the number of handloom weavers declined rapidly, from 2800 in the town in 1817 to 320 in the mid-1830s (*ibid*, 3). Of the 42 mills recorded in the Ashton area in the 1840s, fifteen were combined (Tables 3.1 and 3.5).

The booms in cotton-spinning mill building in the Lancashire textile industry in 1823-5 and 1832-7 saw ten and four new mills built respectively in Ashton (Appendix 1). This activity was mostly concentrated around the western end of Ashton town and along the Ashton Canal, especially from 1832 onwards. By the mid-1850s fourteen mills were strung along the Ashton Canal from Guide Bridge to County Bridge, while a further two mills were built on the banks of the Hollinwood branch of the Ashton Canal through Bardsley (Ashmore 1974, 90-1; Haynes 1987, 22, 31-2 35, 42). The building of Whittaker's and Harper mills in 1847 and 1855 marked the resurgence of Hurst as a cotton mill area (Haynes 1987, 39, 41). In 1843 a total of 595,276 mule spindles were in operation in the town, while 10,520 people were employed in the industry (*ibid*, 3).

The cotton famine of 1861-5 marked a significant watershed in Ashton's development, bringing to an end over 80 years of, at times, rapid growth. In the 1860s the number of textile sites in the area reached a maximum of 56 (Table 3.1), and although spindleage continued to increase, the number of textile sites and firms steadily fell during the remainder of the nineteenth century. The cotton famine also had a serious effect on the population of Ashton. Between 1801 and 1861 the population of the town had leapt from about 6500 to 34,886, but between 1861 and 1871 it declined to 31,984, only Stalybridge among the local cotton towns suffering worse depopulation (see Chapter 2). In the second half of the nineteenth century the populations of Ashton, Dukinfield and Stalybridge saw the slowest increase of any cotton town in the North-West, that of Ashton reaching 43,890 in 1901 (Williams with Farnie 1992, 27; Table 2.1). Furthermore, the number of operatives involved in the textile industry in Ashton had peaked in 1861, at 11,343, and from then on declined (Haynes 1987, 4).

In the second half of the nineteenth century joint-stock companies began to gain ground in Ashton, the

Chapter 3 The Textile Industry

Plate 3.2 Cavendish Mill, Ashton.
Cavendish Mill, built in 1884-5, replaced the earlier Bankfield Mill of 1820-1. In size the building is typical of the larger mills of the late nineteenth century in Tameside. It was constructed by the Cavendish Spinning Co Ltd, one of two mill-building companies founded in the 1880s in Ashton. When first opened it contained 72,360 mule spindles. Cavendish Mill closed in 1934, one of eighteen out of 32 mills to close in Ashton during that decade.

area eventually becoming the leading centre of the movement in Tameside (Williams with Farnie 1992, 28). The first two joint-stock companies in Ashton, Brassey's weaving mill and Knowles' spinning mill, were founded in 1861 but it was not until the second joint-stock boom in the Lancashire textile industry in the years 1873-5 that such companies properly established themselves in the area. Twelve were formed in this short period, although half of these took over existing mills (Haynes 1987, 4). However, family or private firms continued to command a large share of the output in Ashton until the end of the century. In 1888 of the 1,775,784 mule spindles in the town's mills 977,296 were in private hands but by 1911, when spindleage had risen to 2,076,728, only 176,980 were in private control (*ibid*, 5).

The number of working combined mills recorded in the Ashton area fell from 24 in the 1870s to seventeen in the 1890s as a result of competition from north-east Lancashire for their weaving goods, as well as from the joint-stock companies in the spinning sector (Table 3.5; Williams with Farnie 1992, 27). Only one specialist weaving firm was established in Ashton town in the late nineteenth century, Carrs Mill, built by the Carrs Manufacturing Co Ltd in 1884 (*ibid*, 181). The remaining twelve mills built between 1875 and 1905 were all large spinning blocks (Haynes 1987, 44) (Plate 3.2).

The last mills to be built in Ashton were erected by the Ashton syndicate of Messrs Barlow, Marland, Coop, Newton, Pollitt and Pownall, which set up seven joint-stock mill-building companies in Ashton

Chapter 3 The Textile Industry

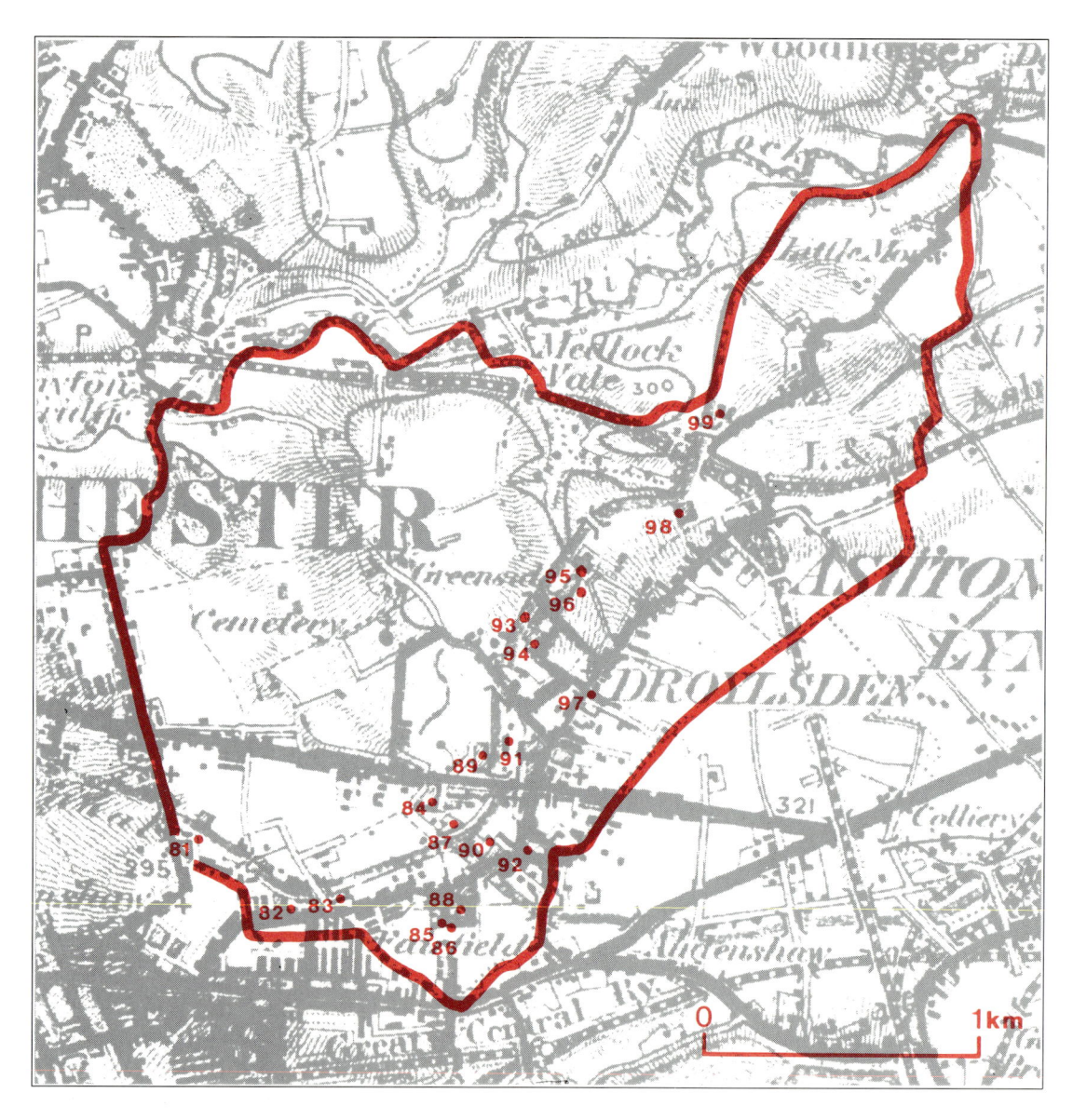

Fig 3.2 The mills of Droylsden.
Key: 81 Edge Lane Mill; 82 Droylsden Copperas/Springfield Print Works; 83 Fairfield Dyeing Works; 84 Victoria Mills; 85 Boys' Boarding Academy; 86 Boys' Sunday School; 87 Angola Mill; 88 Nos 21 & 22 Fairfield Square; 89 Fairfield Mills; 90 Droylsden Mills; 91 Greenside Lane Dyeworks; 92 John Hammond's Factory; 93 Albion Mill; 94 Beetle Dyeing and Finishing Works; 95 Oakfield Mill; 96 Saxon Mill; 97 Swindell and Booth's Factory; 98 Royal Mill; 99 Lumb Mill.

between 1891 and 1905. These new mills, Atlas, Cedar, Curzon, Minerva, Rock, Texas and Tudor, were largely responsible for the continuing increase in Ashton's total spindleage, adding a total of 550,710 spindles to the town's capacity. They specialized in the spinning of Bolton counts from Egyptian cotton, but did so on the old fashioned mule spindle. In the 1920s five of these mills, Atlas, Cedar, Rock, Texas and Tudor, became part of the Atlas Mills Ltd group, accounting for nearly 400,000 spindles (*ibid*, 48-53).

Despite the lack of technical innovation in those mills built by joint-stock companies, ring spinning had been introduced into Ashton during the 1880s and by 1911 there were about 300,000 ring spindles in nine mills, eight of which were run by five combined firms. The town reached its peak spindleage in 1920 when there were 2,084,026 spindles in operation along with 11,182 looms, this last figure being virtually the same as in 1911 (*ibid*, 5). The problems of the severe textile depression of the 1920s were partly offset by the lack of participation by Ashton firms in the recapitalization boom of 1919-20, although three Ashton mills closed during this decade (*ibid*, 6). The major crisis in the local textile industry had been postponed only by a few years. Eighteen mills, out of 32, closed in the Ashton area during the 1930s, with those producing coarser counts of yarn from American cotton being particularly hard hit (*ibid*, 4; Appendix 1).

Droylsden

Droylsden experienced two phases of cotton expansion, the first in 1785-1806, during the pioneering period of the industry, the second in 1835-60, led by the building of steam-powered cotton mills along the Hollinwood branch of the Ashton Canal. The failure of the early industry was probably a result of Droylsden's lack of suitable water and coal supplies and its relative isolation from the surrounding cotton centres. The resurgence of the industry in the 1830s may owe its origin to the increasing cost of setting up new businesses in nearby Manchester and the decreasing number of suitable sites in Ashton. The industry was dominated by single-unit family firms. Although combined firms were common by the mid-nineteenth century there was also a strong bleaching and dyeing industry, which had its roots in the eighteenth-century domestic linen industry. By the early twentieth century the area specialized in medium-sized combined firms, although the dyeing industry was still strong. The industry was able to weather the crises of the 1920s and 1930s tolerably well.

The present survey has identified nineteen textile sites established between 1785 and 1906. These comprised thirteen spinning and combined mills, three bleaching and dyeworks, a print works, a weaving mill and a cotton warehouse (Appendix 1; Fig 3.2).

In the early to mid-eighteenth century there was a domestic-based linen industry in Droylsden, composed of handloom weavers and linen bleachers. Although references to weavers in seventeenth-century Droylsden are quite common, in the eighteenth century bleachers, or whitsters, dominate the evidence. Higson records bleachers with bowkhouses at Greenside Farm, Greenside Lane Farm and Old Clockhouse. In the 1700s the Ashton parish registers record four whitsters from Droylsden, while Speake and Witty list fourteen from throughout the eighteenth century (Speake & Witty 1953, 86, 88; Higson 1859, 88-9; Brierley 1928).

The cotton-spinning factory was first introduced into the township by Robert Booth who, in partnership with a Mr Swindells, built a three-storey factory adjoining the White Hart Inn about 1785. This failed after a short time, although Joseph Lowe, who had married Robert Booth's daughter, took over these premises in 1790 (Speake & Witty 1953, 87; Higson 1859, 89, 91).

In the Moravian settlement of Fairfield three purpose-built cotton factories were erected around 1790, built to the same style as handloom weavers' cottages found elsewhere in the Borough. Joseph Mallalieu of Fairfield used a horse gin to drive spinning jennies in a house in the settlement in 1786, but by 1790 he had moved his operation to a purpose-built building. After Mallalieu retired in about 1793, the factory was used by a number of cotton spinners until it was converted into the Boys' Sunday School around 1800 (Speake & Witty 1953, 138-9). A second factory in Fairfield was erected in about 1790 by a Mr Nalty and was equipped with 144 hand-turned spindles. However, the business failed and the building was converted to the Boys' Academy in 1803 (*ibid*, 139). A third purpose-built cotton factory was erected in 1790 by John Hammond on Fairfield Road. This was a three-storey building housing a carding machine, turned by a horse gin in an adjacent cottage. It lasted until about 1793 when it was converted to the Bull's Head Inn (Higson 1859, 90-1).

As well as these factories a cotton warehouse was established at Fairfield in about 1786, by Ignatius Hindley, and can still be seen today on the northern side of the chapel square. It is now divided into two three-storey brick houses. This warehouse survived in use until about 1813 (Speake & Witty 1953, 138).

The only long-term successes of this pioneering period were the bleaching and dyeing works founded around 1800. The Droylsden Copperas Works were established at the southern end of Fairfield Road around 1800 by a Mr Miller and shortly afterwards a Mr Cowley erected a second works on this site. Both works were purchased in the 1820s by Edmund Buckley, whose family remained in charge until the 1870s (*ibid*, 94). The dyeworks on Greenside Lane were established a little later, around 1806, by James Brundret (Higson 1859, 101). Although Speake and Witty refer to a dyehouse on this site in 1770, the present survey has failed to find any evidence to support this (Speake & Witty 1953, 93). In the middle of the nineteenth century the site was used for dyeing silk and may be a silk mill referred to in 1887 (Worrall 1887, 121).

Speake and Witty argue that the main reason for the failure of the early businesses in Droylsden was the rapid pace of technological change in the period 1780-1810, which quickly displaced hand- or horse-powered jennies, as used in Fairfield, with water- or steam-powered mules (Speake & Witty 1953, 139). Despite the failure of the spinning factories, weaving continued for a while to be a part of the economic basis of the Fairfield settlement. William Howarth and John and Benjamin Howarth are listed as check manufacturers in directories of 1808 and 1811 (Dean & Co 1808 & 1811). However, it is not clear whether the figure of 30 to 40 handloom weavers achieved during the 1790s was maintained in later years (Speake & Witty 1953, 139).

The cotton industry was not firmly established in Droylsden until the 1830s, when three steam-powered cotton mills were opened. The first was Edge Lane Mill, a weaving mill built by Samuel Ollerenshaw and

Chapter 3 The Textile Industry

opened in 1835. This was followed by Fairfield Mills, opened in 1837 as a combined mill but originally built by William Christy as a hat factory. In 1839 the first purpose-built combined mill in the township, the Droylsden Mills of Messrs Worthington, Benson & Co, was opened (*ibid*, 91). Although only one mill was erected in the 1840s, the next decade saw the industry in the township leap forward with the establishment of a dyeworks (Fairfield Dyeing Works), a combined mill (Royal) and a weaving mill (Angola), one other combined mill (Lumb) being added in about 1860 (Appendix 1).

Thus from there being only two industrial textile sites in the township in 1830, a bleach works and a dyeworks, by the early 1860s there were ten textile sites occupied by as many firms: seven cotton mills and three finishing works. Most of these early factories were combined mills and the Droylsden cotton industry was to remain dominated by single-unit combined companies (Table 3.5). In the nineteenth century only one man owned more than one textile site in Droylsden and that was Edmund Buckley, who ran Droylsden Copperas Works and built Victoria Mill in 1845 and Angola Mill in 1850, although these last two were rented to other companies (Speake & Witty 1953, 91). This period of maximum growth in the Droylsden cotton industry was matched by the rapid growth of the township's population. Between 1831 and 1861 this rose from 2996 to 8798, increasing to 11,087 in 1901 (Table 2.1).

The seven early steam-powered mills were established on or, in the case of Victoria Mill, near to the Hollinwood branch of the Ashton Canal, which had been opened through Droylsden as early as 1796 (Hadfield & Biddle 1970, 464). That Droylsden did not take part in the rapid expansion of steam-powered cotton mills visible in Ashton and Stalybridge in the 1810s and 1820s may in part be due to the lack of local coal supplies. Even the opening of the Audenshaw bypass section of the Manchester to Salters Brook turnpike in 1825, through the southern part of the township, did not immediately encourage the growth of the cotton industry in Droylsden (Bowman 1960, 358). The late growth of the industry may partly be the result of the failure of the initial cotton enterprises of the pioneering period in the 1780s and 1790s, while Farnie has argued that the cotton industry only expanded to areas such as Droylsden because of the increasing costs of locating in nearby Manchester (Williams with Farnie 1992, 21).

After 1860 growth slowed in the Droylsden cotton industry, with only two new mill sites (Albion in 1869 and Oakfield in 1877) and one dyeing and finishing works (Beetle in 1863) being added in the last 40 years of the nineteenth century (Appendix 1). Like the earlier cotton mills, these new textile sites were built along the Ashton Canal and were occupied by single-unit firms. The only multi-unit firm in late nineteenth-century Droylsden was Joseph Byrom & Sons which took over Albion, Royal and Victoria mills in the 1870s, acquiring 117,000 spindles by 1895, out of a total of over 300,000 spindles in the township (Worrall 1895; Speake & Witty 1953, 92-3).

The last mill to be built in Droylsden was the steam-powered Saxon Mill, a large spinning mill with over 80,000 spindles, built by the only mill-building company ever formed in the township. This was the Saxon Mill Co Ltd, formed by the Ashton syndicate of Messrs Barlow, Marland, Coop, Newton, Pollitt and Pownall, which was responsible for building seven mills in Ashton between 1891 and 1905 (Haynes 1987, 50). With the completion of Saxon Mill, Droylsden reached its peak spindleage in 1911 at 406,492 (Worrall 1911). Despite the dominance of single-unit firms in the township, the cotton industry fared well during the difficult decades of the 1920s and 1930s, with only three sites closing, the Victoria and Royal mills of Joseph Byrom & Sons and Springfield Print Works.

Dukinfield

The development of the textile industry in Dukinfield followed a slightly different path to that seen in other Tameside townships. The industry did not establish itself in Dukinfield until the 1790s and then saw steady, rather than spectacular growth; along with Ashton and Mossley, Dukinfield was the only district of the Borough to witness new building activity in each decade of the nineteenth century (Table 3.2). Although combined mills became popular in the mid-nineteenth century, the township was always dominated by single-unit spinning firms.

The present survey has identified 26 textile sites within the western part of Dukinfield, comprising 23 combined and spinning mills, one purpose-built cotton-weaving mill, one woollen mill and one bleaching and dyeing works. These were founded between *c* 1792 and 1900 (Appendix 1; Fig 3.3).

Little is known of the textile industry in Dukinfield before the advent of cotton spinning in the 1790s. Holme's directory of 1788 lists William Boyer as a woollen clothier and directories of the 1790s name William Kirk, Thomas Mellor and John Wrigley as woollen manufacturers, all of Dukinfield (Holme 1788; Haynes forthcoming). St Helena's, a carding mill run by James Heginbottom, was in existence on the Tame near Dukinfield Bridge from about 1807 to 1836 (Haynes forthcoming) but there were no other such woollen mills in this part of Dukinfield. This lack of evidence suggests that the township took only a

Fig 3.3 The mills of Dukinfield. *Key:* 100 Union Mill; 101 Barn Meadow Mills; 102 Stanlet Wood Mill; 103 Dukinfield Hall/ Dog Lane Mill; 104 Old Hall Mill; 105 Dukinfield/Aqueduct Mill; 106 Waterside/Alma Mill; 107 St Helena's Mill; 108 Warbrick's Mill; 109 Furnace Mill; 110 Bridge Eye Mills; 111 St Helens Mill; 112 Dukinfield New Mill; 113 Astley Mill; 114 Victoria Mill; 115 Chapel Hill Mill; 116 Albert Mill; 117 Dukinfield Old Mill; 118 Park Road Mill; 119 Queen Mill; 120 River Mill; 121 Oxford Road Mills; 122 Tameside Mills; 123 Tame Valley/Crescent Mills; 124 Tower Mill; 125 Sandy Vale Bleach Works.

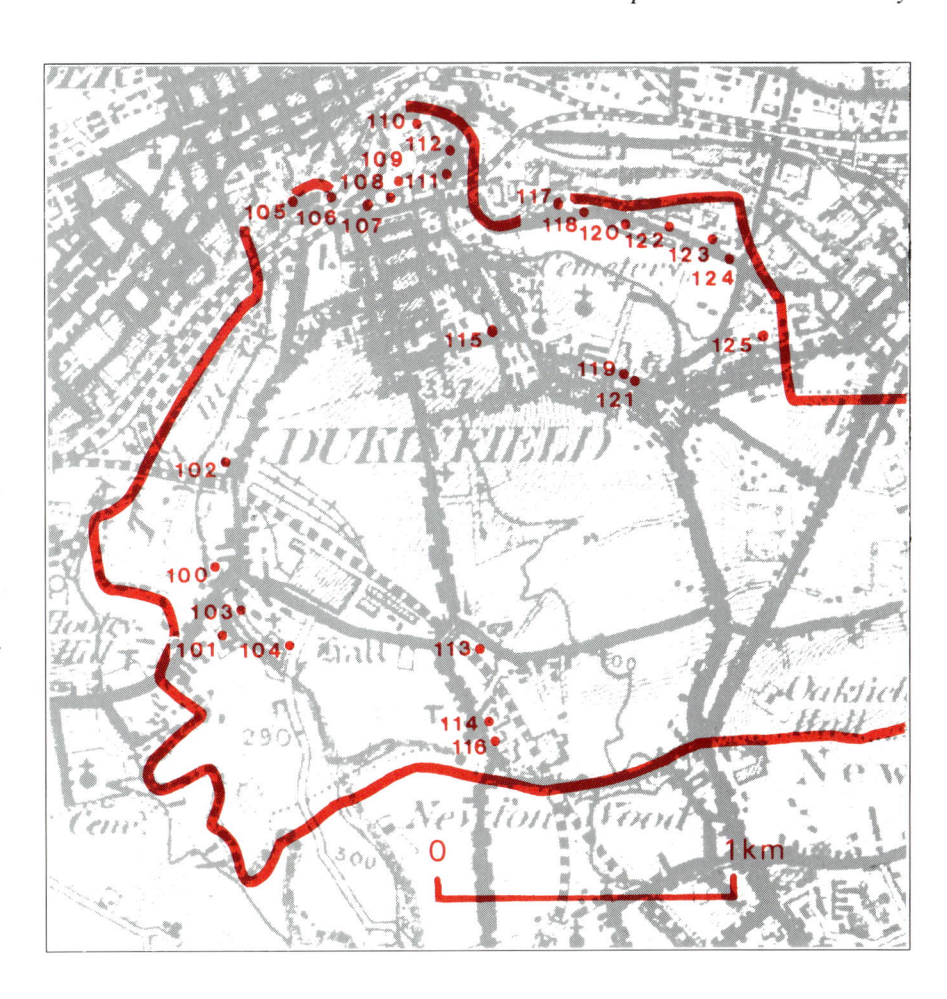

small part in the boom in the woollen industry more evident further upstream in Stalybridge and Mossley (Table 3.4).

The cotton industry was slow to establish itself in Dukinfield during the pioneering phase of expansion in the late eighteenth century. This was perhaps due to the lack of fast flowing streams more typical of Ashton, Mossley, Stalybridge and Longdendale. The two earliest known mills were water-powered cotton-spinning mills established in the Bridge Eye area of the Tame around 1792, these being Dukinfield Old Mill and Furnace Mill which was built on the site of Sir John Astley's ironworks. According to Haynes, James Sandiford established a cotton warehouse known as Chapel Hill, also around 1792, near the old Moravian settlement. This may have contained a steam engine, the first in Dukinfield, by 1803 when it had been converted to spinning (Haynes forthcoming). However, 'James Sandford, cotton manufacturer' of Dukinfield is included in Holme's directory of 1788, so that it is possible that this mill was the earliest in Dukinfield. A further spinning mill, the first purpose-built steam-powered cotton mill in Dukinfield, was built in 1802 by Robert Lees and Robert Davies, of Dukinfield Old Mill, and was therefore known as Dukinfield New Mill (*ibid*).

It was not until the 1810s that the industry began to expand again, finally using the benefits of local coal supplies and a good transport network in the form of the Peak Forest Canal and the Ashton Canal. In 1811 the first four cotton mills contained a total of 32,160 mule spindles, according to Crompton's survey. By 1846 the total had climbed to 178,344 spindles and 2476 looms (Haynes forthcoming). This expansion was not achieved by great spurts in mill building, as can be seen in neighbouring Ashton or Stalybridge, nor was the industry dominated by a few families, as in Hyde or Mossley. Rather there was steady growth, with two or three new mills being founded in each decade from the 1810s to the 1880s (Table 3.2). In the 1820s powerloom weaving was introduced into the township and by 1833 four mills were combined (Haynes forthcoming). Around 1825 Dukinfield's only dyeworks, at Sandy Vale, were started by Thomas Brierley and by 1855 a bleach works had been added to the site (CRO QDV2/148; PP 1854-5 xviii, 56).

The Manchester to Sheffield railway, through the southern part of the township, opened in 1841 and the Guide Bridge branch of the Manchester to Leeds railway, along the Tame valley, in 1849 (Bairstow 1986, 19; 1990, 20). This prompted the development of a second mill centre, between these railways and the Peak Forest Canal. Steam-powered mills had already been built along the canal in the 1830s (Barn Meadow

Chapter 3 The Textile Industry

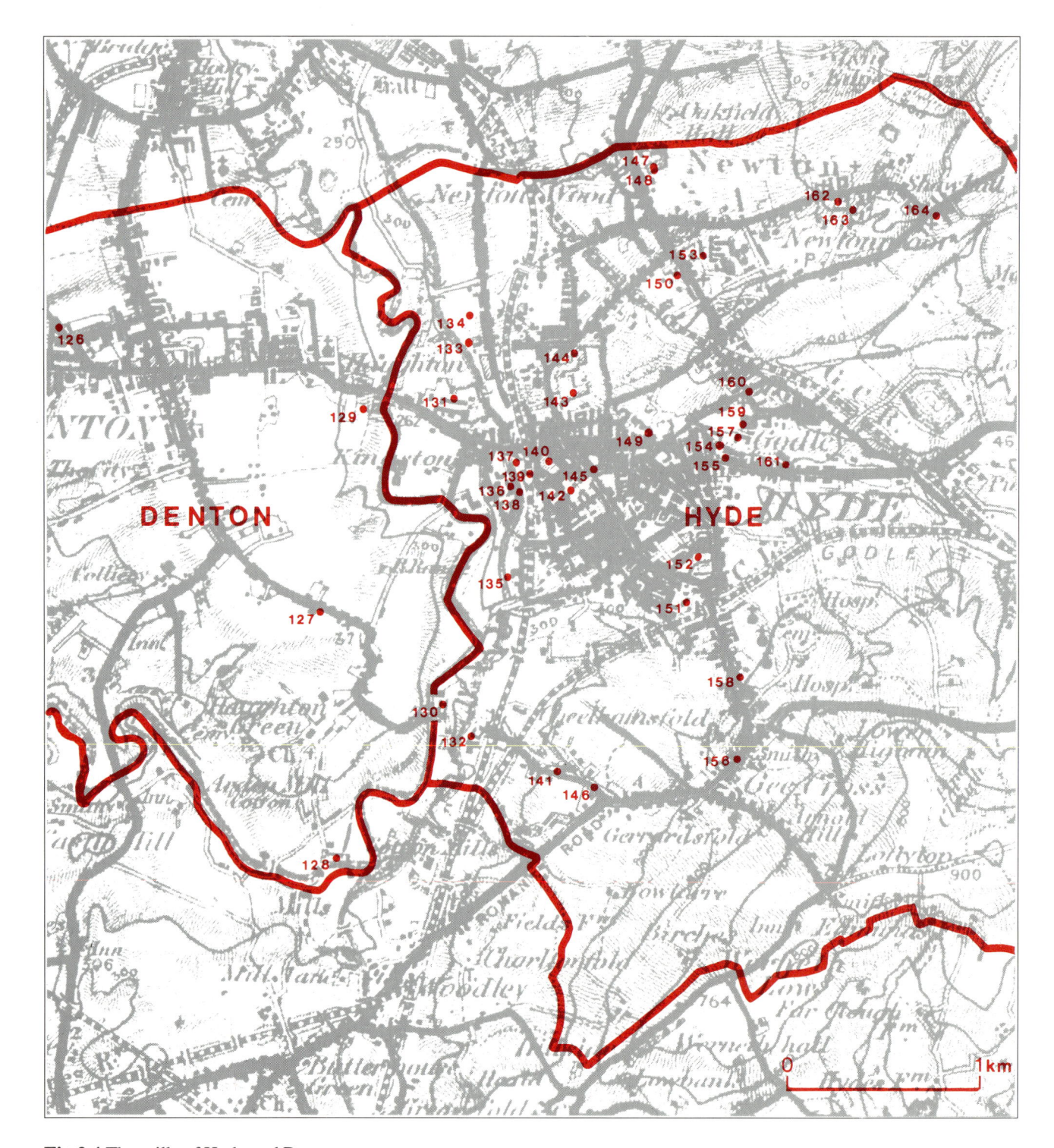

Fig 3.4 The mills of Hyde and Denton.
Key: 126 Alpha/Phoenix Mill; 127 Moorfield Mill; 128 Haughton Dale/Meadow Factory; 129 Broomstair Mill; 130 Gibraltar Mill; 131 Kingston Mills; 132 Gee Cross/Apethorn/Linnet New Mill; 133 Throstle Bank Mill; 134 Wharf Mill; 135 Providence Mill; 136 Barnfield Mill; 137 Birch Mill; 138 Millwood Mill; 139 Birchfield Mill; 140 Greencroft Mills; 141 Doctor's Factory; 142 Greenfield Mill; 143 Carrfield Mill; 144 Bayleyfield Mills; 145 Longmeadow Mill; 146 Gerrard's Mill; 147 Johnson Brook Mill; 148 Hyde Mill; 149 Newton Bank Print Works; 150 Marler's Mill; 151 Spring Bank Mills; 152 Slack Mills; 153 Newton Moor Mills; 154 Boston Mill No 1; 155 Boston Mill No 2; 156 Flash Brook Mill; 157 Highbank Mill; 158 Clough Gate Mill; 159 High Street Mills; 160 Godley Mill; 161 Bone Mill; 162 Lees Factory/Middle Mill; 163 Lees Street Mill; 164 Shaw Hall Mill.

and Dukinfield Hall mills) and to these were added Dukinfield and Waterside mills by 1841 and Union Mill in 1850.

With the opening of Park Road along the southern bank of the Tame in the early 1850s, cotton mills began to spread eastwards along the river towards the Sandy Vale dyeworks and bleach works and Stalybridge. The earliest in this area were the Tameside Mills of John Chadwick and the Tame Valley Mill of George Wainwright (Haynes forthcoming).

The Dukinfield cotton industry reached its peak, in terms of the number of sites, in the late 1870s when nineteen mills and one bleach and dyeworks were in operation (Appendix 1). Spindleage increased rapidly in the late nineteenth century, rising from 425,000 in 1884 to 837,000 spindles in 1913 (Haynes forthcoming; Worrall 1913). However, the number of looms fell by a third between 1884 and 1887, largely as the result of the closure of the combined Bridge Eye Mills, part of the general trend towards specialization in the cotton industry during the late nineteenth century. In Dukinfield most mills concentrated on spinning and by 1900 there were only two combined mills, run by two firms, left (Haynes forthcoming). The only specialist weaving firm in Dukinfield was that of George Bolden & Co at Chapel Hill Mill, which was converted from a combined mill to weaving in 1874. Old Hall Mill, a weaving mill erected in 1864, was always run by a combined firm (*ibid*).

The most important company in late nineteenth-century Dukinfield was C Koch & Co, run by Christian Valentine Koch, a native of Switzerland. His was one of the few multiple-unit companies in the town, running Tame Valley Mill from 1874 and building River Mill in 1877 and Tower Mill in 1885. In the mid-1880s the company employed around 600 people and had a total of 120,000 spindles. When Koch died in 1895 the firm became a limited company (*ibid*).

In 1861 the first joint-stock company in the township, the Newton Moor Spinning Co Ltd, built Victoria Mill, on the Newton border (*ibid*). This company also erected Albert Mill in 1873-4. In the same decade a number of limited firms took over existing cotton mills and further joint-stock companies were formed during the boom of the 1880s. A single mill-building limited liability company, the Astley Mill Co Ltd, built Astley Mill in 1883-4, with a capacity of 84,000 spindles. The last two mills to be built in Dukinfield were also erected by limited liability companies. Park Road Mill was built by the Park Road Spinning Co Ltd in 1892 and had close links with the Astley Mill Co Ltd. Queen Mill was built by Queen Mill (Dukinfield) Ltd in 1900. Each was designed for spinning and contained 92,280 and 100,000 mule spindles respectively (Worrall 1892; 1901).

Although no new mills were built in Dukinfield after 1900, limited liability companies continued to be formed from existing operators and a number of mills were extended during the Edwardian boom (Haynes forthcoming). At Old Hall Mill, the only purpose-built weaving mill in Dukinfield, capacity rose from 300 looms in 1884 to 550 looms in 1906, when the mill was partially rebuilt. The Victoria and Albert mills were extended around 1911 and again around 1914 raising their joint spinning capacity from 105,000 mule spindles in 1903 to 134,000 in 1920 (Worrall 1903; 1920).

By the end of the First World War there were eleven spinning mills, two combined mills, two weaving mills and one print works in Dukinfield, run by thirteen firms, with a total spindleage of 899,040 and 971 looms. There were no mill closures during the crisis of the 1920s and in 1930 capacity stood at 832,768 spindles and 961 looms. However, Haynes is doubtful as to how much of this machinery would have been working in 1930 and his caution is probably borne out by the closure in the 1930s of six of the sixteen textile sites (Haynes forthcoming; Appendix 1).

Hyde (including Denton)

The Hyde area, encompassing both banks of the lower Tame, was dominated by combined firms in the early to mid-nineteenth century and then by weaving and limited liability companies from the late nineteenth century onwards. One family, the Ashtons, played a key role in the development of the industry of this area. They were responsible for the early introduction of powerloom weaving around 1810 and for the re-invigoration of the Hyde textile industry from 1890 onwards.

The present survey has identified 39 textile sites established in the old townships of Denton, Godley, Haughton, Hyde, Newton and Werneth. These encompass print works, combined mills and specialist spinning and weaving sites, founded in the period 1780-1905 (Appendix 1; Fig 3.4).

By the mid-eighteenth century a number of tenant farmers in the Hyde area had turned to cloth production as a way of supplementing their incomes and groups of fustian and linen handloom weavers could be found at Ralph Fold in Werneth, Walker Fold in Hyde and Harrison Fold in Newton (Bann 1976, 14-15). In the late eighteenth century many handloom weavers' cottages were built in the Gee Cross area around Mottram Old Road, in Newton around Muslin Street (now Talbot Road) and in Hyde along Red Pump Street (now Market Street) (*ibid*, 15). Several of these buildings can still be seen in Gee Cross along Knott Lane and Mottram Old Road.

Chapter 3 The Textile Industry

During the 1780s the first water-powered cotton factories in the area were erected, these being Doctor's Factory, and Flash Brook, Godley and Kingston mills. The focus of this activity was the fast flowing streams running down the north-western slopes of Werneth Low through Gee Cross and into the Tame. By 1800 ten such factories were built in this area, mainly distributed along Wilson/Godley Brook and Gerrards Brook (Appendix 1).

Instrumental in this initial expansion, and indeed throughout Hyde's later development, was the Ashton family. In the late sixteenth and seventeenth centuries they were tenant farmers at Gerrards Farm in Werneth (Butterworth 1827, 304; CRO DAR/I/16). The first member of the family to enter the cotton trade has been identified as Benjamin Ashton, born in 1718. He began as a linen weaver, selling the cloth in Manchester, and later became a putter-out for the Manchester merchants Touchett's (Ashmore 1982, 98; Bann 1976, 16). One of the earliest cotton factories in the Hyde area, Gerrards Mill, was built by his son Samuel Ashton, near Gee Cross in about 1795 (Bann 1976, 24). In the early nineteenth century his sons expanded the business and by 1821 owned four mills, Carrfield, Gerrards, Greencroft and Newton Moor, as well as Newton Bank Print Works. When the brothers' partnership ended in 1821-3, Samuel took Gerrards Mill, later taking over the nearby Apethorn Mill and building Woodley Mill in Stockport; Thomas took Carrfield Mill, building Bayleyfield Mills in 1824 and establishing the firm of Ashton Brothers; and John and James took over the Newton Moor Mills, founding the firm of J & J Ashton which later took over Lees Factory and Lees Street Mill in Newton (*ibid*, 20; Ashmore 1982, 98-9).

Another influential family in the early Hyde cotton industry was the Sidebothams. During the boom in water-powered mill building this family owned four mills along both banks of the Tame (Cronin 1985, 54-5). The earliest was Kingston Mill on Wilson Brook in Hyde, founded by Nathan Sidebotham in about 1784. Haughton Dale Mill, in Haughton, was established around 1790 by William Sidebotham, who also rented Gibraltar Mill around 1800 (CRO QDV2/499).

The last water-powered mill to be erected in Hyde was probably Gee Cross Mill (later Apethorn Mill), built by Richard Wych in 1804 on Gerrards Brook. This coincided with the introduction of steam power to the area, at Greenfield Mill around 1800 and Greencroft Mill in 1805. The rise to dominance of steam power by the 1820s in Hyde was undoubtedly due to the local supplies of coal. Many new coal pits opened in the first quarter of the nineteenth century, and the distribution of steam-powered cotton mills is closely related to the location of coal pits in the area, with the main focus of cotton activity shifting northwards by the 1820s to the coal seams around Flowery Field and Newton Heath (Bann 1976, 21-2; CRO QDV2/499).

Another significant development in the early nineteenth-century textile industry in the township was the widespread adoption of the powerloom and the rise of the combined firm. Although powerlooms had been installed by the Ashton brothers at their Newton Moor Mills around 1810, it was not until the 1820s that they gained widespread acceptance (PP 1834 xx, D1, 55 no 40). They were installed at Carrfield Mill in 1817, Slack in 1819, Greenfield in 1820, Longmeadow in 1822 and Bayleyfield in 1824-5 (*ibid*, 57-61 nos 41-4). Other mills which installed them during the 1820s included Godley, Kingston, Apethorn, Gibraltar and Boston (Bann 1976, 24-5). By 1845, when there were 23 mills in the district most of which were combined, Hyde contained more powerlooms than anywhere else in Tameside and a quarter of the total in England (*ibid*, 23; Williams with Farnie 1992, 26).

The hatting depression of the 1840s and 1850s stimulated some diversification in the industry of the Denton and Haughton area, and two new mills were established on the western bank of the Tame during this period, Moorfield and Broomstair, followed by Alpha Mill in 1862. Across the river in the Hyde area the number of recorded working textile sites reached a peak in 1872 at 28, with the opening of Johnson Brook Mill (Appendix 1).

The depression in the cotton industry from the mid-1880s saw at least four mills, all combined, close in Hyde, but the population of the town continued to expand (Appendix 1; Table 2.1). This was in part due to a diversification into other industries such as hatting. Nevertheless, the cotton industry was able to adjust to these harsher times by adopting the private limited company more extensively than any other local cotton town (Williams with Farnie 1992, 29).

The Ashton family was partially responsible for this renewed vigour in the textile industry during the late nineteenth century, taking part in the last mill-building boom in Hyde, as they had in the first. With the rebuilding of Bayleyfield Mills in 1890 the firm of Ashton Brothers became one of the pioneers in the use of steel in the construction of mills (*ibid*, 28-9). Ashton Brothers also gave the combined firm a boost with the pioneering introduction of the highly efficient Northrop automatic loom into the British cotton industry in 1904 and the construction of a new weaving block known as Wharf Mill (*ibid*, 29; Bann 1976, 33). The firm of J & J Ashton was active in moving towards specialization. In 1891 the firm sold its spinning mills in Newton to concentrate on weaving and in 1905 a new weaving shed was added to Slack Mills (*ibid*, 30).

The spinning sector in Hyde was also changing in the early twentieth century with the advent of the large joint-stock company. Two such mills were built in 1906. The Linnet New Mill was built by the Linnet New Mill Co Ltd, as a replacement for the old Apethorn Mill, and could house 110,000 spindles. Hyde Mill, built by the Hyde Mill Co Ltd, contained 116,000 ring spindles, the first mill to have them installed in the Hyde area (*ibid*, 33).

The recapitalization boom of 1919-20 resulted in five new cotton firms in Hyde, but no new mills. These firms in particular fared badly during the crises of the 1920s and 1930s, which resulted in the closure of eleven of Hyde's twenty mills, comprising a weaving mill, a cotton winding mill, three spinning mills and seven combined mills (Appendix 1). Between 1923 and 1933 alone spindleage fell from 793,000 to 475,000. Firms which were part of larger concerns, or had moved towards specialization in weaving, were capable of surviving this turbulent period more readily. Between 1904 and 1921 the number of looms in use in the borough had increased by nearly 50% and by 1934 Hyde was the fourth most important weaving centre in the Lancashire textile district, rivalling the traditional seat of weaving, north-east Lancashire (Bann 1976, 37; Williams with Farnie 1992, 29, 46).

Longdendale

To understand the development of the textile mills in the Longdendale district it is necessary to set them within their wider context, for they formed part of the general textile development of the Longdendale valley, dominated by the cotton town of Glossop. Textile mills in western Longdendale, the part of the valley within Tameside, flourished very early, from the 1780s to the 1800s, as small-scale hand-, horse- or water-powered factories. In the early to mid-nineteenth century the industry was dominated by a few large spinning and printing firms. Longdendale was the only region in Tameside in which water power remained the chief motive source until the second quarter of the nineteenth century. Although there was a renewed spurt of mill-building activity in the mid-nineteenth century, probably prompted by the coming of the railways, the cotton famine of 1861-5 marked the beginning of the protracted decline of the industry in this area.

The present survey has identified eighteen textile sites in Longdendale, encompassing twelve cotton-spinning mills, a cotton waste mill, two purpose-built combined mills, two print works and an engraving mill. These were founded between *c* 1763 and *c* 1887 (Appendix 1; Fig 3.5).

Longdendale had one of the oldest textile traditions in Tameside. During the seventeenth century 19% of all surviving inventories from the parish of Mottram-in-Longdendale mention some item of textile equipment, and in the late seventeenth century the domestic spinning and handloom weaving of wool were on the increase (Powell 1976, 27). In the eighteenth century this domestic industry was common in the Glossopdale area of the Longdendale valley, and by the second half of the eighteenth century individuals such as William Sheppard of Glossop were running large concerns based on the putting-out system (Hanmer & Winterbottom 1991, 75).

The growth of the woollen trade in the uplands of Tameside in the latter part of the eighteenth century saw the establishment of a number of water-powered woollen textile mills, probably for fulling, along the River Etherow in the Longdendale valley. The earliest of these mill sites was probably Hodge Mill, on the site of the later Hodge Print Works. This is first referred to in the Mottram parish registers of 1763 and in 1789 was described as 'formerly a Cloth mill' (CRO MF41/1-9; DTW 2477/B/10). Further upstream, in Glossopdale, a fulling mill at Brookside is recorded in the period 1764-7 (Hanmer & Winterbottom 1991, 77). Along Gnat Hole Brook and Glossop Brook, tributaries of the Etherow, four woollen mills were founded during the period 1780-91 (*ibid*, 82-4).

The golden age of the cotton industry in western Longdendale coincided with the initial regional mill-building boom from the mid-1780s to the early 1800s. The main focus of this activity was the River Etherow and its tributaries, since many of these mills were water-powered. Hand- or horse-powered spinning jennies were also in use and in this pioneering phase Mottram proved to be an important centre. In the 1780s nine mills were set up in the Glossop area and four in Mottram and Hollingworth. By 1800 there were nine cotton mills, a woollen mill and a print works in western Longdendale and fifteen cotton mills and five woollen mills in Glossopdale (*ibid*, 76-7; Appendix 1).

The chief promoters of these new cotton factories in western Longdendale were the Sidebottom family. The founder of this family was John Sidebottom (1727-1802/3), a nailer from Stayley. John married Elizabeth Kelsall, whose brother Henry built Best Hill Mill on the Derbyshire bank of the Etherow in Broadbottom and probably ran Dog Kennel Mill in Hollingworth. In 1789 John built Millbrook Mills, on Hollingworth Brook. The Mottram parish registers indicate the size of the family. John and Elizabeth had six sons, William, James, John, George, Joseph and Thomas, and four daughters, Sarah, Mary, Betty and Ann, all born between 1760 and 1784. Four of the sons became involved in the cotton industry. William and

Chapter 3 The Textile Industry

George founded Broadbottom Mills (later Broad Mills) in 1801-2, their younger brother Joseph joining the business later on. In 1820 William and George bought the Hillend estate in Mottram and with it Lowe's Factory. James took over the running of Millbrook Mills when his father died in 1802-3, later expanding his side of the business by taking over Waterside Mills in Glossop (*ibid*, 111; CRO QDV2/217).

In Hollingworth weavers' cottages were built at Wednesough Green as early as the 1770s (see Chapter 9). During the boom of the 1780s and 1790s farmers in the Mottram area also took to building housing for handloom weavers. Many such cottages were built within Mottram village itself. In 1789 Samuel Cocke, local farmer and innkeeper at the Packhorse Inn, took out a lease to erect three three-storey cottages, with loomshops on the third floor, nos 19-23 Ashworth Lane, which can still be seen today. Outside the immediate area of the village a set of cottages was also erected in this period on the Mudd, opposite Parsonage Farm (CRO DTW 2477/F/12).

As well as building such loomshops, local farmers also set about converting barns or erecting new sheds to house hand- or horse-powered spinning jennies. Perhaps the foremost of these local farmers to speculate in the cotton industry was John Wagstaffe, a member of a large yeoman family living at Old Post Office Farm in Mottram town. In 1786 Wagstaffe converted a barn adjoining the farm into a cotton shop. Around 1797 the land tax returns indicate that he had a second cotton factory opposite the first, this one being known as Dry Mill, though whether he ran both together is not clear (see below).

The pioneering era of the farmer-cum-clothier ended with the founding of Broadbottom Mills in 1801-2. This marked the beginning of the rise of the large water-powered cotton factory in Longdendale and by 1820, on the evidence of the land tax returns, all of the small hand- or horse-powered spinning factories of the 1780s and 1790s and most of the loomshops in the Mottram area had closed (CRO QDV2/299).

After Broadbottom Mills, no other textile site was established along the lower Etherow until 1861. This was because water power remained the chief motive source in this area until at least the 1830s, steam power being introduced as late as the 1820s (Hanmer & Winterbottom 1991, 98, 107, 112). After 1802 suitable unoccupied water-powered sites were only available in the Glossopdale area. Thus the focus of textile activity shifted eastwards, as mill-building activity continued in the Glossop area, eight new sites being added in the period 1802-10 and ten in 1811-20. By 1820 there were over 40 mills in the Glossopdale area,

whereas the number in western Longdendale had declined to ten (*ibid*, 76; Appendix 1). Most of the more suitable sites had now been occupied and Longdendale as a whole took little part in the mill-building boom of the 1820s, noticeable elsewhere in Tameside.

Instead of new sites being established, western Longdendale saw the expansion of existing firms. Broadbottom Mills expanded rapidly with new spinning mills being added to the site in 1814 and 1824, and weaving being introduced around 1834 (see below). The 1824 mill was one of the last water-powered spinning mills to be built in Tameside. At Hodge Mill the arrival of Samuel Matley in 1805 also ushered in a period of rapid expansion, with the old cotton mill being converted, first to a bleach works, and then by the 1820s to a print works (see below). By 1851 the Matleys were employing 450 workers, while in 1861 the Sidebottoms were employing around 1200. The size of these firms compared favourably with two of the largest establishments in Glossop during the mid-nineteenth century; Howardtown Mills employed 1200 in 1842 and Waterside Mills 1500 in 1856 (Hanmer & Winterbottom 1991, 98, 112).

The period 1852-61 witnessed renewed mill-building activity in the Longdendale valley. Four new steam-powered cotton-spinning mills were established in western Longdendale; Victoria Mill in Mottram, Limefield Mill in Broadbottom, and Bent Mill and Mersey Mills in Hollingworth. Two mills were also built in Glossopdale (*ibid*, 80, 112; Appendix 1).

The cotton famine of 1861-5 marked the beginning of the decline in the cotton industry in western Longdendale. The two largest firms of Samuel Matley & Son and W & J Sidebottom suffered particularly badly and by the early 1870s both had sold their sites to new companies (see below). West End Mill in Broadbottom was built in 1869 but Victoria Mill in Mottram appears to have closed at about this same date, with two further mill closures in western Longdendale in the 1870s and no new mills being built in the area in that decade. The last mill to be built in western Longdendale was Spout Green Mill at Roe Cross in Mottram in about 1887, but this was offset by the closure of Millbrook Mills earlier in the decade, in 1882 (Appendix 1).

Expansion in Glossopdale continued until the end of the 1870s, with three new mills being added (Hanmer & Winterbottom 1992, 110). Long-term decline set in with the national depression in trade in the 1880s, as markets began to be lost overseas, the Glossopdale industry being heavily dependent on the production of calico cloth for the Far East. This decline is reflected in a fall in production and employment from the mid-1880s at the three biggest firms in

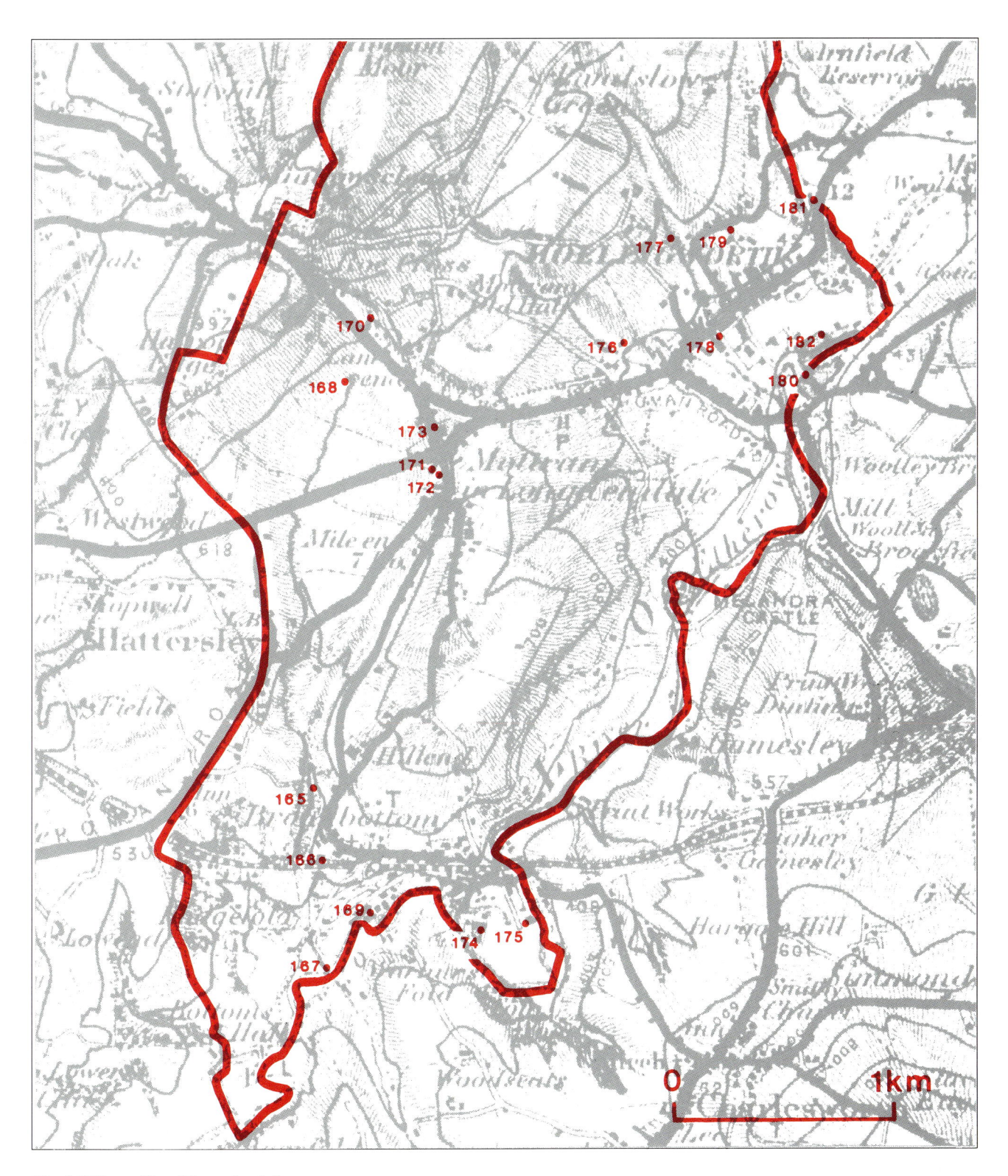

Fig 3.5 The mills of Longdendale.
Key: 165 Lowe's Factory; 166 West End Mill; 167 Moss/Wharf/Hodge Mill; 168 Mottram Old/Roe Cross Mill; 169 Hodge Print Works; 170 Spout Green Mill; 171 Wagstaffe's Factory; 172 Dry Mill; 173 Victoria/Albert/Roughfield Mill; 174 Broadbottom/Broad Mills; 175 Limefield Mill; 176 Albion Mill; 177 Dog Kennel Mill; 178 Cardwell's Factory/Arrowscroft Mill; 179 Bent Mill; 180 Mersey Mills; 181 Millbrook Mills; 182 Hollingworth Bleach and Print Works.

Chapter 3 The Textile Industry

Glossop, based at Howardtown Mills, Waterside Mills and Wren Nest Mills (Hanmer & Winterbottom 1991, 114). It is perhaps significant that the area took no part in the boom in joint-stock company formation during the last quarter of the nineteenth century (Farnie 1979, 234).

From the 1880s there was a stream of cotton-spinning factory closures in the Longdendale valley and by the time of the textile crisis of the 1920s many of the firms prominent in the nineteenth-century cotton industry had long since disappeared. In Glossopdale Gnat Hole, Hawkshead, Hurst and Waterloo mills all closed in the 1880s, followed by Arundel Street, Cowbrook and Primrose mills in the 1890s (Hanmer & Winterbottom 1991, 110). The biggest casualty in the Glossop area was the last element of the Sidebottom family empire, Waterside Mills, which went into liquidation in 1896 (*ibid*, 114). Western Longdendale, which had seen the onset of decline even before the crisis of the 1880s, was to witness further closures around the time of the First World War – Hodge Print Works in 1913, Spout Green Mill in 1909-14 and Bent Mill and West End Mill in about 1914 (Appendix 1). By 1926 the total spindleage of Longdendale had fallen from 1,158,000 in 1893 to 839,000 (Williams with Farnie 1992, 46). Furthermore, although western Longdendale suffered no closures in the 1920s, two of the remaining six textile sites, Mersey and Broad (formerly Broadbottom) mills did not survive the crisis of the 1930s.

Mossley

Along with Longdendale, Mossley was the oldest woollen textile area within Tameside, with a flourishing domestic trade in the eighteenth century (Barnes 1979, 47-9). It was the last area in Tameside to embrace cotton production, which was not firmly established here until the 1830s. The heyday of this industry was a rapid expansion from the 1830s to the 1880s producing an industry dominated by a few large, family-owned cotton-spinning firms, one of which became the largest in the world. Over-reliance on specific overseas markets, and under-investment, led to the stagnation of the Mossley cotton industry from the 1880s onwards, leaving the industry in a weak position to cope with the crisis of the 1920s. As a result of the collapse of the cotton industry in Mossley during the 1920s and 1930s, woollen production, which had always maintained a foothold in the area, experienced a resurgence in popularity, once more becoming the staple industry.

The present survey has identified 44 textile sites established between 1765 and 1900 within the old borough of Mossley. Because of a number of conversions between the woollen and cotton branches of the textile industry these were split between 24 woollen mills, 32 cotton mills (only five of which were combined mills) and two calico print works (Appendix 1; Fig 3.6). The textile industry of Mossley is today dominated by the woollen industry, as it was in the eighteenth century.

In the eighteenth century Mossley was split into three districts, divided between three counties. West of the Tame were Mossley in Lancashire and Quick, in Saddleworth parish, in the West Riding of Yorkshire; east of the Tame was Micklehurst in Cheshire. The river was to play an important role in the development of the textile industry of the town. As the industry grew in the late eighteenth century the fast flowing streams of Micklehurst (Car and Tum brooks) and the Tame itself were found to be ideal situations for the establishment of new water-powered scribbling and fulling woollen mills. The Quick and Mossley districts were not to come into their own until the introduction of steam-powered cotton-spinning mills during the first quarter of the nineteenth century.

During the eighteenth century the woollen branch of the textile trade in Mossley was originally domestic-based. Saddleworth parish, which included the northern third of Mossley, concentrated on producing broadcloths and these were probably the main textile product of Mossley as a whole (Smith 1987, 89; Wild 1970, 219). This industry formed part of a wider woollen textile belt which encompassed much of West Yorkshire (Giles & Goodall 1992, 4-5). In Saddleworth, Wild's study of the parish registers has shown that textiles, mostly woollens, dominated the local economy during the eighteenth century; as the century progressed, the population specialized further in textiles at the expense of farming activities, with the percentage of full-time farmers falling from 11.4% in the mid-1720s to 1.6% around 1790 and declining further by the end of the century (Wild 1970, 220-4). Kenworthy has shown that in the mid-eighteenth century Mossley was dominated by two types of worker – small, family clothier-cum-farmers, and specialist clothiers. There is very little evidence in either Mossley or Saddleworth for the putting out of raw materials to a dependent class of spinners until the end of the eighteenth century (Kenworthy 1928, 3-4; Wild 1970, 223). From about 1760 in Saddleworth parish large numbers of weavers' cottages were built or existing buildings converted, as the industry continued to expand (Barnes 1983, 26). This expansion can be seen in Mossley, where a number of three-storey stone cottages containing loomshops still survive (Fig 3.7).

The increasing production of broadcloths in the area also led to an increasing demand for scribbling and fulling mills. The earliest fulling mill in Mossley

Chapter 3 The Textile Industry

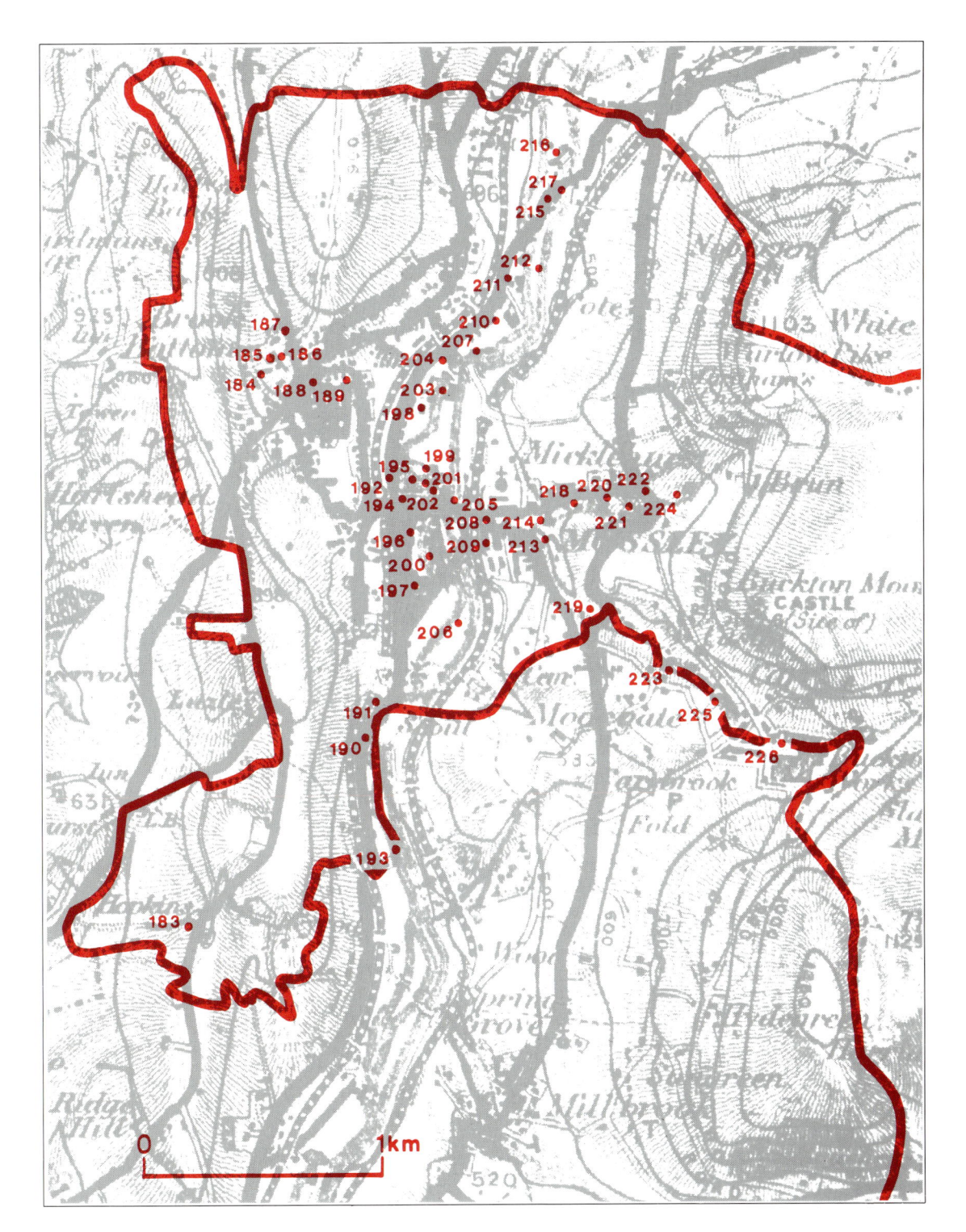

Fig 3.6 The mills of Mossley.
Key: 183 Hopkins Farm; 184 Smeath Meadows/Waterton Mill; 185 Brookbottom Mill No 1; 186 Brookbottom Mill No 2; 187 Hart/Valley Mills; 188 Albion Mill; 189 Westhill Mill; 190 Weir Mill; 191 Scout/New Scout Mill; 192 Britannia Old Mill; 193 Black Rock Mill; 194 Longlands Mill; 195 Britannia New Mill; 196 River Mill; 197 Albert Mill; 198 Border/Mossley Brow Mill; 199 Victoria Mills; 200 South End Mills; 201 Queen Street Mills; 202 Bottoms Old Mill; 203 Milton Mills; 204 Creswell/Carr Hill Mill; 205 Croft Mill; 206 Bottoms New/Bankside Mill; 207 Quickwood/Woodend Mill; 208 New Hollins/Victoria Mill; 209 Albert/Brunswick Mill; 210 Stamford Mill; 211 Andrew/Roughtown Mill; 212 Platt's Mill; 213 Springbank Mill; 214 Oldham Stair/Hollins Mill; 215 Bank Mill; 216 Spring/Una Mill; 217 Union Mill; 218 Doctor Mill; 219 Castle Clough Mill; 220 Squire Mills; 221 Greaves/Vale Mills; 222 Brick Mill; 223 Castle Mill; 224 Clough Mill; 225 Carr Mill; 226 Buckton Vale Print Works.

was Andrew Mill, built in 1765 on the western bank of the Tame in Roughtown by John Andrew, to which a second fulling mill was added in 1769 and a scribbling facility by the 1780s (Barnes 1980, 7-8). A further fulling mill was established on the Tame at Bottoms around 1777. Scout Mill is recorded in 1777, although it is unclear what process was carried out before its conversion to cotton spinning. Also on the Tame, a scribbling mill was founded at Carr Hill in 1793 (Appendix 1). There is record of only one woollen-spinning mill in Mossley in the late eighteenth century, and that was Black Rock Mill, again on the Tame, where water frames for the production of yarn for the worsted trade had been installed by 1785 (Eckersley 1991, 25). Away from the Tame scribbling mills were founded along a number of tributaries. Along Tum Brook these included Clough Mill in 1778, Hollins Mill in the 1790s, Doctor Mill in 1797 and Brick Mill in 1804. Along Car Brook Buckton Vale was founded around 1777, and Castle Clough and Castle mills in the 1790s (Appendix 1).

The majority of these early mills were only small concerns, employing few people, and the owners were usually supplementing their farming incomes, as was the case with John Andrew of Andrew Mill and Thomas Platt of Platt's Mill (Kenworthy 1928, 6; Barnes 1980, 7-8). The number of woollen sites reached a peak around 1800 at twelve. With the completion of Brick Mill in 1805 the boom in the woollen industry of Mossley came to an end.

The textile industry of the area was entering a new phase, characterized by the initial spread of cotton spinning, frequently in converted woollen mills.

The conversion of Scout Mill to cotton spinning sometime before 1793 marked the beginning of the rise of the cotton industry in Mossley (Kenworthy 1928, 12). Initially, the industry was confined mostly to existing water-powered woollen sites, no doubt because the best locations had already been taken (*ibid*, 14). Buckton Vale Mills were converted to cotton spinning in about 1800 and Black Rock Mill in about 1810, while a cotton-spinning mill was added to the existing fulling mills at Andrew Mill in 1805 (Appendix 1). The first purpose-built new site was that of Carr Mill, on the Car Brook in Micklehurst, built by William Heaps in 1799 (*Manchester Mercury* 22/10/1799). By about 1810 there were six cotton factories in Mossley, compared to ten woollen mills.

The initial centre of the steam-powered cotton mill in Mossley was in the vicinity of Brookbottom, on the western side of the Tame. Mossley had no ready supply of coal, which had to be brought in from the major mining areas around Oldham and Ashton, and from 1797 this had been facilitated by the opening of the Ashton to Uppermill section of the Huddersfield Canal. However, it was not until 1813 that Nathaniel Buckley, the son of a woollen manufacturer, erected the first steam-powered mill in the area, Smeath Meadows Mill, rated in 1819 at 12hp (Kenworthy 1928, 14-15). In 1824-5 Giles and Mark Andrews built the steam-powered Brookbottom Mill on a small stream to the east of Smeath Meadows. Steam engines were also installed at previously water-powered mill sites, such as Carr Hill Mill in 1818 (Barnes 1980, 8).

Water-powered mills continued to be built. Charles Kershaw erected a water-powered cotton-spinning mill, Valley Mills, in 1819-21 on a small stream to the north of Smeath Meadows (*ibid*). In Micklehurst a water-powered cotton-spinning mill, New Hollins, was built in 1829-31 on Car Brook, which now had five textile factories along its length. A new woollen mill, Bottoms New Mill, was built on the Tame, also in 1829-31, and may have been water-powered, although the evidence is not clear. By 1829 the numbers of woollen and cotton mills were fairly evenly balanced (Appendix 1).

Nearly all of these establishments were single-unit textile firms, but that was about to change with the arrival of George and John Mayall by 1831 (Farnie & Yonekawa 1988, 176). They came to Mossley at a time when communications were improving, with the opening of the turnpike from Ridgehill to Holehouse in Saddleworth in 1827, and the rebuilding in 1832 of the Ashton to Standedge turnpike (Kenworthy 1928, 29). Their business sense and vigour initiated a period of rapid growth in the Mossley cotton industry which not only eclipsed the woollen trade but also led to the founding of the largest cotton-spinning firm in the world during the mid-nineteenth century.

The expansion of Mossley's spinning capacity in the period 1831-72 has been described as 'remarkable in its rapidity' (Williams with Farnie 1992, 27). There are no reliable data as to the number of spindles in the Mossley cotton mills at the end of the 1820s but it was probably considerably less than 100,000, compared to over 350,000 in neighbouring Stalybridge (Haynes 1990, 6). When John Mayall relinquished control of his company in 1872 that firm alone was running 300,000 spindles (Farnie & Yonekawa 1988, 185), and by the end of the 1870s Mossley had overtaken Stalybridge in terms of spindleage, with over 1,120,000 spindles in operation (Eckersley 1991, 80; Williams with Farnie 1992, 46).

This more than ten-fold rise in spinning production was carried through by four multi-unit firms. John and George Mayall began in partnership, renting Bottoms Old Mill by 1831, in which they installed 7000 spindles (Eckersley, 1991, 8). Shortly afterwards they leased Scout Mill and in the early 1840s built two new mills on Queen Street (*ibid*, 81). When the partnership

Chapter 3 The Textile Industry

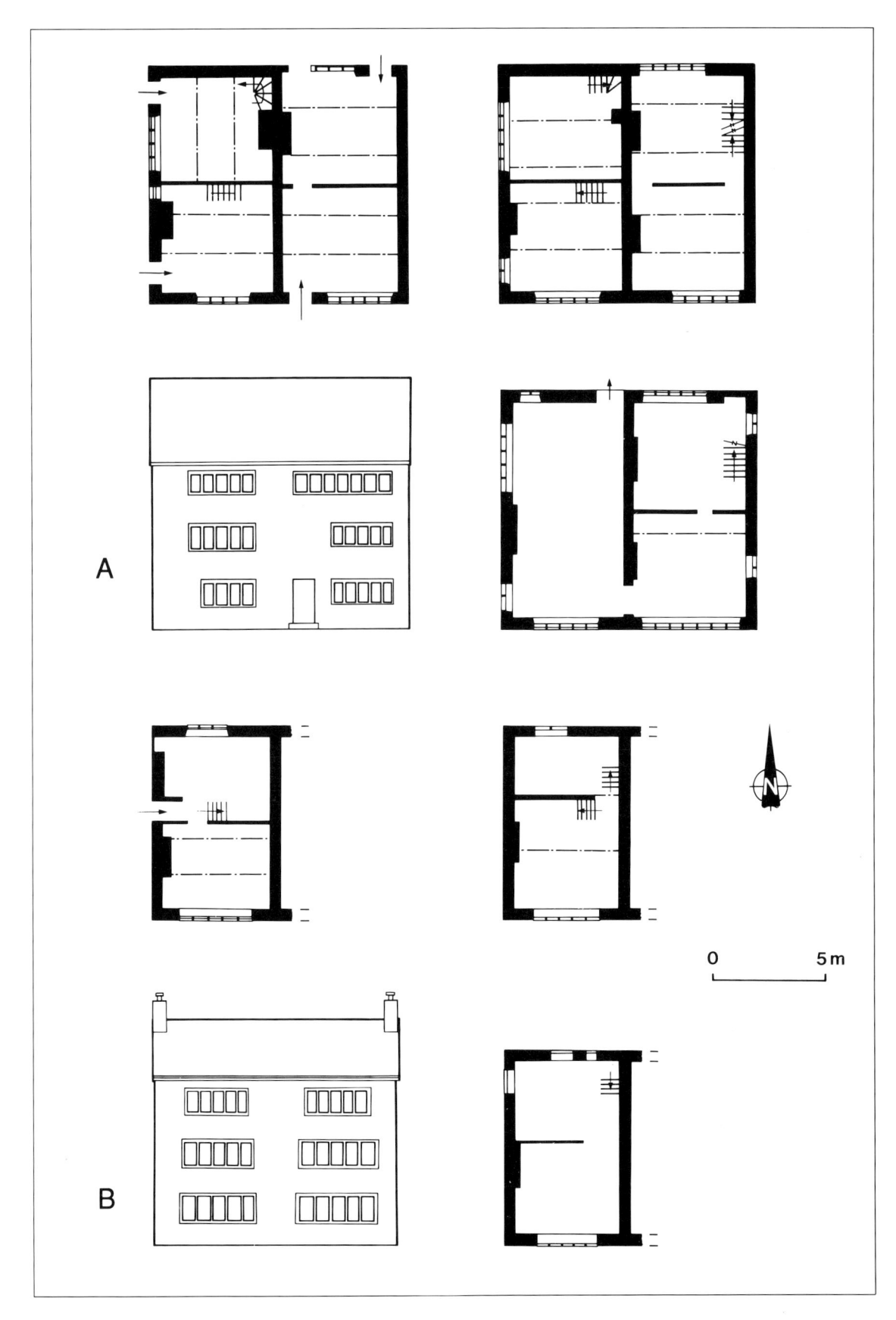

Fig 3.7 Weavers' cottages – no 18 Carhill Road, Mossley (A), and nos 1 and 2 Higher Croft, Stalybridge (B). Mossley and Stalybridge had a strong domestic-based textile industry in the eighteenth century. The buildings which housed this industry were characterized by three storeys, with the third storey having long ranges of mullioned windows to allow plenty of light for weaving.

Chapter 3 The Textile Industry

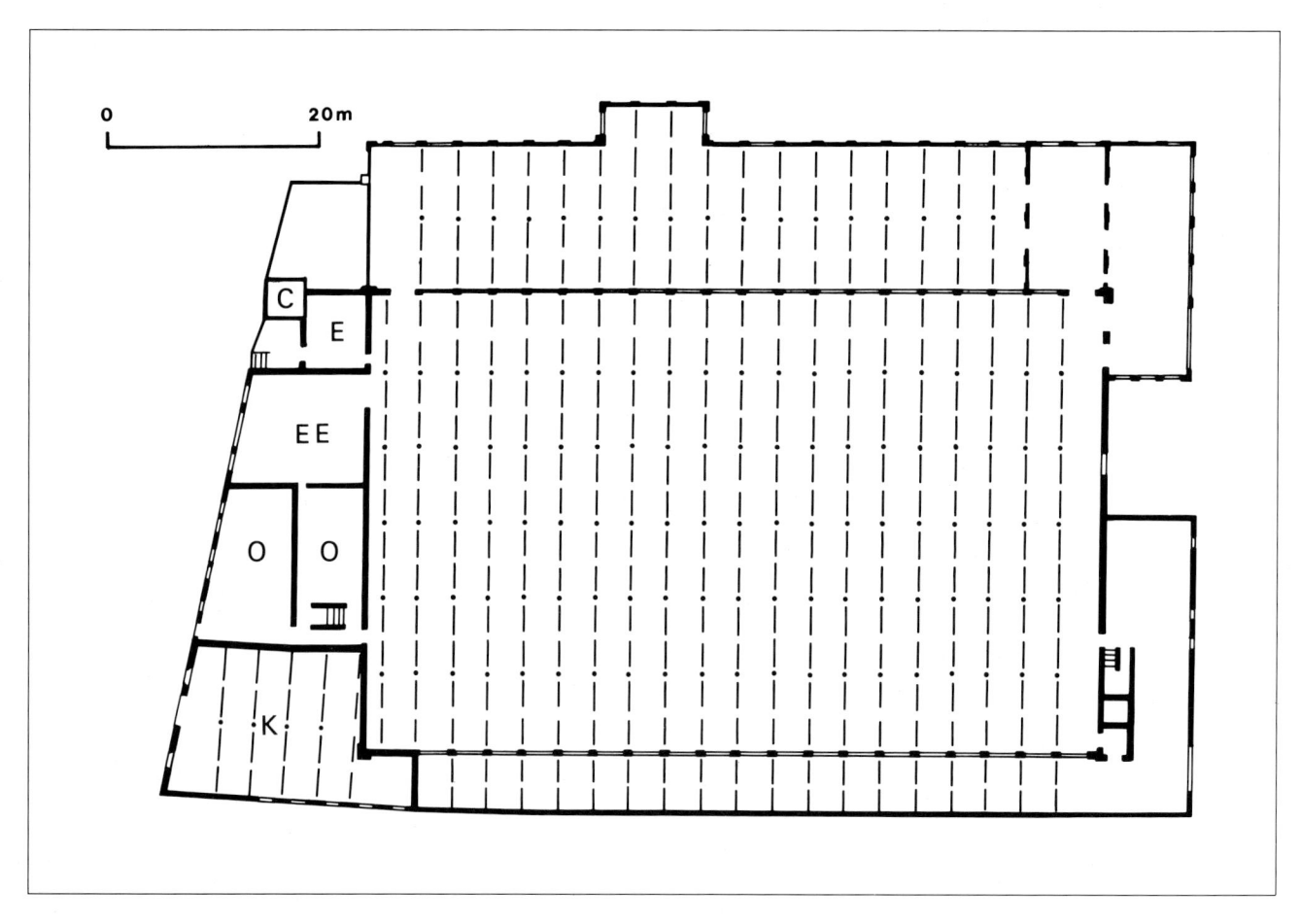

Fig 3.8 Brunswick Mill, Mossley.
Key: E – early engine house; EE – *c* 1890 engine house; O – offices; C – chimney; K – canteen.
This was one of the last, and largest, spinning mills to be built in Mossley, being erected around 1890. Although of typical late nineteenth-century plan, it incorporated the engine house and offices of the earlier Albert Mill which stood on this site.

was dissolved in 1846, John took Bottoms and Scout mills, and George took Queen Street Mills, each having about 40,000 spindles (Kenworthy 1928, 16). Both rapidly expanded their firms in the 1850s and early 1860s, spurred on by the opening of the London & North Western Railway from Leeds to Manchester, via Mossley, in 1849 (Bairstow 1990, 19). This followed the western bank of the River Tame, passing immediately west of the complex of mills owned by the brothers Mayall. When John built Britannia Mill in 1849 he was able to connect the new site with the railway sidings in Mossley via a tunnel under the turnpike road, allowing direct delivery of the raw cotton from Liverpool (Eckersley 1991, 12-13) (Fig 8.6). On its completion Britannia Mill was the largest cotton-spinning factory in the world, with 100,000 spindles. In 1857 the firm of John Mayall became the biggest cotton-spinning concern in the world, with 160,000 spindles. This position was maintained by the building of South End Mill No 1 in 1859-62, increasing the spindleage to 260,000, and of Longlands Mill in 1871, which increased the spindleage to 300,000 (Farnie & Yonekawa 1988, 184-5). South End Mill No 2, built in 1881-2, added a further 89,000 spindles but was not fully equipped until 1892, by which time, with the opening of the rebuilt River Mill in 1889, the company had reached its maximum size at 444,000 spindles. However, the firm of John Mayall was by that time only the third largest spinning operation in the world, having lost its primacy in 1891 (*ibid*, 173; Williams with Farnie 1992, 27).

The second largest firm in Mossley was that of Robert Hyde Buckley & Sons, one of the few firms in Mossley to specialize in combined mills. A Robert Buckley, cotton spinner, of Wall Bank House, appears in Pigot's directory for 1841 and Slater's for 1843. In 1848 Robert built a steam-powered cotton-spinning mill at Woodend, and followed this by taking over Albion and Croft mills. In 1860-1 the firm built two mills, Albert Mill and Stamford Mill, and expanded further by taking over Andrew/Roughtown Mill in 1871 (Barnes 1980, 8). By 1887 R H Buckley & Sons occupied six mills in Mossley with a combined total of 200,000 spindles and 450 looms (Worrall 1887).

George Mayall's company was not as large as his brother's but nevertheless saw rapid expansion in the 1850s and 1860s with the building of Victoria Mills in 1853, and the further expansion of Queen Street Mills. By 1879 the firm was running five mills with a total spindleage of 180,000. Approximately the same number of spindles, together with 536 looms, were in operation at the Carr Hill Mill of Nathaniel Buckley & Sons, one of the few combined firms in Mossley (Eckersley 1991, 81).

The golden era of the Mossley cotton industry saw fourteen new spinning mills built in the period 1833-62, with one other converted from a woollen mill. In the same period only one new woollen mill was established, Carr Mill, formerly used for cotton spinning (Appendix 1). Although Mossley was badly affected by the cotton famine of 1861-5, with only one fifth of the 5060 cotton employees of the area working full time in 1863, trade returned quickly and the 1870s were a very profitable period for the local cotton firms. By the end of that decade the two Mayall firms were employing over 4000 operatives (Eckersley 1991, 37, 61, 81).

From the mid-1880s the cotton industry in Mossley stagnated, ironically since the town was incorporated as a municipal borough in 1885 (Wilkins-Jones 1978, 71). In 1884 spindleage reached its nineteenth-century maximum at 1,250,000, a figure which was not exceeded until 1908, when it reached 1,420,000, and again for a brief period after the First World War (Williams with Farnie 1992, 46). In 1884-5 a severe depression hit the industry, and trade in Mossley remained bad throughout the 1890s. Mossley's population fell steadily after 1891, and the same decade saw the closure of Nathaniel Buckley & Sons (*ibid*, 28; Barnes 1980, 8). After the early 1870s, when Longlands and Border mills were built and Oldham Stair/Hollins Mill was converted from a woollen mill, the only cotton mill to be built in the last quarter of the nineteenth century was Brunswick Mill, constructed in about 1890 and replacing the earlier Albert Mill (Fig 3.8). The last textile mill to be built in Mossley was the cotton-spinning Westhill Mill in 1900, the borough taking no part in the great Edwardian mill-building boom (Appendix 1).

The reasons for the long-term decline of the industry in Mossley are difficult to assess. Poor transport communications were not a problem, the Midland Railway company opening a second line through the borough, on the eastern bank of the river, in 1885 (Bairstow 1990, 21). A resistance to the new limited liability company may have been more significant. Only three mill-building limited liability companies were ever formed in the township, the Mossley Building and Manufacturing Co Ltd in 1862, the Mossley Spinning Co Ltd in 1873-4 and the Milton Spinning Co in 1891-2. Although the firm of John Mayall became a limited company in 1895, this development has itself been seen as a symptom of Mossley's decline (Eckersley 1991, 92; Farnie & Yonekawa 1988, 185). A further problem was the dependency of Mossley on the spinning of coarser counts of cotton, for which the competition from Oldham was particularly strong in the 1890s and 1900s. This may explain why John Mayall Ltd expanded into the spinning of weft during this period. It is also apparent from Eckersley's recent study that the Mossley firms were unwilling or unable to invest in the new ring-spinning technology of the early twentieth century (Eckersley 1991, 116-17).

As a consequence of this under-investment, when the short-lived boom of 1919-20 ended the cotton industry was badly placed in Mossley, with mills full of old technology, and companies with little capital to support them through lean times (*ibid*, 117-18). The result was the most severe collapse of the cotton industry in any of the Lancashire regions, with spindleage falling by more than two thirds from 1,289,000 in 1926 to 370,000 in 1933 (Williams with Farnie 1992, 46). Between 1930 and 1938 nine cotton mills closed permanently, the biggest casualty being John Mayall Ltd which closed in the autumn of 1931 (Appendix 1; Eckersley 1991, 119).

As the cotton industry in Mossley stagnated from the mid-1880s onwards, interest began to revive in the woollen industry, which was less prone to sharp periods of boom and bust (*ibid*, 83-95). In the late 1880s and 1890s the first new woollen mills to be built in Mossley for over 50 years, Springbank and Milton mills, were erected, while Oldham Stair/Hollins Mill was converted back to woollen production. The great shift back to woollen production was not to come until the early 1930s, in response to the collapse of the cotton industry in Mossley. During this period four cotton mills were converted to woollen production, and amongst the leading employers in the town was the new Mossley Wool and Spinning Co Ltd, formed in 1933, woollen production once more becoming the main business of the town (Appendix 1; Dupont-Lhotelain 1982, 13).

Stalybridge

Stalybridge was amongst the earliest districts in Tameside to adopt the new textile industry of the late eighteenth century. Cotton production had displaced woollen manufacture as the chief source of employment by 1800. Stalybridge had the fastest growing population of Tameside during the first half of the nineteenth century, especially in the 1820s. This expansion was abruptly halted by the cotton famine of

Chapter 3 The Textile Industry

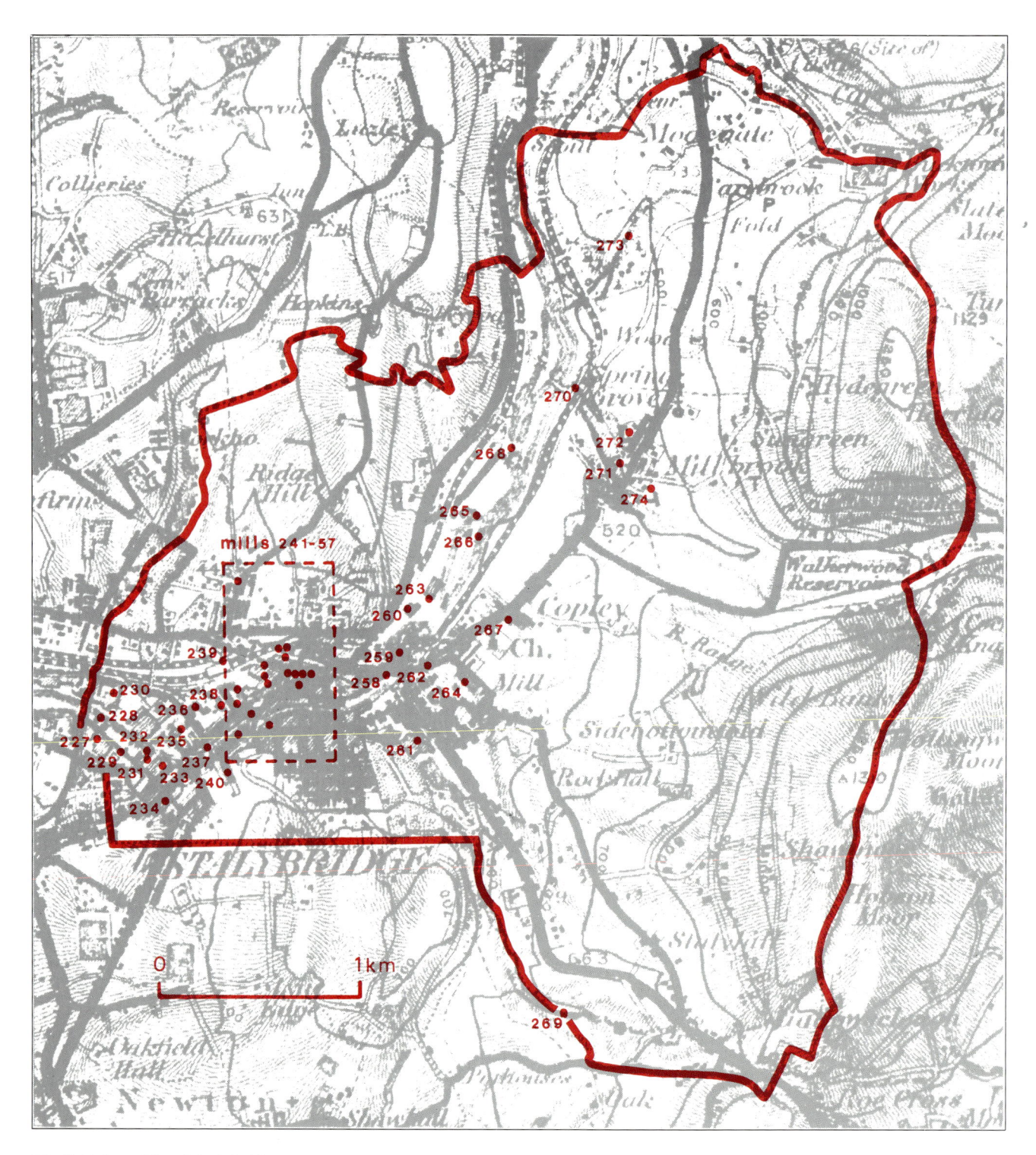

Fig 3.9 The mills of Stalybridge.
Key: 227 Premier Mill; 228 Ray Mill; 229 Clarence Mill; 230 Victor Mill; 231 Phoenix Mill; 232 Aqueduct Mills; 233 Robinson Street Mill; 234 Hollins Mill; 235 Castle Mill; 236 Bayley Street Mill; 237 Bridge Street Mills; 238 Stalybridge Mill; 239 Kershaw Wood Mill; 240 Quarry Street Mills; 241 Bayley's Mill; 242 Johnson Side Mill; 243 Lilley's Mill; 244 Rassbottom Mill; 245 Wareing's Mill; 246 Harrop Street Mills; 247 The 'Old Soot Poke'; 248 Grosvenor Street Mills; 249 The 'Hen-cote'; 250 Garside's Mill; 251 Water Street Mill; 252 Bayley's/Hope Mill; 253 Queen Street Mill; 254 Castle Street Mill (Hall's); 255 Adsheads' Mill; 256 King Street Mill; 257 Castle Street Mills; 258 Stalybridge Woollen/Corn Mill; 259 Stokes Mills; 260 Higher Mill; 261 Bankwood/Cheethams Mill; 262 Albion Mills; 263 Riverside Mill; 264 Staley New Mills; 265 River Meadow Mills; 266 North End Mill; 267 Copley Mills; 268 Heyrod Mill/Hartshead Print Works; 269 Valley Mill; 270 Spring Grove Mill; 271 Staley Textil; 272 New Mill/Oakwood; 273 Crows i' th' Wood Mill; 274 Staley/Howard's/Castle Hall Mill.

1861-5, the area experiencing the lowest growth in terms of output and population among the cotton towns of Tameside during the latter part of the nineteenth century. Although most firms concentrated on spinning, there were also a significant number of combined concerns, even in the late nineteenth century, and many of these mills were still owned by the families who had founded them. Stalybridge saw renewed building activity during the Edwardian boom and can claim to be the site of the last cotton mill built in Tameside.

The present survey has identified 48 textile sites which were established between 1775 and 1908 within the area of the old borough of Stalybridge and the township of Stayley (Appendix 1; Fig 3.9). Most of these were cotton-spinning mills, although there were nine purpose-built combined mills, five woollen mills, two print works and one weaving mill. Haynes's recent study of the cotton industry in Stalybridge provides the most authoritative account of the rise and fall of that industry in the township, and has been especially useful in compiling the following discussion (Haynes 1990).

By the mid-eighteenth century a domestic-based textile industry was well established in Stalybridge, with the evidence suggesting that cotton and wool were being produced for the worsted trade in Nottingham (Baines 1836, 554; Haynes 1990, 3). In 1795 Aikin was able to comment that Stayley township

'has been famous, for a great length of time, for woollen cloth, dyers and pressers, as well as weavers. These branches still continue to flourish. Here and in this neighbourhood commences the woollen manufactory, which extends in various directions as we proceed to Saddleworth' (Aikin 1795, 230).

The earliest textile factory to be established in Stalybridge was the water-powered fulling mill known as Higher Mill on the western bank of the River Tame, which was in existence by 1775. Like other woollen mills in the area it was converted to cotton spinning, in this case by 1803 (Haynes 1990, 22). The first cotton factory to be established was in a reused building which later came to be known as the Old Soot Poke (*ibid*, 16). This was probably founded by Neddy Hall in 1776, and was also the first mill in Stalybridge to be fitted with a steam engine, in the period 1790-3 (*ibid*, 4). Heyrod Mill, built by 1786 by Matthew Faulkner, Thomas Brown and Matthew Etchells, was almost certainly the first purpose-built cotton factory in Stalybridge (*ibid*, 17).

During the initial industrialization of the textile industry in Stalybridge, both the woollen and cotton branches witnessed rapid expansion. Of the ten textile sites founded in the period 1775-99, six were cotton mills and four were woollen mills (Appendix 1). The early industry was dependent on water as the chief motive power and was concentrated to the north of the present town centre, along the banks of the River Tame and its fast flowing tributaries of Mill Brook, Swineshaw Brook and the small stream that runs through Crows i' th' Wood.

It is no coincidence that the beginnings of significant population growth in Stalybridge, from c 1800 to c 1830, coincided with a rapid expansion of the textile industry. During this period 21 new mills were built in three major bursts, in the early 1800s, the late 1810s and the early to mid-1820s, coinciding with mill-building booms in Ashton and in the region's textile industry as a whole (Appendix 1; see above). This expansion may in part have been stimulated by the improving transport network of the area, with the opening of the Huddersfield Canal through Stalybridge in the late 1790s enabling coal supplies from Ashton, Dukinfield and Hyde to be transported with ease (Hadfield & Biddle 1970, 322). Thus the new factories were steam-powered cotton-spinning mills, concentrated in the heart of the modern town, between the River Tame and the Huddersfield Canal.

Unlike in most parts of Tameside, this rapid expansion was not led by a few prominent businessmen or families, but by a whole series of different individuals. In part this may be due to the strength of the eighteenth-century woollen industry in Stalybridge, and the extent to which the woollen merchants and clothiers of the late eighteenth century switched to the cotton industry. Holme's directory of 1788 records only one cotton manufacturer in Stalybridge but twelve woollen clothiers, whereas in 1797 Scholes's directory records 20 cotton manufacturers and five woollen manufacturers. Bancks's directory in 1800 records similar figures, with 21 cotton manufacturers and five woollen manufacturers. Hugh Kershaw and John Orrell, who are recorded as woollen clothiers in 1788, had by 1797 become cotton spinners, at Adsheads' and Water Street mills (Haynes 1990, 18, 21).

By 1811 the spinning capacity of the town, at about 100,000 spindles, exceeded that of Ashton, and by 1823 had doubled to 200,000. It was also in this period that powerloom weaving was introduced into Stalybridge. The mill-building boom of the 1820s saw spindleage leap by over 150,000 in the years 1823-5 alone (*ibid*, 6). The new mills of the 1820s included sites erected by Aaron, George and James Adshead at Staley New Mills, James Bayley at Albion Mills, Daniel Howard at Robinson Street Mill, John Wagstaffe at Aqueduct Mill, J & W Wareing at Wareing's Mill and James Wilkinson at Copley Mills (*ibid*, 29-32).

In contrast to this rapid expansion in the cotton

Chapter 3 The Textile Industry

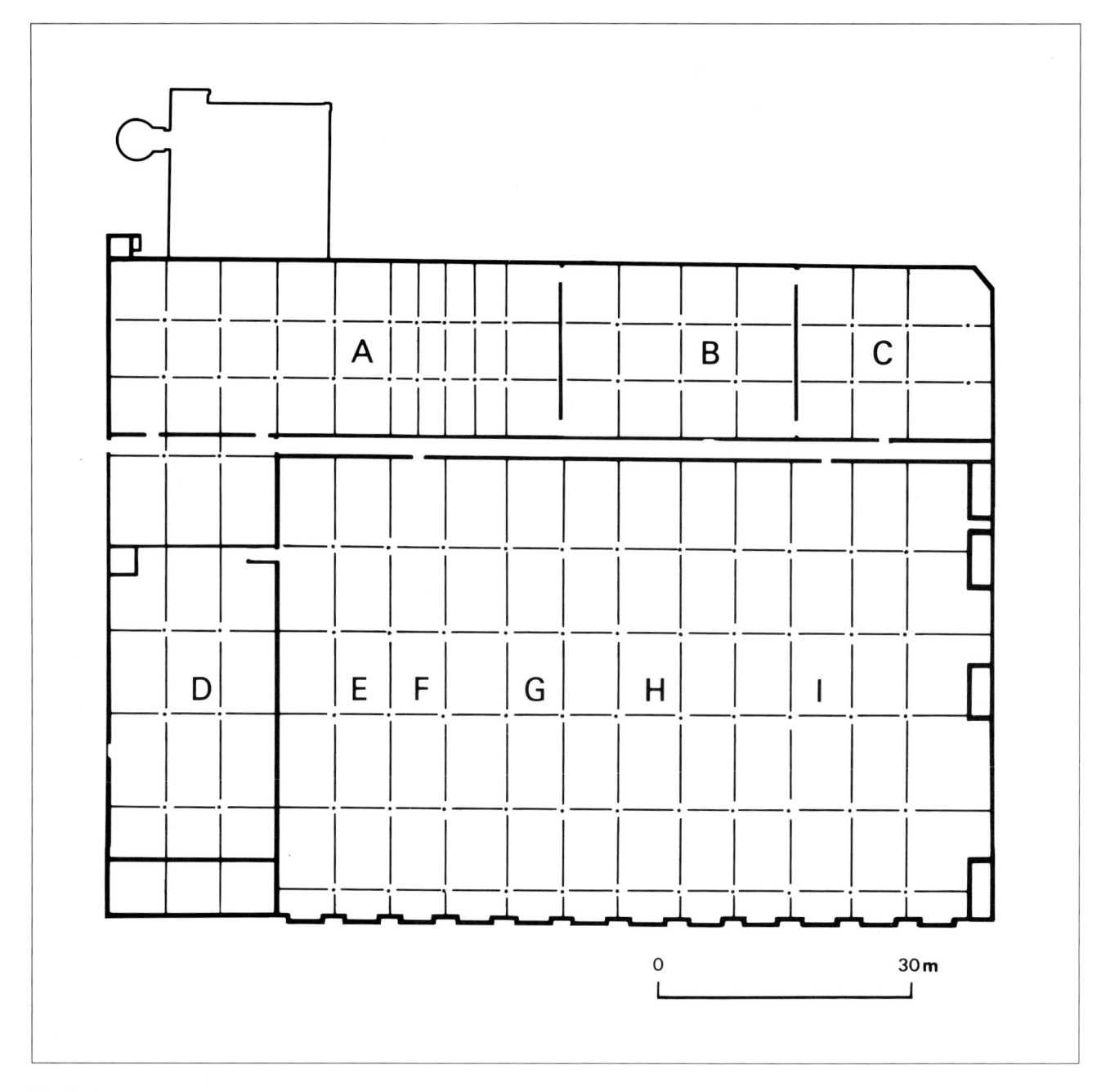

Fig 3.10 Premier Mill, Stalybridge.
Premier Mill is notable as the earliest purpose-built electrically powered cotton mill in Tameside, and for its unusual design. Despite being a combined mill, it was built along the plan of contemporary weaving mills – a large single-storey shed with a multi-ridge roof. Areas A, B and C on the south-west side of the mill housed the ring doubling frames, the quick traverse winding frames and the twist ring frames; area D housed the scutchers; and areas E to I housed the carding machines (E), drawing frames (F), slubbing frames (G), roving frames (H) and twist ring frames (I).
Source: The Museum of Science and Industry in Manchester, the Fine Spinners & Doublers Association Ltd Collection, Acc A9524.

branch, the last woollen mills to be built were probably Crows i' th' Wood around 1795, in an isolated spot north of Millbrook, and the water-powered mill which later became Stalybridge Corn Mill, in about 1800. As the wealth of the cotton industry increased, two woollen mills were converted to cotton spinning, Higher Mill in 1803 and Lilley's Mill in 1802-7. Stalybridge Corn Mill was converted from a woollen mill in the period 1821-5 (Appendix 1).

After the excesses of the mid-1820s the cotton industry nationally entered a period of depression which lasted until the early 1830s. As trade revived four new mills were opened in Stalybridge during the 1830s, including the first purpose-built combined mill, Bankwood Mill, erected by George Cheetham & Sons (Appendix 1; Haynes 1990, 32). The spindleage in the

Stalybridge mills continued to rise, reaching 565,680 by 1843. Perhaps the most significant change in the industry during this period was the growth of the powerloom at the expense of the handloom weavers. By 1843 a total of 5579 powerlooms were in use in the Stalybridge local board area, whereas a survey undertaken by the Manchester Statistical Society in the years 1834-6 counted only 32 handloom weavers (*ibid*, 7). Ten years earlier the Manchester-based manufacturer Robert Gardner had been able to employ between 1000 and 1500 handloom weavers in the Ashton, Stalybridge and Stockport areas (PP 1835, xiii).

The advent of the railways in the late 1840s provided a much needed boost to the industry, no new mills being built in the period 1837-51. Three lines were built through, or directly to, Stalybridge; one by the Manchester, Sheffield & Lincolnshire Railway, which was the first to open, in 1845; a second by the Lancashire & Yorkshire Railway, which opened in 1846; and a third by the London & North Western Railway, which opened in 1849 (see Chapter 8). The improved communications provided by these railways no doubt encouraged the building of five new mills in the period 1851-62, while in 1869, with the building of Phoenix Mill, the industry in Stalybridge reached its maximum extent of 35 working sites (Appendix 1).

The cotton famine of 1861-5 heralded the end of expansion in the Stalybridge textile industry, and although new mills continued to be built, from the 1870s the number of firms, sites and employees in the industry steadily declined. Between 1870 and 1900 spindleage remained around 1,100,000, while the number of looms peaked in the 1860s at around 7500, and thereafter declined (Williams with Farnie 1992, 46; Haynes 1990, 10). This latter trend was part of the regional specialization of the late nineteenth century, with south-east Lancashire concentrating on spinning. Nevertheless, woollen production reappeared in Stalybridge in response to this stagnation, the cotton-spinning mills at Spring Grove and Staley/Howard's being converted to woollen production in 1868 and 1896 respectively (Appendix 1).

It is perhaps symptomatic of this stagnation that of the nineteen limited companies formed in Stalybridge in the period 1871-92 only three were public mill-building companies, the others being either public companies formed to take over existing mills, or family firms which became private limited companies (Haynes 1990, 10). The three new mills which were built in Stalybridge in the late nineteenth century – Stalybridge in 1881, Riverside in 1883 and Castle in 1891 – were matched by the closure of twelve sites in the period 1870-1900 (Appendix 1).

The last spurt of mill building in Stalybridge came in the Edwardian period with the erection of three mills by the same syndicate: Victor Mill in 1903, Premier Mill in 1906 and Ray Mill in 1907. Victor was the first purpose-built ring-spinning mill in Stalybridge, Premier the first combined mill to be built in Stalybridge since Clarence in 1862 and the first electrically powered ring-spinning mill in Tameside (Fig 3.10), and Ray Mill, the last completely new cotton mill to be built in Tameside. These three mills were the most technically advanced, in design and equipment, in Stalybridge, and it is perhaps no coincidence that they were the last to close, in 1982 (Haynes 1990, 38-9). Thanks to these new mills Stalybridge reached its all time peak spindleage in 1911, at 1,273,814 (*ibid*, 11).

Although the Stalybridge cotton industry prospered in the Edwardian period, like the industry nationally it suffered in the post-First World War years from the permanent loss of overseas markets and the recapitalization boom of 1919-20 (*ibid*, 12). From the early 1920s onwards the industry in Stalybridge remained in decline, although compared to other areas of Tameside, this was initially far less severe, with only two textile sites closing permanently in the 1920s, Robinson Street Mill, owned by C H Nuttal & Co, and the Heyrod Print Works, run by the Calico Printers Association (*ibid*, 12, 17). The main period of mill closure in Stalybridge was to come in the depression of the 1930s, when five out of 23 mills closed.

3.4 Selected Textile Building Complexes

A total of 274 textile sites have been identified by the present survey, a summary of which can be found in Appendix 1. These were established in Tameside between 1763, when the woollen mill at Hodge in Broadbottom is first mentioned, and 1907 when the last mill to be built in the Borough, Ray Mill in Stalybridge, was begun. Less than a dozen sites are now engaged in the textile trade, but the survey of mills in the county, carried out in the mid-1980s by the Greater Manchester Archaeological Unit and the Royal Commission on the Historical Monuments of England, recorded over 100 sites in the Borough which still had extant buildings (Williams with Farnie 1992, 197-8). The GMAU/RCHME survey also included detailed surveys of three of these mills, Carrs Mill and Good Hope Mill in Ashton, and Copley Mill in Stalybridge (*ibid*, 181-4). A further six examples were chosen for the present survey as a representative sample of the range and type of textile sites present in Tameside. These are discussed below.

Hodge Print Works, Broadbottom, c 1763-1913

The earliest textile site in the Borough associated with the Industrial Revolution, and uncovered by the

Chapter 3 The Textile Industry

present survey, is that of Hodge Print Works (SJ 989 935). The site was occupied by the textile industry for 150 years and was converted from a woollen mill, to a cotton-spinning mill, to a bleach works, and finally to a bleaching and printing complex. It is the only example of this latter branch of the textile trade to have been examined in detail in Tameside.

The first reference to a mill on this site occurs in 1763 when the Mottram parish registers record the baptism of a child of James and Susan Scholefield of 'Hodg Mill', which was probably then being used as a woollen mill (CRO MF41/1-9). In 1789 John Swindells, a cotton manufacturer from Hurst in Ashton-under-Lyne, along with Edward Moss and Strettie Seddon, leased the site. Swindells's lease was redrawn in 1799 for 32 years at an increased rent, but according to the land tax returns in 1804 Hodge Mill was sublet to John Dale and in 1805 to Samuel Matley, a calico printer from Red Bank, near Scotland Bridge in Manchester. Matley continued to sublease the mill from Swindells until at least 1813 but by 1822 he was the sole tenant (CRO DTW 2477/B/10, B/12, F/12; QDV2/299; Graham 1846, 423; Powell 1988, 2).

It seems likely that Samuel Matley set about adding new buildings to the old Hodge woollen mill as soon as he took over the site in 1805, for the value of the rent more than doubled between 1805 and 1809. In 1813 the site was described in the Mottram rentals as a 'bleaching factory'. New leases on parts of the complex were drawn in 1818 and 1827, and the rentable value of the property once more doubled in this period, suggesting that the site was again extended (CRO DTW 2477/B/12, F/12; QDV2/299; Powell 1988, 2).

By 1821-2 the Matleys were described as calico printers of 'Hodge-mill' and in 1826 the site itself is named as Hodge Print Works. The much expanded bleaching and printing works included a set of three reservoirs on the northern side of the site, first mentioned in 1826 (Pigot & Dean 1821-2, 308; CRO DTW 2477/B/13). These new buildings appear on a plan of the site in a sale catalogue of 1841 for the Mottram estate of Lord Tollemache (Powell Collection). This plan also indicates that the site had a gas works, with an early gas holder. The site appears to have achieved its maximum extent in this period (Fig 3.11), for comparison with the plan accompanying the sale catalogue of 1919 indicates little change in the layout of the buildings in the latter half of the nineteenth century (Powell Collection).

Samuel appears to have given control of the company to his son Richard by 1821-2, when it is first called Samuel Matley & Son (Pigot & Dean 1821-2, 308). Under Richard's guidance the firm grew to be one of the largest employers in the area, with 450 workers in 1851. By then workers were housed in cottages at Summerbottom and at Crescent Row, built in 1837. Richard and his wife Esther had nine children, four boys and five girls, but all of his sons and two of his daughters died before him. On his death in 1865 the works were left to his two unmarried daughters who in 1870 sold the business to Ludwig Hammill, keeping Hodge Hall for themselves (TLSL MF Census returns; Powell 1988, 2-3).

After this date the business seems to have fared badly, running through a succession of owners. In about 1872 Hammill sold the print works to two brothers, Arnold and John Ledeboer; in 1889 Harry Costabadie with Milner Gibson bought the works, which in 1902 they sold to the Calico Printers Association Ltd, of which Gibson was a director. Hodge Print Works finally closed in 1913 (Powell 1988, 3; *Ashton Reporter* 5/4/1913).

The surviving remains of Hodge Print Works consist of the foundations and leat of the 1763 woollen mill, bleach baths relating to the bleaching processes on the site, and Hodge Cottage, a probable late eighteenth-century loomshop. Of these remains the most instructive are those comprising Hodge Cottage. This is a two-storey building, built of watershot stone, 9.3m (*c* 30 feet) by 10.9m (*c* 35 feet), with a hipped stone slate roof, and was added to the northern gable of the original woollen mill. The original building of the late eighteenth century had a single room on the second storey which was probably used as a loomshop. The northern elevation was cut into the side of the hill, so that the second storey opened onto ground level, through a taking-in door. Entrance into the first storey was from the western elevation, although later alterations to this storey have removed all trace of the original internal plan. It seems likely that this building was erected by John Swindells in the period 1789-1805 as an extension to the old eighteenth-century woollen mill, by this time a cotton-spinning mill, which lay immediately south of this building (Nevell forthcoming).

In 1992 the foundations of this mill were exposed to the south of Hodge Cottage. They comprised a loading bay to the north, and a wheel-pit, with associated leat, to the south. At least three periods of construction were visible. The earliest building was a rectangular structure of at least three storeys approximately 11m (36 feet) by 20m (68 feet), with a wheel-pit 4.7m (15½ feet) by 2.8m (9 feet) in plan. Water was supplied to the wheel via a sluice above a weir across the Etherow, east of the print works site. Sometime in the nineteenth century this building was extended southwards by 8m (26 feet) by the addition of an extra bay. The precise use of this extension was unclear, due to the amount of rubble covering this end of the site. However, local tradition asserts that this was the site

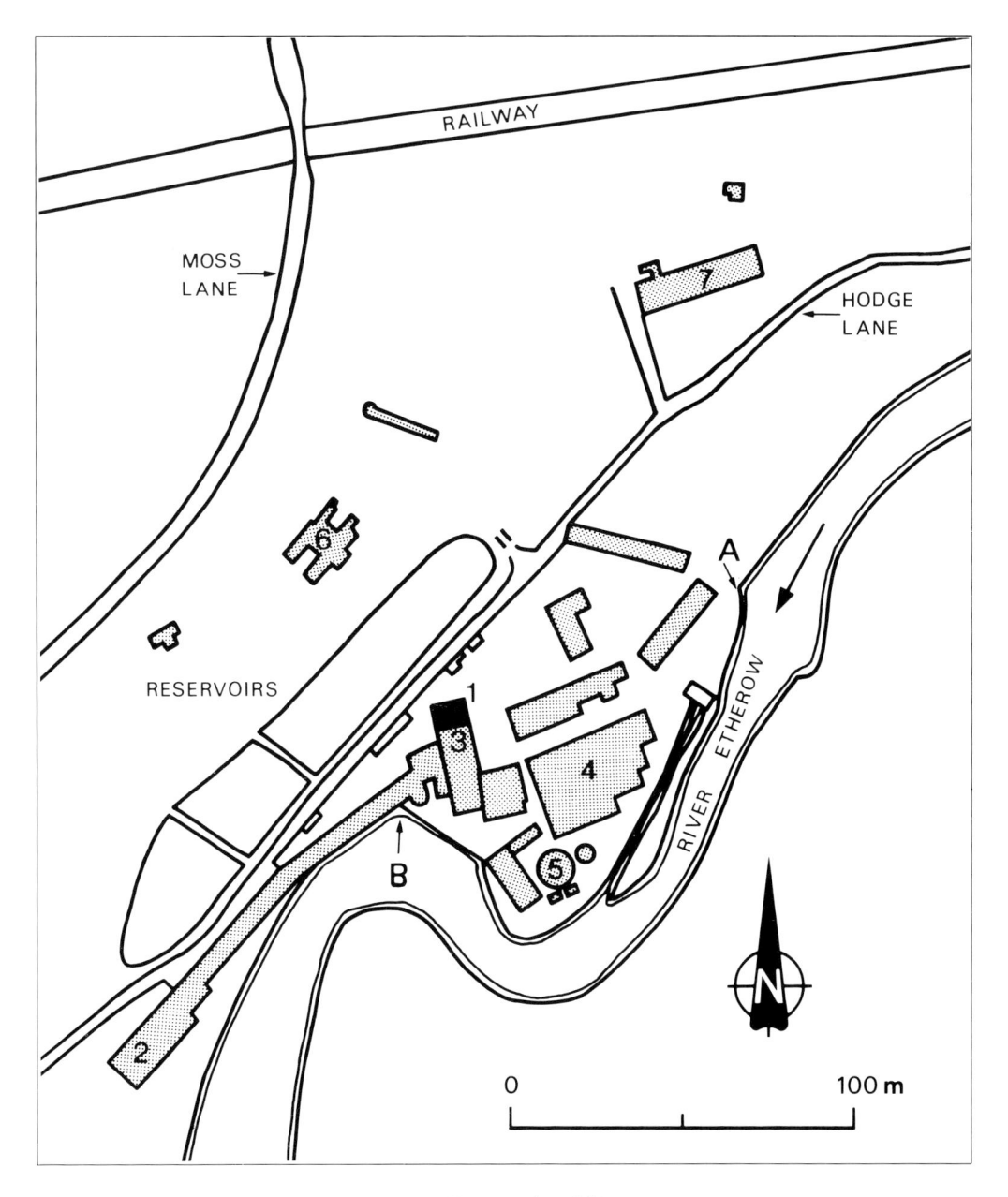

Fig 3.11 Plan of Hodge Print Works, Broadbottom, in 1841.
This is the earliest known textile site in Tameside, the complex being involved in one or other branches of the industry from 1763 until 1913. The earliest building on the site was the mid-eighteenth-century woollen mill (3), later converted to a cotton-spinning mill. Between 1789 and 1805 a loomshop was added to its northern end, the present Hodge Cottage (1), and in about 1790 the weavers' cottages known as Summerbottom were constructed (7). From the early nineteenth century, when the Matley family took over, the site was used for bleaching cloth and the bleaching baths can still be seen today (2). The print works (4) were added in the early 1820s, while the site was lit by its own gas works (5) from around 1834. The Matley family lived nearby at Hodge Hall (6). A and B mark the intake and outfall of the leat supplying the mid-eighteenth-century woollen mill.

of the boiler house for the print works, housing a pair of Lancashire boilers. Perhaps slightly later than this addition was the insertion of a double loading bay across the north-eastern corner of the building and the eastern facade of Hodge Cottage.

In the mid-1980s three groups of stone bleaching baths were excavated by the Greater Manchester Archaeological Unit on the western side of the print works site, comprising two sets of twenty baths and one of ten baths. Each is internally c 1.6m (5 feet 3 inches) by 1.8m (5 feet 11 inches) in plan, and 1.6m deep, and the slab walls are tenoned together and held by 25mm (1 inch) square wrought-iron stays. They are terraced into the hillside and each group is arranged in

Chapter 3 The Textile Industry

Plate 3.3 Dry Mill, Mottram.
Now converted into cottages, this building was erected in the 1790s by John Wagstaffe, probably for the hand- or horse-powered spinning of cotton. There were many such structures in the Longdendale area during the initial cotton boom of the 1780s and 1790s, but this is the only known surviving example.

rows either side of a deep central drainage channel. This drainage channel emptied into a split-level settling tank system, prior to returning the water/effluent to the river. It is likely that these baths date from the expansion of the site undertaken by Samuel Matley in the period 1805-9.

Wagstaffe's factories, Mottram, 1786 - c 1813

The earliest surviving building specifically built for the textile industry in Tameside is Dry Mill (SJ 9930 9556), located on the corner of Market Street and Back Lane in Mottram. With Wagstaffe's Factory it formed a pair of horse- or hand-powered spinning jenny mills established in the late eighteenth century.

These two mills were erected by John Wagstaffe, a member of a large yeoman family which can be traced in the town from the early seventeenth century. Although principally yeomen farmers, they were involved in the domestic spinning of textiles during the early to mid-eighteenth century. In 1786 John Wagstaffe converted a barn on his land into a horse- or hand-powered spinning jenny mill (CRO DTW 2477/B/10). This was on the western side of Back Lane (SJ 9929 9556) immediately south of Old Post Office Farm and was known as Wagstaffe's Factory (Fig 3.12).

Dry Mill, constructed on land opposite Wagstaffe's Factory, was a purpose-built cotton manufactory, for a lease of 1804, mortgaging the site to Robert Newton of Heaton Norris, describes it as a 'new building and workshop lately erected' (CRO DTW 2477/F/12). Now converted into cottages, this is a stone-built two-storey building, of three by two bays, with a gabled slate roof and chimneys, the latter probably dating from its conversion. Original features of the western elevation include a door with a small single light to its right on the ground floor and on the first floor a four-light flat-faced stone mullion window, of which only the central mullion survives. The eastern elevation is much altered, the three windows with stone sills and lintels to the first floor and that to the ground floor all being later additions (Plate 3.3). The northern gable has a blocked window on the first floor.

The mill was probably built in the mid-1790s. A lease of 1799 to John Ashton of Hollingworth indirectly mentions the mill, when it describes a plot of land for building a house bordered on the northern side by the cotton factory of John Wagstaffe, on the eastern side by Mottram (Market) Street, on the western side by Back Lane, and on the southern side by land belonging to Thomas Cardwell (CRO DTW 2477/F/12). Although the land tax returns do not mention the site by name until 1799, the plot of land concerned, valued at 3s 4½d, can be traced in entries for 1797 and 1798 (CRO QDV2/299). In 1796 the land tax returns record John Wagstaffe as owning a cotton mill in Mottram, assessed at the higher rate of 3s 9d but this may refer to Wagstaffe's Factory established in 1786. It is possible that Dry Mill was built in 1796-7 as a replacement for Wagstaffe's Factory, although the land tax returns after that date may include the earlier site in other lands owned by Wagstaffe in Mottram.

Dry Mill did not remain in use for very long and was soon converted into cottages. This had probably occurred by 1813, for the Mottram rental of that year does not mention the cotton factory by name, and may have been as early as a remortgage of 1804 (CRO DTW 2477/B/12, F/12).

Broad Mills (Broadbottom Mills), 1801/2 - c 1938

Broad Mills (SJ 995 934) were the largest of a chain of textile works founded along either side of the River Etherow in the period 1790-1863. This particular mill complex was in operation for over 130 years, for much of that time as a combined mill, only closing in the 1930s when the company was liquidated. The buildings were demolished following a fire in the late 1940s, but in the 1980s a programme of clearance and conservation was commenced at the site, which is now open to the public. The surviving remains and the development of the site have recently been discussed by Arrowsmith (1992), and the following account is largely taken from that work. The site is notable for the remains of the various power systems which illustrate the evolution from water power to steam power in an early textile mill. This type of development was

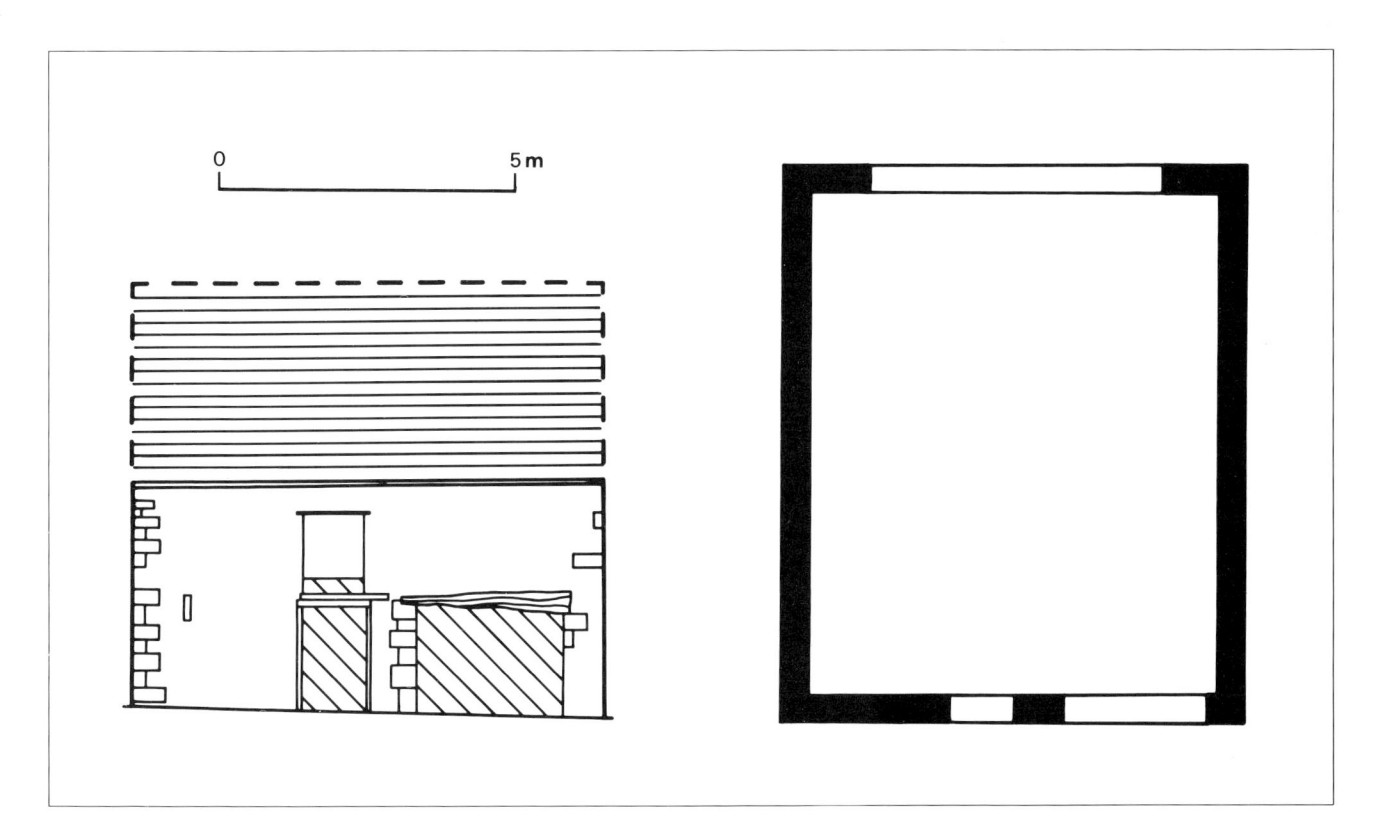

Fig 3.12 Wagstaffe's Factory, Mottram.
An example of one of the many barns converted to cotton spinning during the initial expansion of the cotton industry in the Longdendale area during the late eighteenth century. This structure, owned by John Wagstaffe, stood at the corner of Market Street and Back Lane. It was converted to cotton spinning around 1786, but had fallen into disuse by 1813. The building was demolished in about 1969.

Chapter 3 The Textile Industry

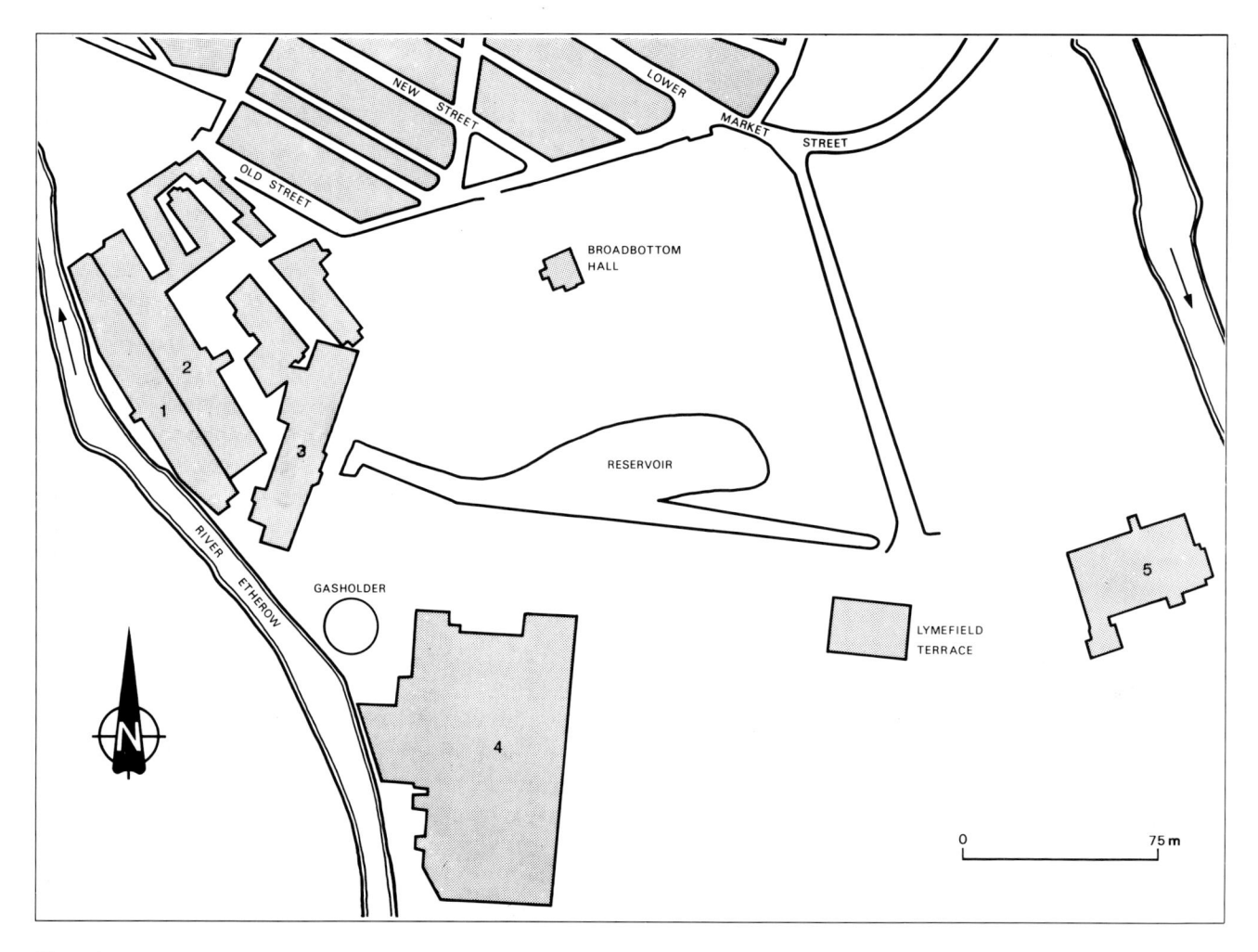

Fig 3.13 Broad Mills, Broadbottom, in about 1900.
Key: 1 single-storey shed *c* 1850, use unknown; 2 Old Mill, built in 1802 and 1814; 3 the 1824 mill, originally water-powered, but with a *c* 1830 engine house added to the south gable; 4 the *c* 1850 weaving shed; 5 Limefield Mill built in 1861, taken over by Broad Mills Ltd in 1904.
This is a complex site in operation from around 1802 to the late 1930s. It shows particularly well the development of the power systems of the nineteenth-century cotton mills from water to steam, and also illustrates the popularity of the combined mill.

common in the early nineteenth century but good archaeological evidence is now rare.

Broadbottom Mills, as they were originally known, were founded in 1801-2 by William and George Sidebottom, two of the six sons of John Sidebottom who owned a cotton mill at Millbrook in Hollingworth (see above). In 1800 they acquired a parcel of land from John Bostock of Broadbottom Hall (CRO QDV2/299). Their first attempt at building a mill on this site, in 1801, is reported to have ended when the building was blown down in a storm. Map and documentary evidence shows that three cotton-spinning mills were built on this site by 1824 (CRO QDP 67 B2/5; CRO QDP 39; PP 1834 xx). The first two of these mills, erected in 1802 and in 1814, were probably contained within Old Mill, a large stone-built structure over 90m (300 feet) long and lying parallel to the river (Fig 3.13). Photographic evidence shows this mill to have been of two phases, the northern twenty bays of the building probably being the 1802 mill and the southern fourteen bays the 1814 mill (Plate 3.1). The 1824 mill, also stone-built, was constructed to the east of, and at an angle to, Old Mill.

Initially these mills were only water-powered, fed by a leat running westwards from the Etherow. By 1834 this had been supplemented by steam (PP 1834 xx), an engine house being added to the south gable of the 1824 mill, and gas for lighting was being produced on site (*ibid*); later plans show a gas house to the north of Old Mill, among a complex of buildings which included warehousing (Tameside MBC, Broad Saw Mill deeds). By 1834 weaving had also been introduced onto the site (Pigot & Sons 1834). The weaving side of the business was expanded in 1849 when Joseph Sidebottom obtained a further area of land from the Bostock family and erected a new weaving shed, to accommodate 1000 additional looms (Broad Saw Mill deeds; Bagshaw 1850, 177). This was a single-storey shed, fronted by a four- or five-storey warehouse. A new engine house and boiler house were added to the 1824 mill in the early twentieth century.

The site reached its greatest extent and influence during the mid-nineteenth century and in 1861 employed 1200 people, making it one of the biggest employers in the valley (J Powell 1977). The cotton famine of 1861-5, however, led to its closure and on the evidence of the directories the mill may not have reopened until 1871, when it was sold by Alfred Kershaw Sidebottom to John Hirst & Sons (Broad Saw Mill deeds). The Broadbottom Mills Co Ltd was established in 1884 and in 1904 was reformed as Broad Mills Ltd which also included the adjacent mill at Limefield (*ibid*). Broad Mills closed in the late 1930s, although Limefield remained in operation.

The most important feature of the complex to survive are the remains associated with the water power system of the 1824 mill (Arrowsmith 1992, 24-5). The elaborate system of channels and sluice gates, set within the basement of this mill block can still be seen. The leat into the eastern side of the mill is bridged by a series of arches which divide the flow into two branches. The southern branch passes through a group of three arches which opened directly into the mill's wheel chamber, where it powered a water-wheel probably of the breast shot type. Opposite the three sluices is a large arched opening marking the outfall from the wheel chamber, which was carried to the river by a stone-lined culvert. The northern branch of the leat passed through the basement of the 1824 mill and ran on through Old Mill where it powered at least one, or possibly two wheels. Its flow was regulated in the basement of the 1824 mill by a branch channel, fitted with a wooden and iron sluice gate and leaving the mill by the outfall from the wheel chamber.

Brunswick Mill, Mossley, c 1890-1990

The first mill on this site (SD 977 018), known as Albert Mill, was built by John Schofield and was described as incomplete in a deed of 1853. Schofield died in 1859 but the mill continued in the family until 1873 when it passed to Edward and John Clementson. The Brunswick Cotton Spinning Co Ltd was formed in 1882. The company was recapitalized in 1920, but failed in 1933 (Dupont-Lhotelain 1982, 13). Brunswick Mill was then taken over by the Mossley Wool and Spinning Co Ltd, along with Milton and Border mills, and concentrated on woollen and manmade fibre production. It remained in the company's possession until its closure and demolition in 1990 (*ibid*, 38; Williams with Farnie 1992, ii).

Little information survives as to the layout and style of the original Albert Mill, for around 1890 it was replaced by Brunswick Mill, a very large spinning mill (Fig 3.8). Parts of the earlier Albert Mill were incorporated into the new structure, giving the building an unusual combination of early and late architectural features.

The main block of Brunswick Mill was in brick and contained an early example of concrete-floored mill construction. Early concrete-floored mills omit the flat roof which later became commonplace. It was probably powered by an advanced inverted compound steam engine in an external engine house adjoining the northern elevation. However, power transmission comprised an upright-shaft system which was more typical of earlier mills, most large mills of the late nineteenth century being powered by rope-drives. The roof was of particular interest, featuring full-length angled glazed panels on both sides creating a well-lit attic. The roof covering was of multiple slate ridges. This type of roof/attic was not particularly widespread.

The northern end of the mill, with the main entrance and offices, incorporated a number of stone-built structures surviving from the earlier Albert Mill. Parts of these were typical of mid-nineteenth-century fireproof construction, with brick-vaulted ceilings supported by cast-iron beams. These buildings also included part of the earlier engine house, which had ornate cast-iron columns and entablature beams of a mid-nineteenth-century double beam engine.

Cavendish Mill, Ashton-under-Lyne, 1884-1934

The original mill on this site (SJ 936 985) was the steam-powered cotton-spinning Bankfield Mill which was built in about 1820 by Richard Stanfield and was the first to be erected beside the Ashton Canal. During the mill-building boom of 1823-5 the factory was doubled in size to six storeys, the extension being occupied by Samuel Earnshaw until the end of the 1820s. The mill subsequently saw a series of occupants. From 1829 to 1848 the mill was occupied by Hugh Shaw & Sons, either solely or as a partner in the firm of Schofield & Shaw. In 1848 the mill was purchased by John Redfern & Sons. In the mid-1860s Thomas Neild & Son occupied the mill. In 1873 the Bank Spinning Co Ltd was formed to purchase the site, running the mill until 1881 (Haynes 1987, 24). In 1884 the Cavendish Spinning Co Ltd, formed with a capital of £70,000 in £5 shares, bought the now empty Bankfield Mill, demolishing and replacing it with Cavendish Mill (*ibid*, 47). This company ran the new mill until its demise in 1934.

The new mill of 1884-5, which still stands, was

designed by Messrs Potts, Pickup and Dixon of Oldham, and initially held 72,360 mule spindles, although by 1920 there were 56,172 mule spindles and 22,588 ring spindles (Worrall 1920). It is notable for its early use of concrete flooring. The building has six storeys, of fifteen by six bays (Plate 3.2; Fig 3.14). The windows are rectangular with flat brick tops and stone sills. It was fireproofed throughout and was the first mill in Ashton, and probably Tameside, to have concrete floors and a flat roof. There is an internal engine house in a five by six bay extension to the east, designed to hold a horizontal twin compound engine built by Hick, Hargreaves & Co of Bolton (Haynes 1987, 47). The mill also has an octagonal stair-well surrounding the lower part of the circular chimney at the south-eastern corner. The late nineteenth-century office building of two storeys with a basement, of three by two bays, still stands. Two brick-built late nineteenth-century warehouses also survive; no 1 is of four storeys and five by four bays, no 2 of one storey and five by one bays.

Premier Mill, Stalybridge, 1906-82

Premier Mill (SJ 951 982) was located between Tame Street and Clarence Street in Stalybridge and was built by the Victor Mill syndicate who also constructed Ray Mill. Premier Mill Ltd was formed in June 1906 with a capital of £70,000 in £5 shares for the building of a combined mill next to Victor Mill and was united in 1911 with Ray and Victor mills under Victor Mill Ltd. The company was taken over by Courtaulds in the 1960s, and Premier Mill ceased production in 1982.

The building itself was designed by Sidney Stott, Oldham's greatest textile architect responsible for 80 designs in the Lancashire region (Gurr & Hunt 1985, 35). It was of a very unusual design, being mainly a large single-storey brick-built shed with a multi-ridge roof (Fig 3.10). It was designed to contain 21,600 ring spindles and 1017 looms. The only comparable combined mill in the county is Cromer Mill at Middleton. Premier was also the earliest purpose-built electrically powered mill in Tameside. The three-phase current was supplied directly from the nearby Stalybridge, Hyde, Mossley and Dukinfield joint board's main generating station, being reduced from 6000V to 400V by three Westinghouse transformers. The shafts to the weaving sheds carried nine 60hp motors and the ring room was turned by a pair of 150hp motors, all made by the British Westinghouse Co, as were all the other electrical motors (*Textile Recorder* xxvi, no 304 (1908), 128-30). With Ray Mill the two sites had a combined motive power of 3050 hp (Haynes 1990, 39).

Little survives of the mill apart from the external walls, although the single-storey office block on Tame Street still stands.

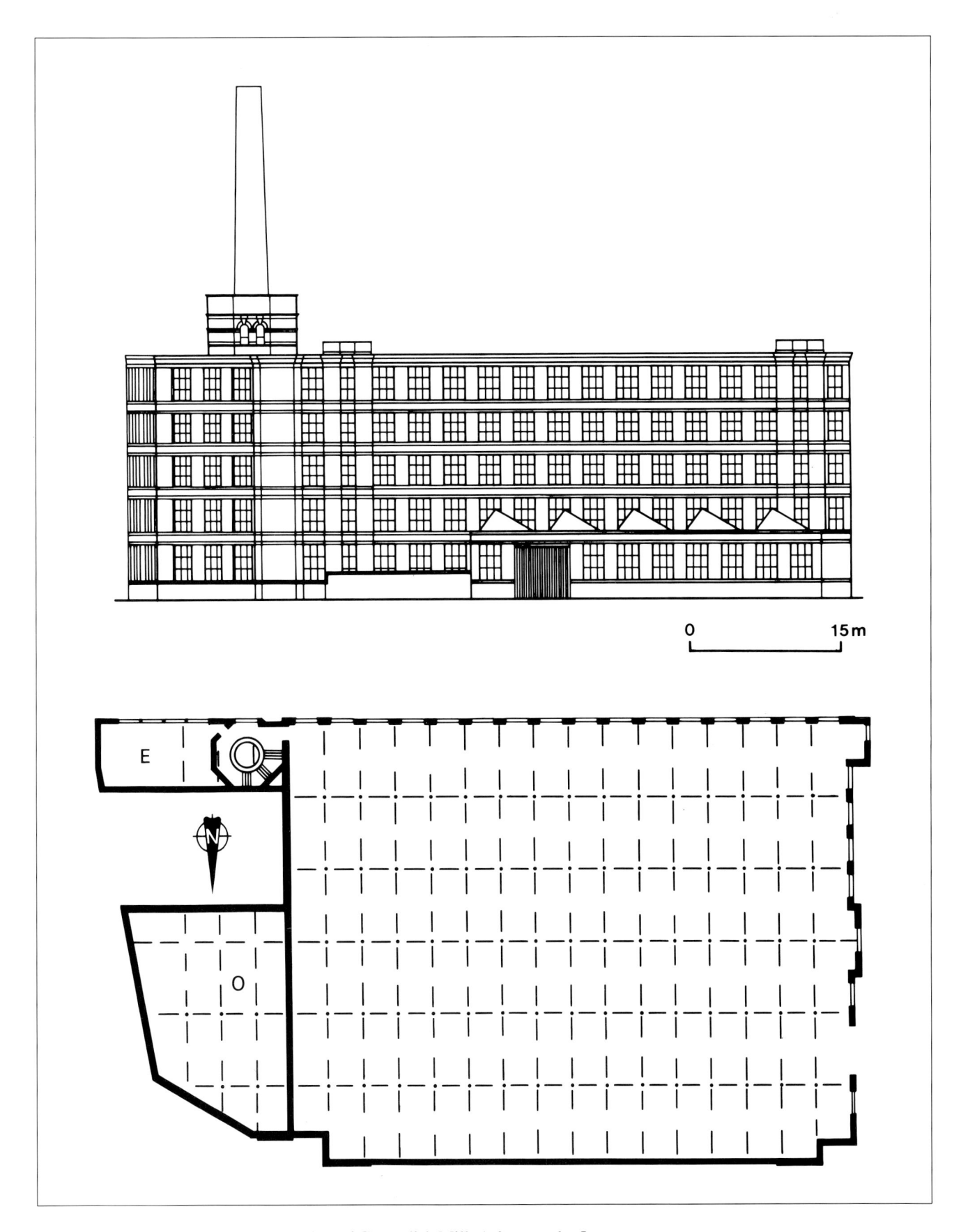

Fig 3.14 Ground-floor plan and elevation of Cavendish Mill, Ashton-under-Lyne.
Key: O – offices; E – engine house.
Built in 1884-5 on the northern side of the Ashton Canal as a cotton-spinning mill, it was the first mill in Ashton, and probably Tameside, to have concrete floors and a flat roof. It also has an unusual octagonal stair-well surrounding the lower part of the circular chimney.

Chapter 4

Hatting

'Over sixty years ago I was a boy, one of a fourth generation of felt hatters, residing at Failsworth, a hatting village near Oldham. In those days felt hat body making was done at home, the hatters working in small shops or outbuildings, though in many instances inside their cottages. The raw material – wool and fur – the felt bodies were made of had to be fetched from their employer's hat works in Oldham, Denton, Bredbury, and Stockport...Working at home in his own shop the body maker was practically his own master...'

(*Hatters Gazette* 15th April 1925, 189)

4.1 Introduction

Denton, along with London, Luton and Stockport, was one of the four great centres of hat making in the country but there were other important areas of hat production within Tameside, particularly Ashton, Gee Cross and Hyde. The industry was dominated by small family firms until the third quarter of the nineteenth century, after which date limited liability companies were established in Denton and Hyde and the family firms declined rapidly. Most of these companies made felt hats for men and women, although straw, silk, tweed, cord and fabric hats have also been manufactured in Tameside. In the Denton area 86 hatting firms have been recorded and in Hyde over 50 are known; many of these were family firms which survived into their fourth generation (Holding 1986, 5; Middleton 1932, 563-7; Powell Collection). Other townships also had hatters, including Audenshaw, Droylsden, Dukinfield, Hattersley, Mottram and Stalybridge. Several studies have been made of the hatting industry in Denton, the best of which are Caffrey's general survey, Holding's survey of the hatting buildings of Denton and Smith's study of the hatting community of Dane Bank (Caffrey 1985; Holding 1986; Smith 1966). The most authoritative and extensive national study of the subject, a doctoral thesis by John Henry Smith, sadly remains unpublished. This contains not only a review of the development of the felt and silk hatting industry in England between 1500 and 1912, but also much original research on the industry in the North-West, and in Denton and Hyde in particular (Smith 1980, I & II). The following chapter of necessity draws heavily on Smith's work.

4.2 The Felt Hatting Process

Hand production

Hat making prior to mechanization in the late nineteenth century involved a number of distinct processes which were carried out in small workshops and domestic dwellings (Smith 1966, 3). Two contemporary descriptions of the felt hatting process can be found in the *Universal Magazine* for April 1750 and the *Penny Magazine* for January 1841. Though separated by nearly 100 years both describe essentially the same processes (Smith 1980, I, 121).

The main element of the preparation process was bowing, in which the raw materials of wool and fur were mixed together on a wooden bench and vibrated to form a layer of even thickness by means of a hatter's bow suspended from the ceiling (Ashmore 1969, 142; 1982, 16; *Penny Magazine* January 1841, 41-2).

Then came the creation of the hat body, the first stage of which was forming, the creation of a basic conical shape by pressing the material into a hood about twice the size of the finished hat (Ashmore 1969, 142; Hellowell 1966, 29-30). Next came planking, or the felting process. During this the hoods were taken to the planking shop where they were alternately bathed in a solution of boiling water and sulphuric acid and rolled with a hatter's pin, gradually shrinking and thickening the material (Holding 1986, 10). The final stage was to shape the hat body on a cylindrical wooden block after which it was dried and dyed (Ashmore 1969, 145; *Penny Magazine* January 1841, 45-8).

The hat was then ready for the finishing processes,

Chapter 4 Hatting

Plate 4.1 Mechanized hat body making in Denton.
Machine hat making was introduced into Tameside in the 1860s and helped to revitalize the hatting industry after a severe depression in the 1840s and 1850s. This early photograph is possibly of the factory of Joseph Howe & Sons, established in 1868 in Annan Street, Denton.

the first element of which was known as blocking and involved pulling, pressing, cutting and ironing the hat, while still on the block. Separate blocks were used to shape the crown and brim. Finally the hats were lined and trimmed according to fashion (Ashmore 1969, 145; *Penny Magazine* January 1841, 45-8).

The organization of the hatting industry in Tameside went through three major phases. In the early eighteenth century the industry was domestic-based, with local farmers supplementing their income by the production of felt hats for agents of the Master Hatters of London (Smith 1980, I, 121). By the beginning of the nineteenth century the production of hats had begun to fragment amongst a number of specialists. The catalyst for this change appears to have been the arrival of the London hatting firms in the North-West, which set up factories in Manchester and Stockport, while subcontracting various parts of the hat-making process to domestic-based individuals in the surrounding townships such as Denton. By the mid-nineteenth century, when this specialization reached its peak, there were specialists for each of the major hand processes, from bowing and planking, to finishing. Although factories had begun to be established in this period, many of the steps involved in the hat-making process, particularly planking and finishing, were often carried out by domestic-based workers known as outworkers (Caffrey 1985, 35). This highly specialized craft industry did not survive the introduction of mechanized hat making, and by the end of the nineteenth century the industry was characterized by large factories, and only the finishing of the hats continued to be carried out on a domestic basis (Plate 4.1).

The most common buildings of the early, premechanized industry were the planking workshops, which were frequently located to the rear of houses or cottages. These were small single-storey buildings, often with chimneys for the kettles, large containers used for boiling the water and sulphuric acid, the rolling process being carried out on wooden boards

Chapter 4 Hatting

Plate 4.2 J Moores & Sons' factory, Denton.
This is a complex site which encompasses six major phases of activity over a 50 year period. This view shows, centre right, the four-storey 'tween' factory built in 1912 for making hats in half sizes and, in the foreground, single-storey workshops.

around the kettle (Caffrey 1985, 32; Smith 1966, 4). Two planking workshops survive in Tameside, at Dane Bank Farm in Denton (SJ 909 949) and at Joel Lane in Gee Cross (SJ 9562 9323) (Fig 4.1). The example at Dane Bank Farm lies at the western end of the farmhouse and is a single-storey stone-built block which has been converted into a garage so that no internal details now survive. The building probably dates from the initial foundation of the business in 1830, and appears to have been superseded in 1861 by a new building which may have housed some of the mechanical processes then being introduced (LRO DRM 1/37; Smith 1980, II, 19). The Joel Lane example survives largely intact, at least externally. This is a single-storey stone-built building with a brick addition at its southern end. Original features include four small steam-release windows in the eastern elevation and a gable chimney stack at the southern end of the building. The date of the building is unclear, although it forms part of a property described in the Werneth estate sale catalogue of 1857 under Lot 50 as consisting of a beer house, two cottages and three hat shops (Powell Collection). The catalogue indicates that the property was rented by a Mr George Oldham and occupied by his wife, and was valued at £3 0s 5d.

Technical improvements

Most of the advances in mechanizing the hatting process in the nineteenth century were developed abroad, particularly in the United States of America where there was a very large hatting industry (Smith 1980, II, 1). The first part of the process to be mechanized was the preparation phase. The Stockport-based firm of T W & J Christy & Co first used a steam-powered blower to separate coarse and fine fur as early as 1821, but the machine was very slow, and did not become popular until improved versions appeared in the later nineteenth century (Giles 1959, 113-14).

Steam-powered hatting machines were patented in England in 1836 and 1837, but it was the 1850s which saw the great leap forward in mechanization in England, led by Christy's of Stockport (Ashmore 1975, 37; Smith 1980, II, 1). In 1850 a machine for making hat bodies was patented, probably a fur former, although the earliest attested use of this type of machine in England was not until 1853. This was followed in 1856 by a patent for a machine to carry out the hardening and planking processes (Smith 1980, II, 2-3). It was not until 1859, however, when Christy's sent two of its owners on a tour of hat factories in the United States, that mechanization really took off in the North-West. The product of this trip was the purchase of a variety of machines including a fur former (Ashmore 1975, 38; Smith 1980, II, 5). Over the next ten years Christy's introduced as many of the new machines as it could, so that by 1868 the firm was almost totally mechanized (Smith 1980, II, 11). The value of this investment in new machinery can be seen in Smith's estimates of the cost of weekly production in 1860, £244, compared to £60 using the new mechanized processes (*ibid*, 9).

The introduction of mechanization in Denton was initially slower than in Stockport, and although Woolfenden's may have introduced some machinery at their Dane Bank site in 1861, it was not until 1864 that its installation became widespread. This was in response to a strike by hatters in Denton during that year, the culmination of a labour shortage in the township since the revival in the hat trade in the late 1850s (Smith 1980, II, 11; see below). As a result of the strike seven master hatters from Denton, Hooley Hill and Bredbury established the Lancashire Machine-made Felt Hat Company, with a capital of £27,000. The initial reluctance of the Denton workers to accept mechanization also led to the growth of a number of new firms in neighbouring Hyde (*ibid*, 12-13).

The mechanization of the finishing process, begun in the 1860s, was not completed until 1900, by which date a number of North-West firms, including Oldham's of Denton, Wilton's of Denton and Perrin's of Hyde, were producing hat-making machinery (*ibid*, 18). Even so, the mechanical processes involved meant that hatting remained a highly labour intensive industry dominated by small single-site firms long after this phase had passed in the cotton and woollen industries. The other major innovation of the late nineteenth century was the introduction of aniline dyes. Their use had been suggested as early as 1874, but technical difficulties prevented a practical application until 1887. In that year a number of firms in Stockport, Denton and Hyde joined together to fund a research post at Owen's College in Manchester, with the result that by the end of the century the use of aniline dyes in the industry had become widespread (*ibid*, 22-4).

The new machinery meant that specialized buildings were needed to house the seven mechanized processes, these being preparation, forming, felting, proofing, dyeing, shaping and finishing (Hellowell 1966, 28-36). As a consequence of mechanization the small domestic-based firm specializing in one part of the process, and the use of outworkers, declined as more firms encompassed the full range of production on one site, with large specialist buildings (Ashmore 1969, 145; Smith 1966, 3-4). The mechanized hat-making site of the late nineteenth and early twentieth centuries was characterized by a range of single- and multi-storey buildings, frequently set around an open courtyard. The main mechanized processes usually took place in the single-storey buildings, which had multi-ridge roofs of glass and were open their entire length. Power was provided initially by an adjacent engine house and from the early twentieth century by an electricity transformer house. The finishing process, and perhaps also the shaping process, was carried out in the multi-storey buildings. These were well lit structures characterized by large windows on each floor and a roof light on the upper floor.

The growth of the small domestic workshop into a large industrial complex is best seen in Tameside at Dane Bank in Denton. Although most of the factory and the associated community has been demolished in recent years, enough survives to trace the development of the site from its foundation in 1830. Joseph Woolfenden bought Dane Shot Bank Farm, now known as Dane Bank Farm, on the edge of Denton moor, in 1820, but did not start making hats until 1830 (Smith 1966, 5-6). Initially he specialized in felt hats but in the latter half of the nineteenth century the company diversified into silk hat production. When John Woolfenden died in 1853, the running of the farm was taken over by his eldest son, Thomas, and the running

Chapter 4 Hatting

of the hatting firm by the remaining four sons, Elias, Henry, James and Joseph (Middleton 1936, 151). The possible supersedence in 1861 of the early planking workshop by a building housing some of the new mechanical processes has already been noted. In 1873 a large factory was built to the east of the farmhouse, for warehousing and the mechanized processes of body making (Holding 1986, 57). The central building was of three storeys, brick-built, and was embellished only by a small clock and the inscription 'J W & Co 1873'. A later addition to the site included a two-storey brick-built block of six by two bays with a basement and its own chimney. This still stands. Houses built for three of John's sons also survive, as does the farmhouse. In 1887 Elias and James retired, Henry and Joseph having died in 1877 and 1879 respectively. The business now fell to their sons John, Joseph and Thomas, the last of whom, Joseph, died in 1911, leaving the firm in the hands of a fourth generation (Middleton 1936, 150).

4.3 The Development of the Felt and Silk Hatting Industries

Early history

Although there is little direct evidence for hatting in Tameside before the mid-eighteenth century, the origins of the local industry can be traced back to the seventeenth century. This was a time when hat making was spreading from its traditional home in London to the north of England. During the early to mid-seventeenth century Chester and, to a lesser degree, Congleton, Manchester and Nantwich became significant centres of activity in the North-West, although production was confined to the coarser felts of wool and coney (Giles 1959, 106-7; Smith 1980, I, 45-6). From 1670 Manchester was the leading centre of hat production in the region, and by 1760 the town and its surrounding area had become the main manufacturing zone in the country, although London remained the commercial heart of the industry (Smith 1980, I, 44).

The earliest known references to hatting in Tameside occur in a will from Hattersley dated 1697, in which William Wagstaffe of Marled Earth Farm left to his son Samuel 'one great Lead now in my dye house and a great plank to make hatts on', and in a will from Ashton dated 1698, in which Joseph Graver left his hatting equipment to his son (CRO WS; LRO WCW). The earliest reference to hat making in Denton occurs in 1702, when a deceased feltmaker named Isaac Gee was mentioned in a document referring to a disputed right of way in Taylor Lane (Young 1982, 20). Booker claims that the Bertenshaws of Haughton Green were employing outside labour in the 1700s, although the present survey has found evidence of the family's involvement in hatting only from 1762, in which year Thomas Bertenshaw of Denton left a will in which he mentioned a shop or work house containing basons, a dye pan, a finishing iron, a kettle and planks (Booker 1855, 10; Caffrey 1985, 29; Smith 1980, I, 97). The only other will of a hatter from Tameside in the first half of the eighteenth century which has been uncovered is that of Daniel Heggenbotham of Hyde in 1735, who had an estate worth £127 18s 0d and a shop containing a bason, a bow, blocks and a plank (Smith 1980, I, 97). It is not until the second half of the eighteenth century that the probate evidence suggests an upsurge in hatting activity in the Borough, particularly in Denton (Table 4.1).

This probate evidence indicates that these hatters were still involved in the whole process of hat making

Township/village	1690-9	1700-9	1710-19	1720-9	1730-9	1740-9	1750-9	1760-9	1770-9	1780-9	1790-9
Ashton	1								1	2	
Audenshaw											2
Denton			1					1		1	2
Droylsden								1			
Hattersley	1										
Haughton								1			
Hooley Hill											1
Hyde					1			1			
Mottram								1	1		

Table 4.1 Probate evidence for hatting in Tameside in the period 1690-1799.
Sources: CRO and LRO wills; Smith 1980, I, 88.

and also that they had a second trade. This was invariably dairy farming rather than arable farming. Smith suggests that this may have been due to the delicate nature of the hatter's hands, which were made soft and liable to cracking by the planking process (*ibid*, 105), but this may underestimate the prevalence of dairy-farming in the region during the eighteenth century.

Probate evidence by itself probably under-represents the extent of hatting in Tameside during this period. The parish registers of St Michael's, Ashton-under-Lyne contain three references to hatters in the period 1711-20 (Brierley 1928). However, hatters appear in the Mottram parish registers only from 1757, although this may be as a result of a general lack of occupational detail. A Joseph Simister, hatter of Mottram, married Martha Garlick on 15th May 1757, and John Platt, hatter of Mottram, buried a daughter on 21st January 1765. The baptismal entries also refer to several hatters of Mottram – Thomas Oldham on 17th April 1765, Thomas Harrop on 9th December 1770, Joseph Simister on 19th August 1781 and Joshua Oldham on 5th March 1782. Beth, widow of Thomas Harrop, a hatter of Hollingworth, was buried on 15th December 1791 (CRO MF41/1-9).

Nationally the eighteenth century was a general period of expansion for the hatting industry, thanks to the English hatting industry's protected position at home and its dominance of the export market in Europe and North America (Giles 1959, 108-9). By the late eighteenth century the main beneficiaries of this growth in the industry in the North-West may have been the emerging group of comparatively wealthy feltmakers in the Manchester area during the 1780s and 1790s; these were a group of individuals identified by Smith from probate evidence who had personal estates valued between £50 and £100. These men may also have been investing their trading surplus in property (Smith 1980, I, 90, 100).

The earliest known hat-making firm, as opposed to individual, in Tameside was Messrs Bromley and Peacock of Denton, who established their works in 1792 (Booker 1855, 10). However, this was probably based on the business founded by Zachariah Peacock in the late eighteenth century, one of the wealthy group of hatters identified by Smith. His will of 1791 states that he had at least one hat shop, as well as two dwelling houses, at Hooley Hill and Crown Point (Smith 1980, I, 92). By 1795 Aikin could describe Denton as

'a long straggling village [which] has increased much of late, and is principally occupied by hatters, cotton-spinners, and colliers' (Aikin 1795, 449).

Another of Smith's group of wealthy hatters, John Ashton, left property in Guide Lane at Hooley Hill, Audenshaw, where a major centre of hat production was developing north of Denton (Smith 1980, I, 92). Of this area Aikin states that

Place/Year	1816	1821-2	1825	1832	1841	1852	1861	1871-2	1879	1892	1901-2
Ashton	3	2	9	4	4	13	9	18	22	11	11
Audenshaw		2	4	14	5	1		2	2	3	1
Denton	11	12	20	12	17	9	22	43	49	47	40
Droylsden		2	1	3	2	1	1	2	1	6	
Dukinfield				11	8		2	4	3		1
Gee Cross			2	3	2	3	4	6	7	2	3
Hattersley					6						
Haughton		3	5	10	5		6	9	9	4	
Hooley Hill		2	6	12	5	2	2	6	12	11	6
Hyde			2	1	4	8	3	14	14	13	13
Mossley					2			3	1	4	
Mottram			1		2						
Stalybridge			4	1	8	4	2	3	5	4	3
Total	14	24	53	71	70	41	51	110	125	105	78

Table 4.2 The felt and silk hat manufacturers and hatters of Tameside, the evidence from selected directories, 1816-1901/2. Sources: Wardle & Pratt 1816; Pigot & Dean 1821-2; Baines 1825; Pigot & Sons 1832; Pigot & Co 1841; Whellan & Co 1852; Slater 1861; Slater 1871-2; Slater 1879; Slater 1892; Kelly & Co 1901; Kelly & Co 1902.

Chapter 4 Hatting

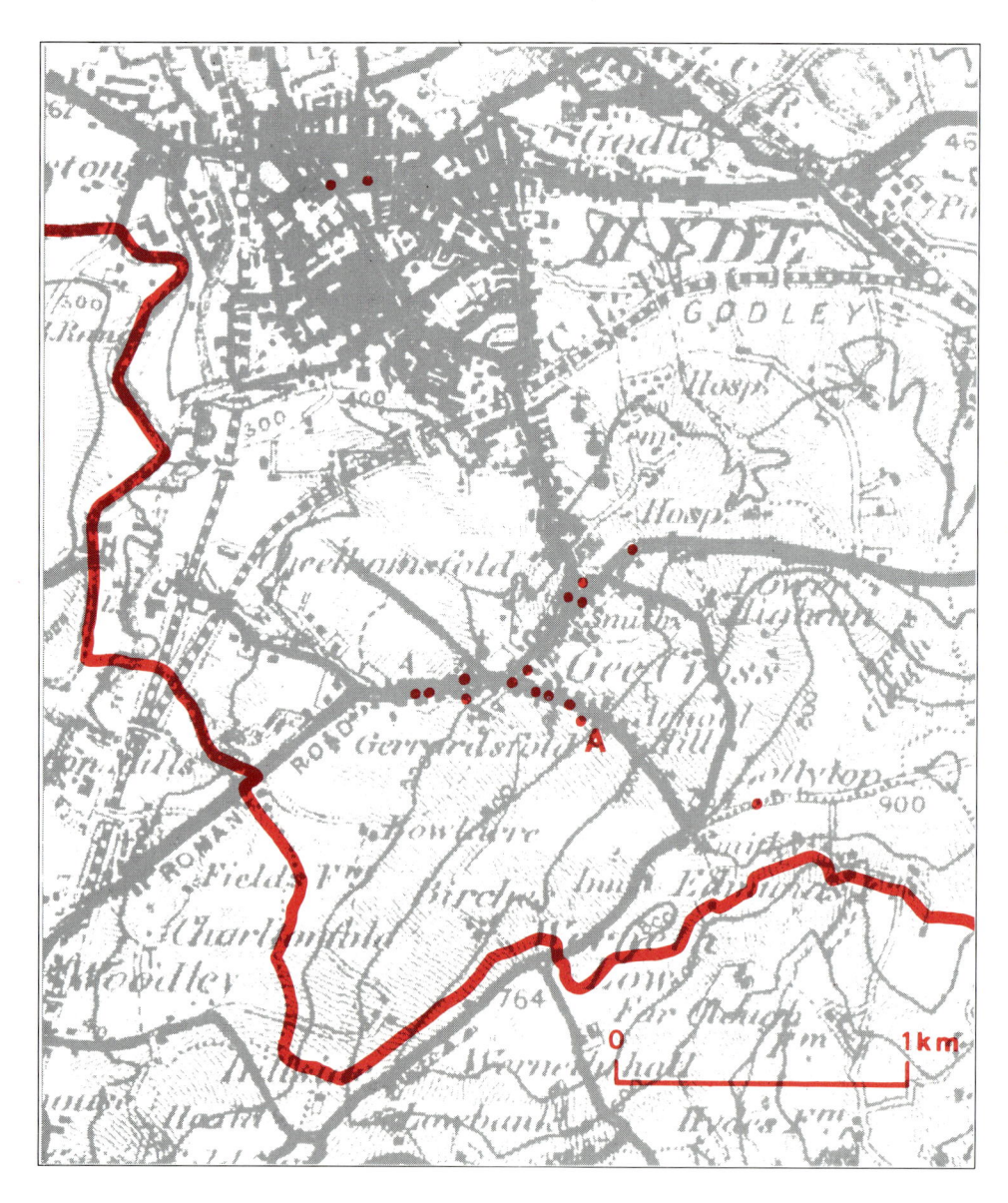

Fig 4.1 Distribution of hat shops in Hyde and Gee Cross in 1857.
Prior to the mechanization of the hatting industry, Gee Cross was the focus of activity in the Hyde area. In 1857 the Werneth estate sale catalogue listed fifteen sites containing a total of 34 hat shops in the village, whereas in the same year only two are known in Hyde town centre. The Joel Lane hat shop (A) is the site of one of only two surviving examples in Tameside of a planking workshop, used in the manufacture of hat bodies.

'the inhabitants of several of the townships near Hooley Hill are employed in a hat manufactory lately set up at a new village called Quebec on the road from Ashton to Stockport' (Aikin 1795, 233).

According to Booker by 1800 there were four felt hatting firms working in the Denton area: Messrs Bond, Bromley and Peacock, George Bowler & Co, Ashworth's, and John, Robert and Andrew Bentley (Booker 1855, 10). In the first quarter of the nineteenth century the industry in Denton saw rapid expansion. According to Baines' directory, in 1825 Denton with 20 manufacturers was the third largest hat-making centre in the North-West, behind only Stockport with 31 and Manchester with 58. It is also clear from Baines that Denton was not the only area of hat production in Tameside at this date. There were ten firms in Audenshaw and Hooley Hill, nine in Ashton, and a few more factories in Droylsden, Gee Cross, Haughton, Hyde and Stalybridge (Table 4.2). Most of these probably produced felt hats. The wills of the early nineteenth century also indicate one-man hat-making establishments in many parts of Tameside. John Leigh of Godley described himself as a hatter and farmer in his will of February 1828, whilst James Horsefield of Werneth and Robert Wagstaffe of Mottram also described themselves as hatters in their wills of September 1828 and September 1829 (CRO WS).

By 1840 2000 dozen felt hats were produced each week in Denton, 100 dozen a week by the single firm of Messrs Peacock & Bros (Booker 1855, 12). This rapid expansion of the industry probably accounts for the upsurge in the combined population of the townships of Denton and Haughton, which grew from 2501 in 1801 to 6759 in 1841 (Cronin 1985, 44; Table 2.1).

The importance of Gee Cross as an early hat-making centre can be seen from the number of hat shops recorded in the Werneth estate sale catalogue of 1857 (Powell Collection). Although the Egertons of Tatton did not own all of the property in Gee Cross, they did possess about three quarters of the village. The sale catalogue indicates that there were at least 34 hat shops in the village, the main concentrations being around the Grapes Inn, at the junction of Stockport Road and Joel Lane, and at the junction of Stockport Road and Mottram Old Road (Fig 4.1). On average each house with a hat shop cost 46s to rent per year.

The number of hat shops recorded in Gee Cross contrasts sharply with the number of hatters and hat manufacturers recorded in the directories around this period (Table 4.2). Even allowing for the likelihood that some of these hat shops may have been disused, it seems that the directories significantly under-represent the number of individuals involved in the hatting industry, at least prior to its mechanization.

During this period an increasing amount of the work began to be done in specialist workshops and buildings, on behalf of a number of London firms who were now establishing factories in the North-West (Giles 1959, 117). Christy's, itself originally a London firm, purchased the works of their Stockport commission firm T & J Worsley in 1826 (Ashmore 1969, 141). They followed this with the building of a large model factory in Fairfield, Droylsden, in 1835. This factory stood in 30 acres of land, had 50 cottages for outdoor work and was reckoned to be worth £12,000 (Giles 1959, 118). In 1837, however, the building was bought by William Christy, one of the Christy brothers, and converted to a cotton mill, being later known as Fairfield Mill (Speake & Witty 1953, 91, 177; Smith 1980, I, 172). There was good reason for this sudden change of use, for in 1836 a trade depression in the felt hatting industry had begun which was to last until the late 1850s (Giles 1959, 131).

Depression

The depression which began in 1836 had two causes. Firstly, the price of beaver fur had steadily risen since 1800, largely due to the over-hunting of the animal in North America, leading to a decline in the production of the beaver hat (Smith 1980, I, 203). Secondly, there was a change in fashion in favour of the silk hat. These had first been produced around 1799, and by 1822 their production was beginning to seriously affect the price of rabbit fur. Firms such as Christy's began to diversify into silk hat production, and the popularity of this product was greatly increased by its use by Prince Albert. Their production was further boosted by the imposition of an import duty on foreign silk hats in 1842. In 1850 250,000 dozen silk hats were made nationally, totally eclipsing the felt hatting branch of the industry (Giles 1959, 131-2).

Denton was not affected until 1841, when there was a serious strike, as a result of which silk hat manufacturers took a large portion of the local felt hat market (Holding 1986, 25). The effects of this depression were acutely felt in Denton because so much of the industry was family based. Wages fell by 35% and unemployment rose sharply, with many entire families being put out of work. As a result the population of the township began to fall as families moved away in search of work, dropping from 3440 in 1841 to 3147 in 1851 (Caffrey 1985, 34; Table 2.1).

This depression seemed to herald the end of the industry and by 1854 there were only twelve firms left in Denton (Booker 1855, 12). Booker noted that in the years 1847-9

'the state of the Denton hatters and their families was pitiable in the extreme. Their trade was irrecoverably lost, upwards of 1,000 families in Denton and Haughton were deprived for the most part of their means of subsistence and, consequently, large numbers left the locality in search of other employment' (*ibid*, 13).

Messrs Peacock & Bros were making only three dozen felt hats per week in 1855 (*ibid*). The first purpose-built silk hatting factory was not established in Denton until 1847 by Thomas and William Walker (Middleton 1936, 152).

The effects of the depression in felt hat making can be seen in Cronin's analysis of the 1851 census returns for the township of Haughton. Not only had the population of the township dropped from 3319 in 1841 to 3042 in 1851, but the chief area of employment in 1851 was the textile industry. This accounted for 47.85% of the occupations in the township, whilst hatting, although the second most common occupation, accounted only for 18.38% (Cronin 1985, 50). Furthermore, of the five master hatters recorded in the census three were retired (*ibid*, 52). No new houses were being built in this year, and 52 of the 630 dwellings recorded were empty. Union Street, in Haughton Green, had fourteen of its fifteen houses unoccupied (*ibid*, 46).

Although the Denton hatting industry recovered, in other parts of Tameside the depression of the 1840s and 1850s, coupled with mechanization from the 1860s, brought an end to the domestic-based felt hatting industry. As noted above, in Droylsden Christy's new hat factory had to be converted to cotton production in 1837. A number of the local felt hat producers turned to silk hat making, and during the 1840s and 1850s there were four silk hatters in the township. However, this industry did not last much beyond the 1850s (Speake & Witty 1953, 94). The effects of the felt hatting depression in the townships of Hollingworth and Mottram can be seen in the census returns

Chapter 4 Hatting

for the period 1841-61. In 1841, at the beginning of the depression, the census of that year records seventeen and nine hatters respectively in these townships, with notable concentrations at Wednesough Green in Hollingworth, where there were five hatters, and Mottram village, where there were six (TLSL MF Census returns). By 1847 there appears to have been only one working hat shop in Mottram, that of Ralph Sidebottom, on the corner of Broadbottom Road and Lower Market Place (CRO EDT 281). By 1851, according to the census of that year, there were no hatters left in Mottram and only five in Hollingworth. Two of these were journeymen hatters, who had no doubt come from other parts of the region to look for work in this area. Although according to the 1861 census there were still five hatters in Hollingworth, it is clear that the days of the small domestic hatter in this part of Tameside were almost over.

Revival in the late nineteenth century

Despite this severe depression Smith concluded that 'by 1860 there can be little doubt that the North-West dominated British hatting' (Smith 1980, I, 167). This was aided by the improvement in trading conditions soon after 1855, resulting from a shift towards silk hat production, increasing mechanization and changing fashion. In the later nineteenth century the introduction of bowler hats in the 1860s, the less formal soft felt hats such as the billycocks and wideawakes shortly after, and the introduction of the homburg and trilby in the 1890s all led to increases in production, employees and firms (Ashmore 1969, 145; Caffrey 1985, 38-9; Smith 1973, 45). In 1871 there were 10,742 people employed in the hatting industry of Lancashire and Cheshire, nearly all concentrated in Denton, Hyde and Stockport (Smith 1980, II, 21). It was during this decade that, according to the directories, the number of manufacturers peaked in Tameside (Table 4.2). Employment peaked slightly later, in 1891 when nationally there were 28,948 people involved in felt, silk and cloth hat manufacture, of whom 17,785 worked in the North-West (*ibid*, 25). Stockport and Denton were the major centres of hat production in the late nineteenth century, although there was significant growth of the industry in Bury and Hyde during this period, while London retained its position as the centre of wholesale, retail and silk production. The only other significant hat-producing area in the late nineteenth century was Warwickshire (*ibid*, 21). This geographical spread of the industry remained unchanged until after the First World War.

The reviving fortunes of the hatting industry can be seen in the growth of new firms in Tameside during the second half of the nineteenth century. This was most marked in Denton, where directory entries indicate a doubling in the number of firms during the period 1861-72 (Table 4.2). It was during this period that a number of the largest Denton hatting firms were founded. The brothers Jonathan and Thomas Moores started a business in a purpose-built workshop next to their cottage in 1862 but soon moved to a new factory in Heaton Street, Denton. Walker, Ashworth & Linney was founded in 1867, William Brown & Sons Ltd in 1872, James Bevan & Co Ltd in 1873 and Messrs Cook, Smith & Co in 1884 (Caffrey 1985, 38). In 1879 there were 49 firms listed in Denton (Table 4.2).

The problems of the industry during the 1840s and 1850s are reflected in the architecture of the new hat factories of the 1860s and 1870s (Holding 1986, 69-71). The new factory of Joseph Howe & Sons Ltd, built in Annan Street in 1868, had upper storeys of normal design, but specially designed ground floors which could be converted into terraced housing if the factory failed (see below). Other similar designs could be seen in factories in Law Street.

The population of Denton was slow to recover after the depression. Having fallen from 3440 in 1841 to 3147 in 1851, in the census of 1861 this had risen to only 3335. By 1871, however, thanks to this surge of new firms, the figure had increased to 5117, a rise of 53% (Table 2.1). By contrast, the population of neighbouring Haughton had recovered by 1861, actually exceeding that of Denton in that year; this early success can be attributed to the greater influence of the cotton industry in that township, which accounted for nearly half of all occupations in 1851 (see above). However, after 1861 the growth of Haughton fell behind that of Denton, reflecting the greater role of hatting in the economy of the latter township.

A second major centre of hat production grew up in Hyde during the later nineteenth century. This was based upon the new mechanized processes, the main sites being located in Hyde town centre and in Gee Cross (Ashmore 1982, 99). This revival began with the founding of John Oldham and James Fogg's factory in Water Street in 1864. The firm moved to George Street in 1866 where the mechanical manufacture of hats was started (Middleton 1932, 563-4). John Cheetham & Sons Ltd was founded in Hyde in 1870 and in 1881 built a large factory in Cooper Street. The firm of James Higinbotham was also established in 1870, in Mount Street, and built the Thomas Street Hatworks in 1887 (*ibid*, 564-5). Thornley & Booth Ltd began in 1877 at Boston Mills as felt hat makers, but after 1904 concentrated on the production of millinery and after the First World War on overalls and head linings (*ibid*, 565-7). Middleton estimated that there were a dozen hat-making firms in the Hyde area in the 1860s to 1880s (*ibid*, 563).

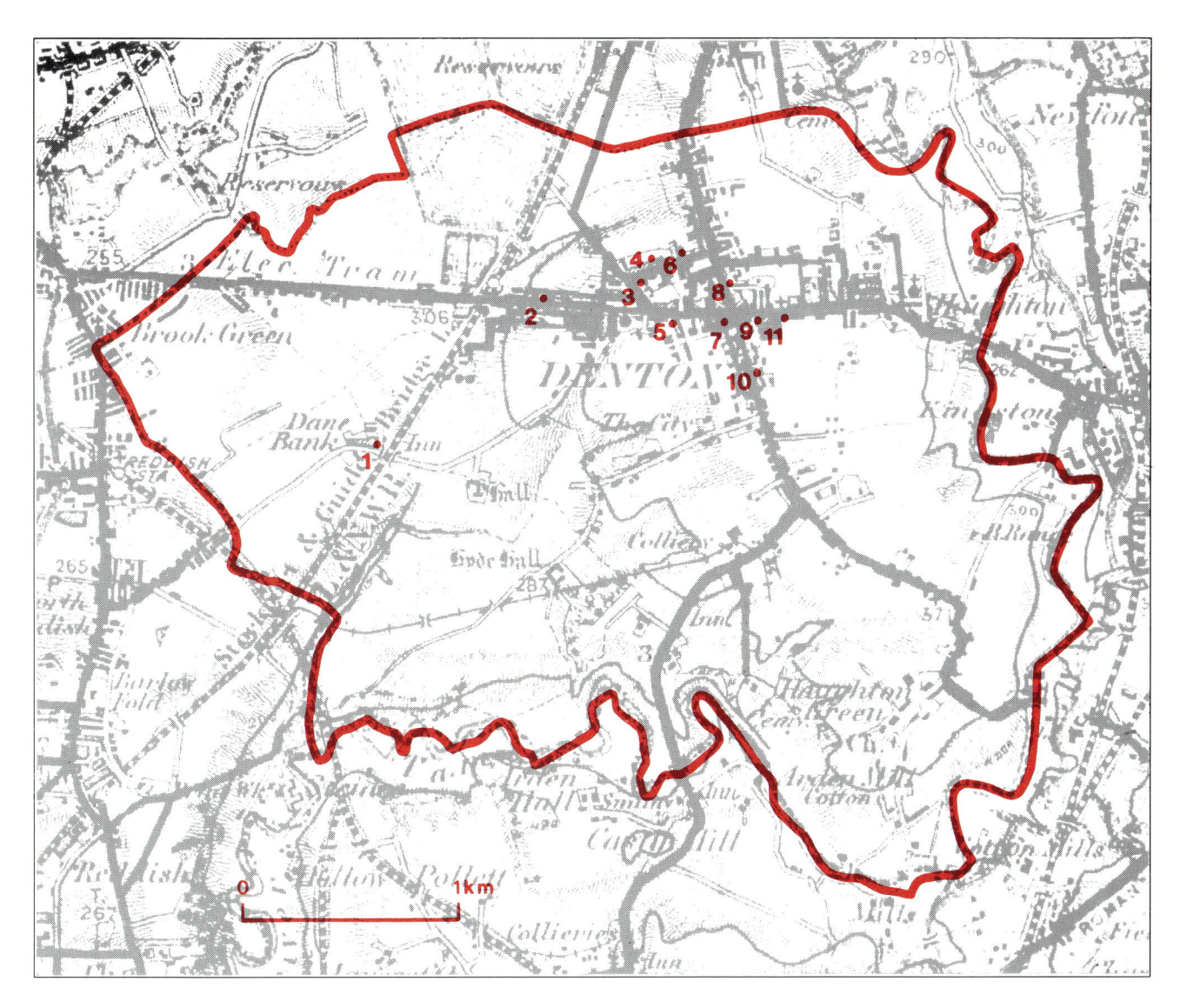

Fig 4.2 Surviving hat factories in Denton.
Key: 1 J Woolfenden & Co Ltd; 2 J Moores & Sons Ltd; 3 Henry Burgess & Co; 4 Denton Hat Company; 5 J W Farron; 6 J Wilson & Sons Ltd; 7 William Robert Bellringer; 8 Joseph Howe & Sons Ltd; 9 Booth & Moores; 10 James Bevan & Co Ltd; 11 C Clermont.

Many of the largest firms became limited liability companies, amongst the first to do so being J Moores & Sons of Denton in 1887 and Thornley & Booth of Hyde in 1897 (*ibid*, 567). New companies continued to be created in Denton during the twentieth century, the Carlton Company being established by Thomas and Robert Gledhill Robinson in 1902, while the Denton Hat Company was founded as late as 1921 (Middleton 1936, 156-7).

Ashton, a town with a long association with the hat trade, also saw a period of strong growth in the late nineteenth century. According to directory entries the number of manufacturers and hatters in the town exceeded those of Hyde in the period 1852-79 (Table 4.2). Unfortunately there is little physical evidence left of this small but significant part of Ashton's industrial heritage. However, the directory entries of the late nineteenth century indicate two main centres of activity, one in Hurst, the other at the eastern end of Stamford Street. During the 1870s there were at least four hat shops along this street, at nos 146, 168, 196 and 270, run by Edward Wood, Samuel Smith, Thomas Hadfield and Thomas Wood. A further two hat shops could be found nearby at no 14 Market Avenue and in the Stamford Arcade, run by James Ollerenshaw and John Shaw (Slater 1871-2, 1879).

Nationally the industry continued to thrive during the last decades of the nineteenth century and the early twentieth century, aided by a rise in exports despite growing competition in the overseas market from Belgium and France (Smith 1980, II, 91-3). According to the directories, between 1879 and 1902 the number of hatting concerns in Tameside decreased by approximately a third (Table 4.2), but much of this decrease

Chapter 4 Hatting

may be accounted for by the disappearance of smaller firms in the face of competition from the largest hatting firms in Denton and Hyde, which alone had the money to invest in new machinery and buildings. After the First World War the rise of the Luton felt hatting industry, and the decline in hat wearing at home and exports abroad, posed a more serious threat (*ibid*, 139). In the borough of Hyde there were just five large firms operating in 1930, four in Hyde town and one in Gee Cross (Middleton 1932, 563-7). However, despite these trading difficulties at the end of the 1920s there were still 3700 people employed in hatting in the old Denton and Haughton townships, accounting for almost half of the working population of 7800 of the new Denton UDC (Smith 1966, 3).

4.4 Straw Hat Making in Tameside

Straw hat production was never extensive in Tameside. The production of straw hats did not need the intensive processes seen in the felt hatting industry and was consequently less skilled. There were four necessary stages. Firstly, the straw was bleached. Then a broad flat plait was made, the edges of which were knitted together by thread. The body of the hat was then formed by winding the plait around a wooden shape and pressing with a hot iron. Finally the hat body was finished with a brim and decoration.

The main centres of production in England during the nineteenth century were Bedford, Buckingham and Hertford. Straw hat making in Tameside never approached the importance of felt and silk hatting but it did enjoy a period of popularity during the depression of the 1840s and 1850s, when production is attested at Ashton, Dukinfield and Stalybridge (Pigot & Co 1841; Slater 1843; Whellan & Co 1852; Slater 1861).

4.5 The Main Hatting Firms

With at least 86 hatting firms in Denton and upwards of 50 known in Hyde, it would be impossible to give a detailed record of every firm. Therefore, the following discussion will concern itself with four hat-making sites where substantial surviving remains highlight the development of the felt and silk hatting industry in Tameside.

Joseph Howe & Sons, Annan Street, Denton

This small but complex site (centred SJ 9257 9565) is noteworthy because of its unusual mid-nineteenth-century architectural details. The firm was founded by Joseph Howe who in 1838 set up a workshop in Denton specializing in the dyeing of hats. By 1859 the business had been extended to include the manufacture of fur and wool hats. By this date his six sons were employed in the business, as were several journeymen. In 1868 Joseph died, and the following year his sons John, Joseph, Richard, Robert, Thomas and William, bought a plot of land along Annan Street in Denton on which they erected a large factory. In 1887 the firm became a limited company under the name Joseph Howe & Sons Ltd (Middleton 1936, 151-2; Hellowell 1966, 18).

The 1868 factory is formed by a long two-storey brick building, of seventeen by two bays, fronting Annan Street. The second-storey windows are rectangular with stone sills and lintels. However, the first-storey windows are alternately rectangular and rounded brick-arched windows. The latter have breaks in the bonding of the brick immediately below them, indicating that they were so designed as to be capable of conversion into the doorways of domestic dwellings should trading conditions worsen. Slightly later than this phase is a small six-bay extension to the east end of the Annan Street frontage. This is particularly interesting in that it is built in the same style with alternate round-headed ground-floor windows also capable of conversion into doorways.

Perhaps slightly later is a brick boiler house, to the rear of Annan Street, at the western end of the range. This has a later circular chimney on an earlier square pediment. Beyond this is a three-storey brick building of four by six bays, with a gable roof with pediments at its northern and eastern ends (phase 2). All the storeys are open, and the wooden floors are supported by cast-iron columns.

A third phase of activity, around the turn of the century, is represented by a range of buildings on the northern and eastern side of the site. This comprises a three-storey, four-bay extension to the phase 2 three-storey structure described above. East of this is a range of single-storey workshops.

J Moores & Sons, Heaton Street, Denton

This factory (centred SJ 9182 9545) was founded by Jonathan and Thomas Moores, the company remaining in family hands. Jonathan worked as a journeyman hatter until he was sacked by his employers for selling his own hats in Manchester. With capital from their father, Jonathan and his brother built a workshop next to their own cottage in 1862. In 1889 Thomas retired, and Jonathan changed the name of the firm to J Moores & Sons, since his three sons and son-in-law were now part of the business. In 1887 the firm was made a private limited liability company with a capital of £100,000 (Middleton 1932, 567).

The 1862 building was a two-storey structure, the

being supported by cast-iron columns, technology acquired from the textile industry. There was also a brick boiler house with a circular chimney, behind which may be a contemporary single-storey workshop. A slightly later addition to the Heaton Street frontage, of nine bays, was made in the same style (phase 2).

In 1912 a 'tween' factory, for making hats in half sizes, was added. This is formed of four main elements, again set around an inner courtyard. The Heaton Street frontage was extended in the same style, apparently in two stages of nine and eleven bays (phases 3 and 4). In the phase 3 extension of nine bays the easternmost bay has a ground-floor loading bay next to an elaborate stone entrance. The phase 4 extension of eleven bays has a large loading bay at its eastern end extending throughout the first two floors. At the western and eastern ends of this range are two four-storey buildings with gable roofs and open floors. The whole of this complex appears to have been built using concrete floors and steel columns. At the rear of the site is a southern range of single-storey brick workshops. A slightly later office block, of two storeys with a terracotta facade, finishes the eastern end of the Heaton Street frontage (phase 5). There are also later, mid-twentieth-century, single-storey workshops to the rear of the 1892 factory (phase 6).

Joseph Wilson & Sons Ltd, Wilton St, Denton

Wilson's hat factory (centred SJ 9230 9580) was founded in 1872 by Joseph Wilson, the son of a hatter who began his career in Godley in 1860 but later moved to Haughton Green (Holding 1986, 64; Middleton 1936, 154). The firm became a private limited company in 1900 and sometime after 1936 was taken over by the Associated British Hat Manufacturers. Wilson's was the last factory in Denton to produce felt hats, closing in the 1980s (Caffrey 1985, 38). This is the largest hatting complex in Denton. In 1936 the firm employed 1100 people and was one of the largest felt hat factories in the world (Middleton 1936, 154). The site is particularly noteworthy for its mixture of construction techniques and architectural styles, reminiscent of some of the local textile mills (Plate 4.3).

The earliest building on the site is a short run of three brick terrace houses of two storeys, probably of the mid-nineteenth century. These lay at the eastern side of the site on Bright Street and probably predate the hat factory.

The primary phase of the factory, built in 1872, lies along Wilton Street, where a three-storey brick-built factory, of seven by two bays, was erected (Fig 4.4, phase 1). As with the factories of Joseph Howe and J Moores, each storey is open, the wooden floors being

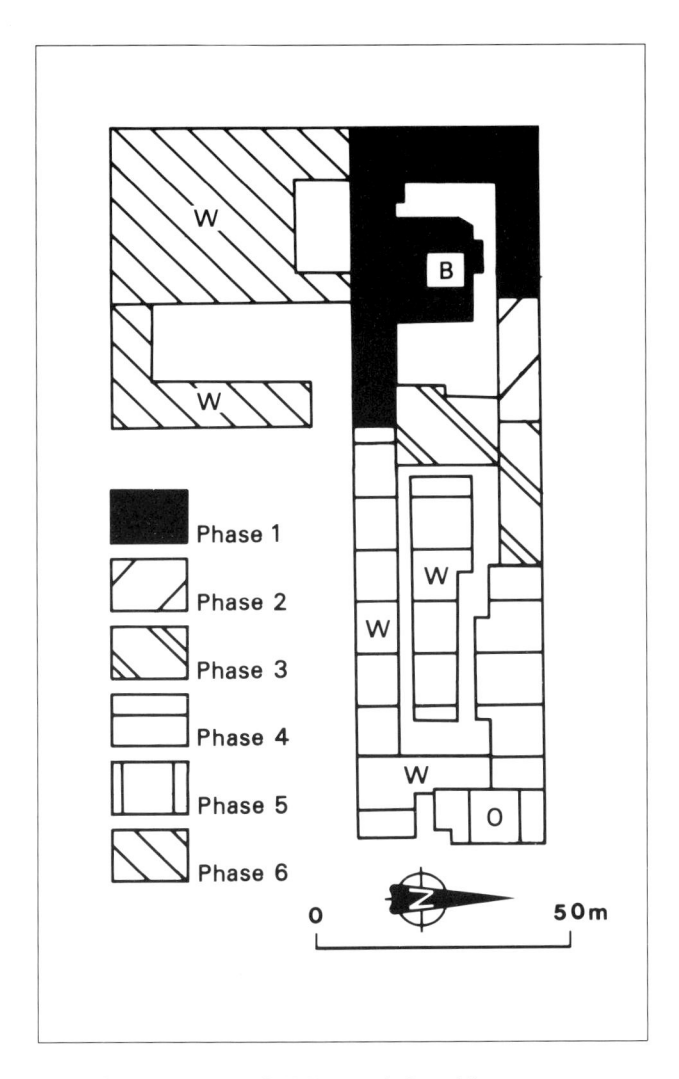

Fig 4.3 Phased plan of J Moores & Sons' factory.
Key: W – workshop; O – offices; B – boiler house and chimney.
The majority of buildings on this site date to the period 1892–1912 and are a mixture of tall, three- and four-storey buildings and single-storey workshops.

ground floor of which could be used for hat making and the upper storey for finishing (Holding 1986, 46). However, like many of the factories built in the 1860s and 1870s, this building could also be converted to dwellings if the business failed. In 1872 new premises were bought in Heaton Street and a new two-storey factory erected (Caffrey 1985, 38). Around 1892 this factory was demolished to make way for the present buildings on the site (Plate 4.2).

The site as it exists today is complex. The earliest surviving buildings relate to the *c* 1892 rebuild, formed by a suite of buildings set around three sides of a courtyard (Fig 4.3, phase 1). The largest of these is an L-shaped brick building, three storeys high, of twelve by thirteen by two bays. As was the case with many of the late nineteenth-century hat factories in Denton, each storey was open, the wooden floors

Chapter 4 Hatting

Plate 4.3 J Wilson & Sons' factory, Wilton Street, Denton.
The largest hat factory in Tameside, the complex is especially notable for its use of mill-building techniques and for the imposing facade on Wilton Street, erected in two phases in the late nineteenth and early twentieth centuries. The three-storey building shown at the far end of this facade is part of the original factory built in 1872.

supported by cast-iron columns. To the rear of this factory is a three-storey brick boiler house with an octagonal brick circular chimney. West of this is a large rectangular building of two storeys with very few windows, and a large skylight running its full length. It has a gable roof and the western and eastern gables are surmounted by pediments. Its use is unclear but it may have been an engine house. Perhaps slightly later was a range of single-storey brick-built workshops to the rear of this building. These had multi-ridge roofs supported by cast-iron columns.

In the late nineteenth century a large extension was built along Wilton Street to the east of the 1872 factory (phase 2). This comprises a four-storey L-shaped brick-built building with a basement, of seven by fourteen by five bays; there is a water tower with a cast-iron tank in the north-west corner. The southern facade of seven bays is embellished by stone coursing between the storeys, and by two pediments on the top of the elevation. There are two loading bays in this elevation, including one linking this facade with the 1872 factory. Behind the Wilton Street frontage the building is twelve by five bays in size. Internally the floors are wooden, being supported by cast-iron columns. A further range of single-storey workshops may have been added to the rear of the complex in this phase.

The third major phase of activity visible on the site probably belongs to the early twentieth century. The Wilton Street facade was further extended to the east, by seven by eight bays, in the same style as the phase 2 addition. On the roof a third pediment was added. Structurally the building was radically different, with concrete floors supported by steel columns, and steel roof trusses. The rear of the phase 2 Wilton Street building was also extended in a similar style, by fourteen by five bays. At the back of the new building was added a third range of single-storey workshops with multi-ridge roofs supported by steel beams, most of which have now been demolished (phase 4). Perhaps contemporary with this phase is a two-storey brick-built electric power house, in the north-eastern corner of the site.

James Higinbotham & Son, Mount Street, Hyde

The firm of James Higinbotham was one of the earliest mechanized hatting firms of Hyde, and was part of the diversification of industries which took place in Hyde as a result of the cotton famine of 1861-5. James Higinbotham began as a hat planker, but at the age of eighteen started work at Greenfield Mill in Hyde. He later established a retail greengrocery business in Clarendon Place in Hyde, with storerooms in Mount Street. It was in Mount Street in 1870 that Higinbotham with two partners, Messrs Morgan and Thornley, established a hat-making firm. The two partners soon left and eventually James brought his three sons into the business. The firm specialized in men's hard and soft felt hats, and ladies' felt hats. The original 1870 factory was extended as the business grew and in 1887 a second factory was built in nearby Thomas Street (Middleton 1932, 565-6).

Although the 1887 factory has been demolished, the extensive Mount Street premises still survive (SJ 9518 9482), these being now divided between three firms. There are at least three phases spread across three main buildings. The earliest buildings probably belong to the original 1870 factory. One is a single-storey brick-built shed with a gable slate roof and may be the original planking house, although there is no evidence of a chimney by this or any other building on the site. The second early building fronts Mount Street and was probably the original finishing premises. This is a large two-storey brick-built structure of six by five

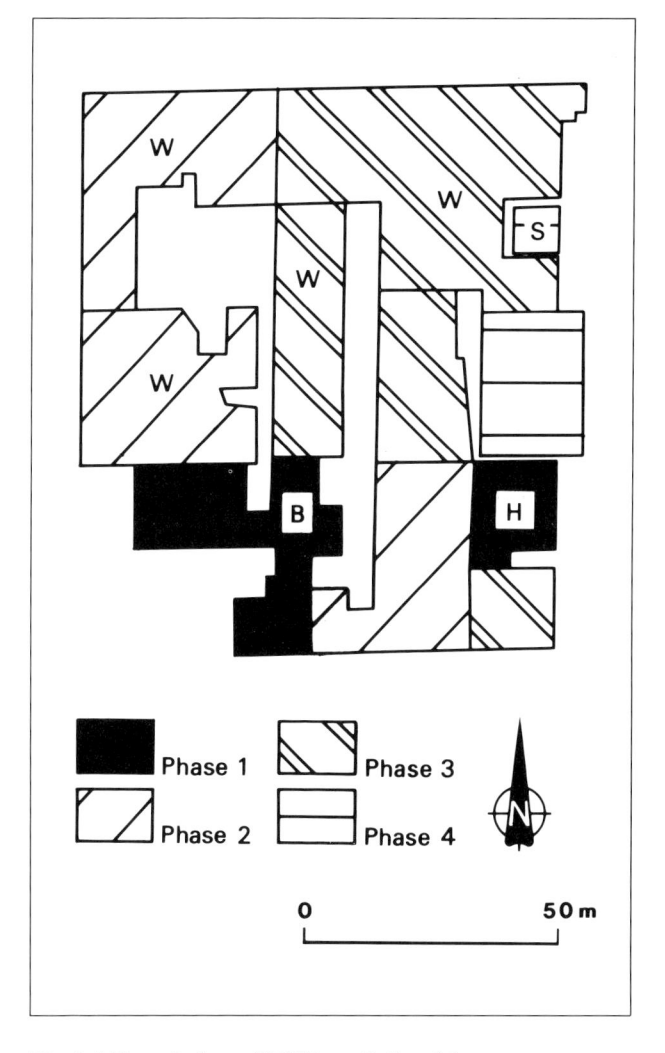

Fig 4.4 Phased plan of J Wilson & Sons' factory.
Key: W – workshop; B – boiler house and chimney; H – housing; S – electricity substation.
Founded on this site in 1872, Wilson's rapidly expanded during the late nineteenth and early twentieth centuries, and by 1936 was employing 1100 people.

bays. It has a flat roof, although this appears to be a later addition. Both floors appear to have been completely open. A slightly later building lies to the west. This is probably the 1870-87 extension mentioned by Middleton and was probably another finishing works (Middleton 1932, 566). This is a three-storey brick-built building, of five by four bays, with a gable slate roof. A later nineteenth- or early twentieth-century three-storey three-bay extension was added to the eastern rear end of the building.

Chapter 5

Agriculture

'The district [south-east Lancashire]...is principally occupied as small dairy farms, there being a great demand for milk and butter; and not much adapted, from the nature of its soil and climate, for arable cultivation'

(Rothwell 1850, 20)

5.1 Introduction

Throughout most of the eighteenth and nineteenth centuries agriculture was an expanding, successful industry, responding to the ever increasing food demands of the new urban communities, as well as providing a ready pool of labour for the new industries of the period. Within Tameside the majority of the population remained on the land until the first quarter of the nineteenth century, many tenant farmers combining cattle or sheep rearing with a second occupation, usually weaving but sometimes hatting or tanning. Nationally it was not until the great agricultural crisis of 1873-96 that the industry entered a decline, although in the North-West the supply of dairy produce to the industrial towns appears to have allowed areas such as Tameside to weather the crisis with relative impunity. This chapter explores the changes in the agricultural landscape of Tameside which took place in the years 1700-1930, beginning with a discussion of the general trends during this period and concluding with a review of farming conditions and the workings of the two largest estates in the Borough.

5.2 Farming before 1750

In the early eighteenth century most of the population of England was still involved in agriculture, the village and farm being the normal centres of working life. In the North-West pastoral farming, usually of cattle in the lowlands and sheep in the uplands, was the most common form of agriculture. Cereals were grown only as subsistence crops. On the Cheshire plain, which was considered to have some of the finest grazing in the country, barley, beans, oats, peas, rye, vetches and wheat were grown in small quantities (Hey 1984a, 129, 151), while Lancashire was a centre of potato cropping from the late seventeenth century onwards (Hey 1984b, 64).

It has been suggested that the size of cattle herds in Lancashire during the early eighteenth century was on average around seven, as against sixteen in Cheshire. Cattle were reared both for their meat and for their milk, although in Lancashire the emphasis was on meat production whilst in Cheshire it was on dairy produce (Hey 1984a, 153-4; 1984b, 63-4). Almost all Cheshire inventories of the first half of the eighteenth century record cheese, and values in excess of £40 were not rare (Hey 1984a, 154). However, farming in both counties was seldom sufficiently profitable or reliable to be the sole support of the many yeomen tenant farmers characteristic of the area, who often worked farms as small as ten or fifteen acres (*ibid*, 149). For this reason the farmer-craftsman flourished, particularly in the Pennine foothills where the vagaries of climatically marginal holdings could be lessened by the domestic production of textiles.

There has been little systematic study of the inventories of Tameside farmers in the first half of the eighteenth century, perhaps because in quality and quantity the eighteenth-century probate records are far more uneven than those of the seventeenth century. However, an examination of the twenty inventories which survive in the Cheshire Record Office for Mottram parish in the years 1704-49 indicates some of the trends. Half of these inventories are for people described as either yeomen farmers (seven) or husbandmen (three). However, farming-related items can be found in all of the inventories. Two of the inventories are of weaver-farmers. Isaac Gee, a weaver from Werneth in 1708, had one cow valued at £3 15s and worth only slightly more than his two looms, valued at £3, while Thomas Simister, a weaver from

Plate 5.1 Hollingworth Hall farmhouse.
Built in the late nineteenth century, this farmhouse was part of an upsurge in new agricultural buildings in Tameside during this period.

Godley in 1724, had two cows worth £4 and looms valued at £1 10s. John Heaworth of Hattersley is described as a tanner in his will and inventory of 1706 but nevertheless had a plough and a harrow valued at £1 1s 10d, as well as £2 6s 8d worth of hay in his barn, some of which he was selling to a Thomas Chadwick; the Stamford rental of 1702 shows that he was renting eleven acres of land in Hattersley at a yearly cost of 6s 10d (John Rylands Library, Dunham Massey MSS, Accession 8/5/92 Box 4/1). Even innkeepers derived some income from farming. Nicholas Hill, innkeeper of the Angel Inn in Mottram in 1728, had two cows, one pig and £2 worth of hay. Jonathan Bennison, an innkeeper in Werneth in 1749, farmed a tenement known as Rhodes Farm.

In the ten inventories where farming is the chief occupation cattle rearing predominates. The value of these inventories ranges from £6 19s to £257 15s, although this latter figure, for Thomas Heaward of Hattersley in 1738, included £216 worth of debts owed to him. Another yeoman who had large debts owing to him was John Worth of Hattersley in 1723, to the value of £52 13s 10d out of an inventory totalling £105 3s 4d. Herd sizes ranged from two to twelve, although the average was around six. Other livestock mentioned included pigs and geese.

Cheese was the most commonly mentioned produce after cattle. James Bulkley of Newton in 1704, William Roads of Stayley in 1718, Thomas Simister and John Worth each had churns and presses, Matthew Carlisle of Hattersley in 1734 had 21 'little cheeses', Robert Collier of Hattersley in 1718 cheese worth £1 4s, and Thomas Booth of Werneth in 1728 five cheese boards, a press and 'half a hundred' of cheese valued at 15s. The only crops mentioned are hay and corn, and these were probably grown for fodder. Joshua

Chapter 5 Agriculture

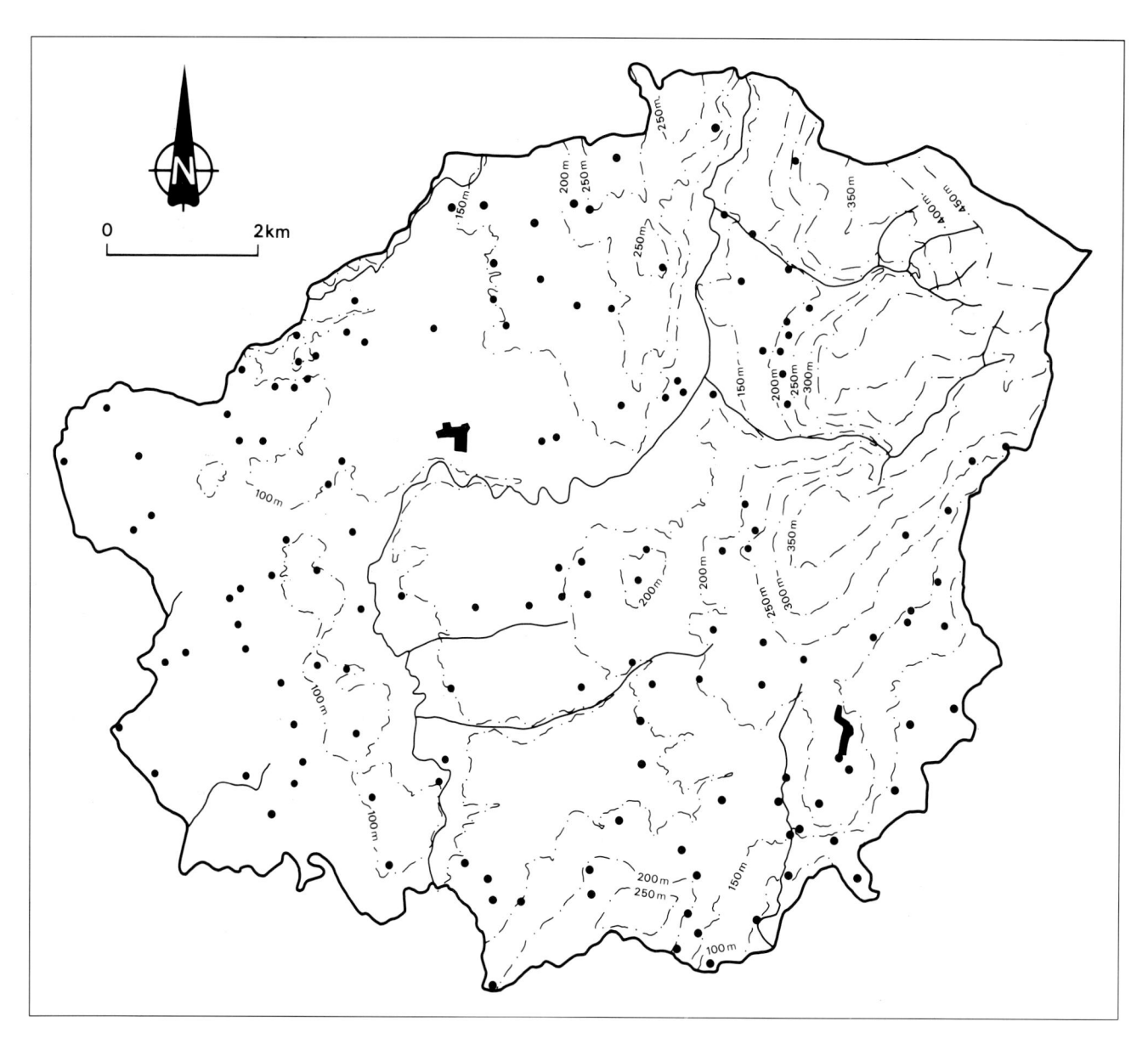

Fig 5.1 Distribution of farmsteads in Tameside in 1700.
Key: ● = farmsteads; ▬ = urban centres; – · – · contours at 50m intervals.
For much of the eighteenth century most of Tameside's population were dependent upon agriculture for their livelihood. The landscape was characterized by 143 known dispersed farmsteads, with only Ashton and Mottram forming significant urban centres.

Hopwood of Hattersley in 1737 had hay and corn worth £17 and twelve cows worth £18 2s, while John Worth had corn and hay worth £14 10s and six cattle worth £15 11s. Even among the avowed farmers a number had a second occupation. James Bulkley had wool and woollen yarn worth £1 2s and Matthew Carlisle had 'some yarn'.

While no survey of the early eighteenth-century inventories has been undertaken for Ashton, study of the parish registers, coupled with analysis of two rentals from the Stamford estate, provides a useful guide as to the nature of agriculture in the lowland part of the Borough during this period. The rentals, dating from 1702 and 1704, give the names of individual tenants, the amount of land which they leased, the rent they paid, whether that land was used for meadow, pasture or arable, and the obligations owed to the lord of the manor, the earl of Stamford (John Rylands Library, Dunham Massey MSS, Accession 8/5/92 Box 4/1; Accession 27/3/92 Box 6). These indicate that the lowland areas of Audenshaw, Ashton and Hattersley and the upland areas of Mossley and Stalybridge were almost uniformly livestock areas, although there is no indication as to what this livestock was. Furthermore, the 1702 rental suggests that farming was the only major economic activity, listing 330 tenants (Table 5.1). Of these only four gave a second occupation, namely a carrier, a collier, a shoemaker and a webster.

The Ashton parish registers for this period present a perhaps more balanced picture (Brierley 1928). Only 36% of the parish register entries which mention trades in the years 1701-10 are related to agriculture. These include occupations such as husbandman, yeoman, labourer and shearman. A further 34% gave the textile trade as a primary occupation, although comparison with the Saddleworth parish registers of the same period implies that most of these individuals were probably also involved in agriculture (Wild 1970, 221).

Those directly involved in farming at this time were divided between freeholders (usually the gentry or wealthy yeomen farmers), smallholders, who rented farms, and labourers, who were hired to help freeholders and smallholders run their estates and farms (Cootes 1982, 3). In Ashton parish these groups may be equated with the yeomen/gentlemen, husbandmen/agricolae and labourers of the registers. As might be expected, the largest group were the labourers, who accounted for 14% of all entries in the period 1701-10, while the husbandmen/agricolae accounted for 10%, and the yeomen/gentlemen farmers for a mere 1%.

Among the surviving examples of farmsteads of this period in Tameside are the Manor Farmhouse, Haughton Green, and Moorgate Farm in the uplands of Stalybridge. The Manor Farmhouse, which has a datestone of 1735, is a stone-built, single-depth structure of two storeys and three bays; the front elevation has a symmetrical arrangement of a central doorway flanked by mullion windows to both floors (DoE 1987, De7/45). In the lowlands of the Borough brick or timber framing were the more usual building materials during this period, and the use of stone at the Manor Farmhouse suggests it to have been a yeoman building of some prestige.

Moorgate Farm, by contrast, was a small marginal holding. In the eighteenth century the farm was rented from the Stamford estate by the Heap family who, it would appear, were dependent upon textile production as a secondary occupation. The 1702 rental records a Robert Heap, yeoman, and a Robert Heap, 'cloathmaker', as jointly renting 17 customary acres (5.27 statute acres) of land at 13s per annum (John Rylands Library, Dunham Massey MSS, Accession 8/5/92 Box 4/1). Daniel Heap, of Moorgate Farm, occurs at the end of the eighteenth century in the land tax returns for Stayley and in his will of 1806 described himself as a woollen clothier (CRO QDV2/393; WS). The present buildings consist of a long, single-depth range, stone-built and very much in the Pennine tradition of the period (Brunskill 1987, 156-7). The oldest element of the complex is formed by a central farmhouse, dating to the seventeenth century. This is of two storeys in watershot stone and squared rubble, with mullion windows to both floors. In the eighteenth century this farmstead was extended by the addition, at the western end, of a range of two two-storey cottages and, at the eastern end, of a shippon and barn with an arched entrance (DoE 1987, St1/164-7).

Township/division	No of tenants	Average farm size in statute acres
Ashton		
Town	56	22.3
Audenshaw	34	27.6
Hartshead	23	32.9
Ridgehill and Lanes	23	29.1
Luzley	22	16.1
Althill	16	58.3
Littlemoss	15	20.2
Hurst	15	25.4
Mossley	11	26.4
Alt Edge	9	51.2
Hazelhurst	8	64.5
Hattersley	41	26
Matley	9	34.1
Stayley	48	30

Table 5.1 Tameside farmers and farm sizes (adjusted from customary acres to statute acres) in the Stamford rental of 1702.
Source: John Rylands Library, Dunham Massey MSS, Accession 8/5/92 Box 4/1.

5.3 Farming 1750-1873

The period 1750-1873 saw wide-ranging improvements in agriculture, which in many parts of the country created much of the modern landscape. Nationally by 1870 agriculture had been transformed by the growth in the average size of farms and the introduction of many new practices and techniques. These included improved breeds of cattle and sheep, improved sowing techniques, new types of manure, new crops in four-course rotation, new forms of drainage, better implements and enclosure of common and waste land (Mingay 1989, 941-5). However, the pace of adoption was often uneven and slow. In Tameside the general success of agriculture in this period is reflected in the increase in the number of farmsteads which rose from 143 known sites at the beginning of the eighteenth century to 273 sites as shown on the Ordnance Survey 6in to 1 mile maps of 1845-72 (Figs 5.1 & 5.2). Much of this growth was the direct result

Chapter 5 Agriculture

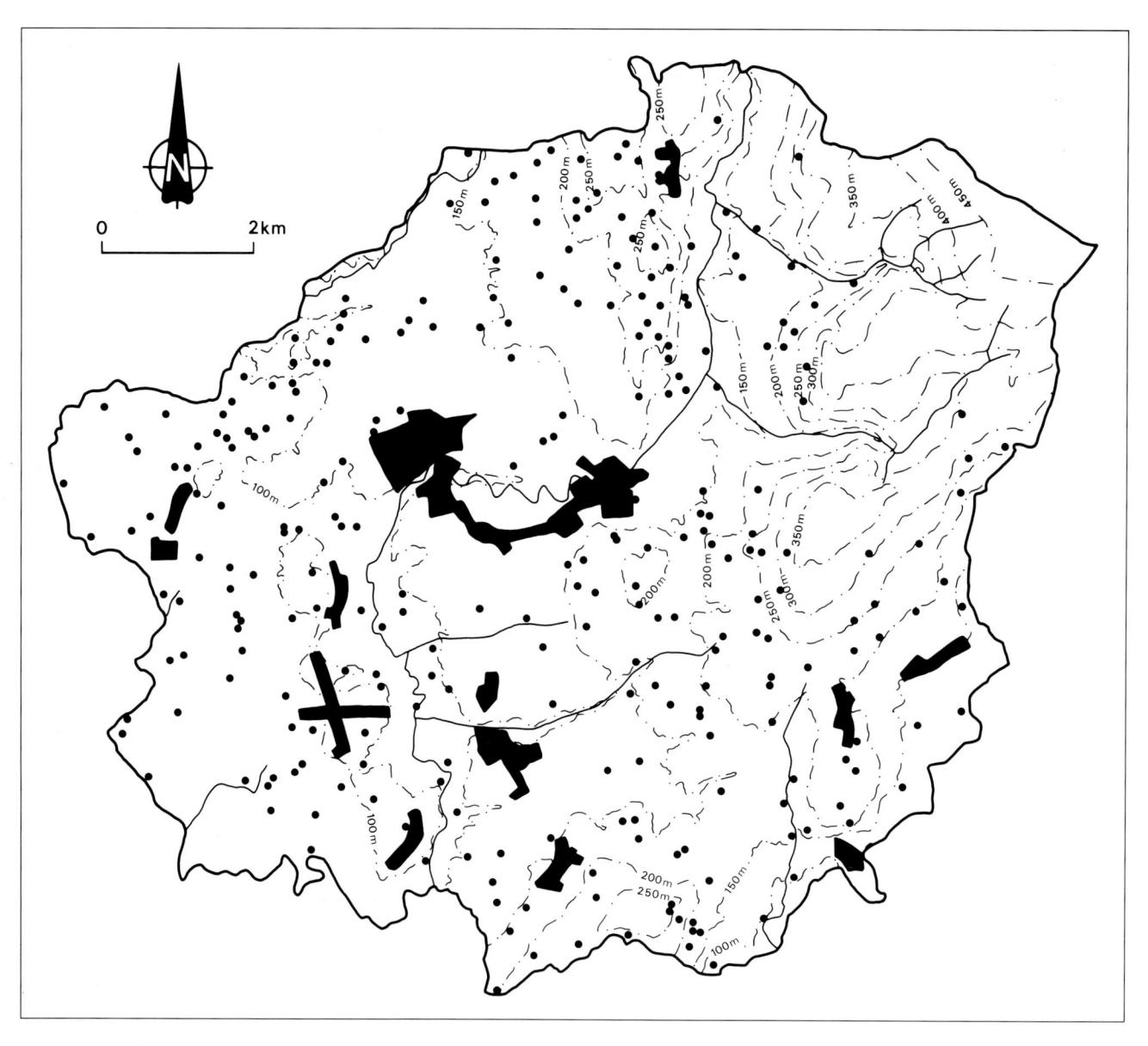

Fig 5.2 Distribution of mid-nineteenth-century farmsteads in Tameside.
Key: ● = farmsteads; ▬ = urban centres; – · – · contours at 50m intervals.
By the eve of the great agricultural depression of 1873-96 the number of farmsteads had grown rapidly, with 273 known in the period 1845-72, spurred by the food demands of the burgeoning populations of the new industrial towns. This expansion was spread evenly across the lowland and upland areas of the Borough.

of the increasing food demands of the new industrial urban centres. Evidence for specific changes in farming practices in the Borough during this period is often fragmentary, although sufficient remains to identify some of the main patterns of development.

Cattle

Throughout this period of change the agricultural base of the North-West remained predominantly pastoral. Despite outbreaks of cattle plague in the 1740s and 1750s which led to a slight shift away from stock rearing, Cheshire in the mid- and late eighteenth century remained heavily committed to dairy farming and Cheshire cheese continued to be the main dairy product, thanks to the area's rich pasture-land (Hodson 1978, 84-8). The same was true of the county in the mid-nineteenth century. Once more this was despite cattle plague, which in 1866 destroyed approximately a third of the dairy herd (Scard 1981, 88-90). In 1867 there were still 112,998 cattle in Cheshire, and a further 201,363 in Lancashire (Lewis 1868, 237). Perhaps not surprisingly, many of the agricultural changes recorded in the region during this period concentrated on improving the quality of pasture-land and the output of the cattle herds.

Terracotta drains were introduced in the first quarter of the nineteenth century and pasture began to be also improved by the use of bone dust and chemical fertilizers (Palin 1845, 90). Palin noted that in Cheshire

> 'during the ten or fifteen years preceding the spring of 1842, a considerable improvement in the management of the land became perceptible' (Palin 1845, 58).

In 1821 20 statute acres of meadow land were spread with bone dust at Swindell's Fold in Godley, while in 1826 a number of fields in Mottram had 'been improved with bone manure', although other land in Mottram at this date 'wanted draining and improving' (Davies 1960, 118; CRO DTW 2477/B/13).

Evidence from Cheshire indicates that by about 1850 dairy farmers were following two systems of farming, either a complete separation between permanent pasture and permanent arable, or a rotation between pasture and tillage (Scard 1981, 72). The dairy herds were usually put out to pasture in early May until early October. From then until Christmas they were pastured during the day and stabled at night. Then from Christmas until May they were kept in sheds. During this period, in February and March, calving usually occurred (*ibid*, 61).

In Tameside perhaps the best evidence of the new farming practices in operation in the mid-nineteenth century is provided by the diary of John Clarke of Hyde. The Clarke family had inherited the Hyde estate, which included the townships of Hyde and Newton in Tameside, in the early eighteenth century from the Hyde family of Hyde and Norbury (Ormerod 1882, 869-70). Extensive records in the form of family papers of the nineteenth century are deposited in the Tameside Local Studies Library. Amongst these are the day books of Hyde John Clarke, covering the years 1819-57, day books belonging to John Clarke, covering the period 1860-1902, and diaries, also written by John Clarke, for the years 1842, 1843 and 1845 (TLSL DD 1/1/1-84). The latter contain particularly useful material giving detailed accounts of the farming of Hyde Hall Farm, the demesne farm of the manor. The extent of the farm is given in John's diary of 1845 which lists ten horses, one bull calf, six 'milch' cows, eight calves, two bulls, nineteen 'feeding' cows, 79 ewes, three rams, 155 'feeding' lambs and thirteen other livestock. There were also 30 statute acres of wheat and 29 statute acres of oats (TLSL DD 1/1/41).

The diary of 1842 gives even fuller details regarding the farming year at Hyde Hall Farm. From January to March the fields were manured with guano and lime, and the cattle kept inside, fed by fodder crops such as oats, potatoes and turnips. The estate was also kept in general trim, with repairs to walls, hedges and the installation of tile drains in fields known as the 'flatts', by the river. April and May were spent sowing two acres of cauliflower, and a number of fields of barley which 'came up in about 14 days'. The cattle were turned out in these months. Turnips, carrots and cucumbers were also sown in the steam-heated hot-house by the hall. By June the farm workers were mowing ryegrass and 'soiling up' the potatoes, while July was spent building a new pigsty and churn house. August saw cheese making, more grass mowing and the start of the barley harvest. By September the crops were in and these fields were being ploughed and harrowed. The biggest events of October appear to have been the hatching of a clutch of 'game chickens', the sowing of wheat at the end of the month and the bringing in of the cattle. Finally, November and December were spent preparing the farm for winter, repairing hedges and fences and installing more tile drains (TLSL DD 1/1/38).

Such labour- and capital-intensive agriculture was typical of Victorian high farming prior to the great agricultural depression of the late nineteenth century. It must be borne in mind, however, that it was probably not typical of the majority of the farms in Tameside during this period, which could not afford so expensive a system.

Sheep

While cattle provided the backbone of Tameside agriculture in the eighteenth and nineteenth centuries, sheep farming continued to form a small but significant part of the livestock economy. Sheep had been raised in eastern Cheshire for their meat and wool long before 1700, and in Tameside the moors above Hollingworth had been used as common land for the pasture of sheep for many centuries (CRO DDX 87/2; Davies 1960, 138; Scard 1981, 87). Despite one correspondent's assertion to Palin that in Macclesfield hundred 'very few *sheep* are kept here, it being considered that in summer they injure the cow-pastures', the Cheshire and Yorkshire parts of Tameside had long been noted for their sheep (Palin 1845, 77). By 1845 Palin estimated that there were about 65,000 sheep in Cheshire, the same number as in 1808 (*ibid*, 71-2). The first accurate total, in the agricultural returns of 1867, showed that there were 266,074 sheep in Cheshire and a further 337,495 in Lancashire (Lewis 1868, 237). As noted above, in 1845 Hyde Hall Farm included a flock of 237 sheep, including 155 lambs, in addition to its herd of cattle.

There were two main sheep-rearing areas in Tameside during the eighteenth and nineteenth centuries, the Longdendale valley and the townships of Mossley and Stayley. Sheep farming is attested in these areas from the sixteenth and seventeenth centuries and

Chapter 5 Agriculture

provided the basis of the domestic woollen industry which thrived in these townships until the early nineteenth century (Nevell 1991, 85; see Chapter 3). Quick moor in Mossley was used as pasturage for sheep by the earl of Stamford from the time of its enclosure in the seventeenth century (Petford 1987, 83). In the late eighteenth century there was sufficient pasturage in Werneth for 1000 sheep, while in the Longdendale valley proper a number of sheep farmers supplemented their agricultural income with the running of inns on the Manchester to Yorkshire pack-horse route (Davies 1960, 138).

Evidence for the rearing of sheep by one farmer on the western fringe of Longdendale is provided by the diary of George Shaw of Godley. Covering the years 1795-1800, this diary was noted by Middleton but cannot now be traced (Middleton 1932, 41-3). Manure seems to have been George Shaw's main fertilizer, one day's 'loading muck' costing 5s in 1795. Potatoes in the 'pottato ground' are also mentioned, and other crops include barley and grain (*ibid*, 42). These crops may have been used as fodder for livestock, for although most of the entries which Middleton quotes relate to ploughing and muck spreading it is clear that Shaw was renting part of Godley Green common, possibly for some of the 55 sheep bought at 'teen and ninepens a pees' in 1799 (*ibid*, 43).

Arable farming

The continuing lesser importance of arable farming in the North-West is demonstrated by the first reliable agricultural returns, collected in 1867; these record 181,972 acres of arable land in Cheshire and 230,490 acres in Lancashire, out of a total farming acreage of 495,617 and 729,892 respectively (Lewis 1868, 236-7). The importance of potatoes, swedes and turnips increased steadily in the region throughout the early nineteenth century; in most cases they were still used as fodder for cattle, but in south-east Lancashire and north-east Cheshire they were also used as market crops for the nearby urban populations. All of these crops are mentioned in the Mottram estate rentals of the period 1799-1826 (CRO DTW 2477/B/10, 12 & 13; Palin 1845, 58; Garnett 1849, 8; Mingay 1989, 296-304). According to a correspondent of Palin, in the mid-nineteenth century the cycle of cropping in the hundred of Macclesfield was very bad, fallow land frequently being planted with potatoes, then wheat, then oats with clover, before being put to grass for two to three years;

> 'the land is consequently so impoverished that it becomes almost useless for several years' (Palin 1845, 67).

The situation was even worse in southern Lancashire where Garnett confidently asserted that 'a regular and scientific system of cropping is rarely met with' (Garnett 1849, 8).

Market gardening and Ashton Moss

Specialized growing of selected crops for the urban market was a nineteenth-century innovation. Market gardening developed in areas such as the Vale of Evesham, the Sandy district of Bedfordshire, but above all around the large urban areas such as London and Manchester (Mingay 1986, 108). In Tameside the chief market garden area was Ashton Moss. Drainage of this large expanse of mossland began in 1831. In that year the notebook of the steward of the Stamford estate recorded that in November a Mr Read began to drain and cultivate the peat, and that out of an area given as 240 statute acres a total of 70 acres would be ready for the cultivation of 'Wheat, Oats, Potatoes & Vetches' by the spring of 1834 (Bowman 1960, 48). In 1843 a further entry in the notebook stated that the moss was 'in a state of partial drainage and cultivation'.

A plan showing the moss in this partially drained state survives from the Stamford records and is now held in the Tameside Local Studies Library (TLSL DDS 1055). Although undated it must have been surveyed between the years 1831, the year in which Rayner Lane and Moss Lodge Lane, both shown on this plan, were formally laid out, and 1846, in which year the railway line from Miles Platting across the northern side of the moss to Ashton town centre was opened, a line which does not appear on the plan. Marked on this same plan are the names of some of the original tenants, Messrs Andrew, Erwood, Goodier and Smith, and the size of the moss in this period, 241 acres. It is possible that Katherine Street in Ashton town, laid out in the late 1820s, was planned as part of the Stamford estate's scheme to exploit this potential market garden area, providing direct access from the moss to the new Market Place, which was opened in 1830 (see Chapter 9).

By the early twentieth century the number of tenants on the mossland had risen to 44, the peatland being divided into 68 parcels. All except Northern Nurseries were private tenants, in 1933 paying on average £2 16s 11d per acre and providing a yearly income for the estate of £686 3s 9d (TLSL DDS 1603; 1616).

Enclosure

Although elsewhere in England the enclosure of common or waste land, largely before 1830, played a major part in the agricultural revolution of the late eighteenth and early nineteenth centuries, this was not the case in Tameside where much of the common land had been enclosed as early as the sixteenth and seventeenth centuries (Nevell 1991, 85-6). The principal areas of common land which remained were Ashton Moss, Godley Green and Newton Heath, in the lowlands, and in the uplands a small part of Werneth Low, the majority of the Low having been enclosed by the seventeenth century *(ibid,* 86). However, in the eighteenth century the remaining commons still attracted the attention of local landowners. Even Quick moor, above Mossley, most of which had been enclosed in the seventeenth century, continued to be parcelled and sold off in the eighteenth century (Petford 1987, 91).

This process was not always carried out unopposed. By the mid-eighteenth century local resentment of the piecemeal enclosure of the residual common land on Werneth Low reached a crisis point in a dispute over herbage rights and common access, prompting the Egerton family to take out an action for trespass (Davies 1960, 75). However, such events can be contrasted with Warhill common in Mottram, which was enclosed prior to Burdett's map of Cheshire of 1777, and Godley Green which was enclosed as late as 1846, both without any recorded complaint *(ibid,* 153). Godley Green was not particularly large, at just over 21 statute acres, but was nevertheless divided between twelve farmers (Middleton 1932, 130). Similarly the enclosure of waste land, almost exclusively in the upland areas of the Borough above 250m OD, has left little record of social disturbance. Hollingworth moor was enclosed by the late 1840s, seemingly without opposition. Much of the uplands of Longdendale, however, remained unstinted pasture until 1925 (Davies 1960, 138).

The mini-rebuilding c 1750 - c 1873

Nationally the period of advancement and prosperity in farming was reflected in an upsurge of farm building which appears to have lasted until the great agricultural depression of 1873-96 (Brunskill 1987, 24-9; Perry 1973, xiii). This activity affected all types of farm building and all levels of landowners and occupiers. Even so Garnett, writing in the middle years of the nineteenth century, was very critical of the way in which most Lancashire farms were arranged,

> 'with little attention paid to ventilation or the economy of space and labour, now considered so necessary in a well-regulated farming establishment' (Garnett 1849, 39).

Within Tameside it is usually on the richer estates that such improvements can best be seen. Denton Hall and Hyde Hall in Denton each received new brick-built farm buildings set around an outer courtyard in

Fig 5.3 Roe Cross Farm, no 49 Old Road, Mottram.
This site shows some of the typical features of upland farms in Tameside during the era of the mini-rebuilding. The central farmhouse dates from the mid-eighteenth century. In the nineteenth century a large barn with an arched entrance was added to the west gable of the farmhouse, while a single-depth stone cottage has been added to the east.

Chapter 5 Agriculture

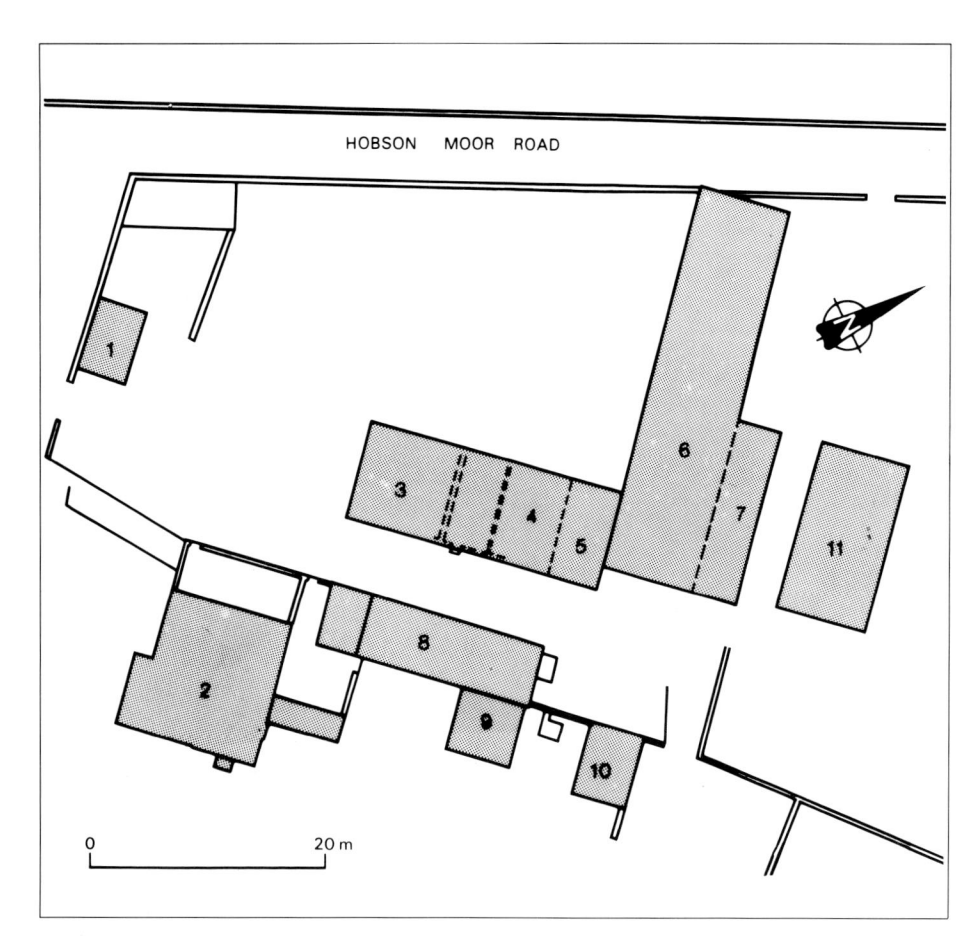

Fig 5.4 Hollingworth Hall Farm in the early twentieth century. *Key:* 1 cart shed; 2 late nineteenth-century farmhouse; 3-5 laithe house with a shippon and hay loft (3), a cottage (4) and a stable and loft (5); 6 barn; 7 shippon; 8 cart shed; 9 fowl shed; 10 bull cote; 11 Dutch barn.
Source: Powell Collection.
This was an ancient site attested before 1700. It contains a wide range of buildings from the eighteenth to the late nineteenth century and indicates the continuing success of upland farms in Tameside throughout the industrial period.

the nineteenth century. Across the River Tame in Hyde, the farm buildings of Hyde Hall had already been improved along these lines in the late eighteenth century (Aikin 1795, 295), as had those around Newton Hall and Stayley Hall. This period of rebuilding is documented in the Tatton and Tollemache rentals. The Tatton manuscripts in the John Rylands Library record extensive rebuilding on the Thorncliffe estate in the late eighteenth century. This was owned at that time by the Egertons of Tatton but had been leased in 1780 to John Lyne of Tintwistle, a shopkeeper, who set about rebuilding the hall, as well as erecting new shippons, a kitchen, buttery and cheese house (Davies 1960, 49). The Mottram rentals of the early nineteenth century contain a number of observations on the state of farm buildings in the township by the land agent who particularly noted buildings in need of repair, as on the farms of Edward Moss and Cicely Shaw, as well as new buildings such as a 'new bay of building' on William Ashton's farm (CRO DTW 2477/B/13).

In the lowland areas of Tameside new farm buildings were usually built in brick with slate roofs, replacing earlier stone or timber-framed buildings. In the uplands of the Borough stone was still the traditional building material. Typical upland ranges of farm buildings of the period can be seen at Roe Cross Farm, no 49 Old Road, in Mottram and on Hollingworth Hall Farm. Roe Cross Farm is a mid-eighteenth-century two-bay, double-depth building of three storeys, built in stone, with a central entrance and mullion windows on each floor (Fig 5.3). To the west is a later, nineteenth-century, two-storey stone barn with an arched entrance, and to the east a two-storey single-depth stone-built cottage (DoE 1987, L4/82). On Hollingworth Hall Farm there is a range of farm buildings to the north of the late nineteenth-century farmhouse, forming what appears to be a laithe house (Fig 5.4). In the centre of this range is an eighteenth- or early nineteenth-century stone-built two-storey farmhouse which is flanked to the east by a stable and loft and to the west by a barn, with opposed cart entrances, part of which was later converted to a shippon.

5.4 Farming 1873-1930

Nationally the last quarter of the nineteenth century was a period of great crisis in farming. Falling prices, land values and rents, frequent bankruptcies, a high turnover of tenants and an increase in untenanted farms were the key features of a widespread agricultural depression. Although the worst of this depression had lifted by the end of the 1890s, many of these problems persisted until 1939 (Perry 1973, xi-xii). Those areas of the country most dependent on arable farming were worst affected. The depression began with five successive bad harvests from 1873 to 1877, and poor seasons continued into the 1890s with a succession of summer draughts. The major causes of the crisis, however, lay in competition from foreign grain and meat imports, and in a general slow down in Britain's economy visible in all major industries in the late nineteenth century (*ibid*, xviii-xix; Cootes 1982, 159-60).

The effects of the crisis across the country were not, however, uniform and, as two studies in particular have emphasized, farmers in Lancashire and Cheshire may have fared better than most (Fletcher 1961; Scard 1981). In many regions the response of farmers to falling grain and meat prices was a shift towards dairy production, with the acreage of pasture-land rising by a third between 1873 and 1896 (Perry 1974, 114). In the North-West, however, cattle rearing had been the dominant form of agriculture for centuries. Furthermore, the introduction of the railways from the 1840s meant that the farmlands of south-east Lancashire and north-east Cheshire were no more than a few hour's travel from the growing urban communities of Manchester and the surrounding towns. This sparked one of the most important changes in the farming of the region, the shift from cheese to milk production (Perry 1974, 23; Scard 1981, 67). Scard has argued that as a consequence local farmers enjoyed a regular monthly income, which could be invested in new livestock, machinery or buildings; more importantly there was an increase in permanent pasture and in cattle numbers during the late nineteenth and early twentieth centuries (Scard 1981, 67-8).

A temporary rise in arable farming in the North-West occurred during the First World War, as part of a national response to falling food supplies, resulting from the U-boat blockade. Nevertheless, the region remained a predominantly dairy area even during the war, and by the early 1920s the local production of cereals had fallen back to its pre-war level (Whetham 1978, 178-9, 182).

The success of Tameside in avoiding the worst aspects of the great agricultural depression may be reflected in the number of new farm buildings erected in the late nineteenth and early twentieth centuries. Those built on the Stamford estate in this period are noted below, but such improvements are also found on smaller farmholdings (Plate 5.1).

5.5 Farms, Tenants and Rents

Size of farms

The most extensive evidence for the size of farms in eighteenth-century Tameside comes from the Stamford estate rental of 1702. This lists 330 tenants farming land in the old townships of Ashton, Hattersley, Matley and Stayley, with an average farm size of 34 statute acres in Ashton, 26 in Hattersley, 34 in Matley and 30 in Stayley. Particularly noticeable in Ashton is the variation in farm size between the lowland farmholdings of Littlemoss at 20.2 acres, Audenshaw at 27.6 and Ashton town at 22.3, compared with the upland townships of Hartshead with holdings of 32.9 acres, Alt Edge with 51.2, Althill with 58.3 and Hazelhurst with 64.5 (John Rylands Library, Dunham Massey MSS, Accession 8/5/92 Box 4/1; Table 5.1). Evidence for farm sizes in the remainder of the eighteenth century and into the early nineteenth century is difficult to come by for the majority of Tameside, but regional estimates give some guide for this period.

Holt estimated in 1795 that most Lancashire farms were between 20 and 50 statute acres in extent (Holt 1795, 19). Fletcher has estimated that the average Lancashire farm size in 1875, of holdings of more than five acres, was 40 acres, slumping to 30 acres in southeast Lancashire, compared with the national average of 80 acres. Furthermore, 8% of the total number of holdings farmed 30% of the agricultural land in the county (Fletcher 1961, 80). According to Scard the average farm size in Cheshire in the same period was approximately 80 acres. However, there continued to be many smaller farms under 50 acres, particularly in central and north-eastern Cheshire, suggesting that the average size of a Tameside farm in the late nineteenth century was closer to the Lancashire average than that of Cheshire (Scard 1981, 60). When the Thorncliffe Hall and Hollingworth Old Hall estates were sold in 1890 the average farm size was 27 acres and 26.5 acres respectively (Powell Collection) (Fig 5.5).

There are two estates in Tameside where the size of farm holdings can be traced with some degree of precision during the late eighteenth and nineteenth centuries, namely the Tollemache estate in Mottram and the Tatton estate in Werneth. Both townships were predominantly dairy regions, although there was a sizeable sheep flock on Werneth Low. Both also included farms which were divided into multiple tenancies.

The average size of farms appears to have remained stable in Mottram during the period 1785-1841, although there are noticeable variations in the size of tenancies. Between 1785 and 1799 there were nineteen farms and two crofts leased, accounting for over 540 acres of the Tollemache estate in Mottram. The average farm size was 25.8 acres, but as a result of a number of these being multiple tenancies the average tenancy size was only 13.6 acres. By 1826 there were 23 farms, the average size being 25.9 acres and the average tenancy 15.3 acres (CRO DTW 2477/B/10 &

Chapter 5 Agriculture

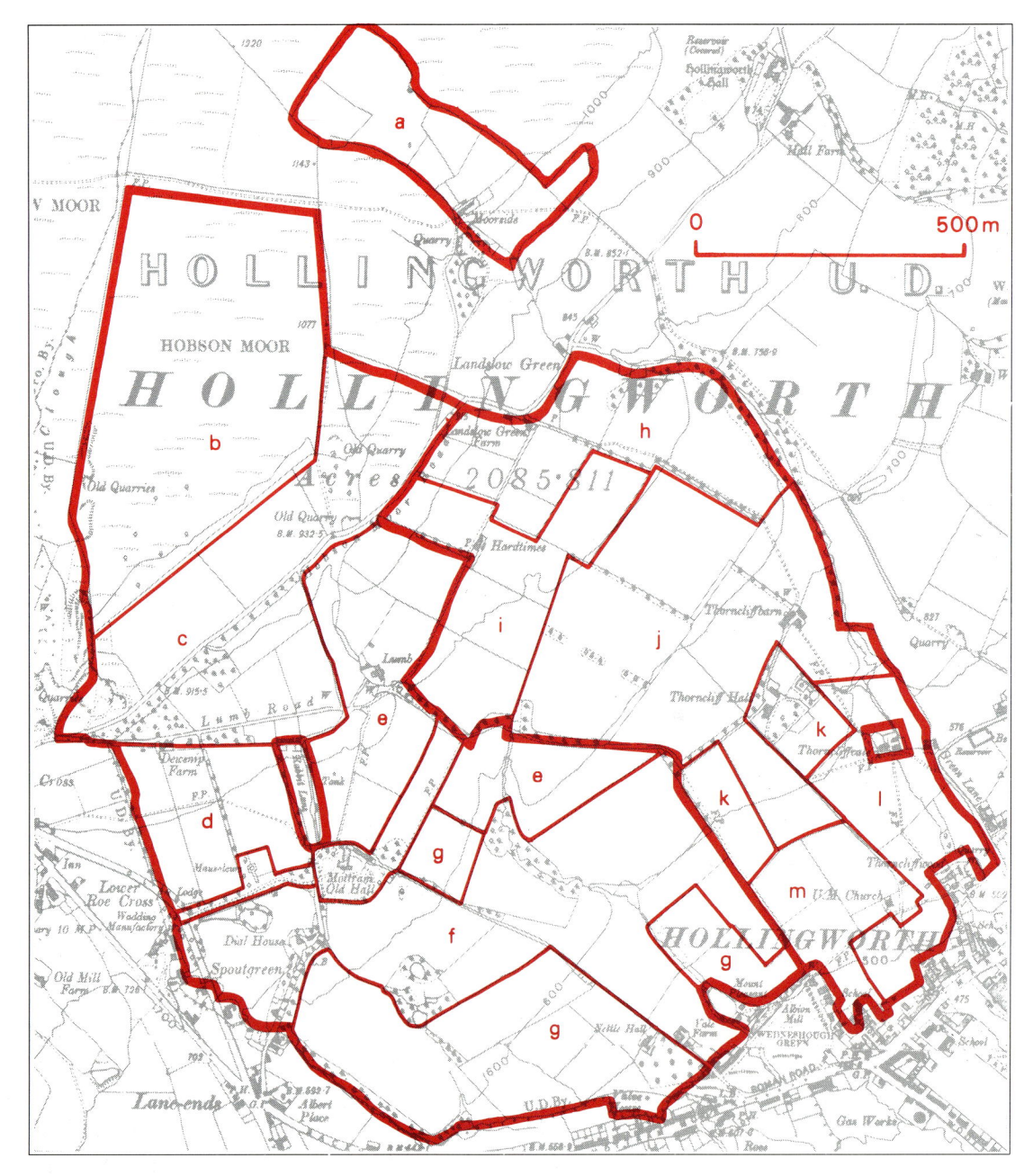

Fig 5.5 Hollingworth Old Hall and Thorncliffe estates in 1890.
Key: a Moorside Farm; b Hobson Moor; c Hobson Moor Farm; d Dewsnap's Farm; e Lumb Farm; f Vale Farm; g Nettle Hall Farm; h Landslow Green; i Hard Times; j Thorncliffe Barn; k Thorncliffe Hall and grounds; l Dog Kennel; m Ogden's Farm.
Source: Powell Collection.

13). The 262 acres of the Mottram estate which were offered for sale in 1841 included seven farms at an average of 26.2 acres each, but the average tenancy size was only 9.7 acres. Between 1841 and 1919 there appears to have been a general consolidation of the Tollemache farm holdings in Mottram, with a reduction in the number of tenants and farms. When the Tollemache holdings in the township were finally sold in 1919, there were only ten farms, the average farm size being 36.1 acres and the average tenancy size 17.5 acres (Powell Collection) (Fig 5.8).

The farm sizes on the Tatton estate in Werneth in the eighteenth and nineteenth centuries follow a similar pattern to that seen in Mottram, despite the greater overall height of the township and the existence of a sizeable sheep-farming industry. During the eighteenth century there were very few farms on the estate above 50 statute acres, the majority being between 20 and 30 acres (Davies 1960, 50). By the time the Egerton family sold the estate in 1857 there were 24 tenants occupying 20 farms, and the average farm size

Chapter 5 Agriculture

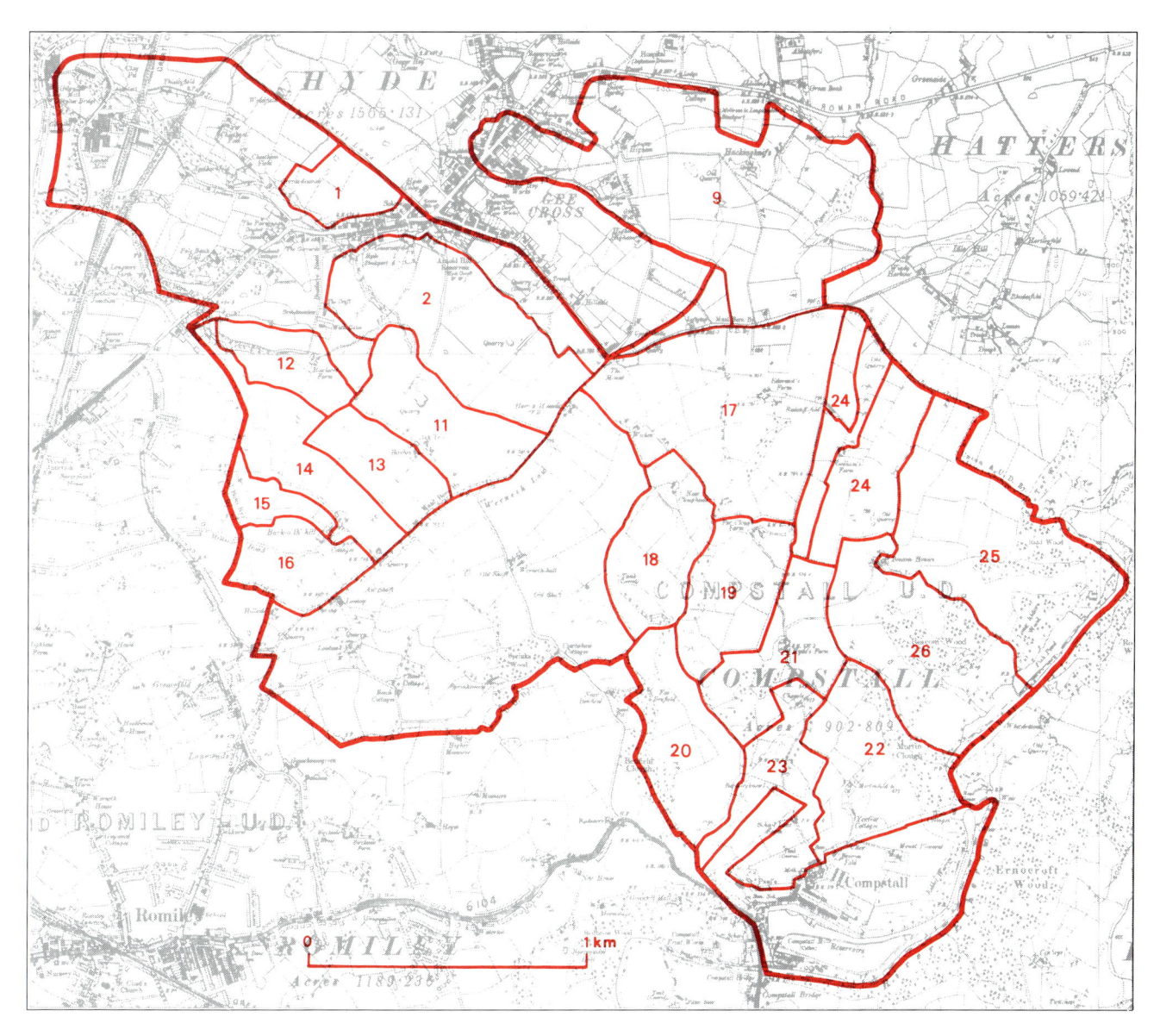

Fig 5.6 Farmholdings on the Tatton estate in Werneth township in 1857.
Key to lot numbers: 1 Spout House; 2 Gee Cross Fold; 9 Higham; 11 Lousythorn; 12 Bowl Acre; 13 Birches; 14 Back-O'-Th'-Hill [I]; 15 Back-O'-Th'-Hill [II]; 16 Back-O'-Th'-Hill [III]; 17 Tobits and Edmunds; 18 Nearer Clough Side; 19 Further Clough Side; 20 Ben Field; 21 Hydes; 22 Mortins; 23 Beacom; 24 Needhams; 25 Beacom House [I]; 26 Beacom House [II].
Source: Powell Collection.

had grown to 51 acres, while the average tenancy was 42.5 acres (Powell Collection) (Fig 5.6).

Leases and rents

In the late eighteenth and mid-nineteenth centuries most Cheshire and Lancashire farms were either let from year to year or for seven, eleven or fourteen years (Holt 1795, 22-8; Palin 1845, 84). Despite one correspondent's comment to Palin that in Macclesfield hundred there were 'very few leases or agreements for terms of years in this district' (Palin 1845, 85), by the mid-nineteenth century farms in Hollingworth and Werneth were usually leased for fourteen years. During the eighteenth century Tollemache land in central Cheshire was let in leases for lives, years and at will (Davies 1960, 14). However, according to the Mottram survey of 1799 all of the farmland in Tameside owned by the estate was let for fourteen years, whereas workshops and factories in the township were frequently leased for 99 years, and cottages for 99 years or three lives (CRO DTW 2477/B/10 & F/12).

Such leases frequently contained restrictions and duties. On the Tatton estate in Werneth the leases of farms during the eighteenth century restricted arable land to a third of the holding. In addition the amount of potatoes which could be grown was limited to that which could be consumed by the farmer's family,

Chapter 5 Agriculture

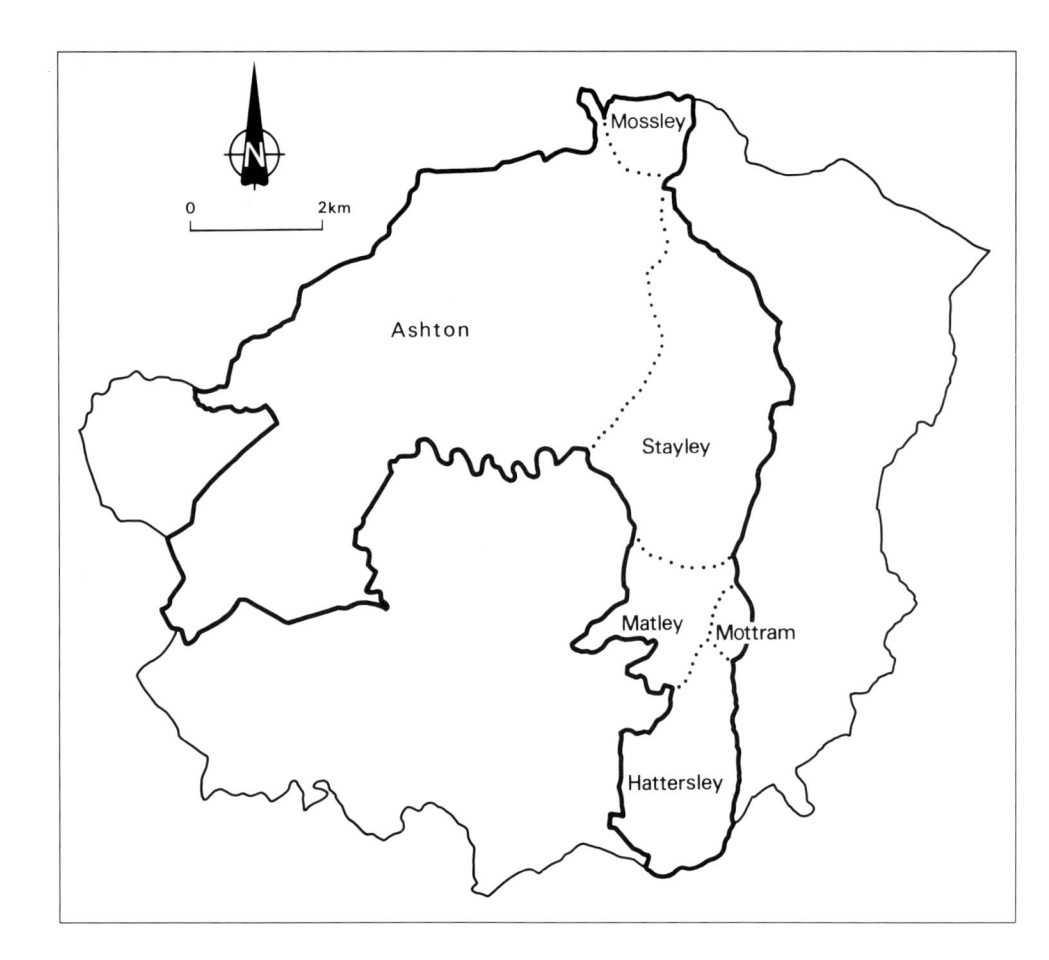

Fig 5.7 The Stamford estate in Tameside in the early nineteenth century. The Stamford estate was by far the largest landowner in Tameside during the period 1700-1930, although from the mid-nineteenth century it sold a number of landholdings, the largest being Hattersley manor. Prior to this the estate held more than 75% of the land in Ashton parish, Hattersley, Matley and Stayley townships, as well as owning most of the Quickmere division of Saddleworth parish, the north-western corner of Mottram township and various scattered estates in Droylsden township.

while the spreading of lime on the estate was made a condition of most leases after 1760 and the felling of trees expressly forbidden except with the permission of the landlord (Davies 1960, 49-50).

With regard to rent, Davies has estimated that the usual payment per statute acre on the Tatton estate in Werneth between 1743 and 1768 was 10s, that after 1768 this rose to 15s per acre, and by 1780 was 20s (*ibid*, 50). In Mottram the average rent per acre was 23s 2½d in 1785 but by 1799 this had nearly doubled to 42s, probably reflecting a national increase in rents during the Napoleonic wars. However, rents per acre of farmland were still around this level in Mottram in 1826 (CRO DTW 2477/B/10 & 13). These figures may be compared with the average rent in 1768-71 of 16s per acre in Cheshire and 22s 6d in Lancashire, and in 1851 of 30s in Cheshire and 42s in Lancashire (Mingay 1989, 1112-13).

The great agricultural depression of 1873-96 tended to drive down the rent per acre in the arable sector of the agronomy, and although the livestock branch fared better rents did not rise significantly in the late nineteenth century. In 1890 rents per acre on the Hollingworth Old Hall estate were only around 40s, and on the neighbouring Thorncliffe Hall estate around 52s (Powell Collection).

5.6 The Stamford and Tollemache Estates

At the beginning of the eighteenth century landownership and the agricultural economy in Tameside were dominated by a few large estates, the most significant being those lands belonging to the earl of Stamford and to Lord Tollemache. As noted in Chapter 2, the land tax returns for the Cheshire part of the Borough in the period 1780-1830 show an explosion in the number of landowners, drawn in particular from the ranks of mill-owners and other manufacturers. Most of these new landowners were concentrated in the urban heartlands of Dukinfield, Hyde and Stalybridge. However, beyond these urban centres the two largest estate holdings of the eighteenth century survived into the early twentieth century. Furthermore, in Ashton parish the Stamford estate preferred to lease rather than sell property. As such the estate not only continued to profit from the increasing industrialization of the area but it also played a key role in the expansion and development of Ashton town.

The Stamford estate

Those lands owned by the earls of Stamford in Tameside formed the largest, and oldest, single holding in the Borough, and the greatest part of the Lancashire estates of the family (Fig 5.7). Unlike other farm estates in the Borough, the Stamford estate had significant income from sources other than agriculture. Partly inherited from the Asshetons of Ashton-under-Lyne through marriage in 1515 and partly acquired from the Asshetons' joint successors, the Hoghtons, by purchase in 1605, these extensive lands encompassed most of the townships of Ashton (9494 acres), Hattersley (1190 acres), Matley (700 acres) and Stayley (2760 acres), although the estate also held significant tracts of land in Droylsden and Quickmere (Nevell 1991, 19-21, 41-3; John Rylands Library, Dunham Massey MSS, Accession 8/5/92 Box 4/1; ESRCA 15). This made the earls by far the largest and most influential landowners in Tameside by the early eighteenth century. Although most of the estate remained in the hands of the Stamford family during the period 1700-1930, land was sold from time to time, the largest single sale being in 1858, when John Chapman bought the manor of Hattersley (Earwaker 1880, 154).

The earl of Stamford's chief residence was Dunham Massey, near Altrincham in Cheshire, but the family also owned property in Leicestershire, Staffordshire, Shropshire, Yorkshire and Worcestershire (Cordingley 1986, i). As absentee landlords the earls managed their Tameside estates through a steward. Although two rentals survive for the Tameside property for the years 1702 and 1704, there is unfortunately little further information regarding the running of the estate during the eighteenth century (John Rylands Library, Dunham Massey MSS, Accession 8/5/92 Box 4/1; Accession 27/3/92 Box 6). Only two stewards are known from this period, Richard Drinkwater, attested in 1703, and John Houghton, attested in 1706-15 (Cordingley 1986, 6a). The income of the earl's lands in Cheshire and Lancashire in the year 1702 is given as £2817 12s 4d, of which £428 2s 11½d came from the Ashton estate, £189 15s 2d from the Stayley estate and £117 15s 4½d from the Hattersley estate. In the case of the Ashton estate this included £234 0s 6d from rents and boons, demesne rents of £97 3s 6d, market rents of £4 16s 6d, market tolls of £1 10s, corn-mill rents of £62, chief rents of £4 0s 6d, rent from coal mines of £15 and from mossland of £2 10s.

Until the late eighteenth century the majority of the income from the estate came from agricultural rents, the estate keeping a tight control over the leasing of property. When Sinderland Hall Farm was leased to Samuel Leech in 1756 for fourteen years, the rent was £50, plus '£5 for each acre plowed more than 10 [acres] in any year'. The lessee was obliged to keep the premises in repair, pay all levies and taxes, spend any profits on the premises, keep windows, causeways, ditches and fences in repair, thatch the buildings and not to plough the meadows (*ibid*, 4).

From the 1780s onwards an increasing proportion of the income of the estate came from the rents for coal mines, new housing and new industrial premises such as cotton mills. Rents payable for coal mining rose sharply from £21 per annum in 1758-9 to £827 14s 1d in 1785 (Bowman 1960, 468, 471). The estate also began to invest in private and commercial housing, between 1787 and 1832 laying out a large planned town around the medieval core of Ashton. This is discussed in greater detail in Chapter 9, but it is worth noting here that the estate was responsible for laying out the grid-iron of streets and then selling the leases for plots of land to builders, while stipulating in the leases the road and pavement widths and the necessity of drainage (Cordingley 1986, 18). The stewards of the estate were also responsible for the acquisition and disposal of land to road, canal and rail companies. The steward in 1802, for instance, Mr H Worthington, witnessed a deed transferring all rights of way and 'the reversion and reversions, remainder and remainders, rent issues and profits tenancy, and every part and parcel thereof' to the Manchester, Ashton-under-Lyne and Oldham Canal Company (*ibid*, 14).

While the income of the estate diversified in the nineteenth century, much of the Stamford lands in Tameside remained agricultural. Although we lack detailed evidence as to the running of the agricultural side of the estate in this period, it is clear from plans deposited in Tameside Local Studies Library that the estate continued to invest in the farms within its control. In particular the late nineteenth and early twentieth centuries appear to have been a period of notable building activity on the farms of the estate. A total of 21 plans exist for improvements to farms in the period 1896-1930, most for the years 1900-14 (TLSL DDS). The most frequently mentioned improvements are new shippons, on eight farms (TLSL DDS 248, 302, 354, 356, 357, 908, 1082, 1476), new or altered farmhouses (TLSL DDS 776, 953, 1095, 1113, 1280, 1307), new stables (TLSL DDS 319, 349, 1233) and new dairies (TLSL DDS 355, 411, 932, 1529). These farms were distributed across the estate, from Audenshaw in the west to Micklehurst in the east.

The Tollemache estate

The Tollemache family had inherited the lordship of Longdendale, comprising the manors of Mottram and Tintwistle, from the Wilbrahams in the 1690s (Nevell 1991, 40). In Cheshire the Tollemache estate consisted of approximately 28,000 acres, of which about 15,000 were located in the Longdendale valley, and a further 5000 in mid-Cheshire on some of the best land in the county. In Longdendale in 1805 there were 6500 acres of rough pasture and 5000 acres of waste land (Davies

Chapter 5 Agriculture

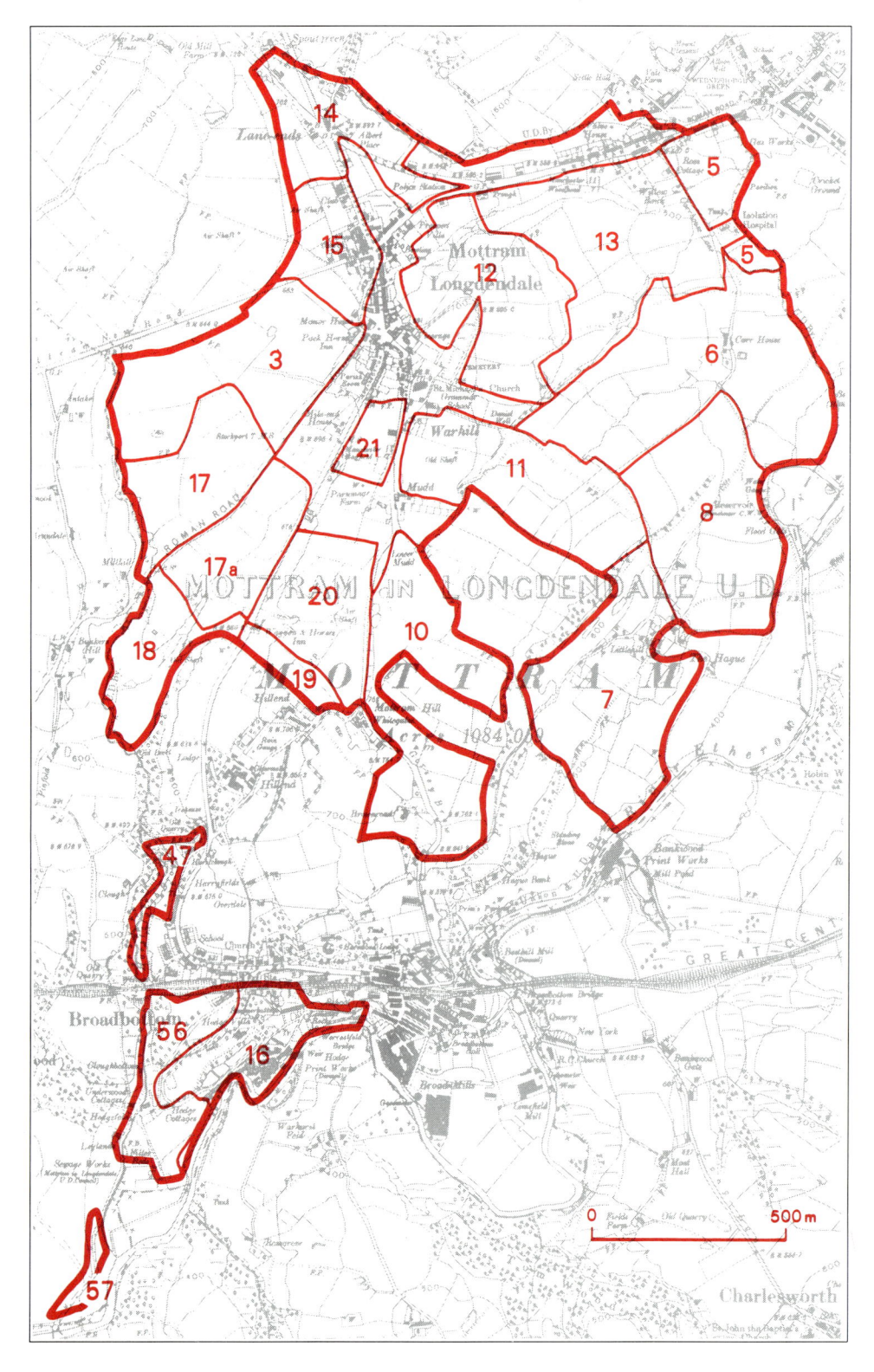

Fig 5.8 Tollemache estate holdings in Mottram in 1919.
Key to lot numbers: 3 'The Pack Horse Inn' and Farm; 5 'The Robin Hood Inn'; 6 Carrhouse Farm; 7 Peartree Farm; 8 The Hague Farm; 10 Brownroad Farm; 11 Warhill Farm; 12 Rhodes Farm; 14 Walter Heys Farm; 15 Post Office Farm; 16 Hodge Print Works; 17, 17a & 18 agricultural land; 19 agricultural land adjoining 'The Waggon and Horses'; 20 & 21 agricultural land; 47 Hurst Clough; 56 meadow land at Hodge Fold; 57 Hurst Clough, part of.
Source: Powell Collection.

1960, 13). These lay within the 14,120 acres which comprised the township of Tintwistle, the Micklehurst division of which is now in Tameside. The estate also included most of the 1079 acres of the old manor and township of Mottram, which was all good dairy land. A set of rentals for the Longdendale estate in the Cheshire Record Office covers the period 1771-1919 and enables its workings to be recovered in some detail.

Being absentee landlords the Tollemache family appointed agents as stewards to look after the Longdendale estate. These agents took an active interest in the running of the estate in Mottram. Many of the surveys from 1771 onwards include remarks on the state of the property and contain valuable details of the acreage and field-names of the farms of the township. Comments in the rental of 1826 by the steward, a Mr

Dearnaley, include such observations as buildings in bad repair on Edward Moss's farm, others which needed to be pulled down on Cicely Shaw's farm and land improved by 'bone manure' on Robert Wagstaffe's farm (CRO DTW 2477/B/13). In that year the income of the Tollemache estate from the Mottram lands was £4198 14s 7d, which when added to other income from increased rents, £148 0s 1d from coal rents, £26 7s 6d from the sale of timber and £19 14s 6d from the sale of stone, gave a total income of £4563 3s 9d. Total expenditure was £2263 3s 9d, giving a profit to Lord Tollemache of £2300 (CRO DTW 2343/F/16).

As the nineteenth century progressed many of the larger landowners attempted to consolidate their holdings. The Tollemache family were no different, having lands spread across many counties. Small plots of land in Mottram were being steadily sold in the late eighteenth and early nineteenth centuries, the largest sale being that of the Hillend estate to Lord Dysart (CRO DTW 2477/B/10). In 1841 about a third of the Mottram estate, 262 acres, was put up for sale, although most went unsold, with only Samuel Marsland buying one lot, Hague Farm (Powell Collection). However, such sales do not compare with the amount of land sold to Manchester Corporation in 1852 in Tintwistle. In that year a large area of the bottom of the Longdendale valley east of Tintwistle village was bought by the corporation in order to build a series of five reservoirs to supply the population of Manchester with drinking water (Davies 1960, 148). The Tollemache family sold all of their remaining estates in Longdendale in 1919. Although the sale was originally withdrawn after the failure to reach the asking price of £3500, it was finally sold for £3000 (Powell Collection) (Fig 5.8).

Chapter 6

Coal Mining

'I do give to...my said daughter Henrietta after she shall have attained the age of twenty one years also full power and authority...to work my coal mines in Dukinfield, Newton and Hyde aforesaid. And I will and direct that the money to be raised from the said mines and by leasing as aforesaid shall be applied in or towards the discharge of the principal money secured by mortgages of the same premises.'

Will of Sir William Dukinfield Daniel, 8th December 1756 (CRO D73)

6.1 Introduction

Coal mining, which had been an element of the rural economy before 1700, formed the last of the four great industries of Tameside, and its impact on the Borough was profound. In the late eighteenth century the industry was a prime initiator of the canal network of the region, which accelerated the rate of economic change. Even more significantly, from the early nineteenth century coal was the single most important power source in the Industrial Revolution, driving local factories and fuelling the second transport revolution, that of the railways.

In its initial period of growth, from the late eighteenth to the mid-nineteenth century, pits were scattered across the Borough, operated by a host of individual owners and companies. In the late nineteenth and early twentieth centuries the number of collieries was drastically reduced, from fifteen or more in the early 1850s to seven in 1900, to only two in 1906. A drift mine was opened in 1912 but proved short-lived and after the closure of Denton Colliery in 1929 only one mine, Ashton Moss, remained in operation in Tameside.

The late nineteenth-century contraction of the industry to a few large pits and its final demise in the twentieth century has meant that its physical impact on the landscape has been largely erased; the pit-head buildings have been dismantled, the slag heaps removed and the communities dispersed. However, an assessment of the development of the industry in the Borough and a review of the main coal-mining zones is made possible by a large body of documentary and cartographic material, together with recent surveys of the industry in Denton, Dukinfield and Hyde (Cronin & Yearsley 1985; Newton 1970; Bann 1976).

6.2 The Development of the Industry

The Lancashire coalfield

Surface outcrops of coal were worked in southern Lancashire during the medieval period, although there is no evidence for its exploitation at this date in Tameside. As the demand for coal increased in the sixteenth and seventeenth centuries, partly because of the falling supply of timber, records relating to coal mining in the Borough occur for the first time (Nevell 1991, 91-2).

The source of this fuel was the exposed coal-bearing rocks of the Lancashire coalfield. These form a crescent running between St Helens in the west, Burnley in the north and Macclesfield in the south, an area which covers more than 800 square kilometres (300 square miles). It is divided into three separate geological zones, with Tameside lying over the East Manchester district. The coal seams in this zone are found at three levels, the Lower, Middle and Upper Coal Measures, the deepest deposits being over 1000m (3270 feet) below ground (Trotter 1954, 199, 203-5).

Technological developments

Until the eighteenth century the coal mined in Tameside was used mostly for domestic heating, although the coal-fired glass furnace in operation at Haughton Green in the seventeenth century provides a notable instance of an early industrial use of the fuel (Nevell 1991, 92-3). The earliest mines in the Borough exploited those seams closest to the surface and were of two types: firstly bell pits, where shallow shafts were sunk from the surface directly into the coal seam

Chapter 6 Coal Mining

Plate 6.1 Hand digging for coal near the Hague, Mottram.
Coal outcrops in the Mottram area had been exploited on Warhill since the early seventeenth century. These deposits near the hamlet of the Hague were mined from the mid-eighteenth century by nearby Hague Colliery. Nevertheless, the hand digging of surface outcrops of coal continued into the 1920s and 1930s.

which was then worked outwards; and secondly drift mines, gently sloping tunnels which were cut into, and followed, outcropping seams. Physical evidence for bell pits may survive on Mottram moor (Nevell 1991, 139), while in the early eighteenth century two drift tunnels were dug from the northern banks of the River Tame in Denton, exploiting the coal seams beneath land owned by the Hyde Clarke family (Cronin & Yearsley 1985, 59).

During the eighteenth century, as coal seams close to the surface were worked out, deeper workings in the Lancashire coalfield were increasingly necessary. By the mid-eighteenth century pits in Lancashire were being sunk as deep as 80m (*c* 260 feet) (Flinn with Stoker 1984, 76). Access to such workings was via a shaft and as the technology of drainage and ventilation developed these shafts reached ever greater depths.

The traditional method of drainage in the early

Chapter 6 Coal Mining

eighteenth century was by means of soughs, tunnels dug from the lowest point of a mine to a nearby stream. However, horse gins might also be used to lift water out of a mine, one being recorded in a deed relating to land rented by Robert Hyde from Mr Hulton in Denton in 1735 (Cronin & Yearsley 1985, 60). Occasionally, water-wheels were employed for the same purpose. In Tameside a water-worked pit is recorded at Old Rocher, in Rocher Vale, while Aikin in 1795 refers to 'a water-engine...belonging to some valuable coal mine of Mr Clarke's' on the Denton bank of the Tame, opposite Hyde Hall in Hyde (Preece 1985, 5; Aikin 1795, 450).

The first Newcomen steam engine to pump water at a Lancashire coalfield colliery was installed by 1733, and nineteen more were in operation in the coalfield between 1734 and 1775 (Flinn with Stoker 1984, 121-2). One such steam engine, known as Fairbottom Bobs, was used by the Fairbottom Coal Company from the 1780s until about 1834 on a site now in Oldham Metropolitan Borough but once in Ashton parish. The water pumped by this engine was carried in a wooden trough to the Ashton Canal at Fennyfield Bridge (Wilkins-Jones 1978, 20; Ashmore 1969, 109). The Fairbottom Coal Company also had a Newcomen engine at New Rocher Pit, above the Park Bridge ironworks; here the pump beam was attached to a waterwheel and was used as an auxiliary power source in case the water supply to the wheel failed.

Engines were used in other Tameside mines of the late eighteenth century. In Mottram a steam engine is mentioned in the 1770s in relation to pits at the Hague (CRO DTW 2477/F/12). The steward's notebook for the earl of Stamford's estate in Ashton refers to a 'fire-engine' used to pump water from a coal pit at Hurst in 1788 (Bowman 1960, 470). A steam engine, possibly of the Newcomen type, was also used for pumping at Hulme's Pit at Denton Colliery. It was modified in 1834 by Musgrave & Co of Bolton and continued in use until the Denton Colliery Company closed in 1929 (Cronin & Yearsley 1985, 61).

The application of steam power to winding was first undertaken by Boulton and Watt in 1788 (Flinn with Stoker 1984, 102). This new technology was adopted at a fairly early date in at least one part of Tameside, for Aikin notes that at Newton moor

> 'the water is pumped out and the coal raised by steam-engines, which are now generally taking place of the former horse-machines' (Aikin 1795, 457).

It was not, however, until the 1840s that steam-powered winding gear became common in the Lancashire coalfield (Ashmore 1969, 103-4; Dickinson 1855, 71-2).

Ventilation of early, shallow workings was allowed to occur naturally, but pits deeper than 60m (c 200 feet) required artificial means to circulate the air (Flinn with Stoker 1984, 128-9). In the mid-eighteenth century fire buckets were introduced, usually located at the bottom of a second shaft and using convection currents to draw air through the workings. In the Lancashire coalfield this remained the usual form of ventilation until the late nineteenth century when steam-powered fans became common. As late as the 1870s new mines in the coalfield were still being ventilated by this primitive method. At Ashton Moss Colliery the 1882 shaft, which was sunk to a depth of 870m (2850 feet), had a furnace halfway down and boiler fires at the bottom (Ashmore 1969, 105; *Colliery Guardian* 5/8/1892, 235-6).

During the late nineteenth century the main focus of technical innovation in the industry was in the area of working methods. In particular there was a slow shift to the mechanical cutting and haulage of coal. The technology necessary for this was invented in the mid-nineteenth century, the first steam-powered haulage machinery being employed in 1841, although it was not introduced into the Lancashire coalfield until 1869 (Ashmore 1969, 103; Preece 1981, 52). Mechanical coal cutters, powered by compressed air, were first used in a Scottish colliery in 1853 but they were not popularized until after 1863 by which time further design improvements had been made (Church *et al* 1986, 328-40). However, by 1900 under 5% of British coal was machine-cut and only 8% in 1913 (Cootes 1982, 168). Machine cutting was not to become popular until the 1930s, when by 1939 61% of British coal cutting was mechanized, compared with over 95% in Germany and Belgium (*ibid*, 267; C Jones 1989, 73).

In Tameside most mines had closed long before that last date. However, it is clear from an inventory compiled for the liquidators of the Denton Colliery Company in 1930 that this mine, at least, had mechanized coal cutting as well as coal haulage to the surface (TLSL DD 83).

Transportation

The eighteenth- and nineteenth-century advances in mining technology and increase in production raised the problem of how to transport the coal quickly and cheaply from the coalfield. In the early eighteenth century inland areas such as Tameside, with little or no access to navigable rivers, were dependent on packhorses to transport coal to the consumer, but according to contemporary reckoning the cost of such land transport doubled the pit-head price every ten miles (Flinn with Stoker 1984, 146). The possibility of an alternative cheaper form of transport was first shown by the

Year	Lancashire coalfield	Great Britain
1700	0.08	2.9
1750	0.3	5.2
1775	0.9	8.8
1800	1.4	15.0
1815	2.8	22.2
1830	4.2	30.5
1840	6.0	42.6
1850	9.6	62.5
1860	12.1	87.9
1870	14.7	115.5
1880	22.2	147.1
1890	25.8	181.7
1900	28.7	225.3
1910	27.2	264.5
1913	28.1	287.5
1920	19.0	229.5
1930	15.0	243.9

Table 6.1 Lancashire coalfield output, 1700-1930 in millions of tons.
Sources: Flinn with Stoker 1984, 26; Church *et al* 1986, 3, 86; Mitchell with Deane 1971, 115-16.

duke of Bridgewater's canal, built in 1759-66, which enabled bulk supplies of coal to be carried from his mines in Worsley to Manchester at a fraction of the cost of using pack-horses (Hadfield & Biddle 1970, 19-27). As a consequence of the Bridgewater Canal's success, coal-owners were frequently supporters of canal projects in the later eighteenth century.

The Ashton Canal, built in the 1790s, was constructed largely to capitalize on the coal reserves to the east of Manchester (*ibid*, 294). A branch led off the canal to the pits at Fairbottom, and a second branch, known as the Beat Bank, was planned to run to the pits at Denton. An act authorizing the Beat Bank was passed in 1793 but five years later the project was abandoned (see below).

The earliest recorded tramway in Tameside was run by the Fairbottom Coal Company and linked New Rocher Pit to the Fairbottom branch of the Ashton Canal. This included a tunnel 150m (490 feet) long, through which trucks were hauled by a horse-powered chain mill (Ashmore 1974, 97; Bowman 1950, 140). The earliest evidence of the line of this tramway can be found on the Ashton estate plan of 1765, although this is a later addition to this map, probably dating from the 1790s when the course of the Ashton Canal was added (ESRCA 15). It seems probable that the line was rebuilt when steam locomotives were introduced in 1865 (Ashmore 1969, 116-17).

By the mid-nineteenth century there were at least three collieries linked by tramway to canals or railways. By 1849 a tramway ran from Dewsnap Colliery in Dukinfield to the Peak Forest Canal and the newly built Sheffield, Ashton-under-Lyne & Manchester Railway (CRO EDT 143/1). Another, built by 1841, linked Broad Oak Colliery with the coke ovens at Lordsfield Colliery immediately north of Ashton town (OS First Edition 1in to 1 mile). Its terminus was on Oldham Road between Boodle Street and Wellington Road, and when in the mid-1840s the Lancashire & Yorkshire Railway was built this tramway ran over the top of the new Oldham Road Station on a high-level bridge (TLSL DDS 2076). By 1872 this had been replaced by a new tramway from Broad Oak Colliery to the Oldham, Ashton-under-Lyne & Guide Bridge Railway, with a terminus at Waterloo in Smallshaw (OS Second Edition 1in to 1 mile). Finally a tramway, opened in 1853, linked the collieries at Denton to the Reddish Coal Wharf on the London & North Western Railway (*Stockport Advertiser* 16/9/1853).

Output and colliery numbers 1700-1850

Although there are no reliable statistics for national coal output before 1854, it has been estimated that between 1700 and 1750 coal production nearly doubled, between 1750 and 1800 trebled and between 1800 and 1850 quadrupled. Estimates for the Lancashire coalfield show a rate of expansion during the eighteenth and early nineteenth centuries well in excess of the national average, with output increasing nearly four-fold in the first half of the eighteenth century, nearly five-fold in the second half and nearly seven-fold in the first half of the nineteenth century (Table 6.1).

Production figures for collieries in Tameside are difficult to find for this period, although a set survives for Fairbottom Colliery from the years 1818-21 (LRO DDRe 6/7). Details of dividends for the Fairbottom Coal Company also survive from the period 1816-37 (LRO DDX 614/19).

In Tameside the expansion of the coal industry in the late eighteenth and early nineteenth centuries is perhaps best illustrated by the growing number of colliery companies and owners. In Ashton Broad Oak Colliery had been opened by 1750, while Hyde Lane Colliery in Hyde may have been worked by 1754; in Mottram Hague Carr Colliery and Mottram Colliery were both being worked by the 1770s. By the 1780s these concerns had been joined by the Fairbottom

Chapter 6 Coal Mining

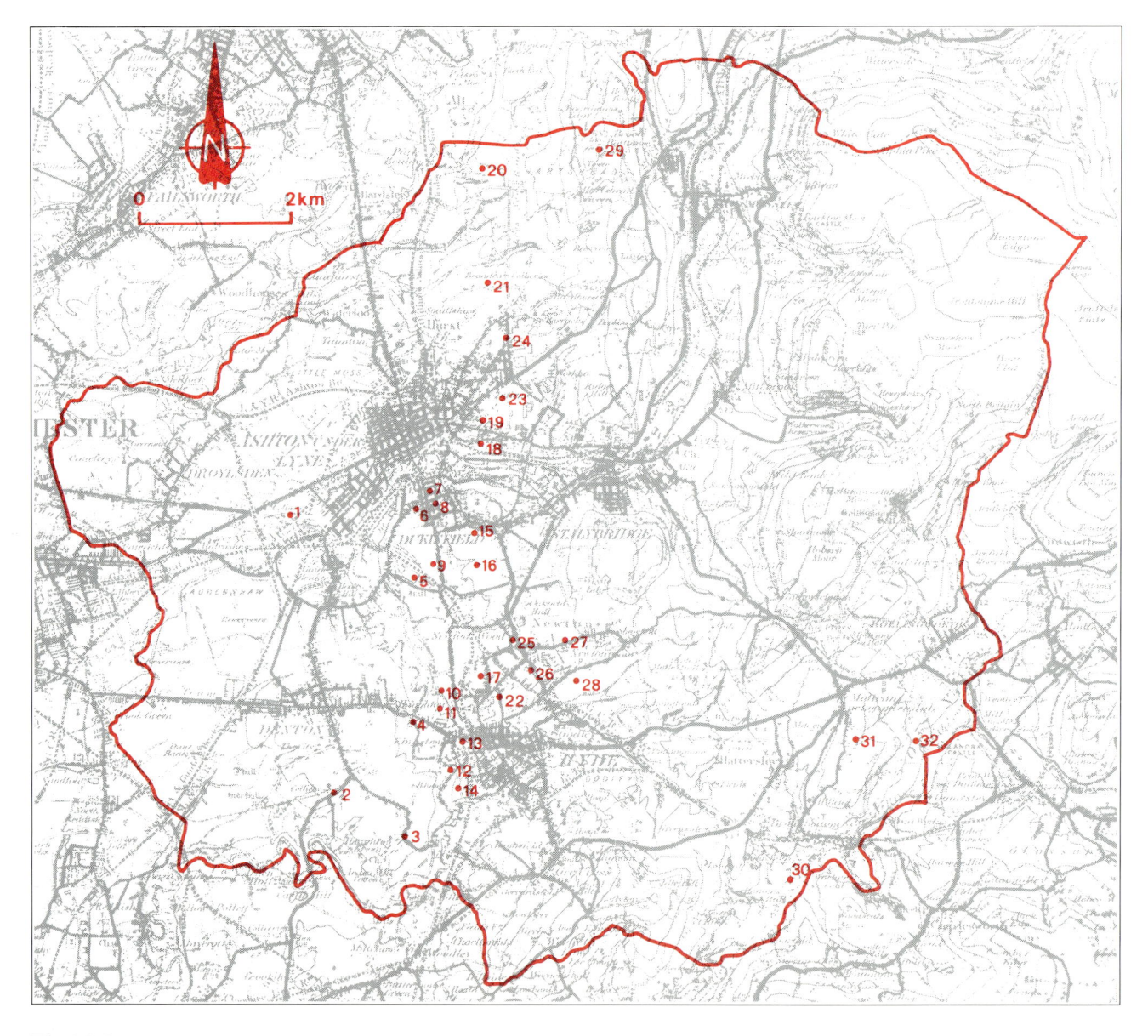

Fig 6.1 Collieries in Tameside.
Key: 1 Ashton Moss; 2 Denton; 3 Haughton; 4 Broomstair; 5 Dewsnap; 6 Dunkirk (Dukinfield); 7 Chapel; 8 Dog Lane; 9 Astley Deep Pit; 10 Dunkirk (Newton); 11 Kingston; 12 Glass House Fold; 13 Hyde Lane; 14 Peacock; 15 Town Lane; 16 Victoria; 17 Flowery Field; 18 Currier Slacks; 19 Crickety Lane; 20 Fairbottom; 21 Broad Oak; 22 Bayleyfield; 23 New Heys; 24 Hurst; 25 Newton Wood/Old Dow; 26 Daisyfield; 27 Muslin Street; 28 Back Lane; 29 Broadcar; 30 Leylands; 31 Mottram; 32 Hague Carr.

Coal Company in Ashton, Denton Colliery in Denton and probably Haughton Colliery in Haughton. By the 1790s pits are also attested at Dukinfield and Newton (see below). The rise of local colliery concerns is reflected in the cartographic evidence. Burdett's map of Cheshire and Yates's map of Lancashire, published in 1777 and 1786 respectively, record a total of eleven pits in operation in the Borough; five in the Hurst area of Ashton, four in the Hague area of Mottram and two at Newton Wood on the Dukinfield-Newton township boundary.

Further new collieries are attested in the first decades of the nineteenth century. By the early 1840s seven collieries were in operation in Dukinfield alone, and five in Newton. In 1855 Dickinson was able to record fifteen collieries in Tameside based upon a survey conducted three years previously (Dickinson 1855, 81, 89, 101-2; Table 6.2).

The number of individual shafts during this period was by any reckoning far greater. In the period 1839-49 a total of 79 are recorded in the Borough, 26 in Ashton, ten in Denton, seven in Dukinfield, 27 in Haughton, one in Hyde, four in Mottram and four in Newton (LRO DRM 1/37, 1/50; CRO EDT 143, 217, 281, 292; Butterworth 1842, 119, 175; OS First Edition 6in to 1 mile, 1848). Six of these – four in Hurst, one in Hazelhurst and one in Haughton – are described as 'old pits' and thus might not be in use. The remaining discrepancy in part represents the severality of shafts which might be used by an individual mining concern, for winding, pumping and ventilation. In the 1840s the Denton Colliery Company had six shafts, the main shaft being Ellis Pit at Burton Nook, on Stockport Road. On the other side of the road were Top Pit and Ladder Pit, separately named on the nineteenth-century Ordnance Survey maps but part of the colliery complex. Connected to this central group were Great Wood Pit, about 500m to the south, with its associated upcast at Ellenfield about 50m to the east, and Hulmes Pit, by the River Tame (Cronin & Yearsley 1985, 64).

Rationalization and decline 1850-1930

Output nationally continued to rise through the late nineteenth century and early years of the twentieth century, more than doubling between 1850 and 1880, and almost doubling again between 1880 and 1913, when production reached its highest ever peak at 287.5 million tons per annum before entering a rapid decline. However, the proportion contributed by the Lancashire coalfield fell from about 15% around 1850 to around 10% in 1913. The coalfield was particularly hard hit by the collapse of the cotton industry in the 1920s (Table 6.1).

Both nationally and regionally the late nineteenth-century rise in production took place against a background of a falling number of collieries and the growth of multi-colliery firms. In 1850 there were over 2500 collieries in Great Britain, of which approximately 12% were located in the Lancashire coalfield (Dickinson 1855, 71). It has been estimated that by 1860 there were 2791 collieries, a figure which had risen to 3307 by 1880. After this date colliery numbers declined, falling to 2705 run by 1400 companies in 1913, and declining further to 2075 run by 972 companies in 1935. In the Lancashire coalfield the number of collieries in operation rose from 406 in 1860 to 480 in 1880, but thereafter fell back to 399 in 1895 and declined further to 335 in 1913 (Church *et al* 1986, 388; Supple 1987, 362).

In Tameside the number of working collieries appears to have peaked in the mid-nineteenth century and from then on to have fallen until by 1906 there were only two in operation, Ashton Moss and Denton. This was partly due to the national trend towards larger companies, this factor being particularly noticeable in Denton where by 1873 the Denton Colliery Company was the only mining operation functioning, having bought its neighbouring competitors. At the same time the reduction in the number of collieries is to be seen as symptomatic of a genuine decline, as workable coal supplies became exhausted.

The Borough's remaining mines faced the regional and national difficulties which affected the industry after its peak in 1913. The last colliery to be opened in Tameside, the large drift mine of Kingston Colliery in Newton, which began operation in 1912, was forced to close in 1925 because of a combination of geological difficulties and poor trading conditions. In 1929 the Denton Colliery Company was forced into closure for similar reasons (Cronin & Yearsley 1985, 68).

6.3 The Collieries of Tameside

Ashton and Audenshaw

Coal mining is attested in Ashton from at least the early seventeenth century. In addition to pits in the north of the township at Fairbottom and Alt, there is also evidence from the seventeenth century for mining in the immediate vicinity of Ashton town itself, including a reference to a 'coal myne neare unto Ashton' in a petition of 1666 (Nevell 1991, 92; LRO QSP/288/4). In the early eighteenth century, in 1722, a shaft

Colliery	Location	Owner
Charlestown	Ashton	William Wild
Fairbottom	Fairbottom &c	Leese and Booth
Heys	Ashton	John Kenworthy and brothers
Hurst Knowl	Ashton	John Whitaker and Sons
Denton	Denton	Jacob Fletcher Fletcher
Denton	Denton	Peter Higson
Haughton	Haughton	Leigh and Bradbury
Haughton	Haughton	Thomas Shaw
Back Lane	Newton	Executors of late George Wooley
Bayleyfield	Mottram	Thomas, James and George Ashton
Dukinfield	Dukinfield	Dukinfield Coal Co
Dukinfield	Dukinfield	F D P Astley
Dunkirk	Dukinfield	Dunkirk Coal Co
Hyde	Hyde	Leigh and Bradbury
Staley Bridge	Staley Bridge	Executors of late George Wooley

Table 6.2 Tameside collieries, their locations and owners as recorded in 1852 (Dickinson 1855).

Chapter 6 Coal Mining

is mentioned near Crickety Lane, to the north-east of the town (Bowman 1960, 468-70).

The great period of expansion in coal production in Ashton coincided with the major era of innovation in the industry, namely the late eighteenth and early nineteenth centuries. According to the manorial accounts the rents from coal production in the years 1758-9, 1768-9 and 1775 were each £21, but by 1785 this figure had leapt to £827 14s 1d (Bowman 1960, 468, 471). The leases attached to these pits by the earls of Stamford were very similar. They allowed the digging of pits, soughs, trenches and other holes, but not within 70 yards of any building. Proper roads had to be built to the mines, which were required to be fenced (*ibid*, 468). In 1795 Aikin was able to talk of the

'coals got at the very edge of the town in abundance, whence they will be conveyed to Manchester by the canal which is now nearly finished' (Aikin 1795, 227).

Expansion in the nineteenth century was rapid. In terms of the number of pits in operation the industry in Ashton appears to have reached a peak in the middle of the century. An indication of output and the continuing importance of the Manchester market at this date is provided by Butterworth's comment in 1842 that

'upwards of 20,000 tons of coal are conveyed from the parish to Manchester' (Butterworth 1842, 119).

The two largest mining concerns in Ashton during the late eighteenth and nineteenth centuries were the Broad Oak and Fairbottom collieries. The oldest of these was Broad Oak Colliery, opened by a Mr Lees by 1750, at which date a 'Coalpitt Road' ran from this site (Bowman 1960, 470). In about 1868 the colliery was sold by Lees and Booth to the Fairbottom Coal Company and after 1872 was run by the Broad Oak Company. The colliery closed in 1904 (Mines Department 1928). Fairbottom Colliery comprised a group of pits in the Medlock valley. Although coal had been dug at Fairbottom from the seventeenth century, serious exploitation only began in the 1780s with the formation of the Fairbottom Coal Company (LRO DDRe 6/7). From the 1790s the company's New Rocher Pit was linked by a tramway to the Fairbottom branch of the Ashton Canal (see above).

Among the other collieries operating in Ashton in the mid-nineteenth century that at Hurst Knowl was run by John Whittaker & Sons in conjunction with their cotton mill, Hurst Mills, the two being connected by a tramway (Hey 1979, 4-5). In the Hartshead area New Heys Pit was opened by the Kenworthy family in 1823 (*Ashton Reporter* 1/8/1857). This family originally worked a shaft by Currier Slacks Lane, near Ashton, but this was closed in 1849 because of the nuisance and danger caused to the neighbourhood (Bowman 1960, 472). Broadcar Colliery, on the top of Hartshead near to the Pike, was opened in 1843 but proved to be short-lived (*ibid*, 471).

In the second half of the nineteenth century the industry in Ashton entered a decline which saw the closure of most of the collieries north of the town. These included the Fairbottom Coal Company, whose last pit, New Rocher Pit, closed in 1887 (Mines Report 1886, C5132; 1887, C5464). When Broad Oak Colliery closed in 1904 only one colliery was left working in the Ashton area, this being Ashton Moss Colliery. Nevertheless, the 1911 census recorded that 4% of the total working population of Ashton was then involved in mining or quarrying (Cordingley 1986, 25).

Ashton Moss Colliery, in Audenshaw, was the last mine to be opened in the Ashton area. Two pits were sunk in 1875 and 1882 in an area previously unaffected by the coal-mining industry. At the time the second shaft, at 870m (2850 feet), was the deepest in the world (Ashmore 1982, 79). The colliery was provided with its own sidings and a branch line to the Oldham, Ashton-under-Lyne & Guide Bridge Railway, as well as an arm from the Ashton Canal (TLSL DD 60).

Denton and Haughton

The first direct reference to coal pits lying within the townships of Denton and Haughton does not occur until the early eighteenth century when two drift tunnels were dug from the northern banks of the River Tame in Denton (Cronin & Yearsley 1985, 59).

It was not until the last quarter of the eighteenth century that mining operations began to expand on a scale similar to that seen in Ashton. Yates's map of Lancashire published in 1786 shows only one colliery in Denton and Haughton, on Two Trees Lane, which was probably the forerunner of Haughton Colliery. Denton Colliery, off Stockport Road and run by the Fletcher family, was opened shortly afterwards in 1788 (LRO DDX 326).

By the 1850s there were five collieries in the area employing 9.5% of the local workforce (Cronin 1985, 50). Two of these collieries were in Denton, run by Jacob Fletcher and Peter Higson (Booker 1855, 13; Dickinson 1855, 89). In Haughton there were three: Haughton Colliery, also owned by Jacob Fletcher; Glass House Fold owned by Thomas Shaw; and Broomstair Colliery owned by Messrs Leigh and Bradbury, who also held Hyde Lane Colliery in Hyde, on the opposite bank of the Tame (Bann 1976, 21; Booker 1855, 136; Cronin & Yearsley 1985, 68; Dickinson 1855, 89; TLSL DD 2/93).

Chapter 6 Coal Mining

Plate 6.2 Ashton Moss Colliery.
This was the last deep mine to be sunk in Tameside, between 1875 and 1882. At 870m, or 2850 feet, the 1882 shaft was the deepest in the world at that time.

The largest and longest-lived coal-mining concern in this area of Tameside was Denton Colliery. Its rise and fall charts the progress of the mining industry in Denton and Haughton. In 1788 William Hulton of Hulton Park, who had bought the manorial estate in 1762, leased coal mines in Denton for 50 years to 'John Fletcher, Gentleman, of Ashton under Lyne, Collier' at an annual rent of £40 and one sixth of the coal raised. The specific area of these mines is not mentioned but in 1789 this lease was replaced by a second in which John Fletcher rented two messuages in Denton, Hardy's Farm and Torkington, both near to the site of the later Denton Colliery (Booker 1855, 34; LRO DDHu 12/32 & 33).

William Hulton found the rents from these mines sufficiently profitable for him to sponsor a canal act of March 1793, which authorized a branch of the Ashton Canal to be built from Clayton junction to Heaton Norris in Stockport, with a spur along the northern edge of the Tame valley to Beat Bank in Denton. The latter's purpose was to give access to the collieries leased by John Fletcher (Hadfield & Biddle 1970, 294). However, two letters now in the Lancashire Record Office indicate that the Ashton Canal Company was not keen on the plan, perhaps because two of the chief shareholders in the company, James and John Lees, were also shareholders in the Chamber Colliery Company based in Werneth in Oldham and thus rivals of the Fletcher family (LRO DDHu 32/3 & 4). In 1798, after poor progress and escalating costs, the plan was abandoned, much to the disgust of William Hulton who had hoped to increase the income from the collieries rented on his land (Hadfield & Biddle 1970, 295-6).

By the third quarter of the nineteenth century the Denton Colliery Company was the only working coal-

Chapter 6 Coal Mining

mining concern in the district. This was partly through the exhaustion of neighbouring collieries, but chiefly because the Fletcher family, and their successors the Denton Colliery Company, acquired most of the remaining collieries in Denton and Haughton. Three generations of the Fletcher family, John, Ellis and Jacob, ran the Denton mines until 1867 when the lease was transferred to Peter Rothwell, the former agent of the Fletchers. In 1872 he helped found the Denton Colliery Company, of which he was the principal shareholder and managing director (Middleton 1936, 158; Cronin & Yearsley 1985, 67-8). In 1873 the company purchased Thomas Shaw's pits at Haughton and Haughton Green (Mines Report 1873, C1056). These were probably the pits at Tib Street (by the Mason Arms) and at Three Lane Ends, and Victoria Pit by the Bay Horse public house on Haughton Green (Bann 1976, 21; Middleton 1936, 158; *North Cheshire Herald* 29/3/1873, 8/11/1873; TLSL DD 83). Glass House Fold Colliery, also run by Thomas Shaw & Sons, had closed around 1870 (*North Cheshire Herald* 5/3/1910). The Denton Colliery Company continued in operation until 2nd December 1929 when it went into voluntary liquidation (TLSL DD 83).

Dukinfield, Newton and Hyde

Upwards of 50 coal seams run along the eastern bank of the Tame from Dukinfield to Hyde and it is perhaps not surprising that some of these had been worked since the seventeenth century (Nevell 1991, 92; Newton 1970, 2). This led to the characteristic riverside distribution of the industry in this part of Tameside. The exception to this were the coal seams at Newton Wood, on the western edge of Newton moor.

These coal deposits were initially exploited by the Dukinfield Daniel family, and their heirs the Astleys, who owned most of the townships of Dukinfield and Newton. Sir William Dukinfield Daniel, in his will made in December 1756, refers to 'my coal mines in Dukinfield, Newton and Hyde' (CRO D73). It is clear from this document that some of these mines were leased and that all were mortgaged, perhaps giving an indication of their relative value at this early date.

In 1795 Aikin could comment that

> 'Dukinfield is very valuable, abounding in mines and quarries that yield a considerable revenue. The coalpits are from 60 to 105 yards in depth, according to the bearing of the strata...One mile from hence is Newton Moor, under which coals have been got for ages at different depths' (Aikin 1795, 455, 457).

The earliest known pit in the Hyde area was Hyde Lane Colliery which may have been worked as early as 1754 and was certainly in existence by 1790 (Bann 1976, 10; CRO D73; Ridgway 1988, 4).

The development of the early coal companies in Newton appears to have been related to the success of the Ashton brothers' cotton factories in the early nineteenth century. The industry's growth can be partly recovered from contemporary deeds and the land tax returns. In 1793 William Sherratt & Co was leasing 'coalworks' from Lord Astley in Newton, probably Flowery Field Coal Pit (*Manchester Guardian* 13/4/1842). In 1805 this company was joined by John Garside and in 1807 possibly by the Muslin Street Colliery, run by John Hilton. Around 1819 an expansion of the industry took place with five collieries in operation: Flowery Field, run by Bateman & Sherratt; Dunkirk Colliery (Newton), worked by John Newton & Company; Muslin Street Colliery run by John Hilton; Bayleyfield Colliery run by the Ashton brothers, the local mill-owners; and Rabbit Hole, or Back Lane Colliery, which was in that part of Dukinfield later transferred to the borough of Stalybridge, on the High Street near the junction with Caroline Street, and which was run by Hampson & Woolley (CRO QDV2/313 & 148).

In Dukinfield a John Ogden is recorded in the land tax returns for 1797 as renting mines from Lord Astley (CRO QDV2/148). The next reference to coal pits in the Dukinfield land tax returns does not occur until 1825, when four collieries were being worked by the Dunkirk Coal Company, Hampson & Woolley, William Wild & Son and Samuel Swire & Company. However, large-scale coal production had begun in Dukinfield at least as early as 1819 for in that year Greenwood's map of Cheshire records coal pits in the area of the later Dewsnap Colliery.

Further expansion in the industry, led by local demand, meant that by 1842 there were seven collieries in operation in Dukinfield, employing a workforce of 150 (Butterworth 1842, 175). These were probably Dog Lane, Dewsnap, Dunkirk (Dukinfield), Chapel, Newton Wood, Town Lane and Victoria. A further five could be found in Newton and were probably Back Lane, Bayleyfield, Daisyfield, Dunkirk (Newton) and Flowery Field. Finally, there were two collieries in Hyde, Hyde Lane and Peacock (Bann 1976, 21). This expansion culminated with the opening of Astley Deep Pit, which was sunk between 1847 and 1858, and at the time was the deepest in the world at 628m (2060ft) (Newton 1970, 5-6; *Ashton Standard* 24/7/1858).

These collieries were run by a variety of owners. In Dukinfield the three main concerns were the Dukinfield Coal Company, the Dunkirk Coal Company and Sir Francis Astley who owned Victoria Colliery (Newton 1970, 3). In Newton in 1852 Back Lane

Colliery was held by the executors of George Woolley, who also held a pit in Stalybridge, while Bayleyfield Colliery was owned by the mill-owning family the Ashtons. The firm of Leigh and Bradbury owned both Hyde Lane Colliery in Hyde and Broomstair Colliery in Haughton (Table 6.2).

By 1875 only the Dukinfield industry remained strong with six collieries producing 336,440 tons of coal per year and employing 1120 miners (Newton 1970, 2). Elsewhere in the area there was only one colliery in Newton, at Bayleyfield, and one in Hyde, at Hyde Lane (Ridgway 1988, 10; TLSL DDS 188).

The exhaustion of coal reserves coupled with geological difficulties such as pit flooding, especially in those mines along the river, were significant factors influencing closure in the Dukinfield area. The Astley Deep, Dewsnap and Chapel collieries were the last to close in Dukinfield, ceasing production in 1901, although their demise was hastened by a wage strike in that year (Pavasovic 1984, 12). The last of the old collieries to close was the Hyde Lane pit, which ceased production in 1905 (Bann 1976, 10).

The final pit to be opened in the area was Kingston Colliery in Newton, in 1912. This was a large drift mine, the site of which is now under the M67. Although employment reached 122 men in 1919, the expected production capacity of 1000 tons a day was never achieved, largely due to geological difficulties. Consequently Kingston Colliery closed on 20th October 1925 (*ibid*, 10).

Mottram

The geology of the Mottram area meant that, as in Dukinfield and Newton townships, coal could be found outcropping on the surface (Plate 6.1). As a result, it had been exploited from the early seventeenth century and possibly from the mid-sixteenth century (Nevell 1991, 91). Partly because of this early exploitation and partly because of the poor quality of the coal, mining in the Mottram area did not become a major part of the local economy in the way in which collieries elsewhere in Tameside did. Indeed Aikin was fairly dismissive of the industry, commenting

> 'coals of an indifferent quality are occasionally got at Mottram' (Aikin 1795, 473).

The course of the exploitation of the coal reserves in the township can be traced through the Tollemache estate records in the Cheshire Record Office. These indicate that deep mining began in the mid-eighteenth century and that the coals dug from the three collieries in the township were never extensive. In 1771 the Tollemache estate raised £10 in rent from the coal mines in Mottram. A general survey of the township in 1800 noted that although there were coals beneath the glebe, on Warhill, they were only of value when worked with the adjoining deep shaft colliery. This may account for the modest rise in value of coals to the estate, which by 1801 had only risen to £16 5s. Even so the steward of the Tollemaches' Longdendale estate must have felt that there was money to be made from coal mining, for in 1828 the estate was paying for prospecting in the Longdendale valley. However, only a small seam, not worth working, was found near Waterside (CRO DTW 2477/A/1; EDP 198/10).

The earliest seams to be exploited by deep mine technology were in the vicinity of Hague Carr. Coal pits below the Hague are shown on Burdett's map of Cheshire published in 1777 and Stockwell's map of Mottram in 1794, while a steam engine is mentioned in relation to mines at the Hague in the Mottram estate rentals of the 1770s (Aikin 1795, 457; CRO DTW 2477/F/12). These pits may have been worked by Messrs Garlick & Co who occur in the land tax returns of the period 1796-1801 owning Hague Farm and paying one of the highest land taxes in the township at £1 4s 9d (CRO QDV2/299). The 2464 loads of coal got by Thomas Cardwell, probably the owner of Arrowscroft Mill in Hollingworth, in 1803 and the 1445 loads got by Cardwell in 1807 may both have been from this colliery (CRO DTW 2477/A/1). The last record of the colliery occurs in 1837 when Hague Carr was put up for sale by a William Thornley (*Manchester Guardian* 18/3/1837). Evidence of coal workings between Hague and Carr farms survived in the form of earthworks, but the area has been recently ploughed and much of this evidence obscured.

The largest colliery in the area was Mottram Colliery, on the Mudd. The seam which this colliery exploited stretched across Warhill from Mottram moor to Hurst Clough and had been worked since the seventeenth century (Nevell 1991, 91-2). According to the parish records of Mottram, in 1768 coal was discovered under the glebe lands near Parsonage Farm by a Mr Wray who 'dug for it and converted same to his own use'. The Mottram estate accounts note that by 1771 Edward Kershaw was exploiting these deposits, while in 1791 the vicar of Mottram, the Reverend Kinder, wrote to the bishop complaining about the coal workings run by John Hadfield. These were probably related to the shaft sunk by Hadfield and mentioned in the general survey of 1800. From about 1818 the colliery was worked by John and James Braddock and in that year 4614 loads of coal were mined (CRO EDP 198/10; DTW 2477/A/1). The Braddock family appear to have run the colliery for the rest of its life. By 1861 the colliery was employing nineteen men and six boys and had a steam engine on site (TLSL MF

Chapter 6 Coal Mining

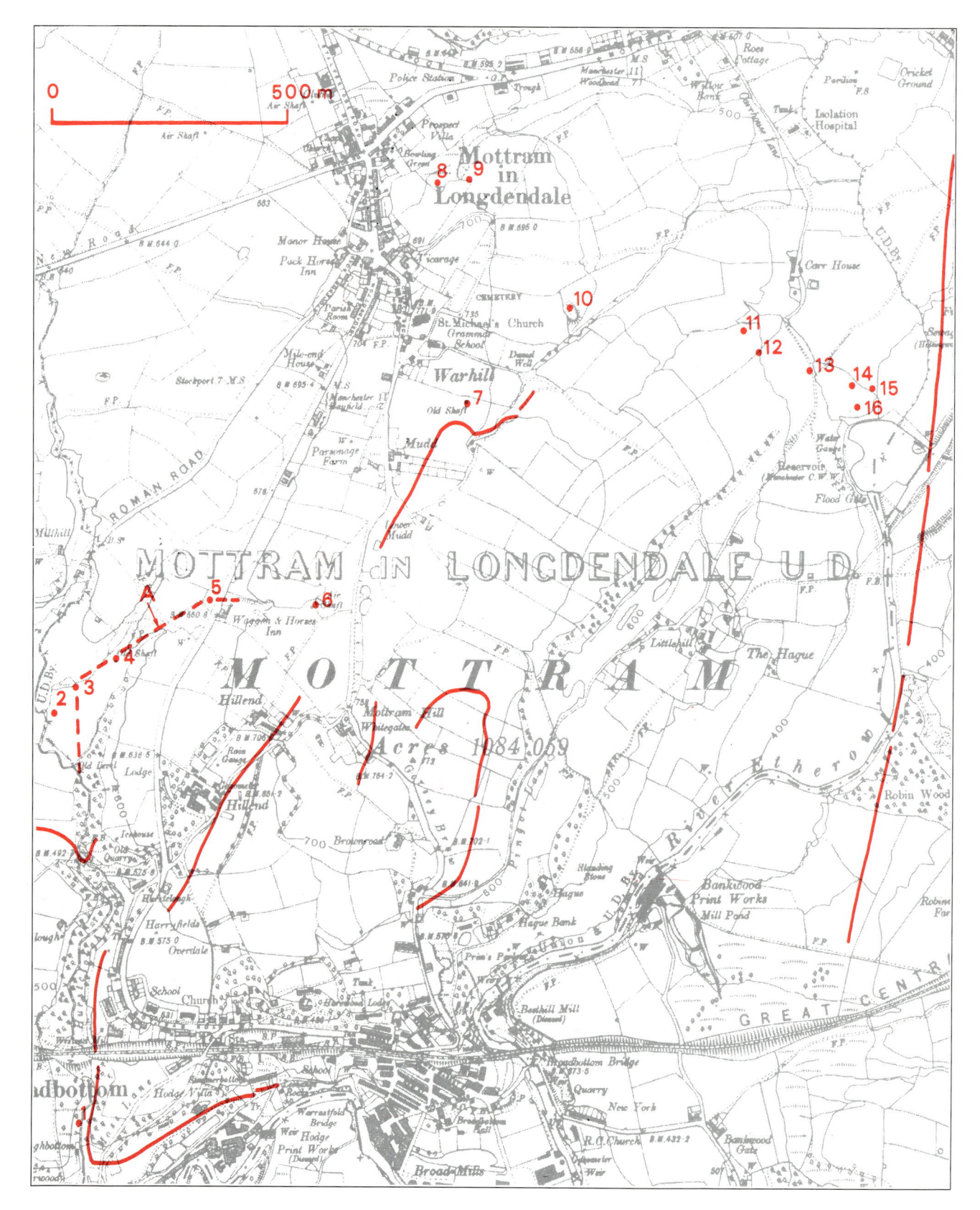

Fig 6.2 Plan of Mottram showing collieries and coal seams.
Key: —— coal seams in the Mottram area; A – the Great Sough, a drainage channel for Mottram Colliery; 1 Leylands Colliery; 2-6 ventilation shafts for the Great Sough; 7 Mottram Colliery; 8-10 coal shafts on Mottram moor; 11-16 coal shafts relating to Hague Carr Colliery.

Coal had been exploited in Mottram since at least the early seventeenth century. By the early nineteenth century there were three working collieries in the township. The industry was never, however, a significant part of the local economy and the last of these pits closed in about 1874.

Census returns). However, the last reference to the colliery occurs in a directory of 1874 and thereafter it appears to have closed (Slater 1874).

The third colliery in Mottram lay in fields opposite Leylands Farm in Broadbottom, now occupied by the sewage works. It was almost certainly the site of the mine dug by John Swindells, who was letting Hodge Mill to Samuel Matley and appears in the Tollemache accounts for 1809 paying rent for mining coal. In 1813 John Swindells mined 2390 loads of coal 'gotten near Hodge Mill'. Swindells was still mining coal in 1817, when the accounts record 2334 loads of coal obtained from the colliery in that year, but the site appears to have fallen into disuse soon after, with only the name 'coalpit field' surviving on the tithe award in 1845 (CRO DTW 2477/A/1; EDT 281).

Chapter 7

Secondary Industries

'JOHN HALL AND SON, FIRE CLAY WORKS, DUKINFIELD Manufacturers of Patent Pressed White Building Bricks. Every description of Terra Cotta made to order. Fire Bricks and Tiles for Gas Furnaces, &c. DEALERS IN GLAZED SANITARY TUBES, &c, &c.'

Advertisement in Morris & Co 1874, 297

7.1 Introduction

While textiles, hatting, agriculture and mining were the main employers in Tameside during the eighteenth and nineteenth centuries, there was a host of secondary industries whose supporting role and impact on the landscape were of great significance in this period. Chief amongst these were the ironworking and engineering industry, the building industry and the retail trade. Each was a response to the essential needs created by the four major industries of the Borough, either in the provision of machinery, the housing of the new industries and the boarding of a growing population, or in the everyday supply of food, clothing and household goods.

Besides these secondary industries there were many other minor manufacturing processes carried out in Tameside. These included the manufacture of chemicals and pharmaceuticals, rubber, margarine, pottery, mineral water, cork, paper and stationery, and the printing of books. The Greater Manchester Sites and Monuments Record (held by the Greater Manchester Archaeological Unit) and Ashmore's survey of the industrial archaeology of the North-West (1982) provide useful summaries of the physical remains of these minor industries, while the local rate books and the census returns from the nineteenth century are probably the most informative documentary sources for an assessment of their impact.

7.2 Ironworking and Engineering

By the mid-nineteenth century the Manchester region, spurred initially by the booming cotton and coal industries and later by the railway network, had become one of the major engineering areas in the world (Musson 1973, 55). The region led the way in new cast- and wrought-iron production techniques and in the building of cheap and efficient machinery for the cotton industry. From 1843 it dominated the world market in textile machines, with exports becoming more valuable than supplies to the home market (Farnie 1990b, 150-2). In the late nineteenth and early twentieth centuries new forms of manufacture were introduced into the North-West, such as the production of electrical power plant, gas and oil engines and motor cars (Ashmore 1969, 83-4).

The towns surrounding Manchester usually had their own engineering sector. Although there were no firms in Tameside which approached the size of Platt Brothers of Oldham, the largest engineering firm in the world during the second half of the nineteenth century, there was a strong machine-manufacturing sector in the Borough.

The main centres of this industry were Ashton, Hyde and Dukinfield. Among the earliest of the engineering firms in Tameside was Hannah Lees & Sons at Park Bridge in Alt, north of Ashton town, a specialist manufacturer of rollers and spindles for cotton mills. The evidence is not entirely clear but it seems likely that Samuel Lees, a local blacksmith, founded the ironworks in 1784 on the site of a water-powered corn-mill. When Samuel died in 1804 his son, also named Samuel, took over the works but appears to have played little part in the day to day running of the site, leaving that to his wife Hannah, whom he had married in 1783 (Holland 1969, 2). She ran the business for many years until her death, the works being subsequently extended by her sons and grandsons. The site did not finally close until 1963 (Ashmore 1969, 86-7).

The rates entry for the works in 1825 shows that the site then included turning rooms powered by water, ten cottages and 'at New Mill more Turning Rooms'

Plate 7.1 Park Bridge ironworks.
Founded by Samuel Lees in the late eighteenth century, Park Bridge was one of the earliest of the industrial ironworks in the Borough. The factory did not close until the 1960s. This view, taken in the early twentieth century, shows the interior of the bright shop where the steel was polished.

(Bowman 1960, 475). By the late nineteenth century the ironworks consisted of a large complex of buildings strung along the northern side of the Medlock valley. Most of these buildings were still standing in 1969, when Ashmore was able to assess the development of the site. The earliest element of the complex, the eighteenth-century water-powered mill which was converted into an ironworks, lay at the western end of the site by the later Oldham, Ashton-under-Lyne & Guide Bridge Railway. In the early nineteenth century this building was replaced by a four-storey brick-built rolling mill, which in turn was converted into a cotton-spinning mill in 1886. During the nineteenth century the site was greatly expanded, partly as a result of the introduction of steel production. In the valley to the east of the original works was built a series of rolling mills, furnaces and forges, the latest and largest of which was a late nineteenth-century five-aisle single-storey rolling mill for wrought-iron bar production; this also contained a bright shop where the steel was polished (Plate 7.1). Among the last buildings to be erected on the site was a new roller-manufacturing works, which was opened in 1886 immediately by the railway (Ashmore 1969, 86-7). In the 1920s the main complex, running eastwards from the railway, included, at the top forge, scrap-metal cutting machines, a small steam hammer and a cogging mill, while the bottom forge contained three rolling mills, seven hand-charged furnaces, a large steam hammer, a helve or frog hammer and two large bar-cutting machines (Holland 1969, 5).

There was an associated community, much of which still survives (see Chapter 9). Initially the works were served by the Fairbottom branch of the Ashton Canal, opened in 1797, from the end of which a horse-drawn tramroad ran up to the site. After 1861 the works were linked by a branch line to the Oldham, Ashton-under-Lyne & Guide Bridge Railway. Coal was supplied locally from the Fairbottom pits (Ashmore 1969, 86-7).

Other iron foundries in the Ashton area during the early nineteenth century included the Bridge End Works on Mill Lane in Ashton town, owned by Henry and Edward Lees, elder sons of Hannah Lees of Park Bridge, and the works of Eli Cryer in Katherine Street, also in the town (Bowman 1960, 475).

The ironworking and engineering industry of Dukinfield, like that of Ashton, began in the late eighteenth century, the main centre being by the River Tame, near the later railway, between Wharf Street and the Ashton Canal (Pavasovic 1984, 12). Between 1759 and 1787 Sir John Astley attempted to establish a large iron foundry and an associated community along the banks of the Tame opposite Ashton. According to Aikin he spent 'a great deal of money...in building works and houses'. However, it was not a success and after a short period under a lease to a Manchester firm the site was closed. It was demolished in 1792 and Furnace cotton mill erected on the site (Aikin 1795, 456; Haynes forthcoming).

In the 1790s the Alma Iron Works, owned by J G Wagstaffe & Co, were operating in Dukinfield, in what is now Station Street. A short canal arm linked this site to the Peak Forest Canal (Pavasovic 1984, 12). The Waterside Iron Works were situated nearby, a large stone-built complex of the early to mid-nineteenth century, while in Foundry Street lay Bevan's Works, established in the mid-nineteenth century. Other ironworking firms in operation in Dukinfield included John Fernihough & Sons, who ran the Victoria Boiler Iron Works on Yew Tree Lane, founded in 1815, and W & J Garforth and J D Somers, both with works near Station Street and established respectively in the early and late nineteenth century (Haynes 1990, 38). Also in the latter part of that century the Barn Meadow Iron Works (SJ 9325 9700) were founded by John Rowley and the Phoenix Works on Astley Street by John Chadderton (Pavasovic 1984, 12).

The most important of the Dukinfield engineering firms was Adamson, Hatchett & Acrow. The company was originally founded in Newton in the mid-nineteenth century by Daniel Adamson, who was noted for his improvements in boiler construction and who was also the first chairman of the Manchester Ship Canal Company. By 1869 he was producing boilers, engines, gas works, hoists, hydraulic lifts, iron bridges, locomotives and steam cranes. In the later nineteenth century the firm moved to a site on Johnson Brook Road in Dukinfield, where it had its own sidings by the Manchester, Sheffield & Lincolnshire Railway (Ashmore 1982, 92; Pavasovic 1984, 12-13).

The last area to develop a significant engineering industry in Tameside was Hyde. In the early nineteenth century the textile firm of Ashton Brothers briefly produced textile machinery in the township (Ashton Brothers & Co Ltd 1961, 3). However, the expansion of the engineering industry in Hyde was largely a product of the mid- to late nineteenth century. The largest firm was Joseph Adamson & Co, founded by a nephew of Daniel Adamson in 1874 and best known for the manufacture of steam boilers for the textile industry. In 1894 the company was the first in the country to produce electrically driven cranes and overhead travellers (Ashmore 1982, 99; Middleton 1932, 367-9). Long ranges of workshops, including a press shop and engine house, still survive, with datestones from 1885 to 1898 (SJ 944 946). Middleton lists a further twelve engineering firms established in the Hyde and Newton area between 1864 and 1912. These were mostly specialist boiler makers but included Turbine Gears, established in Newton in 1912 (Middleton 1932, 569).

In the Denton area a number of firms specialized in the manufacture of hat-making machinery including rollers, body-felting machines, fur-blowing and finishing equipment and ironing machines (Holding 1986, 81; Oldham & Son Ltd 1949). The main firm was J Oldham & Son Ltd, founded in 1865, although others, such as Wilton & Co, also made machinery. By 1887 Oldham machines were used for 90% of felting in the hatting industry (Smith 1980, II, 21). Frederick Cheetham patented a machine for making hat linings and another for stitching hat leathers, and these were produced by his hatting firm of John Cheetham & Sons Ltd in the late nineteenth and early twentieth centuries (Middleton 1932, 565). Other hatting machinery firms included Perrin's in Hyde, begun in the 1870s (Smith 1980, II, 13).

Wadsworth & Co Ltd of Droylsden manufactured Jacquard looms for the textile industry. The company was founded in 1860 by John Wadsworth, who invented the double sift double cylinder Jacquard machine (Speake & Witty 1953, 171). In Stalybridge Taylor Lang & Co Ltd ran the large complex known as the Castle Iron Works, established in the mid-nineteenth century between Back Grosvenor Street and the Huddersfield Canal; the works produced a variety of machines for the textile trade, including cotton waste cleaners, scutchers and mule spindles (Hill 1907, 53).

Among the new engineering industries of the late nineteenth and early twentieth centuries was the Wellington Works of the National Gas Engine Co Ltd, in Ashton (SJ 929 991), founded in 1889 by Henry Neild Bickerton. These works produced two-cycle gas engines which were widely used in electric power plants, cotton mills and other works. The firm became a limited company in 1897 and eventually became part of the Stockport firm of Mirlees, Bickerton & Day Ltd, co-founded by Bickerton in 1907 to produce diesel engines (Bowman 1960, 479-80). By the time

Chapter 7 Secondary Industries

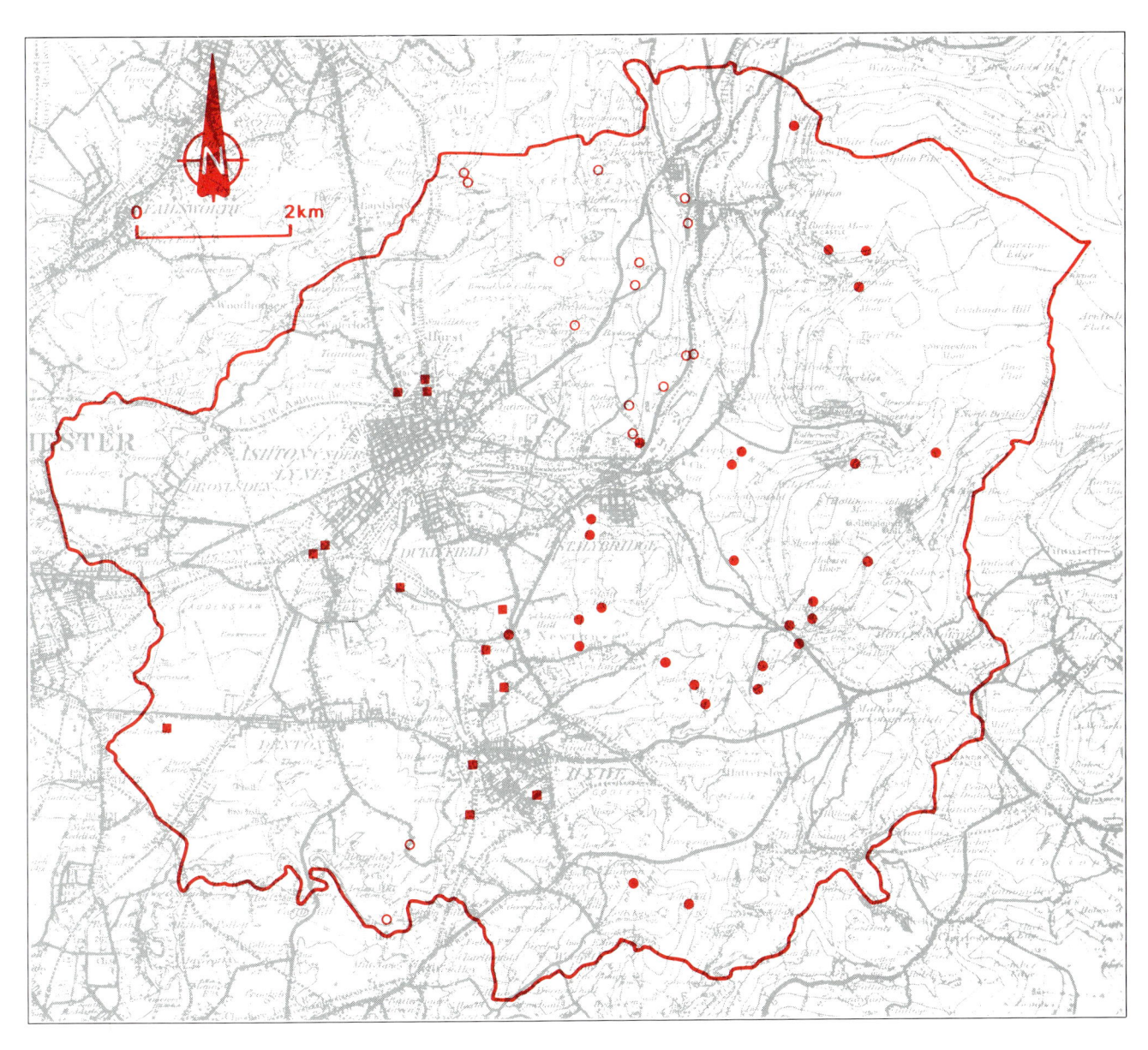

Fig 7.1 Distribution of quarries and brick works in mid-nineteenth-century Tameside.
Key: ■ = brick works; ○ = sandstone quarries; ● = millstone grit quarries.
The distribution reflects the underlying solid geology of the Borough, with the quarries being concentrated in the upland areas and the brick works on the clay lowlands.

of Bickerton's death in 1929 the firm was one of the largest producers of gas and oil engines in the world.

In Droylsden the Glyco Metal Co Ltd was founded in 1901 to produce anti-friction metals and bearings for the engine- and motor-manufacturing industries (Speake & Witty 1953, 173). The works comprised a brass foundry, white metal alloying department and machine shops. The Latex Engineering Co was also founded in Droylsden in the early twentieth century and specialized in producing machinery for the rubber-making industry (*ibid*, 172).

7.3 Building Trade

The upsurge in building activity associated with the industrialization and urbanization of Tameside has left its mark on the landscape both in the present building stock and in the many extractive sites still visible in the Borough. There were two sides to the industry, the extraction and processing of the raw materials, stone and clay, and the building process itself.

Raw materials

Although details of the sources of the raw materials in Tameside are scanty for the eighteenth and nineteenth centuries, most building materials were evidently obtained locally, with brick buildings predominating in the lowland districts of Audenshaw, Ashton, Denton, Droylsden, Dukinfield and Hyde, and stone buildings

Chapter 7 Secondary Industries

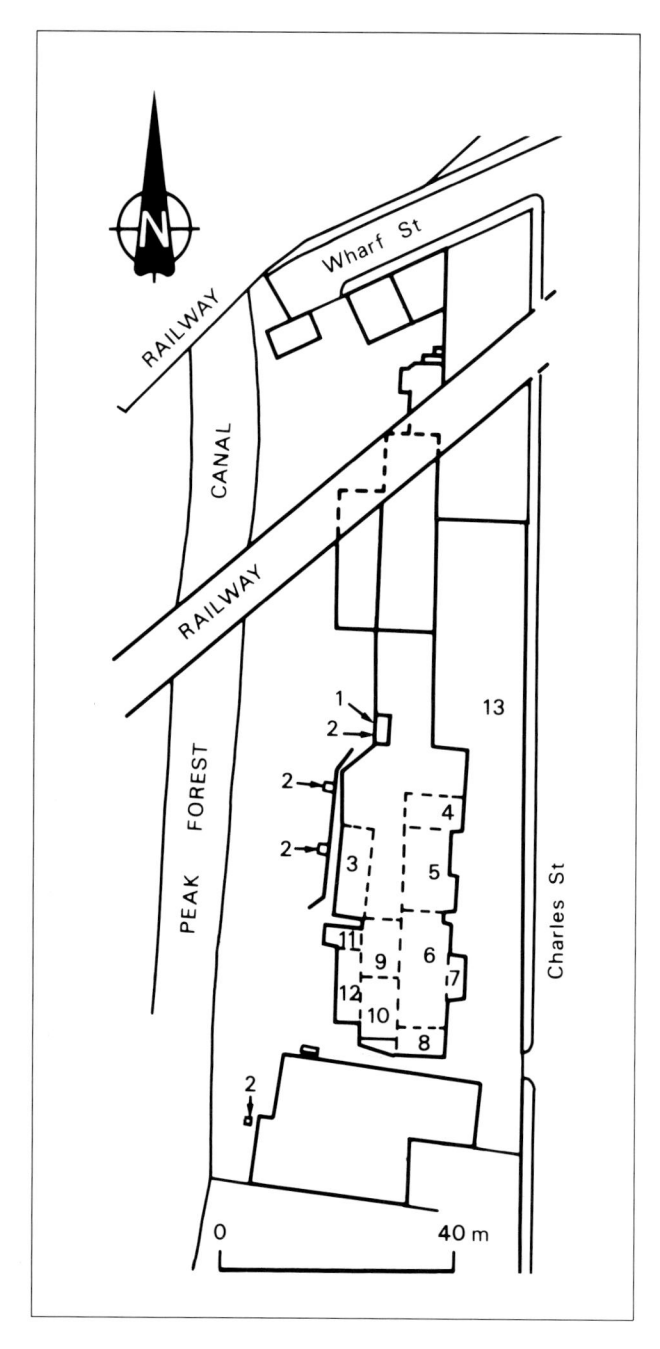

Fig 7.2 Plan of John Hall & Son (Dukinfield) Ltd, tile and brick makers (after Lamb 1968).
Key: 1 double chimney; 2 kilns; 3 apprentice pattern makers' shop; 4 pugging machine; 5 pre-1929 engine house; 6 shafting, butts and grinding mill; 7 grinding mill for pipes; 8 automatic brick press; 9 moulding shed above the drying shed; 10 post-1929 engine house; 11 pre-1929 boiler house; 12 post-1929 boiler house; 13 clay yard.
This was the largest and amongst the earliest tile and brick makers founded in Tameside, the site being worked from 1792 until 1967.

in the upland districts of Longdendale, Mossley and Stalybridge.

Stone in the form of limestone, gritstone and sandstone was used as paving stones, stone slates and building stones. In Tameside both gritstone and sandstone were extensively extracted and many small quarries are still extant. A total of 41 sites are recorded on the Ordnance Survey 6in to 1 mile First Edition maps of Tameside for the period 1845-72 (Fig 7.1). Fifteen are described as sandstone quarries; the remaining 26 are referred to only as quarries and were almost certainly used for the extraction of gritstone. As might be expected, these quarries are located in those parts of the Borough where the underlying solid geology outcrops, the greatest concentrations being on Harrop Edge in Mottram and Hartshead Pike to the north of Ashton.

Clay was used for making bricks and tiles. Only three groups of brick kilns are recorded in Tameside on the 1845-72 Ordnance Survey maps, two in Dukinfield and one in Ashton. However, a further ten brick fields are shown in the lowland townships of Ashton, Denton, Dukinfield and Hyde (Fig 7.1). The longest working tile and brick manufacturing site in the Borough was that of John Hall & Son (Dukinfield) Ltd, which opened in 1792 and finally closed in 1967 (Lamb 1968). The site lies on the eastern bank of the Peak Forest Canal (although it was founded two years before the construction of the canal was authorized by Parliament), from where its products were shipped to Hall's Manchester wharf on the Rochdale Canal near Great Ancoats Street. The company produced all types of fire-clay ware, from caps to mill chimneys, but the processes involved were largely carried out by hand. A steam engine was installed in the nineteenth century from which rope-drives ran the grinding mill, hoppers and mixers, whilst in the twentieth century machines such as a brick press, a pipe machine and a pugging machine were introduced. In its final form the site consisted of a variety of nineteenth-century buildings, including seven kilns, stables and moulding and drying sheds (Fig 7.2). A tramway connected the site with a clay pit to the east.

Among the earliest records of individuals involved in the building trade in Tameside are the Ashton parish registers. In the first decade of the eighteenth century 5.4% of the entries which name an individual's occupation relate to the building trade, these occupational descriptions being bricklayer, dauber, glazier, joiner, mason and plasterer (Brierley 1928).

Nationally a great upsurge in the trade occurred in the late eighteenth and early nineteenth centuries. In Tameside during this period the rise in building activity can be traced in the many new mills erected, in the construction of the new Georgian and Regency town at Ashton, and in the growth of the neighbouring small urban centres of Dukinfield, Hyde, Mottram and Stalybridge (see Chapters 3 and 9). Perhaps not surprisingly, those areas which saw the greatest activity also record the largest numbers of individuals engaged

Location	Bu	Jo	Pa	Pl	Plu	Gl	SM	BM	Su	Total
Ashton	2	4	11	2	6	1	1	1		28
Denton	1	1			1	1				4
Droylsden		1								1
Dukinfield	2	4	1		2	1		2		12
Gee Cross		1			1		1		1	4
Hollingworth					1	1				2
Hyde	2	5	2	2		1		2		14
Mossley		2	1	1		1	3			8
Mottram	1	4	2	2	1	1	1			12
Stalybridge	1	2	1	1	6	6	3	1		21

Table 7.1 The distribution of the building trade professions in Tameside in 1841.
Key: Bu – builder; Jo – joiner; Pa – painter; Pl – plasterer; Plu – plumber; Gl – glazier; SM – stone mason; BM – brick maker; Su – surveyor.
Source: Pigot & Co 1841.

in the trade; Pigot's directory of 1841, for example, lists 106 such individuals in the Borough, of whom 28 were located in Ashton, 21 in Stalybridge, fourteen in Hyde, and twelve in both Mottram and Dukinfield (Table 7.1).

The evidence of this directory suggests a local industry still dominated by individuals and small family concerns. However, the increasing demand in the region for large industrial buildings also led to the emergence of large integrated building firms, a major market being the textile industry. In the early nineteenth century the design and construction of a mill was spread between the millwrights, engineers and builders. By the mid-nineteenth century specialist firms, such as that run by David Bellhouse of Manchester, were designing and constructing mills in the region (Williams with Farnie 1992, 78-9). Bellhouse was also the designer of one of the most impressive industrial buildings in Tameside, the Ashton Canal Warehouse at Portland Basin in Ashton, built in 1834 (see Chapter 8).

In Tameside, as in other areas around Manchester, the booms and lulls in the mill-building industry appear to have been strongly echoed by the progress of house building (Lewis 1965, 87). From 1851 assessment of the building cycles within Tameside is facilitated by the increasing availability of registers of plans held by local authority surveyors. This evidence has been collated by Lewis to create an index of building cycles in the Borough, excluding only the urban district of Longdendale and covering the period 1851-1913. The earliest records began in Ashton in 1851, with the inclusion of Hyde from 1864, Stalybridge from 1868, Dukinfield from 1880, Denton from 1888, Droylsden from 1896, Audenshaw from 1897 and Mossley from 1899. This material indicates peaks in building activity during the early 1850s, the early 1860s, the mid- to late 1870s, the mid-1880s, the late 1890s and the mid-1900s (*ibid*, 301, 313-15).

7.4 The Retail Trade

The growth of the retail trade

The Industrial Revolution of the late eighteenth and early nineteenth centuries also engendered a commercial revolution, as new methods of distribution were required to provide foodstuffs and other goods for the growing populations of the new industrial communities. The result was a dramatic rise in the retail trade, which found expression in the rapid increase of fixed shops and the construction of new market places and halls.

The importance of fixed shops in the expanding industrial centres has been emphasized by recent studies of the retail trade in Manchester (Mui & Mui 1989; Scola 1992). Between 1783 and 1822-3 the number of shops in the town rose over six-fold from 156 to 951 (Mui & Mui 1989, 67-9). In Tameside this early growth may be paralleled in the growing urban centre of Ashton-under-Lyne. At least one Georgian shop front, no 120 Stamford Street, survives from the original planned town of the period 1787-1803, indicating that fixed shops were an integral part of the scheme (Plate 10.1). The important role of fixed shops in the commercial life of Ashton by the early nineteenth century is illustrated by directory entries of 1821-2 and 1825 which are dominated by shop-based trades (Pigot & Dean 1821-2; Baines 1825).

In Ashton the fixed shops operated alongside the old medieval market, and from the mid-nineteenth century new market halls and places were established in the major urban centres of the Borough. Ashton's new Market Hall and Place were established in 1830, Stalybridge Market Hall in 1831, Hyde Market Place by 1851 (the market hall was not built until 1927) and Denton Market Place in 1863 (Bowman 1960, 296-7; March 1957, 100; Middleton 1932, 150; Middleton 1936, 14).

Although the new nineteenth-century markets were restricted to the larger urban centres, the retail trade also extended to the smaller industrial communities in the form of fixed shops. Mottram township had a flourishing retail trade by the late eighteenth century, a phenomenon which is probably directly related to the growth of the town, from the 1780s onwards, as the centre of the local cotton industry (see Chapter 3).

Chapter 7 Secondary Industries

Village	1821-2	1841	1869	1902	1914	1934
Broadbottom	0	14	33	29	43	32
Hollingworth	2	34	56	38	54	53
Mottram	34	69	59	24	35	37
Total	36	117	148	91	132	122

Table 7.2 The distribution of shops in Longdendale by village, 1821/2-1934.
Sources: Pigot & Dean 1821-2, Pigot & Co 1841, Slater 1869, Kelly & Co 1902, Kelly & Co 1914, Kelly & Co 1934.

Tollemache estate surveys of the late eighteenth century record eight retail outlets in Mottram in 1785, this figure rising to eleven in 1799; specifically named retailers in these early surveys, however, are confined to public houses, of which three are mentioned in 1785 and four in 1799, and a butcher's shop, erected in 1796 (CRO DTW 2477/B/10). The rise of the retail trade in Mottram was noted by Aikin who commented that

'formerly there was not sufficient business in Mottram for one butcher...At present the town affords a tolerable livelihood for five' (Aikin 1795, 462).

A Grocer's Hall is mentioned in Mottram in the land tax returns but does not appear to have been a success, being attested only for the years 1799-1804 (CRO QDV2/299). The continuing rise of the fixed shop, however, is documented in trade directories of the first half of the nineteenth century, although as with other trades and industries it is likely that this evidence is incomplete. Of the 36 retail outlets listed in Longdendale in 1821-2, 34 lay in Mottram, the remaining two being in Hollingworth; by 1841 the number listed in Mottram had risen to 69 (Table 7.2).

The directories also chart the rise of two other retail centres in Longdendale, at Broadbottom, which lay within Mottram township, and at Hollingworth, both of which witnessed the growth of new industrial communities from the late eighteenth century onwards (see Chapter 9). Although initially the needs of these communities may have been largely served by Mottram, by the early 1840s both had evidently developed their own local retail trade. In 1841 fourteen outlets are listed in Broadbottom and 34 in Hollingworth, these figures rising to 33 and 56 respectively by 1869 (Table 7.2). Allowing for the unevenness between directories, after the last date the number of outlets within both communities appears to have remained fairly static through to the 1930s. In Mottram itself, however, the number sharply decreased, seemingly reflecting a demographic and industrial decline in the late nineteenth and early twentieth centuries.

Directories serve as a guide not only to the comparative development of local retail trades but also provide an indication of the relative numbers of shop types. In Longdendale, for example, outlets selling consumable household goods, principally food and drink, remained dominant throughout the period 1821/2-1934, accounting for 61-78% of the total number, followed by retailers of clothing, at 12-25%, and of hardware and other durable items, at 3-9%. The directories also indicate the growing diversity of specialist shops, largely selling new leisure goods, during the first decades of the twentieth century (Table 7.3).

Co-operatives

One of the most significant developments in the retail business of Tameside from the mid-nineteenth century onwards was the growth of the co-operative movement. Co-operatives were set up by low-paid workers to sell, and in some cases also to manufacture, better quality goods, at cheaper prices, than those being offered by local shopkeepers and mill-owners. Goods were produced and distributed on a non-profit-making basis, any surplus monies being distributed as a dividend among the members of the co-operative. Members were also encouraged to save by leaving their dividend in the business as shares on which interest would be paid.

The traditional date for the beginning of the movement is 1844 when the Rochdale Pioneers opened their first shop, the success of which led other workers to follow their example. However, the origins of the co-operatives lay in the previous decade and the Owenite movement inspired by the mill-owner Robert Owen. In Tameside a number of short-lived co-operatives were begun in the 1830s and included stores in Mossley in 1830 and Ashton in 1838 (Bowman 1960, 489). The most successful of these early ventures was the Flowery Field Co-operative Society, which ran from 1832 until 1849 (Middleton 1932, 199). However, it was not until the late 1850s and early 1860s, a period of rapid expansion for the co-operative movement nationally, that co-operatives were firmly established in Tameside.

The largest of the new co-operatives were those of Ashton, Hyde and Stalybridge. The earliest of these to be formed was Ashton-under-Lyne Working Men's Co-operative Society Ltd, in 1857. The original shop was in Mill Lane but in 1870 central premises were established in Portland Street (Bowman 1960, 489-90). As a result, the membership grew from 94 in 1861 to 4606 in 1906, while profits rose from £254 3s to £24,463 11s in the same period. In the late nineteenth century the society was able to provide charitable

Group	1821-2	1841	1869	1902	1914	1934
Group I Clothing						
Clothes brokers			1			
Drapers	1	1	10	6	7	5
Hatters & tailors	2	9	6	3	1	1
Milliners & dress makers		2	6	1	6	4
Shoe, clog & boot makers/repairers	2	11	14	7	8	5
% for year	13.9	19.7	24.7	18.7	16.7	12.3
Number of shops	5	23	37	17	22	15
Group II Consumable household goods						
A Food:						
Bakers						1
Butchers	2	6	6	5	10	8
Cheesemongers, confectioners & fruiterers			1	4	17	13
Corn & flour dealers	6	1				
Fried fish dealers & fishmongers				1	6	6
Grocers & tea dealers	8	6	14	16	16	14
B Drinks:						
Beer retailers		15	16	5	5	2
Public houses, inns & victuallers	10	19	19	18	15	13
C Sundries:						
Chemists & druggists	1	4	5	1	2	1
Co-operatives			3	3	3	3
Tallow chandlers	1	2				
Shopkeepers		35	28	10	16	27
% for year	77.8	75.2	61.3	69.2	68.2	72.1
Number of shops	28	88	92	63	90	88
Group III Household goods & hardware						
Cabinet & chairmakers	1	1	3			
Coopers	1			1		
Fellmongers			1	1	1	2
Furniture brokers				4		
Ironmongery & hardware	1	1	3	2	5	2
Picture frame makers					1	
Seedsmen		1	2			
Upholsterers						1
Watch makers		1	1	1	1	
% for year	8.3	3.4	9.3	5.5	6.1	4.1
Number of shops	3	4	14	5	8	5
Group IV Specialist services						
Booksellers, newsagents & stationers		1	7	3	5	3
Cycle repairers/garages					1	4
Hairdressers		1		1	3	4
Music sellers				1	1	
Photographers					1	1
Tobacconists				1	1	1
Wireless dealers						1
% for year	0	1.7	4.7	6.6	9.1	11.5
Number of shops	0	2	7	6	12	14
Total number of shops in survey	36	117	150	91	132	122

Table 7.3 Shop trades in Longdendale, 1821/2-1934. Sources: see Table 7.2.

help, to make educational grants and even to publish its own newspaper (TLSL DD 271, DD 174/5, DD 73/4; Thompson 1907, Appendix). The Stalybridge Good Intent Co-operative Society Ltd was founded in 1859, the first week's takings amounting to £84. By the early twentieth century it had over 3500 members and twenty branches (Hill 1907, 197; TLSL DD 250). Hyde Co-operative Society was founded in 1862 when the society bought the Market Street, Hyde branch of the Dukinfield Co-operative Society for £1000. By 1887 there were ten branches in the Hyde area, and by 1930 the society had 5341 members and sales of over £200,000. The society also provided reading rooms, scholarships and educational courses (Middleton 1932, 199; TLSL DD 250).

Of the co-operatives outside the three major urban centres, the Mossley Industrial Co-operative Society was founded in 1856, a year before the Ashton society. By 1935 it had a membership of 3734, ten branches, an educational department and a library (Mossley MB 1935, 59; TLSL DD 246). The Dukinfield Co-operative Society was founded in 1858, and the Denton and Haughton Equitable Co-operative Society in 1867; this originally sold only groceries and provisions but by 1887 had expanded into clothing and footwear (Marsh 1985, 79-80). A co-operative shop was established in Droylsden in 1859 as a branch of the Dukinfield co-operative. In 1861 it became a separate organization, the Droylsden Industrial Co-operative Society Ltd, with a membership of 71 and a capital of £140 4s 1d. The first year's profits were £120 5s 3½d. By 1875 membership had risen to 1101 and profits to £4162 7s 11d. At this time Droylsden was little more than a large village. Indeed as late as 1876 it was stated that Droylsden 'was not a Market town, it was a country township' (Speake & Witty 1953, 168-9; TLSL DD 153/1).

Other co-operatives established in the 1860s included, in the Ashton area, the Higher Hurst Co-operative Society, the Hurst Brook Co-operative Society and the Waterloo Co-operative Society (TLSL DD 268-70). In the same decade two co-operatives were founded in Longdendale. The Hollingworth Industrial Co-operative Society had two branches, one in Hollingworth, the other in Mottram. The Broadbottom Industrial Co-operative Society Ltd had a single shop (Slater 1869; J Powell 1977, 23).

Joseph Booth's grocer's shop, Broadbottom

A valuable insight into the development of the retail trade in mid-nineteenth-century Tameside is provided by Joseph Booth's grocer's-cum-general store at nos 43-43a Market Street in Broadbottom. Not only does the building still stand but the documentary evidence

Chapter 7 Secondary Industries

Name	Type of Supplier	Address
Benjamin Andrew	paint supplier	not given
G H Bancroft	wholesale grocers and importers of Irish butter	Stamford St, Ashton-under-Lyne
Buckley & Newton	millers, corn merchants and cheese factors	Stalybridge Corn Mills
John Clayton & Co	lime	Marple Lime Works, Marple
James Cook	silk merchant, linen and woollen draper	Rassbottom St, Stalybridge
John Cooper	men's shoes	Apethorn, Hyde
Josuah Cooper	boot maker	Friendship Arms, Hollingworth
Mary Cooper & Son	tallow chandlers	Mottram
Samuel Dean	not given	Stockport
James Downs	wholesale cheese factor	Market Place, Stockport
Matthew Gibbons	brush and shoe manufacturer	70 Shudehill, Manchester
William Gibson	dealer in china, glass and earthenware	Rassbotton St, Stalybridge
James Heginbotham	wholesale and retail grocer, tea and coffee merchants	16 Market Place, Stockport
R Holliday & Co	manufacturers of washing powder, etc	Bradford
Henry Ollerenshaw	brush manufacturer	27 Thomas St, Manchester
John & Henry Rolling	corn millers	Oxspring Mills, near Barnsley
James Sheppard	corn, flour and cheese factor, importer of Irish butter, etc	Park Street, Stockport
James Sidebottom & Co	tea importers and coffee merchants	21 St Mary's Gate, Manchester
James Smith	wholesale grocer and tea dealer	3 Market Place, Stockport
Wall, Buxton & Co	soap dealers	30 Shudehill, Manchester
William Webb	linen and woollen draper	Market Place, Stockport
R & J Whitworth	wholesale grocers, tea dealers and importers of Irish butter	26 Withy Grove, Manchester
D Woolley	dispensing family chemist	6 Millgate, Stockport

Table 7.4 Some suppliers of Joseph Booth's shop in 1849.
Source: Powell Collection. The details are taken, where possible, from the bill or receipt heading.

for the business includes the rare survival of a series of receipts and bills which were found in the attic of the shop during restoration work, still impaled on a bill hook.

Joseph Booth was born in Charlesworth in 1810, and married another native of that township, Sarah. Their first two children, Robert (b 1836) and Thurstan (b 1837), were born in Charlesworth but their last three children, Eliza (b 1838-9), Mary Jane (b 1846) and Joseph (b 1849-50), were born in Mottram township, suggesting that Joseph and his family moved to Mottram in the period 1837-9. The 1841 census records a Joseph Booth as living on Market Street and gives his occupation as a cotton worker. However, a directory of 1841 lists a Joseph Booth, shopkeeper, of Mottram, suggesting that he either began his business in this year or ran a shop as a second occupation (Pigot & Co 1841, 87). Joseph's new business quickly prospered. The Mottram sale catalogue of 1841 indicates that nos 43-43a Market Street had not yet been built, but by the time the map for the tithe award was drawn in 1847 the shop had been erected and was rented by Joseph Booth (CRO EDT 281; Powell Collection).

The 1851 census indicates that Joseph's business was sufficiently successful to enable him to employ a house servant, Jane Senior. The business continued to flourish during the 1850s and in 1858 the Mottram rate book shows that Joseph Booth had bought the land on which his shop stood and that he was also renting nineteen acres of land from John Bostock. The shop was estimated to be worth £21 9s a year and the land £60 per year. The house next door to the shop, no 45 Market Street, had also been built by Joseph by 1858, when it was occupied by William Beaumont and John Ridings (Powell Collection).

On the eve of the cotton famine in 1861 Joseph's fortunes had risen still further. The census of that year describes him as a grocer and farmer of eighteen acres, employing two men, a shop assistant and a carter. His son, Robert Booth, now occupied part of the house next door, which had been converted into a butcher's shop. John Ridings, described as a stone quarryman, still inhabited the rest of the house. It seems likely that the eighteen acres of land rented by Joseph were used to supply the butcher's shop.

The surviving receipts and bills from Booth's

Plate 7.2 Joseph Booth's grocer's shop and Robert Booth's butcher's shop, Broadbottom
Joseph Booth's shop (left), now converted into two cottages, was built in 1841-7 as part of the growing retail trade in the flourishing textile village of Broadbottom. In the 1850s Booth built the adjoining property (right) to lease to tenants. In about 1860 half of this building was converted into a butcher's shop, run by his son Robert, the large shop window to the left of the doorway being a surviving feature of that conversion.

grocer's shop number 217 and cover the years 1846-79 (Powell Collection). Nearly a third of the receipts and bills, 66, date to the year 1849 and list no less than 23 suppliers (Table 7.4). Of these seven are located within modern Tameside: one each in Ashton, Apethorn in Hyde, Hollingworth and Mottram, and three in Stalybridge. A further seven suppliers are from Stockport, five are from Manchester, one is from Marple and one each from Barnsley and Bradford. The use of suppliers in the two Yorkshire towns may indicate the impact which the burgeoning rail network was having on the retail distribution system. The Sheffield, Ashton-under-Lyne & Manchester Railway, with a station at Broadbottom, opened in December 1845, while the Lancashire & Yorkshire Railway's line from Leeds to Manchester via Stalybridge was completed in August 1849 (see Chapter 8).

Joseph Booth's shop on Market Street still stands, although much altered and divided into two properties, nos 43-43a (Plate 7.2). It appears to have been a purpose-built shop, which from the evidence described above was built in the period 1841-7. The building is a two-storey stone-built structure of four by two bays, with a loading bay at its western end and a stone slate roof with two ridge chimneys. Immediately east of the shop is the building erected by Joseph Booth in the period 1851-8. This was originally a double-fronted house, with a central stone-arched doorway, flanked by rectangular windows with stone lintels and sills. The building is stone-built with two storeys, two by two bays, and two ridge chimneys. By 1861, according to the census of that year, part of the building had been converted into a butcher's shop, for use by Joseph's son Robert (see above). Corresponding with that division, an additional doorway, now infilled, was inserted in the facade, along with a shop window.

Chapter 8

The Infrastructure

'The intermediate districts including Glossop, Hyde, Mottram, Newton, Dukinfield, Ashton Under Lyne and Staley-Bridge will be, by this railway, so united to Manchester, as to derive all the advantages for conducting the trade of that extensive and important place and at the same time retain those peculiar to their several localities'

Prospectus of the Sheffield, Ashton-under-Lyne & Manchester Railway, May 1836
(Bairstow 1990, 16)

8.1 Introduction

The infrastructure of Tameside in the period 1700-1930 was composed of two main elements, the first being concerned with transport (the roads, canals and railways), the second with the delivery of services (water, gas and electricity). The two differ both in the broad nature of the industries concerned and in the degree to which public as well as private investment was involved.

The turnpike roads in the Borough, built between the 1730s and 1830s, the canals built in the 1790s and 1800s, and the railways, built between the 1830s and 1880s, were all the result of private speculation, responding to the needs of the expanding regional and local economy and encouraging further growth. All of these industries were first established in the Borough through initial bursts of rapid expansion, followed by periods of steadier growth which saw the completion or infilling of the skeletal systems established in the first wave of enthusiasm.

Direct involvement by local government in the transport infrastructure of Tameside was initially restricted to the maintenance of public highways, although between the 1830s and 1880s these responsibilities increased considerably as control of the turnpikes passed from private trusts to local authority boards. From the 1890s the municipal authorities also began to take over the running of passenger transport systems from private companies, running firstly horse-driven trams and later, from the early 1900s, new electric tramways.

Of the service industries, the provision of water and gas supplies to the growing towns of the Borough in the early nineteenth century was largely spearheaded by private investment. However, from the mid-nineteenth century local authorities established their own waterworks undertakings, while in the late nineteenth century some local authorities took over private gas companies. Public electricity supplies were established in Tameside at the turn of the twentieth century in association with the electric tramways. By this date the principle of municipal service industries was so well established that almost from the outset local authorities and private investment shared this new market.

8.2 Transport I: Turnpikes

Until the late seventeenth century the maintenance of roads and highways was the sole responsibility of the local parish or borough, and as the volume of traffic increased so did the financial burden on parishioners or burghers. To alleviate this problem turnpike acts were introduced before Parliament, designed to improve the quality of roadways by defining a stretch of road under the jurisdiction of a trust. The trust was responsible for maintaining a roadway in good repair, and in return was allowed to levy a toll from the highway's users, using a system of toll houses and gates.

The first act for turnpiking was passed in 1663 and related to a section of the Great North Road in Cambridgeshire but it was not until after 1706 that trusts became popular (Armstrong 1989, 97-9; Pawson 1977, 341). Between 1706 and 1750 over 400 turnpike acts were passed by Parliament, mainly affecting the major routes. The rate of expansion rapidly increased during the turnpike fever of 1750-90, which saw more than 1600 new acts; by 1790 approximately 24,000 kilometres, or 15,000 miles, of roads had been brought

Plate 8.1 Portland Basin, Ashton-under-Lyne. The basin was constructed in the 1790s where the Ashton and Peak Forest canals meet on the northern side of the River Tame and was originally known as Ashton New Wharf. During the mill-building boom of the 1820s it became the focus for a string of new steam-powered cotton-spinning mills.

into the system, at an average of about twelve kilometres, or seven and a half miles, per trust. Between 1790 and 1830 the progress of road improvement decelerated, so that although 2450 turnpike acts were passed in this period these related to only 8000 kilometres, or 5000 miles, of new turnpike roads (Cootes 1982, 88; Armstrong 1989, 99-101). In the 1830s and 1840s competition from the railways virtually ended long-distance road haulage and coach traffic. The decline of the turnpike system was further hastened by the Highways Act of 1835. This enabled local authorities to take over turnpike trusts in their area by allowing the levying of a highway rate, and neighbouring parishes to unite to form highway district authorities which could employ labour to maintain the roads in good repair. As a result of these developments the number of turnpike trusts fell steadily in the mid-nineteenth century as control of the highways became increasingly concentrated in the hands of local authority boards. The end came in 1888 when responsibility for highway maintenance was passed wholly to local authorities and turnpike trusts were abolished, although by that date very few were still functioning.

This national picture is largely reflected in the development of turnpikes in Tameside (Fig 8.1). The earliest, and most important, turnpike trust in the Borough dates from the initial, early eighteenth-century period of growth. This was the Manchester to Salters Brook turnpike, an act 'for repairing, widening, and amending the road leading from Manchester

Chapter 8 The Infrastructure

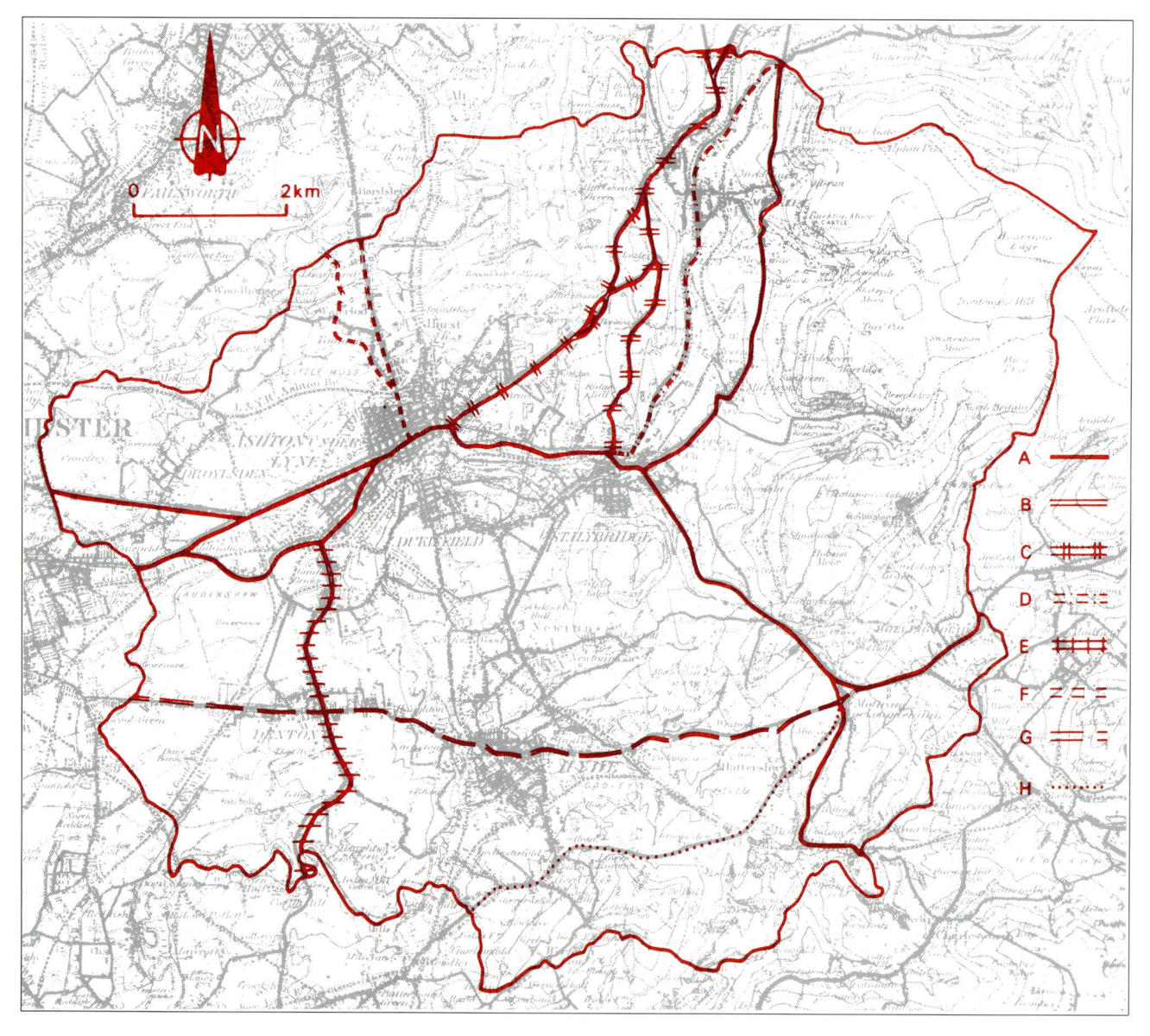

Fig 8.1 The turnpikes of Tameside.
Key: A – Manchester to Salters Brook, 1732; B – Ashton to Standedge, 1793; C – Ashton to Doctor Lane Head, 1765; D – Ridgehill to Holehouse, 1825; E – Stockport to Audenshaw, 1765; F – Ashton to Oldham, 1799; G – Manchester, Hyde and Mottram, 1818-32; H – Bredbury to Mottram, 1765.

in the County Palatine of Lancaster to Salters Brook in the County of Chester' being passed by Parliament in 1732 (Pawson 1977, 344). In Tameside the trust ran through Fairfield, Audenshaw, Guide Bridge, Ashton, Stalybridge and Mottram, and from there along the Longdendale valley to Woodhead. Initially there were two turnpike gates along the road in Tameside for the collection of tolls. One lay in Audenshaw, although its exact location is not known; in 1756 this was replaced by a toll house near Deanhead Farm in Audenshaw. The other was located at Three Lane Ends in Mottram. In the late eighteenth century the tolls charged by the Salters Brook trust were 2s for four-wheeled wagons, 1s 6d for a coach and four horses and 1d for a single unladen horse. Pedestrians and horses carrying the mail were allowed free passage (TLSL TTM 1).

The trust carried through various improvements, including the cutting of new alignments. The most impressive of these in Tameside, indeed along the whole route, was the deep cutting on the road from Stalybridge to Mottram, designed to avoid the steep climb over Harrop Edge. The enabling act for this was passed in 1799 but work was not finished until 1826. The debris from the excavation was used to form the embankment on which the road was continued to Three Lane Ends. Here another new cut was made, Backmoor, bypassing Mottram moor and causing the junction to be renamed Four Lane Ends.

Proposals put forward in 1825 suggested further improvements to the line, including a section of new road cutting across the southern portion of Ashton Moss, now Manchester Road (TLSL An Act for the diversion of the Manchester to Salters Brook Turnpike Trust, 1825). A branch route to Broadbottom was also approved in that year. The increase in heavy traffic to the mills at Broadbottom, and the growth of a substantial population there, meant that the precipitous road to the Salters Brook turnpike via Gorsey Brow was inadequate and dangerous. The old road from Broadbottom as far as Hillend Lane followed a tortuous path which was recut into the smooth curve followed by the modern Mottram Road. From Hillend Lane to Mottram a completely new road was cut across the fields, the modern Broadbottom Road, and a toll house was erected at the junction with Hillend Lane. Some of the expenses involved are recorded in the Mottram church wardens' accounts (CRO P25).

The Salters Brook turnpike was not only the first turnpike to be opened in Tameside but also the last to be closed, in 1884 (TLSL TTM 964). In its final year the income from tolls amounted to £4640; a traffic count records that in 24 hours 448 vehicles passed through the toll gate in Audenshaw (TLSL TTM 965).

The turnpike fever of 1750-90 saw no fewer than three new turnpikes in the Borough being authorized in a single year, 1765. The first of these was the turnpike from Ashton, through Mossley to Doctor Lane Head in Saddleworth (for which two toll houses still stand, one on Wakefield Road in Stalybridge, the other on Manchester Road in Mossley). The second was the turnpike from Saxon's Lane End in Audenshaw to Stockport. These first two new routes were built by the renowned road maker John Metcalfe of Knaresborough. The third of these turnpikes was established along the existing route from Bredbury to Mottram (Wilkins-Jones 1978, 12).

In the late eighteenth and early nineteenth centuries new and existing roads continued to be turnpiked in Tameside, no doubt spurred by the rapid economic growth of the Borough. In 1793 a turnpike was authorized for the route from Ashton, via Stayley township, to Standedge in Saddleworth, while in 1799 a turnpike was authorized from Ashton to Oldham, later being extended to Huddersfield, via Rochdale and Blackstone Edge (Hyde 1980, 5). A scheme was presented to Parliament for a new road from Manchester to Mottram, via Hyde, in 1818. Although the route from Manchester to Hyde, now Hyde Road, was quickly built, it was not until 1832 that the Hyde to Mottram section was begun (Middleton 1936, 13). This later section was a new road cutting across farmland in Godley, Matley and Hattersley, now known as Mottram Road. The act was repealed in 1877 (TLSL TTM 1188/2). In 1825 a turnpike was proposed for a route from Ridgehill, in Ashton, via Heyrod and Mossley, to Holehouse in Saddleworth (CRO QDP 67 1/2). The extension of the Manchester and Hyde turnpike to Mottram in 1832 was the last new project in the Borough. After this date competition from the railways, and the growth of local authority boards in the Borough, eroded the commercial base of the trusts.

A glimpse of the services made possible by the trusts in Tameside immediately prior to the arrival of the railways, and the consequent decline of the turnpikes, is given by Pigot's directory of 1841. From Ashton there were hourly coaches, and three daily through coaches, to Manchester, two daily coaches to Glossop, three daily coaches to Sheffield and a daily coach to Stalybridge. In addition there were sixteen carriers offering daily services for the transport of goods to Barnsley, Glossop, Holmfirth, Manchester, Mossley, Mottram, Oldham, Sheffield, Stalybridge, Stockport, Tintwistle and Uppermill. The only competition which these carriers had to face was the daily long-distance canal services from Ashton Old Wharf to Manchester, Huddersfield, Wakefield and London (Pigot & Co 1841, 11).

8.3 Transport II: Canals

National background

In the early eighteenth century water transport, by both river and sea, was cheaper and quicker than using the unreliable road system. Even with the rise of the turnpike trusts in the mid-eighteenth century the transportation of bulk loads was still slow and expensive by land (Armstrong 1989, 96; Cootes 1982, 93). An answer to these problems was provided by the development of an artificial inland water system.

The canal-building boom of the late eighteenth century grew from the knowledge acquired by new river navigations in the early part of the century (Hadfield & Biddle 1970, 15-16). The catalyst which showed the value of the canal as a means of cheap, reliable transport for bulk goods was the construction of the Bridgewater Canal, built by the duke of Bridgewater in the years 1759-66, initially to carry coal from his collieries in Worsley to Manchester (*ibid*, 19-27). This canal proved to be the first stage in an extensive network of inland waterways in the Midlands and northern England. The mania for canal building reached a peak in the years 1791-6, during which period many new, successful canals were established and other, unrealistic projects were begun and quickly abandoned (Cootes 1982, 95).

By 1830 the country had 6500 kilometres, or 4000 miles, of navigable waterways, which with the developed turnpike road system provided Britain with an extensive and reliable transport system (*ibid*, 96-7).

Chapter 8 The Infrastructure

Barges which could carry between 30 and 100 tonnes at a time allowed the raw materials of the Industrial Revolution, coal, iron and cotton, to be transported cheaply and regularly to the industrial heartlands and, conversely, the finished products of these industries to be distributed to their markets (Armstrong 1989, 96). The reason why the golden age of the canals came to such an abrupt end in the 1840s was the onset of the railways and the greater speed, reliability and flexibility of this new transport network. Although most canals continued to function, the canal companies were quickly absorbed by the new railway companies and the slow decline of the system began.

The building of the canal system in Tameside

During the boom in canal building in the 1790s three narrow-boat canals were constructed in Tameside (Fig 8.2). Since all three shared many of the same shareholders and committeemen and even used the same Altrincham-based solicitors, the Worthingtons, these canals can be seen as creating one system. Although the 'establishing and carrying on a thoroughfare Trade from Hull to Manchester' encouraged co-operation between the three canal companies, the immediate aim of the projects was to capture local and regional trade. As part of this aim Ashton formed a key focus for the three schemes, being an important coal-mining centre in this part of the Lancashire coalfield. The act for the Manchester, Ashton-under-Lyne and Oldham Canal (the Ashton Canal) gave mine-owners powers to build canal branches up to four miles long, and indeed the Fairbottom branch to the Fairbottom Colliery, a length of 1.8 kilometres, or 1⅛ miles, was built using these powers (Hadfield & Biddle 1970, 296-8).

Two major studies have dealt in depth with the history of these canals, Hadfield and Biddle's survey of the canals of the North-West (1970) and Keaveney and Brown's history of the Ashton Canal (1974). Company minutes for all three canals are held on microfilm at the Tameside Local Studies Library.

The Ashton Canal was the first to be built, construction taking place in the years 1792-7. The primary course was from Piccadilly in Manchester to near Dukinfield Bridge in Ashton, with a branch heading northwards to New Mill near Oldham (Hadfield & Biddle 1970, 294; Paget-Tomlinson 1993, 98-9). Opening in late 1796, the Manchester to Ashton section cost approximately £170,000 (Hadfield & Biddle 1970, 464-5). The Stockport, Hollinwood and Fairbottom branches opened the following year. However, the Beat Bank section, which was due to link the Denton collieries to the Stockport branch, was abandoned in 1798. The cost of the project was escalating and the need to gain income from the transportation of coal from Denton may have been removed by the opening of the Hollinwood and Fairbottom branches, which gave the company access to the Werneth coal pits in Oldham and the Fairbottom pits in Ashton (*ibid*, 295-6). There is also evidence to suggest that some of the Ashton Canal shareholders, who also had a share in the Werneth mines, were reluctant to see the scheme succeed (see Chapter 6).

By 1825 40 carriers were using the Ashton Canal. Peak annual tonnage was reached in 1838 when 522,469 tonnes were carried, bringing in an income of £17,363 and a dividend of 7% (Hadfield & Biddle 1970, 305).

The Peak Forest Canal, constructed in the years 1794-1805, with a northern terminus with the Ashton Canal at Portland Basin in Ashton, gave access to the limestone quarries of the Peak District (Paget-Tomlinson 1993, 178-9). Originally planned as a branch of the Ashton Canal in 1793, the canal was separately funded in the 1794 act, probably due to the heavy financial commitments of the Ashton Canal shareholders, the total cost being £177,000 (Hadfield & Biddle 1970, 306, 312). The line chosen was from the Ashton Canal's Dukinfield aqueduct, through Hyde and Marple to Chapel Milton, and from there by railroad to the limestone quarries near Doveholes. It rose 63 metres, or 209 feet, via sixteen locks, from Portland Basin to Marple. Not only was the canal designed to carry limestone but its line also exploited the coal traffic in Dukinfield and Hyde (*ibid*, 306-7).

The last canal to be opened in Tameside was the Huddersfield Canal (Paget-Tomlinson 1993, 146-7). The canal was constructed in the years 1794-1811 with the intention of capturing trans-Pennine trade from Hull to Manchester, in particular the traffic of coal, corn, lime and limestone, but in the early years the biggest annual tonnage was represented by general 'merchandise' (Hadfield & Biddle 1970, 331). The route chosen ran from the eastern end of the Ashton Canal up the Tame valley and across the Pennines to Sir John Ramsden's broad canal at Cooper Bridge near Huddersfield (*ibid*, 322). The nearly 32 kilometre, or twenty mile, length of the canal was intended to rise 103 metres, or 338 feet, above its Ashton start, culminating in the Standedge tunnel, originally five kilometres, or three miles and 198 yards, long (*ibid*, 323). The Ashton to Stalybridge section opened in November 1796, and the section from Stalybridge to Uppermill in August 1797. The cost in 1793 had been estimated at £178,748, with five years needed to cut the Standedge tunnel. In the event the tunnel took seventeen years to build and the final cost of the project was just over £400,000. Furthermore the rival Rochdale Canal, which furnished a Pennine route 24 kilometres, or fifteen miles, shorter, had been built and

Chapter 8 The Infrastructure

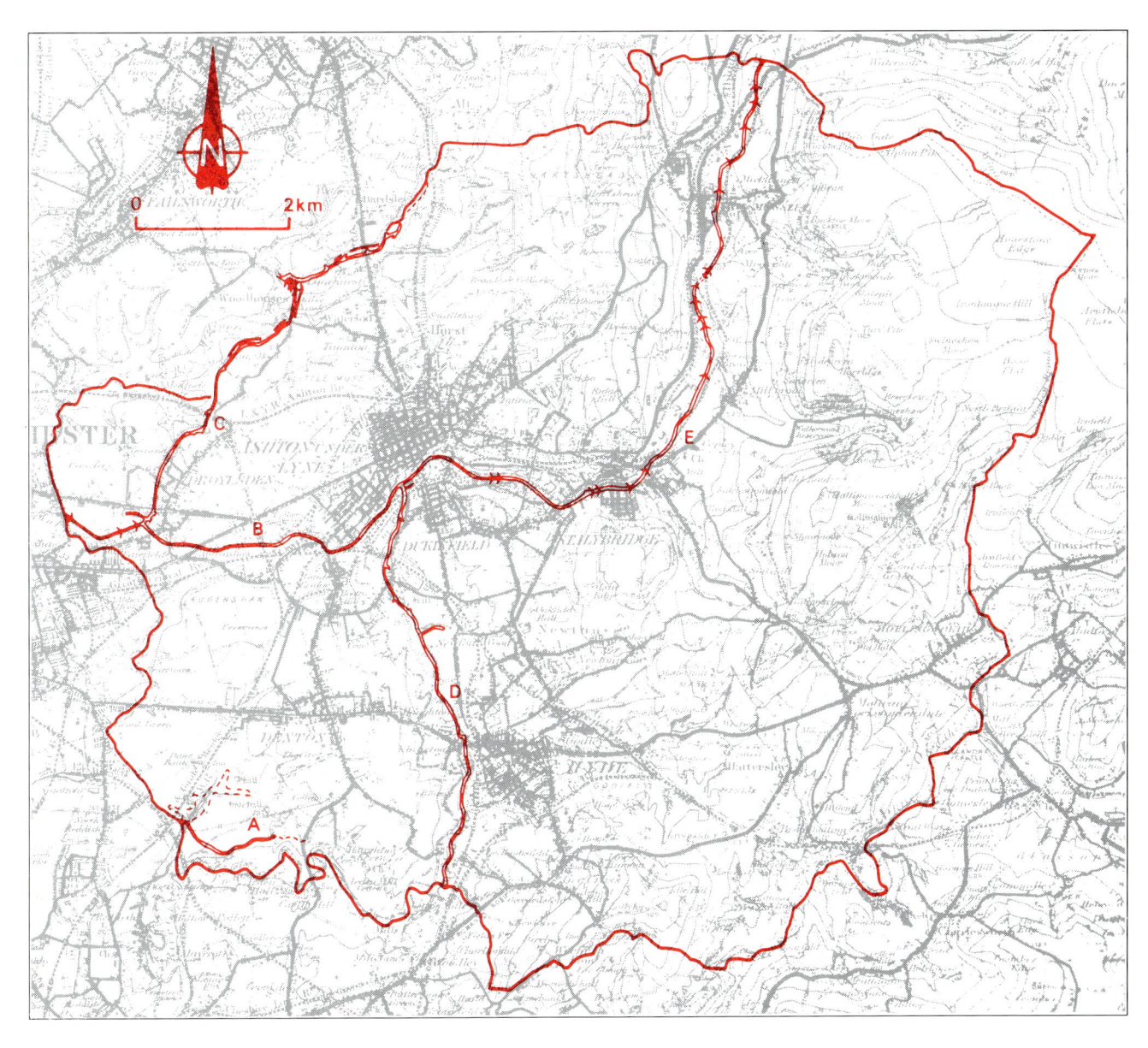

Fig 8.2 The canals of Tameside.
Key: A – the unfinished Beat Bank section of the Ashton Canal, abandoned in 1798; B – the Ashton Canal, built in 1792-7; C – the Fairbottom branch of the Ashton Canal, built in 1797; D – the Peak Forest Canal, built in 1794-1805; E – the Huddersfield Canal, built in 1794-1811; – – – intended reservoir for the Beat Bank branch of the Ashton Canal.

opened over six years previously (*ibid*, 328-9). The long-term result was a price war with the Rochdale Canal and continuing financial problems for the Huddersfield.

The Tameside canals and railway competition

By the 1830s all three Tameside canals were enjoying a period of sustained prosperity with rising traffic tonnage as well as annual dividends being paid to shareholders. However, the success of the Liverpool to Manchester railway, which opened in 1830 and was making substantial profits by 1831, marked the beginning of the end of the canal-building age, although serious competition was not to take place in the North-West until the railway boom of the 1840s. The danger which railways might pose to the canals was nevertheless recognized at an early date. In 1825 the Huddersfield Canal Company threatened the Ashton Canal Company with the promotion of 'a new communication by Rail Road or otherwise from the Huddersfield Canal to Manchester', if the Ashton Canal was not converted to double locks so as to ease traffic congestion (Hadfield & Biddle 1970, 302).

The trans-Pennine railways which opened in the 1840s, from Manchester to Leeds via Standedge and from Manchester to Sheffield via Woodhead, marked the end of commercial independence for the Tameside canals and the beginning of a protracted period of decline. The canals could not compete with the speed

Chapter 8 The Infrastructure

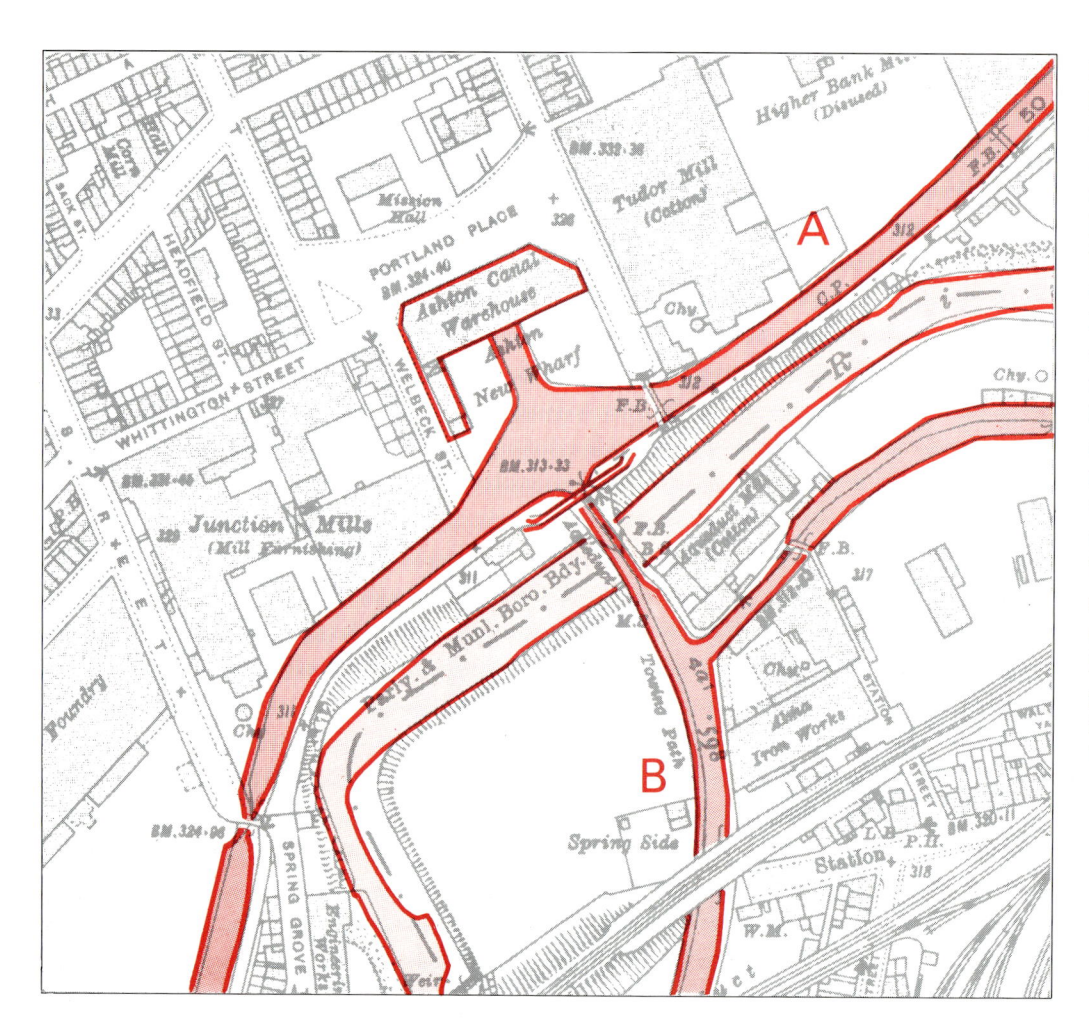

Fig 8.3 Portland Basin, Ashton-under-Lyne. *Key:* A – Ashton Canal; B – Peak Forest Canal. This was the junction of the Ashton and Peak Forest canals, opened in 1797; traffic from and to the Huddersfield Canal also had to pass through the basin. It was thus the hub of the canal trade in Tameside during the early nineteenth century with coal, limestone and cotton goods passing through Ashton New Wharf.

of railway transport nor with the flexibility of the network, handicapped as they were by the lack of a central booking scheme. As profits and tonnage fell, the canals were bought by the railway companies.

The first canal in Tameside to be bought by a railway company was the least successful. This was the Huddersfield Canal which was sold in 1844 to the Huddersfield & Manchester Railway, henceforward the Huddersfield & Manchester Railway & Canal Company. The canal was leased to the London & North Western Railway in 1847 (*ibid*, 335). Within a few years of the sale of the Huddersfield Canal, in 1846 and 1848, the Peak Forest Canal and the Ashton Canal were both sold to the Sheffield, Ashton-under-Lyne & Manchester Railway (*ibid*, 305, 315).

All three canals continued in service. Traffic along the Huddersfield Canal remained between 150,000 and 200,000 tonnes per year until the end of the century. Although regular through traffic ceased around 1905, the lowland western and eastern ends of the canal continued to be actively used until the First World War and were only abandoned by the London Midland & Scottish Railway in 1944 (*ibid*, 445-7). Likewise traffic tonnage on the Ashton Canal, though less than half that in 1838, was still around 240,000 tonnes per year in 1905, the most important goods carried being coal at over 103,000 tonnes that year (*ibid*, 442). Furthermore pleasure traffic was encouraged on this and the Peak Forest Canal in the early twentieth century (Owen 1977, 76). However, the rapid growth of road haulage in the 1920s, coupled with colliery subsidence along the branches in Hollinwood and Fairbottom, destroyed commercial traffic on the Ashton Canal (Paget-Tomlinson 1993, 98-9). The Peak Forest Canal was at first the most successful of the canals under railway ownership, the limestone business of the Doveholes quarries remaining profitable until the end of the nineteenth century. As the quarries declined so did the fortunes of the canal. The railway company gave up its own fleet of boats on the canal in 1892, and freight per year fell from around 384,000 tonnes in 1858 to 138,000 in 1905. The last loads of limestone were carried in 1925 (Hadfield & Biddle 1970, 444-5; Owen 1977, 75-6; Paget-Tomlinson 1993, 178-9).

The surviving canal fabric

Most of the canals in Tameside still survive as navigable watercourses, having been restored from the

Chapter 8 The Infrastructure

1960s onwards (Owen 1977, 80). They include eighteen locks on the main section of the Ashton Canal, and although the Hollinwood and Fairbottom branches are no longer navigable much can still be seen. The whole of the Peak Forest Canal can still be traversed, as can most of the Huddersfield Canal except for a short section in Stalybridge town centre. Much of the related infrastructure of the canals, barges, warehouses and wharfs, however, has been lost but a notable exception is Portland Basin, the heart of the canal system in Tameside (Fig 8.3; Plate 8.1). Here Ashton New Wharf (SJ 934 985) marks the junction of the Ashton and Peak Forest canals, opened in 1797. A fine single-arch towpath bridge of 1835 spans the Peak Forest Canal, which is carried over the River Tame by a three-arch sandstone aqueduct, designed and built by Benjamin Outram and Thomas Brown. To the east of the junction, across the Ashton Canal, a steel footbridge, dating from the 1950s, has replaced an original timber footbridge built by Isaac Watt Boulton in 1843.

The most impressive remains are those of the Ashton Canal Warehouse, built in 1834 (Fig 8.4). This stands on the northern side of the wharf in Portland Place, and was originally a three-storey building with a fine southern stone facade fronting the canal wharf, and with timber floors supported by cast-iron columns. Unfortunately much of this structure was destroyed by fire in 1972, so that only the first and second storeys remain, although the eastern half has been converted into a museum. The original building was constructed by David Bellhouse for the Ashton Canal Company at a cost of £8901 13s 3d, as their third warehouse, two others being designed and built by David's father at the Manchester terminus of the Ashton Canal in 1798 and at the Heaton Norris terminus in 1799. The main southern facade has three arched shipping-holes flanked on either side by two large cart openings allowing the transhipment of goods. The cranes used for unloading these goods were originally operated by hand, but during the years 1839-41 a 0.9m (3 feet) wide, 7.5m (25 feet) diameter, water-wheel was installed at a cost of £1078 0s 6½d. Situated at the eastern end of the warehouse, it was fed from the Ashton Canal and the northern exit of the leat debauched into the River Tame (Owen 1977, 84-5).

Another site which combines a number of elements of canal fabric is Fairfield Locks, a pair of double locks on the Ashton Canal immediately west of the junction with the Hollinwood branch in Droylsden (SJ 900 979). By the eastern pair of locks on the northern side of the canal, of which only one has been restored, can be seen a single-storey, single-roomed, brick-built toll house, a two-storey lock keeper's house and a single-arch stone footbridge. A long stone-built boathouse, large enough for one narrow boat and built in 1833, lies immediately to the west (Ashmore 1982, 91-2; Owen 1977, 82-3).

Among the surviving canal warehouses in Tameside is the fine brick-built warehouse at Hyde Wharf on the Peak Forest Canal, built in 1828 (SJ 943 951). This is a two-storey structure with a basement, of five by three bays, with semi-circular arched windows and a loading opening on the canal side. It has timber floors supported by cast-iron columns. On Melbourne Street in the centre of Stalybridge a brick-built warehouse of the 1820s stands next to an old canal bridge alongside the infilled course of the Huddersfield Canal. The warehouse is rectangular in plan with a stone basement and brick superstructure of three storeys and retains the fittings for hoists.

Fig 8.4 The Ashton Canal Warehouse.
Built in 1834 at a cost of £8901 13s 3d, the remains of the warehouse still stand on the northern side of Ashton New Wharf. It is the most impressive surviving piece of canal-related infrastructure in Tameside.

Chapter 8 The Infrastructure

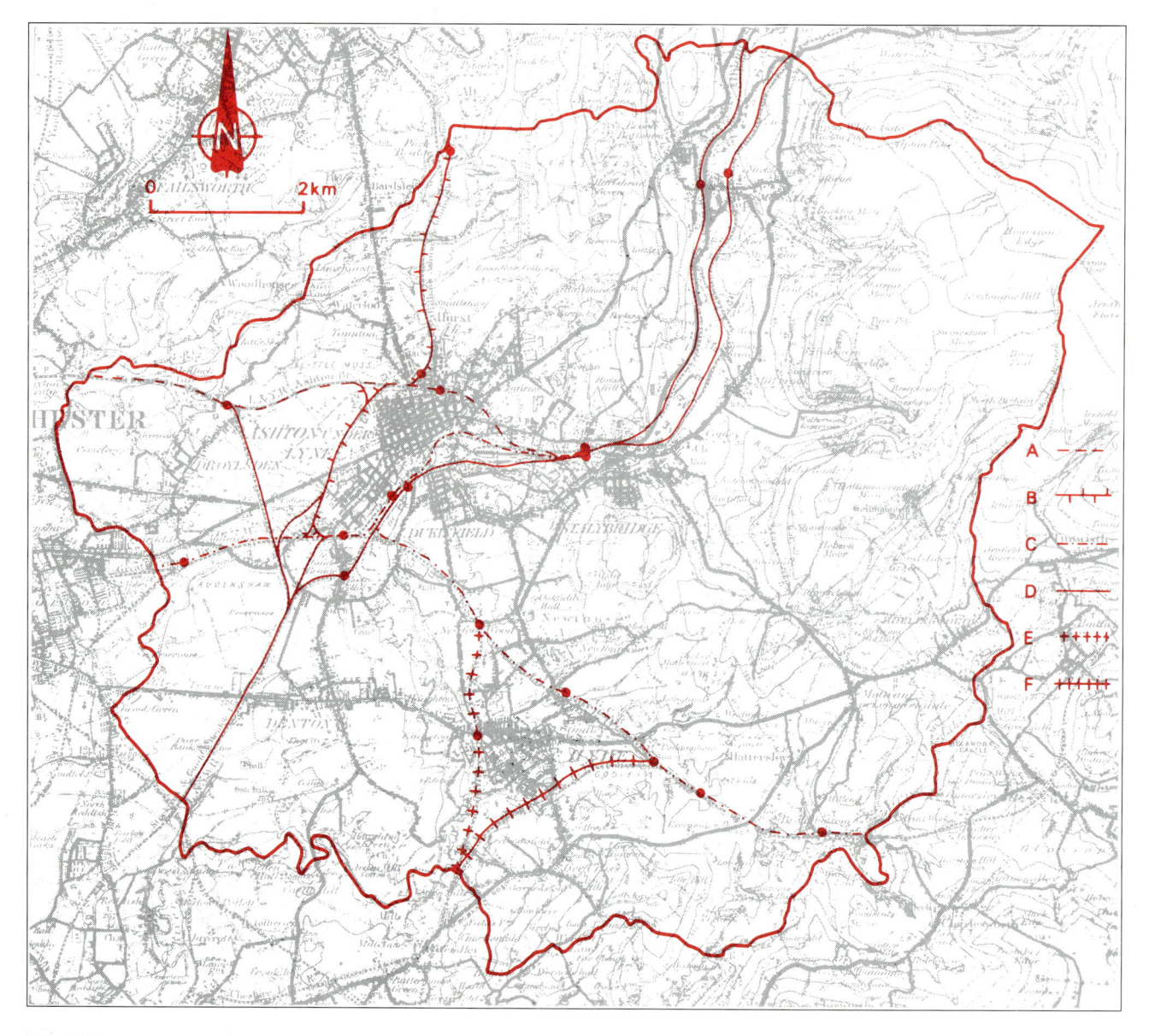

Fig 8.5 The late nineteenth-century railway network of Tameside.
Key: A – the Lancashire & Yorkshire (L&Y); B – the Oldham, Ashton-under-Lyne & Guide Bridge (OA&GB); C – the Great Central (GC), formerly the Manchester, Sheffield & Lincolnshire (MS&LR); D – the London & North Western (L&NWR); E – GC and the Midland; F – GC and the Midland; ● = stations.

8.4 Transport III: Railways

The railways of Tameside

Despite the opening of the first passenger-carrying steam railway in 1804, between Croydon and the River Thames, the potential of the railways as public transport was not grasped until the Stockton to Darlington line was opened in September 1825. The railway mania of the 1830s and 1840s was sparked by the high profits made by the Liverpool to Manchester railway, opened in 1830. The result of this mania was the cessation of canal building and the demise of the long-distance horse-drawn transport of goods and people. There were two main periods of railway expansion, the first covering the 1830s and 1840s. The second was from about 1855 to 1875 and increased the total length of track in Britain from 12,900 to 25,031 kilometres, or 8016 to 15,554 miles (Armstrong 1989, 105; Cootes 1982, 139-42).

Most of the railway system in Tameside was built during the first boom in construction, in the 1830s and 1840s. The Borough was the beneficiary of the race to link Lancashire and Yorkshire via two new railways, the Woodhead line built by the Sheffield, Ashton-under-Lyne & Manchester Railway Company (the SA&MR) in 1836-45, and the Standedge line, built by the Lancashire & Yorkshire Railway Company (the L&Y) and the London & North Western Railway Company (the L&NWR) in 1844-9 (Fig 8.5).

Chapter 8 The Infrastructure

The events surrounding the construction of these lines can seem bewildering but two excellent studies by Bairstow give clear and concise histories of each line (Bairstow 1986; 1990). The earliest railway through the Borough to be planned and opened was the line from Manchester to Sheffield. The first proposal for a passenger railway line linking the two towns was made in 1830 but this failed due to the technical difficulties of the route chosen (Bairstow 1990, 16). In 1836 the SA&MR was launched, with a proposed line via Ashton, Glossop, Woodhead and Penistone, and a short branch linking Stalybridge into the system. Construction began in February 1837, and although the line had reached Godley by 17th November 1841 the complete route was not opened until 22nd December 1845 (Holt 1978, 146-8; James 1983, 34-5). The act for the branch line to Stalybridge was passed in July 1844. Despite the collapse of the nine-arch viaduct at Ashton in April 1845, the first train ran to Stalybridge on 23rd December in the same year (Bairstow 1990, 20-1).

Through Tameside the main SA&MR line ran eastwards across the southern edge of Ashton Moss, through Guide Bridge, before turning south-eastwards to pass to the north of Hyde and on to Godley and Broadbottom, and so up the Longdendale valley to Woodhead. There were four stations in the Borough, at Fairfield, Guide Bridge (Ashton), Newton and Broadbottom, and a further two on the Stalybridge branch at Dukinfield and Stalybridge itself. By 1846 these stations were served by 22 trains on weekdays, the fastest taking one hour 27 minutes from Manchester to Sheffield (*ibid*, 19).

In 1847 the SA&MR amalgamated with the Sheffield & Lincolnshire Junction Railway, the Great Grimsby & Sheffield Railway and the Grimsby Docks Company to form the Manchester, Sheffield & Lincolnshire Railway Company (the MS&LR), linking the River Mersey and the River Humber (*ibid*, 21). In 1897 the company was renamed the Great Central, as a consequence of opening its new London extension (*ibid*, 46). During the mid-1920s the company was merged with other northern lines to form the London & North Eastern Railway (*ibid*, 61).

The second major element of the railway system to be built in Tameside was the line from Manchester to Leeds via the Standedge tunnel. Although trans-Pennine communications had been established by railway between Manchester and Leeds in 1841, the route was very circuitous and involved a journey of three hours. A more direct line had to await developments in the mid-1840s (Holt 1978, 149). The first section of this new route was to be the L&Y's line from Miles Platting via Droylsden to Stalybridge; this was approved by Parliament in July 1844, with the L&Y's station at Stalybridge opening on 5th October 1846 (Bairstow 1986, 18; James 1983, 41).

The opportunities offered by a direct link from one or other of Stalybridge's two stations to Huddersfield, and thus on to Leeds, were great enough to encourage two new companies to be formed in 1845: the Leeds, Dewsbury & Manchester Railway and the Huddersfield & Manchester Railway. After much manoeuvring both companies were taken over in July 1847 by the L&NWR, which quickly came to an agreement with the L&Y over the running of the line (Bairstow 1986, 18-19). The result was the opening of a passenger service from Manchester to Leeds via the Standedge tunnel on 1st August 1849 (Holt 1978, 150). There was also a branch line through Guide Bridge and Denton to Heaton Norris in Stockport, which opened on the same day (James 1983, 57). The Manchester to Leeds rail link proved so popular with both freight and passenger traffic that the single-track Standedge tunnel was joined by a second tunnel, also single-track, in 1871; the rest of the line was initially twin-track but was widened to four tracks in the 1880s (Bairstow 1986, 20).

The course of the line through Tameside began on the western side of the Borough, which it entered via Droylsden, moving eastwards across the northern edge of Ashton Moss, and passing to the north-east of Ashton before reaching Stalybridge; the track then followed the western bank of the River Tame northwards towards Greenfield, Saddleworth and Standedge. There were four stations in Tameside, at Droylsden, Ashton, Stalybridge and Mossley. In 1850 there were sixteen through trains per weekday and nine others stopping or starting at Stalybridge, run by the L&Y. Trans-Pennine journeys took about two hours on the fastest trains (*ibid*, 37-8).

The post-1849 additions to the railway network of Tameside were mainly local lines and made little advance to the basic pattern. The most significant of these was the line of the Oldham, Ashton-under-Lyne & Guide Bridge Railway Company (the OA&GB), opened in 1861 to link Ashton and Oldham, and the Micklehurst Loop, on the Standedge line, opened in 1885.

Although Oldham was linked to the railway system in 1842, the route was via a branch line from the Manchester & Leeds Railway, leading from Middleton to Werneth in Oldham, with a steep incline of 1 in 27 (*ibid*, 71; James 1983, 36, 89). The need for a better route into this growing manufacturing town was clear but commercial wrangling between a number of railway companies prevented an effective link being proposed until the OA&GB railway was suggested in 1857, to be run by the L&Y and the MS&LR (Marshall 1981, 56-9). Opened in July 1861, the line ran

127

Chapter 8 The Infrastructure

Plate 8.2 Broadbottom viaduct.
This lithograph of the 1840s shows the original viaduct designed by C B Vignoles and built for the Sheffield, Ashton-under-Lyne & Manchester Railway, with wooden arches supported on brick pillars. In 1858 the viaduct burnt down and was replaced by the present iron and steel construction.

from Guide Bridge to the west of Ashton, northwards across Ashton Moss, through Park Bridge and on to Oldham. A link between the southern end of the railway and Denton Junction, on the Stockport to Ashton line, allowed trains from Stockport to Oldham to commence in 1876 (Bairstow 1986, 71).

The Micklehurst Loop was opened in 1885 as a response to the overcrowding of the Standedge line. Engineering difficulties in widening the Stalybridge to Standedge section of the railway to four tracks resulted in a new twin-track alignment which kept to the eastern bank of the River Tame (Marshall 1981, 50-4).

Other minor improvements to the railway network of Tameside included the opening of a line from the MS&LR at Hyde Junction to Hyde in 1858, with later extensions to Marple in 1862 and Godley in 1866, the latter being jointly owned by the MS&LR and the Midland Railway (Holt 1978, 154-5). The last substantial line to be built in the Borough was by the L&NWR, which in 1882 opened a link across the Tame from Denton to Dukinfield, avoiding the railway trouble spot of Guide Bridge. This was extended to Stalybridge in 1893 (*ibid*).

The impact of the railways

The immediate impact of the railways on the landscape of the Borough was severe along the line of the railways themselves. Deep cuttings, such as those on the L&NWR's Standedge line along the west bank of the River Tame between Ashton and Mossley, or high embankments, such as those across Ashton Moss, scarred the landscape and severed farmsteads from their fields. These were the immediate localized

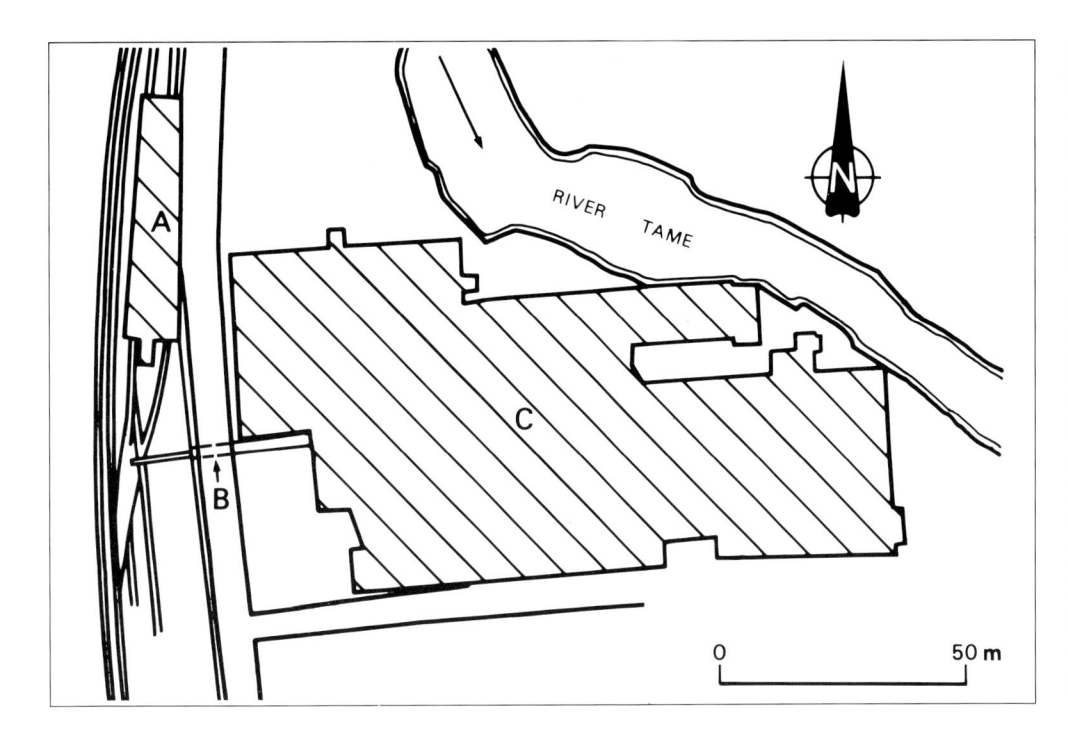

Fig 8.6 Britannia Mill and the L&NWR through Mossley (after Eckersley 1991). *Key:* A – railway shed and sidings; B – tunnel; C – Britannia Mill. The value of the new railways to the mill-owners of Tameside is illustrated by the siting of John Mayall's Britannia Mill in 1849 adjacent to the new L&NWR line. The mill was connected to the line via sidings and a tunnel under the turnpike, allowing the direct delivery of cotton from Liverpool docks.

consequences. In the long term the arrival of the railways further enhanced those urban centres already well established, Ashton, Dukinfield, Hyde and Stalybridge, rather than creating whole new communities as occurred in Cheshire at Crewe.

Outside these urban areas, where the stations were among the most prominent railway buildings, the most lasting impact on the wider landscape were the viaducts. Park Parade Bridge in Ashton, a brick-built viaduct with seven arches, was erected in 1861 on the new OA&GB line across the gorge of the River Medlock on the northern side of the Borough. The Broadbottom viaduct across the gorge of the River Etherow on the Manchester to Sheffield line, designed by C B Vignoles, has nineteen arches, originally of wood supported on brick pillars but rebuilt in 1858 in iron and steel (Plate 8.2).

Economically the impact of the railways was considerable in both the manufacturing and agricultural industries. The resulting impact on the profits of the local canal companies, and the consequent takeovers, has already been noted above. The value of the distribution network supplied by the railway system was quickly realized by the textile mill-owners. In Mossley John Mayall's Britannia Mill, built in 1849, was directly linked to sidings on the L&NWR's Standedge line via a tunnel under the turnpike road (Eckersley 1991, 12-13; Fig 8.6). In the 1870s the mill-owners of Mossley were instrumental in supporting the planned Micklehurst Loop from Stalybridge to Standedge on the eastern side of the valley, largely in an effort to break the monopoly on haulage charges which the L&NWR had in the town at that time (*ibid*, 14-15).

The establishment of direct links with the new railways was not, of course, limited to the textile industry. In the engineering sector, the Park Bridge ironworks of Hannah Lees & Sons had been initially connected to the Fairbottom branch of the Ashton Canal via a horse-drawn tramway. When the OA&GB railway was opened in 1861 the ironworks were provided with their own station and sidings, giving direct access to the towns of Ashton and Oldham. Tramways had long been used by the coal-mining industry to link collieries with the canals, and with the advent of the railways some colliery-owners in the Borough built new tramways joining with the railway network (see Chapter 6).

The significance of the introduction of the railways for agriculture in Tameside was far reaching. The new lines allowed fresh milk to be transported to the urban populations of the region and so spurred the shift from cheese to milk production which helped the dairy farmers of the Borough to weather the agricultural crisis of the late nineteenth century (see Chapter 5).

Apart from encouraging these established industries the railways also generated their own industry. Although this was never particularly extensive in Tameside there were two engineering works of some significance. In 1856 Isaac Watt Boulton, a former apprentice of the railway engineer Peacock who had engineering works in Gorton, set up his own works in Portland Street in Ashton (TLSL DD 13/17/11). His main business was the reconditioning of second-hand locomotives for use as industrial shunting engines, which he later hired out, but Boulton also built portable and stationary engines. By 1864 the works had

Chapter 8 The Infrastructure

expanded into North Street and Boulton had his own sidings attached to the OA&GB railway. Business declined in the 1880s and in 1898 the engineering works were sold (TLSL DD 13/22/2). Shortly afterwards the Great Central Railway was forced to expand its Gorton engineering works due to the demand for new rolling stock. In 1903 the railway purchased 30 acres of land off Globe Lane in Dukinfield from the Dukinfield Astley estate and established a new carriage and wagon works there which were in full production by 1910 (TLSL DD 112/1).

8.5 Transport IV: Buses and Tramways

The development of a passenger transport system in the new urban communities of the region began in 1824 when the first horse-drawn omnibus service was begun in Manchester. From the early 1860s interest was aroused in horse-driven trams which ran on fixed rails. This culminated in the Tramways Act of 1870 which enabled local authorities to run their own concerns, although the usual practice was for the local authority to establish a tramway and then lease it to a private company (Hyde 1978, 7).

The first horse-driven tramway in Tameside was authorized in 1878 when Ashton Corporation empowered the Manchester Carriage & Tramways Company to build a line from Stalybridge town hall, through Ashton to Audenshaw. The line opened in 1881 and was later extended to Manchester, linking it with the rest of the company's network. The first fares from Stalybridge to Audenshaw were 6d inside the saloon and 4d outside on the upper deck, although larger and more frequent trams enabled these prices to be quickly reduced (Hyde 1980, 9). The following year, 1882, the company introduced horse-driven trams in Denton.

In 1898 a conference of Manchester Corporation and Denton and Gorton district councils agreed to allow the larger authority to run tramways on behalf of the smaller (TLSL DDTR 7/1/7). As a consequence, in the same year Denton UDC purchased those lines of the Manchester Carriage & Tramways Company within its jurisdiction and agreed to lease them to Manchester Corporation for an initial period of 21 years (TLSL DDTR 7/1/10). Not to be outdone, in 1900 Ashton Corporation applied to Parliament for powers to construct, operate and purchase its own tramways. The first line to be built, linking Ashton with Hurst, opened in 1902 (Hyde 1980, 31-2).

In the meanwhile a new mode of public transport had been introduced into Tameside – the electric tramway. In June 1899 the Oldham, Ashton and Hyde Electric Tramway Company was launched with the backing of the British Electric Traction Company. The thirteen kilometres, or eight miles, of line were the first electric tramway in the Manchester area and operated from Hathershaw through Ashton, Guide Bridge and Denton to Hyde (*ibid*, 12-20; TLSL DDTR 3/1, 4 & 6).

In November 1899 the success of this electric tramway led the British Electric Traction Company to apply to Parliament for permission to extend the service in Hyde. However, the bill was opposed by the borough of Hyde which wished to promote a scheme of its own (TLSL DDTR 3/4 & 6). The interest shown by Hyde and other local authorities in electric tramways culminated in 1901 with the foundation of the Stalybridge, Hyde, Mossley and Dukinfield Tramways and Electricity Board (the SHMD), which had the dual function of providing electricity to its component districts (Hennessey 1972, 22-3; TLSL DDTR 5/1). The first line to be built by the board ran from Stalybridge to Ashton and opened in 1903. In 1915 a further act was passed authorizing the board to construct and operate tramways in the districts of Glossop, Hattersley, Hollingworth, Matley, Mottram, Saddleworth and Tintwistle. In the same year in which the SHMD's electric trams began operation, 1903, the Manchester Carriage & Tramways Company's lease of their horse-driven tramways in the borough of Ashton expired; Ashton Corporation purchased all the lines and set about converting this horse-driven tramway system to electricity (Hyde 1980, 10). New routes were added, to Mossley, Dukinfield and Hyde, and in February 1904 a through service commenced to Manchester (Hyde 1978, 43).

When the lease of the Oldham, Ashton and Hyde Electric Tramway Company expired in 1921 the four Tameside local authorities through which the company's routes ran, namely Audenshaw, Ashton, Denton and Hyde, purchased these lines for a total of £125,000 (TLSL DDTR 3/19). Manchester Corporation operated the lines in Audenshaw and Denton on behalf of those local authorities; the SHMD operated the lines in Hyde; and Ashton Corporation operated the lines in its borough, quickly extending its routes to Denton in 1922 (Hyde 1978, 43). By establishing links with the Manchester Corporation's tramways in Denton, the SHMD was now able to operate a through service to Manchester, and a through service to Stockport was also introduced (*ibid*, 47).

The 1920s, however, saw electric tramways facing increasing competition from motor-buses. Of the two forms of transport, tramways were the less flexible, with their fixed routes, the problems of road maintenance, and the constant repair and upkeep of the overhead power lines. A further problem was the fragmented nature of the system. South Lancashire, for instance, had 47 tramway authorities, a problem wors-

Chapter 8 The Infrastructure

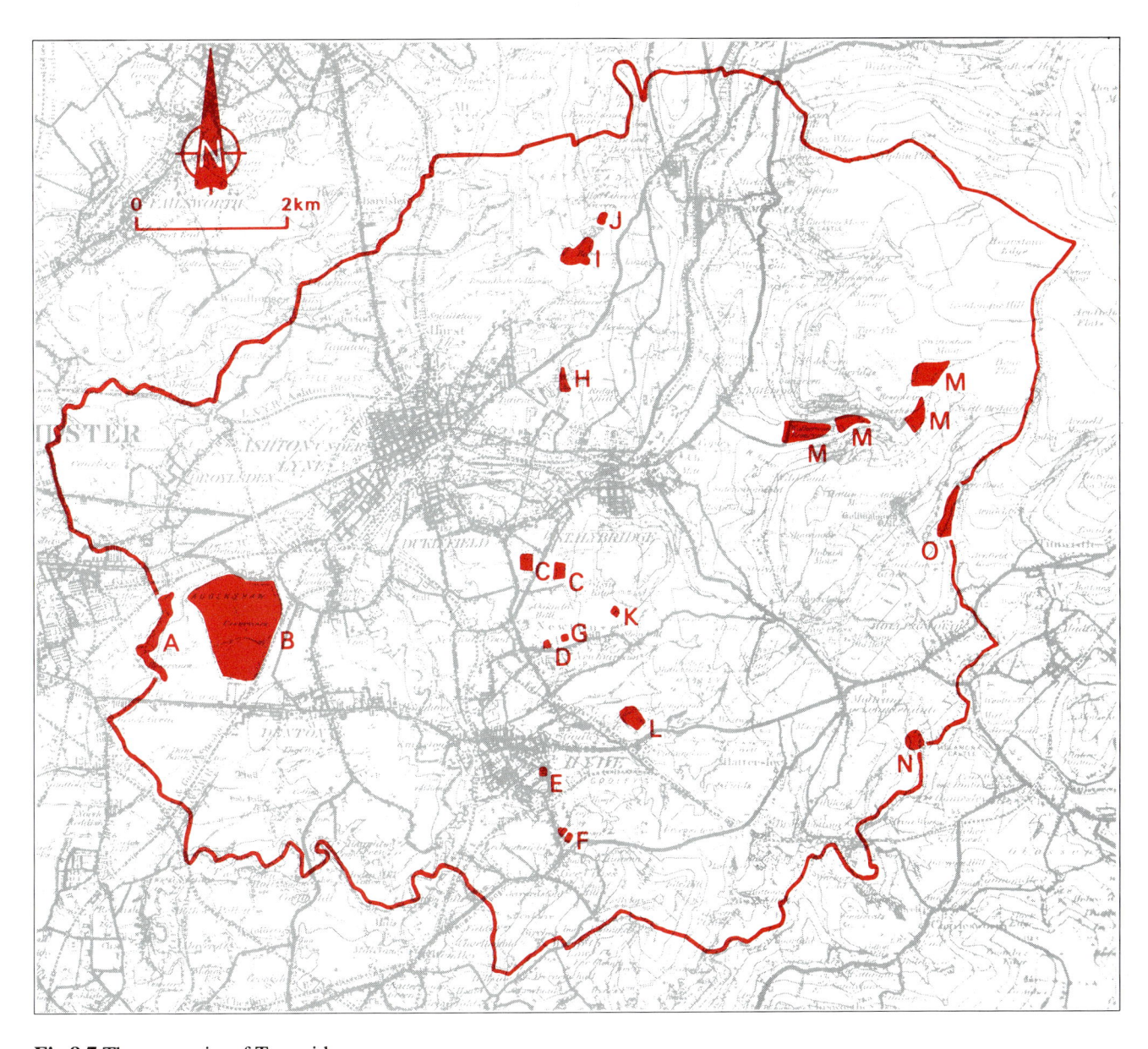

Fig 8.7 The reservoirs of Tameside.
Key: A – Gorton; B – Audenshaw; C – Higher; D – Harbour; E – New and Arnold Hill; F – Gee Cross and Tinker's; G – Blue Bell; H – Park Hall; I – Knott Hill; J – Tombottom; K – Newton House/Line Edge; L – Godley; M – Brushes; N – overflow reservoir; O – Arnfield.

ened by the lack of a standard gauge (Hennessey 1972, 153-4). This left the tramway system vulnerable to the great period of expansion in public motorized transport during the 1920s. In 1923 the first motor-bus service started from Chester Square in Ashton, to Smallshaw. In 1925 the Ashton to Oldham tramway run by Ashton Corporation was converted to a trolleybus service, while the SHMD also introduced its first motor-bus service in the same year (Hyde 1980, 60; 1978, 48). The remaining electric trams were gradually replaced. In Tameside the last electric tram ran in March 1938 from Manchester to Ashton town centre (Hyde 1978, 44).

8.6 Water Supply

Prior to the nineteenth century the main means of water supply in Tameside was by wells or streams. Even the population of Ashton, the only sizeable town in the Borough, could still rely on wells for all

> 'except about two months in the summer, when the inhabitants are obliged to fetch their soft water in carts from the Tame' (Aikin 1795, 227).

A notable exception to this was the piped water system built by Sir John Astley in the late eighteenth century for his Dukinfield estate. Water was pumped from the River Tame to a reservoir on the hill where Dukinfield

Chapter 8 The Infrastructure

New Chapel now stands. This reservoir, which may have given the adjacent Fishpond Yard its name, fed the houses of the estate workers, in particular those of the Circus (*ibid*, 453; see Chapter 9).

Such philanthropy in eighteenth-century Tameside was the exception. It was not until the early nineteenth century, with the rapid urbanization of Ashton, Hyde and Stalybridge, that the need for a clean water supply became acute, as wells and rivers became polluted by the new industries. As was the case with the early gas supplies, mill-owners were among the first to supply their workers with piped water, largely because they had built and now owned a large amount of the housing stock of the Borough.

The first formal water supply in Hyde was provided as early as 1808 by the mill-owning Ashton family. However, it was not until 1831 that the first reservoir was built in Hyde under an act 'for the better supply of water to the several townships of Hyde, Werneth and Newton'. This was Gee Cross reservoir, which was followed shortly afterwards by Tinker's, New and Arnold Hill reservoirs (Fig 8.7). All were built by Thomas Mottram and run by a private undertaking, the Hyde, Werneth and Newton Waterworks Company. The Godley reservoir, jointly run with the Manchester Corporation's waterworks, was added to this system in the 1850s. In 1870 an act was passed which enabled the Hyde local board to purchase the company. The Hyde Joint Waterworks Undertaking later acquired the privately run water supply of Newton from the trustees of the mill-owning firm J and J Ashton in 1920. This included the reservoirs of Newton House (later known as Line Edge), Blue Bell and Harbour (TLSL DD/WW/2/1-57; Middleton 1936, 195).

By the early 1820s Ashton's water supply was in crisis. Under an act of 1825 a private waterworks company was set up to supply the town with piped water from a series of reservoirs running from Tombottom reservoir, through Park Hall reservoir to Ashton, where further small reservoirs were built. The company was re-established under an act of 1835 and the reservoir at Tombottom replaced by the larger fifteen-acre Knott Hill reservoir (Bowman 1960, 332-3).

In 1832 the need for an adequate public water supply was highlighted by the outbreak of cholera in Ashton. Such epidemics prompted Parliament to set up a commission to investigate public health and living conditions. The resulting *Report on the Sanitary Conditions of the Labouring Population (1842)*, compiled by Edwin Chadwick, indicated how bad the situation was. In Ashton alone there were 6832 unsanitary dwellings, mostly occupied by the poor, of which 700 houses had no form of water supply and a further 3132 had no proper drainage (Bowman 1960, 328).

In Ashton the provision of the water supply was taken under municipal control in 1856 when the borough purchased the private Ashton Waterworks Company. Seven years later, in 1863, the boroughs of Ashton and Stalybridge proposed a new scheme to build a series of reservoirs, Brushes, in the Swineshaw valley, the enabling act being passed in 1864 (TLSL DD/WW/86). In 1870 a further act added Dukinfield township to this joint waterworks undertaking and authorized the building of the Higher reservoir to supply the township. Parliament had earlier rejected a scheme proposed by Oldham Corporation to build reservoirs in the Greenfield and Chew valleys in Saddleworth, in favour of a comprehensive water-supply system for the whole of the Tame valley. As a consequence, the 1870 act also made provision for the supply of water to Hurst, Mossley and Saddleworth, via three new reservoirs to be built in the Greenfield and Chew valleys (Bowman 1960, 331; Lawton 1989, 3-4).

The involvement of Manchester Corporation in the reservoir system of Tameside dates from its acquisition in 1846 of the Manchester and Salford Waterworks Company, a private company which had built the Gorton reservoirs on the south-western border of Tameside in 1823 (Quayle 1988, 4). By the early 1840s the water supply from the Gorton reservoirs was inadequate and in 1844 Manchester Corporation proposed the building of reservoirs in the Swineshaw valley to supply the Manchester population with drinking water. The plan was vigorously opposed by Stalybridge mill-owners and by Ashton borough and was soon abandoned by Manchester Corporation in favour of a larger scheme (Lawton 1989, 3). This was the construction of the Longdendale reservoirs (which included, in Tameside, Arnfield reservoir and an overflow reservoir in Mottram), authorized by an act of 1847. The service reservoirs at Audenshaw, built in 1875-84, completed this system (*ibid*, 52).

8.7 The Gas Industry

Coal gas as a source of lighting had been demonstrated in 1792 by William Murdoch, and in 1798 he was asked by the leading steam engineers Boulton & Watt to provide gas lighting for their Soho Foundry in Birmingham (C Jones 1989, 81; Richardson 1986, 165). In 1805 the industry became established as a commercial entity, with the building by Boulton & Watt of their first order for gas plant, and the establishment of the first specialist gas-engineering firm by Samuel Clegg, in Manchester (Wilson 1991, 4). By the second decade of the nineteenth century gas lighting had been installed in several of the largest Manchester mills, the gas being produced and stored on site (Williams with Farnie 1992, 73). In Tameside

Fig 8.8 Plan of Ashton gas works, 1822. *Key:* A – manager's house and offices; B – retort house; C – workshop and coke shed; D – stables; E – lime house. Source: ESRCA 19. The first public-supply gas works in Tameside were those of the Ashton-under-Lyne Gas Undertaking, between Katherine Street and Gas Street, founded in the period 1820-2.

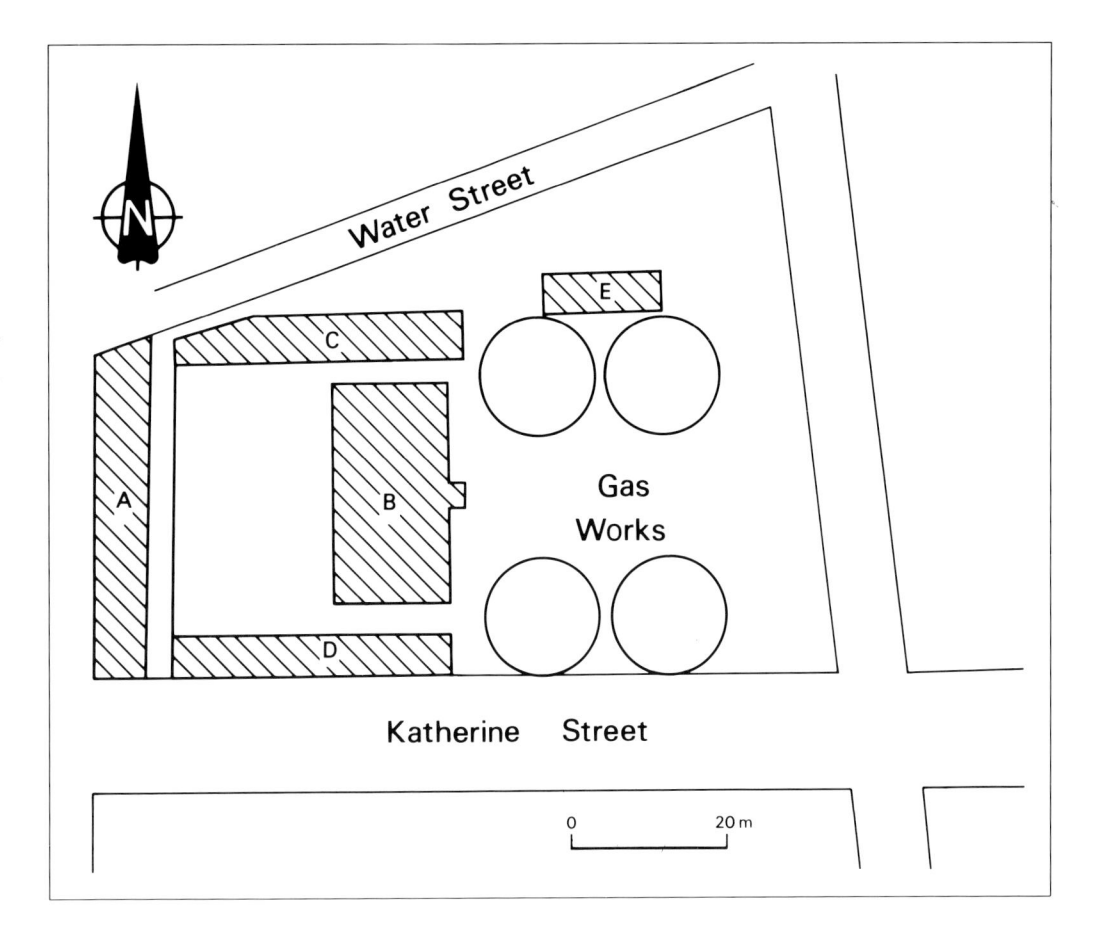

gas lighting was installed by Samuel Clegg in the cotton mills of Samuel Ashton in Hyde as early as 1812 (Wilson 1991, 39).

In that same year the first public-supply gas company was registered, receiving a royal charter to supply gas to the cities of London and Westminster (C Jones 1989, 81; Richardson 1986, 165). The success of the London company engendered an expansion of the industry, so that by 1826 there were 21 public gas companies in the North-West (Wilson 1991, 8-10, 37). Among these was the Ashton-under-Lyne Gas Undertaking, the first public-supply gas works in Tameside; this was established in the period 1820-2 and became a company in 1825 (*ibid*, 27; ESRCA 17, 19; Fig 8.8).

Given the early role of the textile industry in the local gas industry, it is perhaps not surprising that much of the impetus for the growth of public gas companies in Tameside came from local mill-owners. The Stalybridge Gas Light Company was formed in 1829 by five local cotton manufacturers. Two of these, Harrison and Cheetham, had already been using gas lighting in their mills for some years, although two other mill-owners who were using gas in the town, John Leech at Grosvenor Street Mill and George Adshead at Staley New Mills, did not take part in the venture (March 1957, 104; Wilson 1991, 38). A similar situation pertained in Droylsden where four cotton mill-owners, all with their own gas plants, sold them to the Droylsden New Gas Company, formed by themselves in 1857 (BGA DNGC 1857). By 1865 £16,000 had been invested in a new centralized system, and the company was so successful that Manchester Corporation bought it in 1869 for £25,000 (Wilson 1991, 40).

Much of the profitability of the early companies was at the expense of an increasing number of smaller or domestic consumers. The attitude of Alfred Reyner, mill-owner and prominent shareholder and director of the Ashton-under-Lyne Gas Light Company, highlights the problems which such individuals could face:

'If I were to find the price charged to me was such that the shopkeepers had it at the same rate, I would put down my own gasworks; the large discounts allowed me, however, makes me take my gas from the company' (Wilson 1991, 138).

In the late nineteenth century local authorities began to acquire gas undertakings, partly through demands for improved standards of supply and a fair pricing policy, and partly because of the profitable nature of these concerns. The Dukinfield Gas Company, founded in 1854, was taken over by the Denton local board in 1877, while in 1885 the boroughs of Stalybridge and Mossley bought the Stalybridge Gas Light Company (Pavasovic 1984, 45, 85; March 1957, 105). The Ashton-under-Lyne Gas Light Company,

Year	Gas produced (in millions of cubic feet)	Gas sold	No of customers	Leakage %
1857	13.154	–	–	–
1858	15.214	–	–	–
1859	17.884	–	–	–
1860	21.701	–	–	–
1861	23.840	–	–	–
1862	21.357	–	–	–
1863	20.962	16.229	2550	22.5
1864	22.705	17.945	2660	21.0
1865	28.872	21.417	2664	29.3
1866	33.518	26.006	2850	20.9
1867	35.228	27.598	2885	21.7
1868	38.006	28.072	2950	26.1
1869	37.288	29.222	3077	21.6
1870	41.945	32.732	3150	21.9
1871	49.850	38.900	3310	22.4
1872	53.834	44.044	3492	18.2
1873	58.117	46.990	3697	19.1
1874	58.811	50.427	3887	14.3
1875	61.424	51.906	3965	15.8
1876	60.862	53.922	3904	11.7
1877	65.644	58.796	4251	10.4
1878	70.739	61.254	4508	13.4
1879	69.676	60.977	4559	8.8

Table 8.1 Output and number of customers of the Hyde Gas Company, 1857-79.
Source: TLSL DDG 2/2/17.

however, remained an independent private company until the nationalization of the gas industry in 1949 (Bowman 1960, 332).

Hyde, likewise, continued to receive its gas from a private company. The town acquired its first supply in 1844, again from a local mill-owner, Isaac Booth. By 1854 there were ten mill-owners supplying gas to the town, or at least to those streets in the immediate vicinity of their mills. This chaotic situation was rationalized in that year by the establishment of the Hyde Gas Company. The driving force of this company was the Hibbert family who held 245 of 2464 £10 shares issued. Samuel Hibbert was appointed chairman of the company and his sons Joseph and John sat on the board (BGA HGCBM 12/2/1855 & 18/6/1855).

The company's output and the number of customers both rose rapidly during the mid-nineteenth century. Production figures survive for the years 1857-79, during which period the amount of gas produced annually rose from 13.154 to 69.676 million cubic feet (Table 8.1). Details of the number of customers and the quantity of gas sold are first given for the year 1863, when 2550 customers were served, this figure rising to 4559 in 1879. Of particular note is the steep decline in the percentage of gas lost through leakage between 1863 and 1879. This fell from 22.5% to 8.8%, with much of this improvement being spurred by tighter safety legislation.

By the early 1860s the range of customers supplied by the Hyde Gas Company was varied and the 2550 consumers in 1863 included private individuals, a mechanics institute, the police station, a church school, the town hall and the Manchester, Sheffield & Lincolnshire Railway, as well as the more traditional users of gas such as local mill-owners, in particular those of Boston Mills (TLSL DD 216/1). By 1879 the company's quarterly income had grown to £7090. In the early 1880s and again in the early 1890s Hyde Corporation unsuccessfully attempted to purchase the company (TLSL DDG 2/2 & 3). The Hyde Gas Company remained independent in the early twentieth century and expanded its business further by the acquisition of gas concerns in Denton and Dukinfield (TLSL DDG 6/21).

8.8 Electricity

The patenting of the electric light bulb by Joseph Swan and Thomas Edison in 1878-9 prompted what Hennessey has described as the 'Electrical Revolution' of 1880-1930, during which period this new industry rose to become a major part of the national economy in terms of employment and power generation (Hennessey 1972, v). In 1882 the Electric Lighting Act gave local authorities the right to supply electricity. The first local authority power station was probably Bradford's in 1889, and by 1896 Bolton, Manchester and Oldham had municipal electricity supplies (C Jones 1989, 88). These power stations, located in the coalfields, were mostly run by the new steam turbine engine, invented in 1884, which could achieve a high enough speed of rotation to generate electricity efficiently (Cootes 1982, 172; Hennessey 1972, 179).

In Tameside Hyde had considered introducing electric lighting as early as 1897, although the borough did not pursue this plan, perhaps because of the prohibitive cost of introducing only electric lighting (TLSL DD 227/1). For this reason the early supply of electricity was closely bound with the introduction of electric tramways. The earliest power station to be established in Tameside was in Ashton, where the Oldham, Ashton and Hyde Electric Tramway Company, launched in 1899, supplied power for lighting to the borough (Hyde 1980, 12). The first joint local authority electricity board in the south Manchester area was the Stalybridge, Hyde, Mossley and Dukinfield Tramways and Electricity Board, the SHMD, which was established in 1901 (Hennessey 1972, 22-3). Its power station, now demolished, was a magnificent Edwardian structure, located by the River Tame in Stalybridge and built in 1904 (*ibid*, 144-5). By 1924 the power station in Stalybridge was producing 6000 volts, and that in Ashton 33,000 volts. Only the Ashton power station was connected to a wider grid covering most of south-east Lancashire and northern Cheshire, via a substation in Droylsden (TLSL DDTR 12).

Chapter 9

Urban Communities

'I thought I would go to Hyde and Newton Moor, where I had lived many years when I was a boy and young man. I went to Gorton and through Denton and Hyde and on to Newton Moor. I stopped a while at Newton Moor and then went through Dukinfield and Staly Bridge and on to Ashton-under-Lyne. It was twenty-eight years since I was on that road before, but now everything was changed. Villages had grown into large towns, and country places where there was nothing but fields are now covered with streets, and villages and large factories and workshops everywhere.'

Extract from the diary of James Garnett, Lancashire weaver, 6th April 1860 (Brigg 1982, 97)

9.1 Introduction

The growth and concentration of industry in specific areas of Tameside during the Industrial Revolution of the late eighteenth and early nineteenth centuries created new urban centres and caused acute housing problems. People came into the towns faster than houses were built, attracted by regular employment and wages higher than those which farming could offer (Garnett 1849, 44). The situation was made worse where landowners were unwilling to give up land for building. This meant that ever more people were packed into existing housing and such areas soon became slums. Where new houses were built it was on an intensive scale, with tenement blocks, back-to-back houses and terraced housing all closely packed together. The object of this chapter is to record the development of the townscape in Tameside, placing the industry and infrastructure of the area in its proper landscape setting. The discussion is divided into two main sections, the first giving a brief review of the main building types of this townscape, the second describing the urban growth of the nine modern towns of the Borough.

9.2 The New Urban Landscape

By the mid-nineteenth century the densest concentrations of housing in Tameside were in those towns which were the first to be industrialized, namely Ashton-under-Lyne, Dukinfield, Hyde and Stalybridge. Two descriptions from the 1840s illustrate some of the conditions which these new factory towns displayed.

Engels, commenting on the view on entering Stalybridge in 1844, observed that

'In coming over the hill from Ashton, the traveller has, at the top, both right and left, fine large gardens with superb villa-like houses in their midst...A hundred paces farther and Stalybridge shows itself in the valley, in sharp contrast with the beautiful country seats...On entering, the very first cottages are narrow, smoke begrimed, old and ruinous; and as the first houses so the whole town. A few streets lie in the narrow valley bottom. Most of them run criss-cross, pell-mell, up hill and down' (Engels 1845, 78).

Angus Reach in 1849, describing the hamlets of Charlestown and Boston to the north of Ashton, noted overcrowded and unsanitary conditions:

'We threaded a labyrinth of noisome courts and small airless squares, formed generally of houses of a fair size, but miserably out of repair, slatternly women lounging about in thresholds; and neglected, dirty-faced children sprawling and roaring in the gutters. The door of one of these houses stood open, showing a steep, dark staircase, black with mud. The plaster had fallen in lumps from the wall showing the lath beneath, and the coating which remained seemed covered with a dark greasy slime' (Aspin 1972, 73).

Not all early industrial housing was this bad and in the Georgian and Regency planned area of Ashton conditions were far better than in many other contemporary northern industrial towns. House building in Ashton was controlled by the Stamford estate, which ensured paved streets and pavements, sewers and proper drainage. This led Engels to note that

Plate 9.1 Dukinfield Circus.
Built by Sir John Astley for his estate workers in the period 1759-87, these buildings are amongst the earliest known examples of workers' housing in Tameside.

'Ashton owes a much more attractive appearance than that of most Factory towns; the streets are broad and cleaner, the cottages bright red and comfortable' (Engels 1845, 77).

Hyde too was noted in the early to mid-nineteenth century for the quality of its housing (Walton 1987, 174).

The explosion of the urban population of Tameside in the late eighteenth and early nineteenth centuries led to the construction of many tens of thousands of new buildings, the majority for housing. In the first half of the nineteenth century much of this housing was built by local mill-owners. This was particularly noticeable in Ashton where Reach in 1849 observed that

'the system of millowners building and letting out comfortable cottages to their workpeople prevails as much, or even more in Ashton than in any town in Lancashire' (Aspin 1972, 76).

House types in the new industrial towns and villages ranged from communal workers' housing to mill-owners' residences. The growth of local government from the late 1820s, and the increasing activities of philanthropic mill-owners, also led to the construction of new types of public and community structures, many of which can still be seen today.

Workers' housing

Perhaps the rarest type of workers' housing in Tameside was the lodging or boarding house. Although there were only a few of these in the Borough, contemporary accounts suggest that they displayed the worst conditions and were generally overcrowded. In Ashton they could be found in Duncan Street in Charlestown and in Crab Street, Old Street and Crickets Lane in Ashton town itself. All of these have long since been demolished but detailed descriptions survive in a report by J R Coulthart in 1844. Coulthart

Chapter 9 Urban Communities

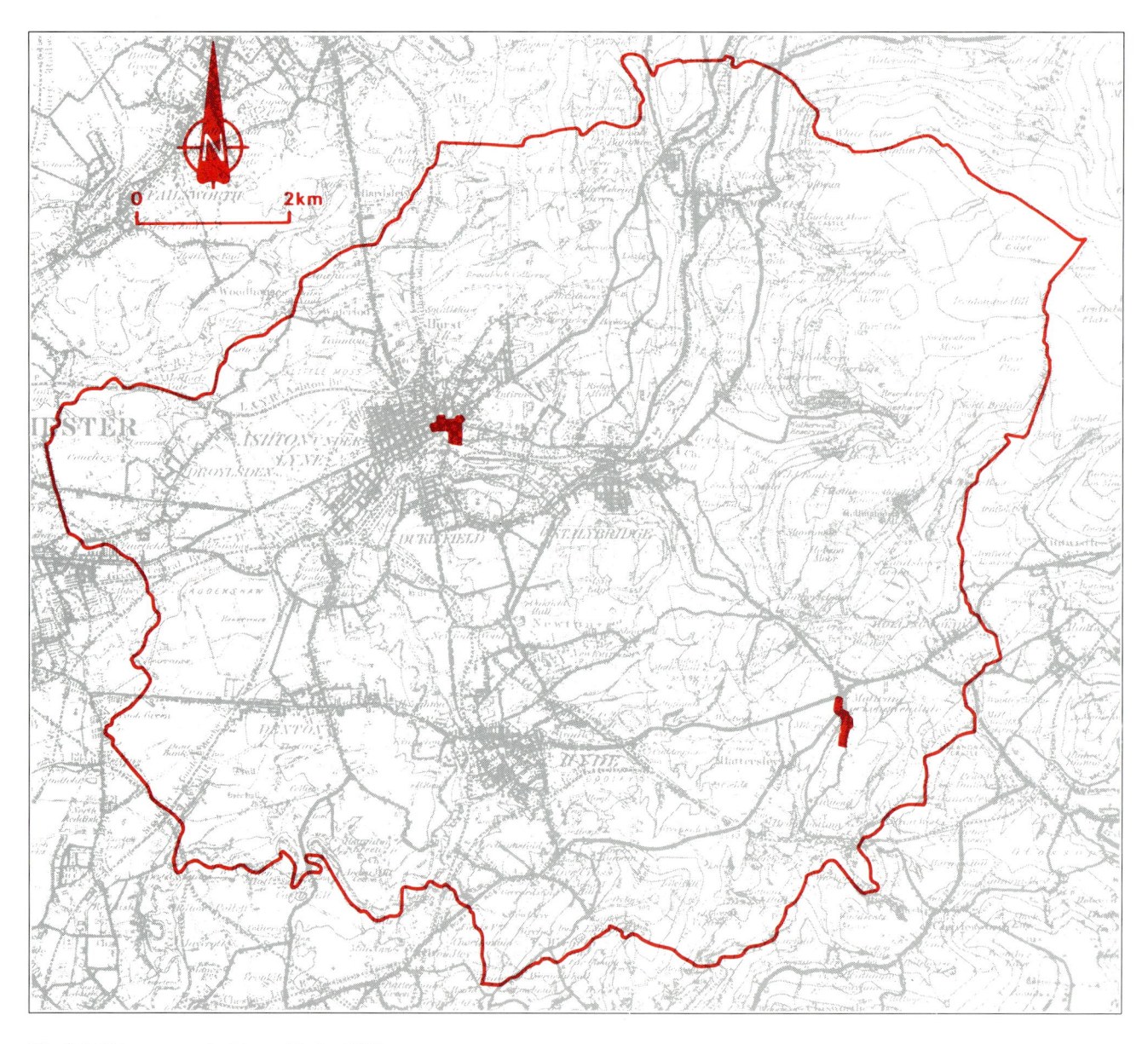

Fig 9.1 Urban areas in Tameside in 1700.
Prior to the Industrial Revolution the economy and society of Tameside were based upon agriculture. The only significant urban areas were Ashton and Mottram, both towns whose origins lay in the medieval period. Even so, their populations were quite small at the beginning of the eighteenth century, that of Ashton being in the region of 500 to 600 people and that of Mottram being around 170.

was a local banker paid by the special survey on the sanitary condition of the labouring population of Great Britain to assess the conditions in Ashton. He visited two lodging houses in Ashton, one in Charlestown, the other in Ashton town. The Charlestown house he described as containing five rooms, the two on the ground floor being used as sitting rooms.

> 'These rooms were crowded with ragged wretches of all ages, sexes, and nations...many of them being wet were drying themselves before the fires, while others, more jovial than the rest, were doing ample justice to the merits of ale, porter, porridge [and] beefsteaks. In vacant corners were hawkers' baskets, pedlars' boxes, musical instruments and beggars' crutches. The sleeping rooms on the second floor were found on entrance to smell strongly of impure air. I ascended to the attic [where] there were 10 beds, which were generally filled with tramps of one sort or another, but it often happens that the whole house is crowded to over-flowing many being obliged to sleep on the floor...At the back of the house, in a very confined situation, is an open necessary which serves about 30 families. The floor of the necessary and the pavement around were covered with ordure and the stench emitted was intolerable. The lodgers are for the most part hawkers, pedlars, knife-grinders, ballad singers, public beggars, impostors, thieves and prostitutes' (Coulthart 1844, 36-7).

Chapter 9 Urban Communities

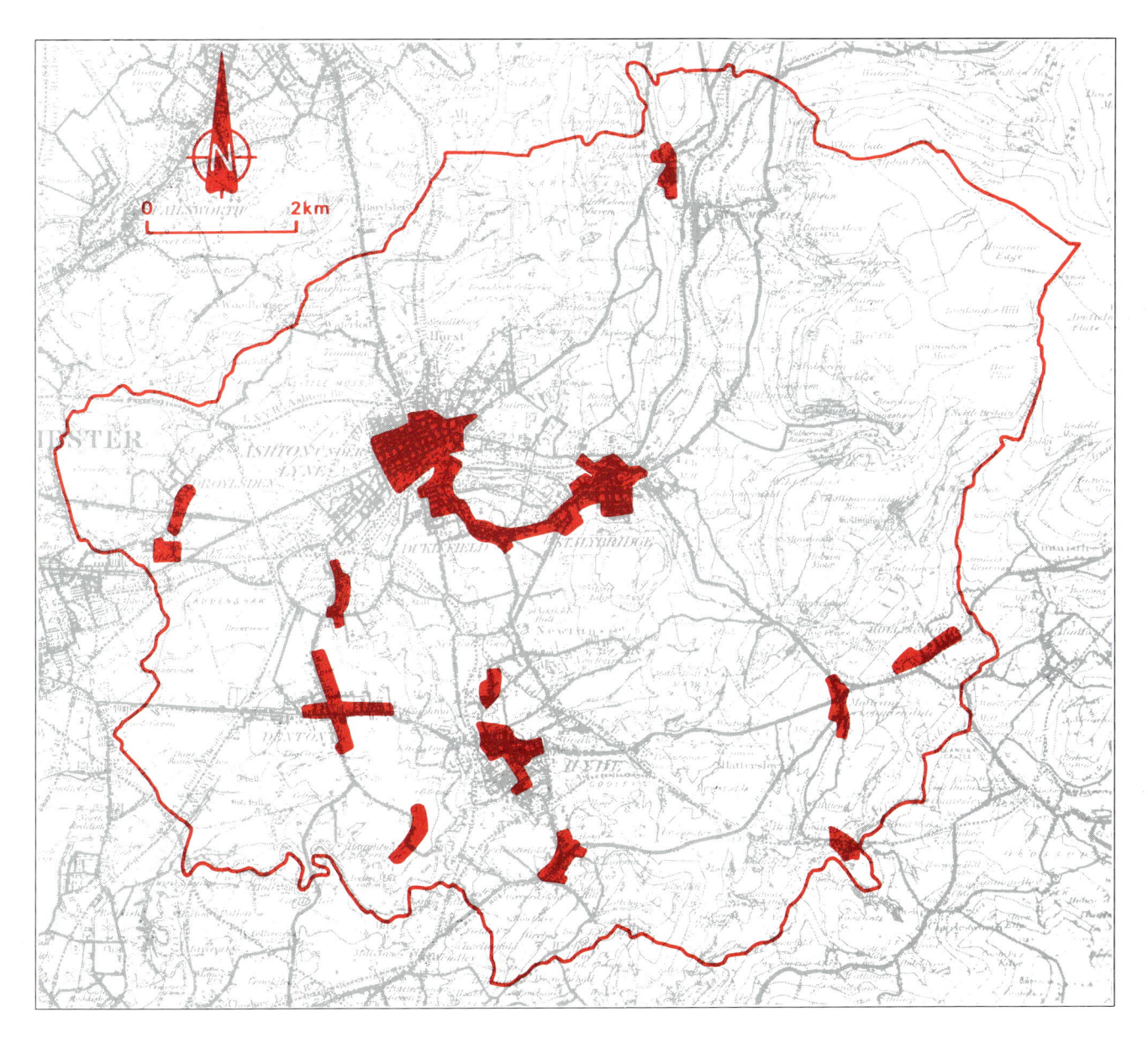

Fig 9.2 Urban areas in Tameside in 1841-2.
From the last quarter of the eighteenth century onwards the rise of the three great industries of the Industrial Revolution in Tameside, textiles, hatting and coal, led to the concentration of people in new manufacturing towns. Ashton and Stalybridge were the largest of these, both seeing phenomenal growth in the period 1775-1841. A clutch of new settlements grew around the factory-based cotton industry in Broadbottom, Droylsden, Flowery Field, Gee Cross, Hollingworth, Hyde and Mossley. In other areas small villages developed around other industries, such as hatting in Denton and mining in Haughton. Although Mottram village saw expansion in the late eighteenth century, this was arrested in the early nineteenth century as the focus of the cotton industry in the township shifted towards the new village of Broadbottom.

The next commonest type of workers' accommodation was the cellar dwelling. Being below ground these were prone to flooding, often resulting in effluent from nearby privies being carried in. Like the lodging or boarding houses, no examples can now be firmly identified in Tameside. However, Coulthart visited a number of cellar dwellings in the 'Little Ireland' part of Ashton, describing them thus;

> '16 [dwellings] open into two enclosed courts, 6 feet below the level of adjoining streets, and each court measuring about 18 yards long by 4 yards wide. There are usually about 100 persons living in the cellars and all that I have conversed with complain of the wretchedness of their dwellings and that their poverty compels them to remain in such miserable abodes...All the cellar dwellings are damp. The light of day is to a great extent excluded, the requisite currents of fresh air obstructed and the confined and tainted atmosphere unfit for human habitation' (*ibid*, 35).

Although back-to-back houses were not widespread in Tameside, Coulthart reckoned that there were 650 such dwellings in Ashton in 1844, accounting for approximately 20% of the housing stock. Further areas of such houses could be found in the vicinity of upper King Street in north-west Dukinfield, Back Percy Street in Mossley and in Stalybridge, although no examples are now known in the Borough. Easy and cheap to build, they consisted of only two rooms; a ground-floor living room and a bedroom above, according to Coulthart seldom more than twelve by fifteen feet, including the stairs and a pantry. As they had only one wall facing outwards they were badly lit and poorly ventilated. Unlike ordinary terraced houses they lacked space for a privy, an inadequate number of which would be set up on spare ground nearby. As with other common privies they were very rarely cleaned. Coulthart described this type of housing as 'exceedingly objectionable' (*ibid*, 34).

The most common form of housing built in Tameside during the nineteenth century was the terraced house, which can be found in all of the major urban areas of the Borough. These were often built by local mill-owners for their workers. Reach, describing the terraced housing in Ashton in 1849, observed that

> 'it is common, particularly in the outskirts to see every mill surrounded with neat streets of perfectly uniform dwellings, clean and cheerful in appearance and occupied by the "hands"...Ranged in rows and squares... each house let according to the number of rooms which it contains...If a garden be attached a few shillings annually are charged in addition...The cottage gardens were, when I visited them, all fluttering with linen drying upon lines and hedges' (Aspin 1972, 76).

Coulthart noted that this type of building was usually built in ranges of ten, twenty or thirty;

> 'the outer walls are 9 inches thick, the inner 5 inches, and are built with the best common brick, at 25s per thousand. The timber is chiefly of the best American pine...and the floors and roofs are usually covered with Yorkshire flags...They are plastered throughout with two coats of excellent plaster, made from Buston lime; and are fitted up in a handsome manner with grates, ovens, and boilers complete' (Coulthart 1844, 32).

Coulthart identified three classes of terraced housing, distinguished by the amount of space to the rear. The best were tenanted by overlookers of factories, handicraftsmen and 'well-conditioned' operative cotton spinners. The second and third classes were occupied by cardroom hands, handicraftsmen and 'well-employed day-labourers' (*ibid*, 32-3).

Many of these nineteenth-century terraced houses survive in Tameside. Notable examples can be seen around Oxford Mills, where a small community of houses was built by Hugh Mason in the period 1845-71, set around two squares and supplied with a school and an institute; at Flowery Field in Hyde, where eight streets of terraced housing were built by the Ashton family in the period 1805-41 for their operatives at the adjacent cotton mills; and at Broadbottom, where stone terraced housing built by the Sidebottom family for their operatives in the period 1802-51 still survives. These three early industrial communities are described in greater detail below. Of the houses built by the local mill-owners Ralph and James Kershaw at Guide Bridge, Reach noted that

> 'the floors were paved with flag stones, but perfectly free from moisture, and generally sprinkled with white glistening sand. In each there was a parlour, a kitchen opening from it, and a yard and proper conveniences behind. The kitchen grate was furnished with a good range, including an oven and an ample boiler; and water from a neighbouring spring laid on, with a sink and all its due apparatus' (Aspin 1972, 76).

A variation of the terraced house, once common in Ashton, Mossley and Stalybridge, was the courtyard terrace:

> 'When 30 or 40 of these dwellings are erected at the same time by a landlord...they are occasionally formed into a parallelogram, with an enclosed area in the centre, which serves as a common back-yard for the whole number' (Coulthart 1844, 33).

Such inward-looking courtyards with access to the street via a covered passageway can still be seen in Mossley, where an especially fine late nineteenth-century example of 50 such houses is set around a central court between Curzon Street and Lorne Street.

Weavers' cottages

The oldest type of workers' housing in Tameside was the weaver's cottage. Many examples of these buildings survive in the historic eighteenth-century cores of Gee Cross, Mossley and Mottram, but rural examples can also be found in Hazelhurst, north of Ashton town. Usually built in stone and of three storeys, they were designed to allow weaving on the top floor and are distinguished by a long row of mullion windows to allow in as much light as possible (Fig 3.7). The lower floors were used as domestic quarters. Fine examples survive in Mottram on Ashworth Road, and in Mossley around the old Market Place and on Anthony Street and Carrhill Road.

Early town houses

Town houses for the professional classes of the eight-

Chapter 9 Urban Communities

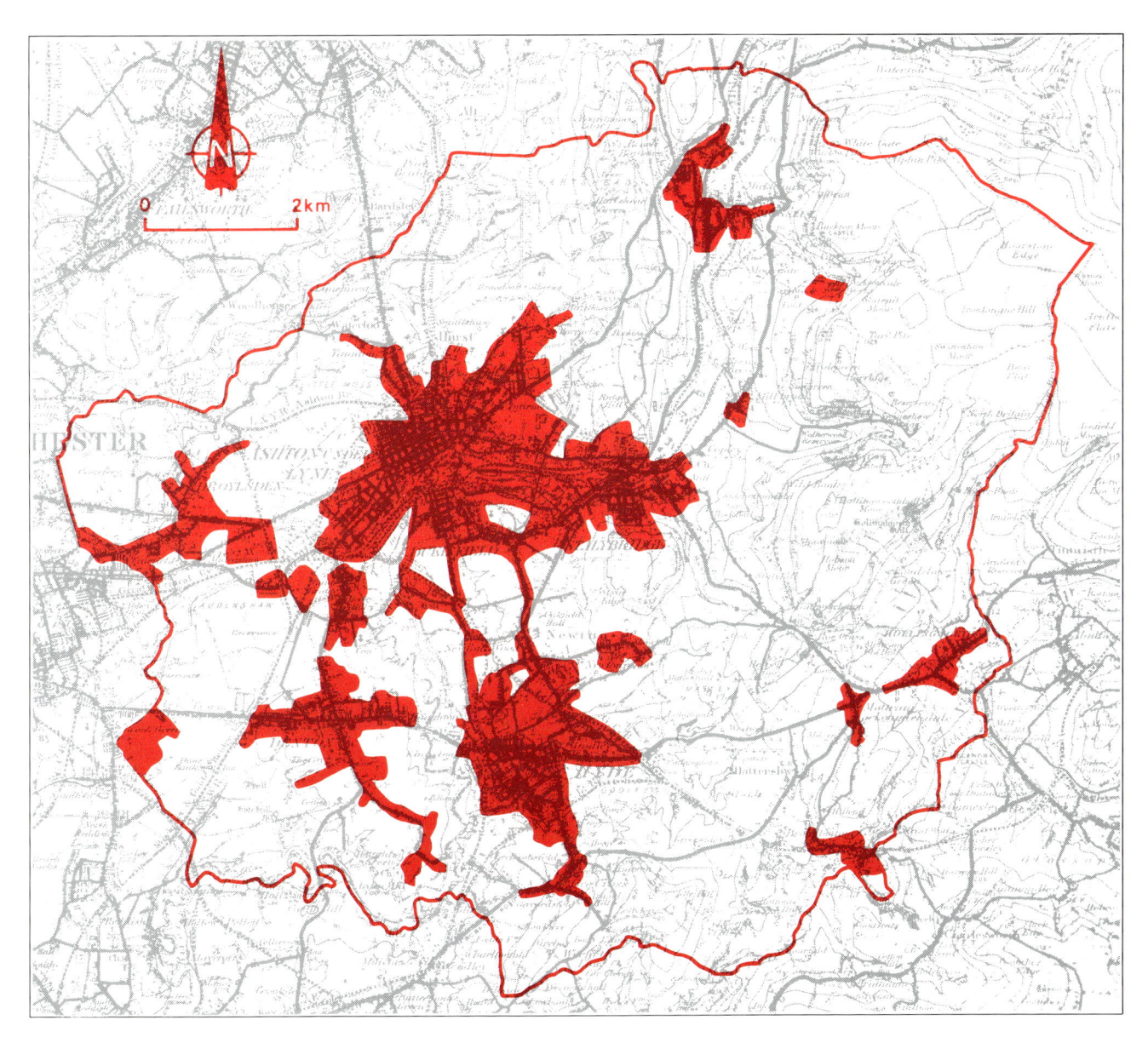

Fig 9.3 Urban areas in Tameside in 1913.
The new industrial towns of the late eighteenth and early nineteenth centuries continued to expand into the early twentieth century. By this time most of the Tame valley between Stalybridge and Haughton had been industrialized, while the chief concentrations of housing and industry, in Ashton, Denton, Dukinfield, Hyde and Stalybridge, had spread to such an extent that these five towns now formed one continuous area of urban development.

eenth and early nineteenth centuries are now only found in Tameside in Ashton town centre around the upper end of Stamford Street, between Old Square and St Michael's church. A row of double-fronted three-storey dwellings was built in this area during the period 1787-1803 as part of the planned Georgian development of Ashton. Most of these buildings have been converted into shops but no 135 Stamford Street survives largely intact, except for some rebuilding at the eastern end. This is of three storeys, with four rooms on each floor, these being equipped with decorated fireplaces and enlivened with cornice moulding, while the entrance has a classical pediment supported by columns.

Manufacturers' houses

The success of many of the largest mills and factories in Tameside enabled the owners to build substantial residences, often in landscaped gardens. Millbrook House, just over the boundary in Derbyshire, was built by John Sidebottom adjacent to Millbrook Mills which he established on this site in 1789; the mill itself has been demolished but the Sidebottoms' grand residence, rebuilt in 1882 and distinguished by its ornate gables and tower, still stands (Hanmer & Winterbottom 1991, 111). In the nineteenth century local manufacturers preferred to build their residences slightly apart from, but frequently still overlooking,

Chapter 9 Urban Communities

their works. The Lees family built Dean House on the southern slopes of Millbrow from where the family had a fine view over their Park Bridge ironworks (Ashmore 1982, 77), while Joseph Woolfenden's sons built three fine detached residences to the south of the Dane Bank hat works as a mark of their rising status (Smith 1966, 6). However, the most impressive manufacturers' houses belonged to the biggest mill-owning families of nineteenth-century Tameside.

William and George Sidebottom of Broadbottom Mills built the extensive property known as Harewood Lodge in the 1820s on the southern slopes of Warhill (CRO QDV2/299). Set in its own grounds, the building is in the Georgian style, stone-built, of five bays, two storeys and a central staircase plan with small symmetrical wings to either side and a wing to the rear (Fig 9.11). There were also neighbouring stables and a gatehouse.

Thomas Ashton, of the great mill-owning family of Hyde, built Pole Bank Hall, set within extensive grounds, to the south of Gee Cross in the early nineteenth century (Maddock 1986, 14). This is a brick building in the Georgian style, of two storeys and a double-depth central staircase plan. The front elevation is enlivened by an entrance defined by a classical porch with Ionic-style columns (DoE 1987, H6/35).

Two fine examples of later nineteenth-century mill-owners' residences can be seen in Ashton and Mossley. Abel Buckley, the founder of Ryecroft Mills in 1832-4, built Ryecroft Hall nearby on Manchester Road in 1860. This is an L-shaped brick building in a Tudor style, of four by seven bays and two storeys (DoE 1987, A4/44). Whitehall, designed by W Williamson and built for George Mayall of Mossley in the years 1861-4, was another large property with great pretensions. Built in the Italianate style, it is of a symmetrical plan of eight bays and two storeys. The stone used for the building is reputed to have come from Macclesfield, while the interior of the house was decorated with heraldic motifs and statuary. Boasting a private reservoir, stables, lodges, glass houses and extensive gardens, the property cost over £60,000 (Eckersley 1991, 48-9).

Community and public buildings

One group of monuments typical of the new nineteenth-century urban landscape were the community and public buildings. Many of these were built with the support of philanthropic mill-owners. Hugh Mason supplied his Oxford Mills community with an institute, library and baths. He was also responsible for the funding of Ashton's public baths, on the southern side of Henry Square. Built in 1870-1 in the Italian Romanesque style to a design by Paull and Robinson, the building is one of the finest pieces of Victorian municipal architecture in the region (Fig 9.4; Plate 2.3). The interior is especially fine with the pool surrounded by paired columns with moulded capitals supporting semi-circular brick arches; above these is a hammer-beam roof (DoE 1987, A4/9). J F Cheetham, the owner of Bankwood Mill, funded the building of Stalybridge Library, designed by J Medland Taylor and opened in 1901 (Preece 1989, 108-10; DoE 1987, St4/182). This was built in a restrained Jacobean style of six bays, with the first storey in stone, the second storey faced with Accrington brick and the roof clad in clay tiles. There are large mullioned windows and stone cornices, while the interior has a central atrium surrounded by arches leading to ancillary rooms. The post office immediately to the north was built at the same time in a similar style and material.

Chapels and churches were another class of urban building which witnessed great expansion during the late eighteenth and nineteenth centuries. Aikin in 1795 records the presence of two churches, in Ashton and Mottram, and seven chapels, two in Dukinfield, and one in each of the townships and villages of Denton, Fairfield, Gee Cross, Mossley and Stalybridge. By the end of the nineteenth century there were 44 Anglican churches and 138 chapels of other denominations in Tameside, mainly Catholic, Congregational and Methodist. Among the most architecturally and historically notable is St Michael's parish church in Ashton, which was extensively remodelled in the period 1821-88. The interior is particularly fine, with dark wood pews and a three-tier pulpit, while the timber panels of the ceiling are enriched by plaster bosses and the walls and arcades deeply moulded with plasterwork (DoE 1987, A4/32).

The Unitarian Dukinfield Old Chapel, behind its 1892 facade, is an unspoilt Gothic building erected in 1840, to a design by Richard Tattersall of Manchester, to replace the original structure of 1707 (Gordon 1896, 1-2). The style is early fourteenth-century and the building is cruciform in plan with a three-sided gallery, box pews, aisles and an organ at the east end. The roof is of ribbed plaster vaulting and there is an octagonal wooden pulpit with a canopy (DoE 1987, Duk3/9).

Hyde Chapel in Gee Cross, a Unitarian foundation built in 1708, was rebuilt in the years 1846-8, to the design of Bowman and Crowther of Manchester. The first fully Gothic Nonconformist chapel in England, the building has a long nave with paired clerestory windows, an open timber roof and a western tower (Middleton 1932, 371-80). The earliest Catholic church still standing in Tameside is St Peter's in Stalybridge, constructed in 1838-9. This is a stone structure built in the Gothic style to the design of M A Hadfield,

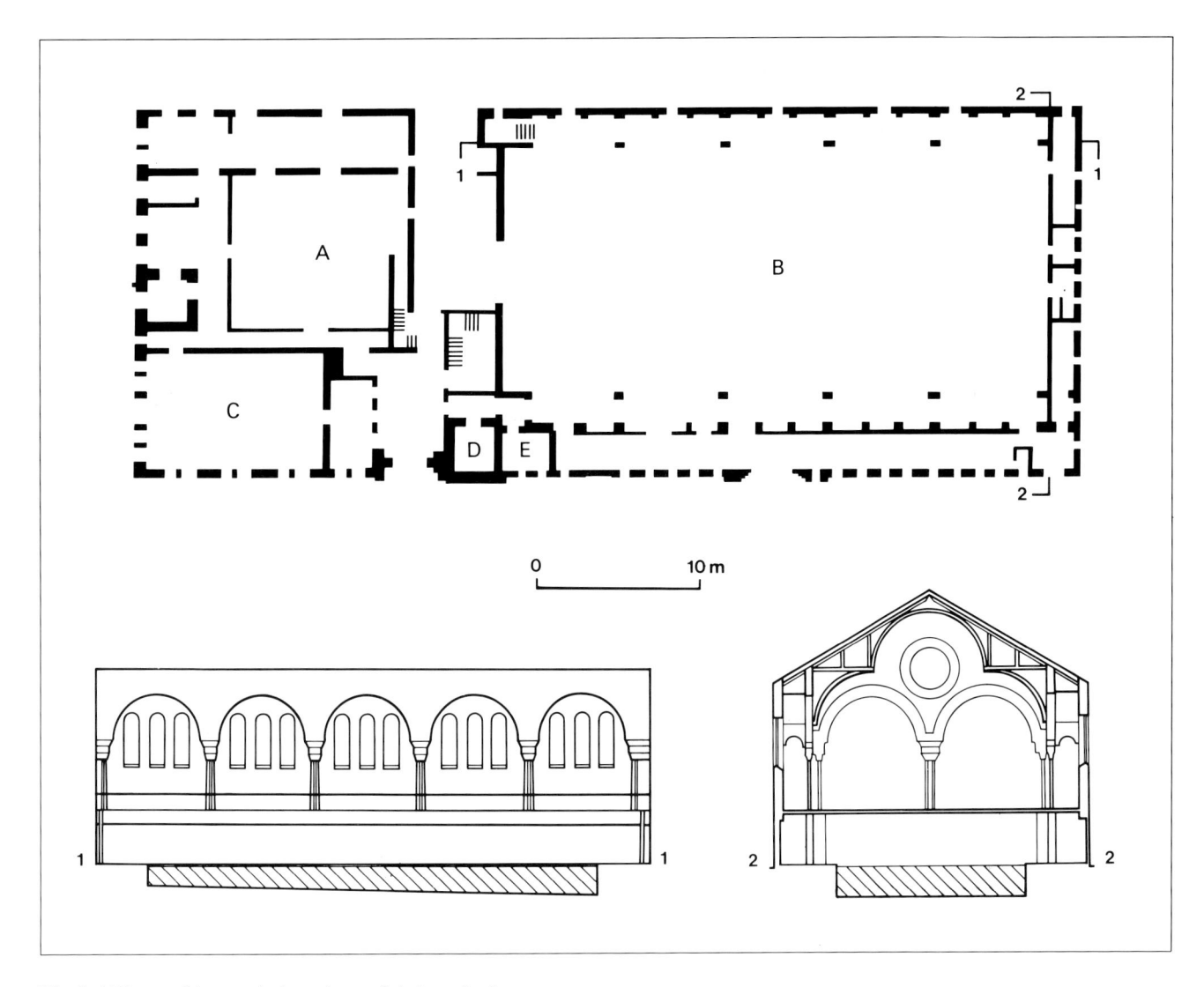

Fig 9.4 Plan and internal elevations of Ashton baths.
Key: A – paddling pool; B – main swimming pool; C – changing rooms; D – chimney; E – boiler house.
Built by Ashton municipal borough in 1870-1 with funds donated by the local mill-owner Hugh Mason, this structure is a notable example of late nineteenth-century municipal architecture.

with seating for 1400. It cost £5000 to build, most of which was raised by contributions from local Catholics (Down *et al* 1989, 9-11).

These religious buildings were themselves often patronized by the wealthy mill-owners of the region. Among the most notable examples is the Anglican St Anne's church in Haughton Green, designed by J Medland Taylor and built in 1881. The funds were provided by E Joseph Sidebotham, a member of the local wealthy industrialist family. Built of brick in the Gothic style but also extensively using timber framing, the church is of a cruciform plan with a tower over the crossing and an undercroft beneath the chancel and transepts. There are notable traceried windows, with glass by Heaton, Butler and Bayne, and the interior is faced in polychromatic brick to great effect. The roof is covered with clay tiles and has an unusual, tile-clad timber tower and spire (DoE 1987, De4/51). Albion Church in Ashton was built in 1890-6 at a cost of £50,000 with the aid of a number of local mill-owners, the Kenworthys, Masons, Reyners and, above all, Abel Buckley who donated more than £23,000 to the cost (Rose 1974, 70). It is the largest Congregational church in England and was designed in the Anglican style by John Brooke, with a nave, aisle passages, clerestory and transepts, and a north-west tower in the Victorian Gothic fashion (Binfield 1988, 173-5).

One group of public buildings which epitomizes the urban growth of nineteenth-century Tameside consists of the town halls erected by the new local authorities. By the beginning of the twentieth century every borough and urban district council in the area had equipped itself with a town hall, and despite the local government reorganization of 1974 many are still in use. Those of Ashton and Dukinfield are of particular note. Ashton town hall was the earliest of the new

Chapter 9 Urban Communities

Plate 9.2 Dukinfield town hall.
Opened in 1901 as a result of the creation of the municipal borough of Dukinfield in 1899, the building was designed by J Eaton and Sons of Ashton.

municipal town halls to be built in Tameside (Stott 1983, 43-4). Constructed in 1840 and extended in 1878 in the same style, it is a statement of the confident civic pride of the new municipal borough. The building is in a classical style to a design by Young and Lee. The main facade fronts the northern side of the Market Place and is of five bays with a central portico of gigantic ashlar columns supporting a pediment. The interior of the building is richly detailed with cast-iron balusters and mural mosaics (DoE 1987, A4/18). Dukinfield town hall, the last to be built in Tameside in this period, was opened in 1901 and is built in a mixture of Romanesque and Gothic styles to a design by J Eaton and Sons of Ashton (Stott 1983, 78). The new-found civic pride of Dukinfield was expressed in the size of the town hall, which matched that of Ashton, although the population of the new municipal borough was much smaller than that of its neighbour. The most striking aspect of the building is the exterior which is faced in alternate bands of red and cream Accrington brick, with a central clock tower (Hickey 1926, 76-8; Plate 9.2).

Amongst the most influential of the new Victorian public buildings were the infirmaries. In the early nineteenth century there was very little provision for health care in Tameside, despite the rapidly increasing populations of the new industrial towns. The creation of the Ashton poor law union in 1837 did not lead to the establishment of a fever hospital in the town until 1847 after a severe outbreak of typhus and cholera. This was eventually replaced by the Ashton-under-Lyne and District Infirmary which opened in 1861, thanks to a donation of £1000 from Samuel Oldham of Audenshaw and the gift of five acres of land near Chamber Hills by the earl of Stamford (Bowman 1960, 337-8).

Public parks

In the mid-nineteenth century the new industrial towns of Tameside had very few leisure facilities. Commenting on Ashton in 1844, Coulthart stated that

> 'no open or convenient spaces for exercise in the form of public parks, gardens or walks have hitherto been found' (Coulthart 1844, 15).

More than twenty years were to pass before a public park was planned, for both Ashton and Stalybridge. In 1865 upon the death of the local mill-owner Abel Harrison, his house and landscaped garden at Highfield House, on the border between the two towns, were purchased for £15,000 with money raised by public subscription and, with a gift of 30 further acres of land from the earl of Stamford, the basis of a public park was formed (Cassidy 1974, 50; *Ashton-under-Lyne Corporation Manual*, 1912-13). The park was laid out by Gregory Hill of Stalybridge whose plans 'were considered to be most practicable, especially on the grounds of expense'. This original section of Stamford Park was opened in 1873. In 1891 a joint committee was formed to manage the park for Ashton and Stalybridge boroughs and quickly began two major projects (Bowman 1960, 340). To the west of the park was a very steep, rocky and picturesque valley, Cock Brook, which contained three defunct water-powered mills, and to the north lay a large reservoir, Chadwick's Dam, which provided them with a head of water. These two pieces of land were acquired by the committee and the reservoir was remodelled and divided into two by an embankment. The mills on Cock Brook were demolished and the valley turned into a wooded dell.

The success of Stamford Park led the other municipal boroughs of nineteenth-century Tameside to provide public parks which were landscaped with walks, formally planted woods, open vistas and playgrounds. In 1897 the mill-owning Ashton family offered the Newton Lodge estate of about 30 acres to the borough of Hyde as a gift to commemorate Queen Victoria's diamond jubilee. Hyde Park was finally opened on 21st May 1904. In 1899 Dukinfield Park was begun by the new borough of Dukinfield. Opened in 1902 it cost £15,000 and lies on the southern bank of the River Tame (Pavasovic 1984, 45). The last major public park to be opened in Tameside was Cheetham Park in Stalybridge, opened in 1931 and formed from the Eastwood estate donated to the borough by John Cheetham and the Priory estate donated by Mrs Wimbush, Cheetham's niece (March 1957, 68). Unlike the other public parks within Tameside, Cheetham Park is notable for the semi-natural state of its grounds and woodlands, with little which is formally laid out.

Urban corn-mills

One urban building type of the nineteenth century often neglected in modern studies is the corn-mill. Before the advent of the railways in the mid-nineteenth century these were vital to the adequate feeding of the mushrooming industrial towns of the North-West, and there was a consequent boom in their building during the late eighteenth and early nineteenth centuries (Ashmore 1969, 152-3). Bott records 190 new mills in Cheshire alone during the period 1702-1850, although many of these were textile factories rather than corn-mills (Bott 1986, 27). Many of the new corn-mills of this period were built on the site of earlier medieval manorial corn-mills, such as those of Ashton or Stayley (Nevell 1991, 54-7; Haynes 1987, 10; 1990, 24).

Within Tameside little evidence survives for the corn-mills of the Industrial Revolution. One of the most unusual examples was the Stalybridge corn-mill (SJ 9665 9855) (Fig 9.5). This had been built around 1800 by John Buckley as a water-powered woollen mill, taking advantage of the new Huddersfield Canal (Haynes 1990, 17-18). After John's death in 1821, the building remained in the family but was converted in 1821-5 into a corn-mill, which it remained until the twentieth century (Morris 1992, 2). The 1820s were Stalybridge's period of fastest growth, the population rising approximately threefold between 1821 and 1831 (Butterworth 1842, 95). This must have led to a great increase in the demand for foodstuffs, and with the woollen industry in long-term decline in the area the Buckley family made a timely decision to change occupations. By the 1830s the Stalybridge corn-mill was one of the new type of steam-powered, town-based corn-mills springing up all over the North-West, which rapidly replaced the older local water- and wind-powered mills.

The Stalybridge corn-mill was a three-phase structure (*ibid*, 3-5). The first phase belonged to the period prior to 1821-5 when the mill was used as a woollen factory and comprised a four-storey stone-built block, of six by four bays, with rectangular windows with stone sills and lintels, and a gable slate roof. The wooden floors were supported by cast-iron columns. A water-wheel was fed from the canal via a leat, now culverted. The second phase dates to shortly after the conversion of the building to corn-milling. In 1831 an engine house and a square chimney on the south-western gable were added. In 1852 a third phase of building activity took place, with the rebuilding of the engine house and the addition of a boiler house extending the building to eleven bays. Sack hoists on the eastern elevation by the canal lifted the grain to the top storey, where it was stored. The grain would then have been emptied through chutes into hoppers above the grinding stones on the floor below; unfortunately none of this internal detail survived in the building by the time of its demolition in January 1993. Although the mill is now demolished, the associated mid-nineteenth-century warehouse of four storeys and four by four bays, linked to the mill, survives, as do offices of *c* 1825, an 1852 gatehouse and associated workers' housing at nos 18-22 Mottram Road (GM SMR 3588).

9.3 Ashton

Outline development

Although Ashton-under-Lyne is perhaps best known as one the most important Lancashire cotton towns of the nineteenth century, its history pre-dates the Industrial Revolution. In origin a medieval market town, Ashton's urban history is particularly noteworthy for the extensive remains which survive of a Georgian and Regency planned town of the late eighteenth and early nineteenth centuries. This planned town was noted by a number of early commentators (Aikin 1795, 226-7; Butterworth 1823, 85-6; Coulthart 1844, 34-6), but in modern times has received little attention beyond passing remarks by Ashworth (1954, 23) and Cherry (1972, 16).

A series of maps in the Stamford records, now held by estate agents and surveyors Cordingleys in Ashton, allows the development of the town to be recovered during this crucial period (ESRCA 14-23; Appendix 2). The earliest of these maps dates from 1765 and indicates that the core of pre-Georgian Ashton centred on four roads, Town Street, Crickets Lane, Old Street and Cowhill Lane (Nevell 1992, 100; ESRCA 15). Little remains of this pre-industrial town, although two buildings marked on the plan of 1765 have survived the later Georgian and Victorian redevelopments: a structure on Old Street, with a datestone of 1742, and Razzles public house on the north side of the old market place.

The first evidence for the grid-iron plan of the modern settlement, centring on Stamford Street, is found on a map of 1787 which shows the proposed layout of Ashton town west of the medieval church (ESRCA 16). The grid-iron pattern of streets in this first Georgian plan extends as far west as Mill Lane, and is bounded on the south by Park Parade and on the north by the medieval road known as Old Street. There is, however, a northern extension beyond Old Street which takes in the area west of Warrington Street and east of Oldham Street. Apart from in this northern extension, by 1787 all the streets in this zone had been named and the land divided into parcels and leased. The core of this development was a principal east-west thoroughfare, Stamford Street, which passed through a circus later known as Old Square. A map of

Fig 9.5 The Stalybridge corn-mill.
This building was originally constructed as a woollen mill around 1800 but in the period 1821-5, during a rapid rise in the population of Stalybridge, it was converted into an urban corn-mill. The first six bays on the left-hand side were the woollen mill. The chimney (A), loading doors (B) and engine house (C) were added after the building's conversion.

the Salters Brook Turnpike Trust, probably of the period 1799-1803, includes a sketch plan of Ashton and shows that all of the land to the east of Warrington Street, or approximately half of the new planned town, had been built upon by that date (St Michael's Parish Church, Ashton-under-Lyne, Collection; Plate 1.2).

By 1820 proposals had been drawn up by the Stamford estate to more than double the area of the original planned town. This new Regency-period scheme, recorded on a map which is undated but probably belongs to the years 1819-20, extended Stamford Street west of Mill Lane through Henry Square and on to the site of St Peter's church (ESRCA 14; Fig 9.6). Although Stamford Street remained the chief axis of the town, five new roads ran at right-angles across the line of the street – Cavendish, Bentinck, Portland, Welbeck and Margaret streets – whilst the northern and southern limits of the plan were defined by Shaw Brook and the River Tame. This new plan even included within its alignment Ashton New Wharf on the Ashton Canal. The development of this plan is recorded on two maps of 1820 and 1822 (ESRCA 17 & 19). This is also the scheme mapped by J Atkinson in 1824 for Baines' directory, published in 1825. When compared with the earlier Stamford estate maps, Atkinson's map indicates how slowly building in this area proceeded, despite the grand design, for by 1824 there were very few buildings west of Portland Street or north of Henry Square.

The third phase of the development of the Georgian and Regency planned town of Ashton took place in the late 1820s and early 1830s (ESRCA 20, 22 & 23). This was the laying out of streets in a similar grid-iron pattern to that seen earlier, around the new Market Place and to the east of Town Street, or Scotland Street as it was now called. The area of the new Market Place was defined by Katherine Street and Stile Barn Road, and incorporated the late eighteenth-century settlement of Charlestown into the area of the planned town. The grid of streets to the east of Scotland Street was defined along its southern edge by the Salters Brook turnpike and a continuation of Stamford Street on a new alignment to the east of Scotland Street, on the east by Montague Road, and along its northern edge by Mossley Road. However, the integrity of this part of the plan was severely compromised by the building of the railway from Manchester to Stalybridge in the 1840s, which effectively severed this proposed new area from the medieval core of the town.

The design of the Georgian and Regency town

It is not known when the idea of developing Ashton as a planned town was first proposed, and there is no evidence to suggest that William Wright and J Sidebottom, who surveyed and laid out the 1787 plan, were the originators. The second and third phases of development, from around 1820, were probably designed, but again not necessarily initiated, by Joel Hawkyard, whose name is attached to all of the Stamford estate plans of Ashton in this period.

It is possible that the fifth earl of Stamford himself, who inherited the property in 1768, was active in the design of the original new town. The names of the new streets have strong Stamford family connections. Aside from the obvious Stamford Street, they include the old family names Booth and Delamere (a reference to Sir George Booth who was the first Lord Delamere), and Grey and Warrington, also names with Stamford family connections. The fifth earl of Stamford was presumably well informed on current ideas concerning planned estates and towns, since he had a London town house in Sackville Street from 1766 to 1778 (Mr F Kelsall, pers comm). The formal estate developments of Cavendish, Grosvenor and Hanover squares had been built in London in the early eighteenth century, while from the 1770s the ideas of John Gwynn, architect of Edinburgh New Town, could be seen in the duke of Bedford's development of Bedford Square in Bloomsbury (Cherry 1972, 10-11). All were characterized by grid-iron street patterns, open spaces and spacious buildings.

Although the Ashton development was on a much smaller scale than either the Edinburgh or London developments, it displays an interesting combination of eighteenth-century town-planning features. In particular it retained the medieval street plan, around which the new town was planned, as well as having an outward looking plan with long vistas and formal open spaces. The decision to retain the pre-eighteenth-century irregular town plan posed the problem of how to join this to the new grid-iron pattern. This was solved by the use of the Circus which allowed the east-west axis of the main thoroughfare, Stamford Street, running at right-angles away from the medieval town on Scotland Street, to be turned through seven degrees so that it ran parallel with Old Street, to the north. The technique of using open spaces to adjust the new town plan can also be seen at the junction of Old Street and Stamford Street, where Henry Square was created to combine the old and new town plans. This technique continued to be used during the Regency period. The positioning of the new Market Place allowed the medieval town plan to be reconciled with the Georgian plan in the area north of Old Street and south of the Charlestown community. Likewise, the new grid-iron development of streets in the south-west of the town reconciled the line of the eighteenth-century turnpike to Stockport by creating an open space at Trafalgar Square. Here the old line of Stockport Road

Chapter 9 Urban Communities

Plate 9.3 Old Square, Ashton, looking westwards along Stamford Street towards St Peter's church.
Originally known as the Circus, Old Square forms the core of the Georgian planned town, and was built sometime during the period 1787-1803. The buildings to the right, on the corner of Stamford Street and George Street, date from this period.

joined the main axis of the new plan as represented by Victoria Street, so as to create a new vista looking south-westwards towards St Stephen's church.

The heart of the vistas and open plan of the original new town was the Circus, or Old Square as it was later known (Plate 9.3). From here there are grand vistas to the west, down Stamford Street, with St Peter's church dominating the skyline, and to the south, where Dukinfield Old Chapel formed the focus of the vista. The latter chapel also formed a second grand vista at the southern end of the north-south axis of Warrington Street, while the northern axis of this street was marked by a later nineteenth-century chapel. Of these landmarks only Dukinfield Old Chapel was in existence in 1787, St Peter's church being built in the period 1821-4 and thus contemporary with the second phase of the development. Smaller vistas were also built into both the Georgian and Regency elements of the new town. The Pitt and Nelson public house, in origin an eighteenth-century establishment on Old Street, was rebuilt with tall, gracefully arched windows, so as to catch the eye at the end of the new George Street. The mid-nineteenth-century development of Market Avenue was marked at its southern junction with Stamford Street by a tall three-storey building, which is in contrast to the more squat three-storey Georgian buildings surrounding it and which can still be seen from Old Square.

Another characteristic of this period of town planning was the rigid social distinction of the town plan, with a strict hierarchy of road widths marking these divisions. The widest roads in Ashton were the east-west Stamford Street and Katherine Street, both sixteen yards wide, marking those areas for the upper and, in particular, the growing middle classes. The main north-south roads of the plan, Warrington, Delamere, Booth, Mill, Cavendish, Bentinck, Portland, Welbeck and Margaret streets, were all twelve yards wide, while the lesser east-west roads were ten and eight yards wide. It was the latter which were designed to house the working classes and artisans of the town. While the social divisions of the Georgian and Regency periods were expressed in the grid-iron pattern of the new town, the plan was still very small

Chapter 9 Urban Communities

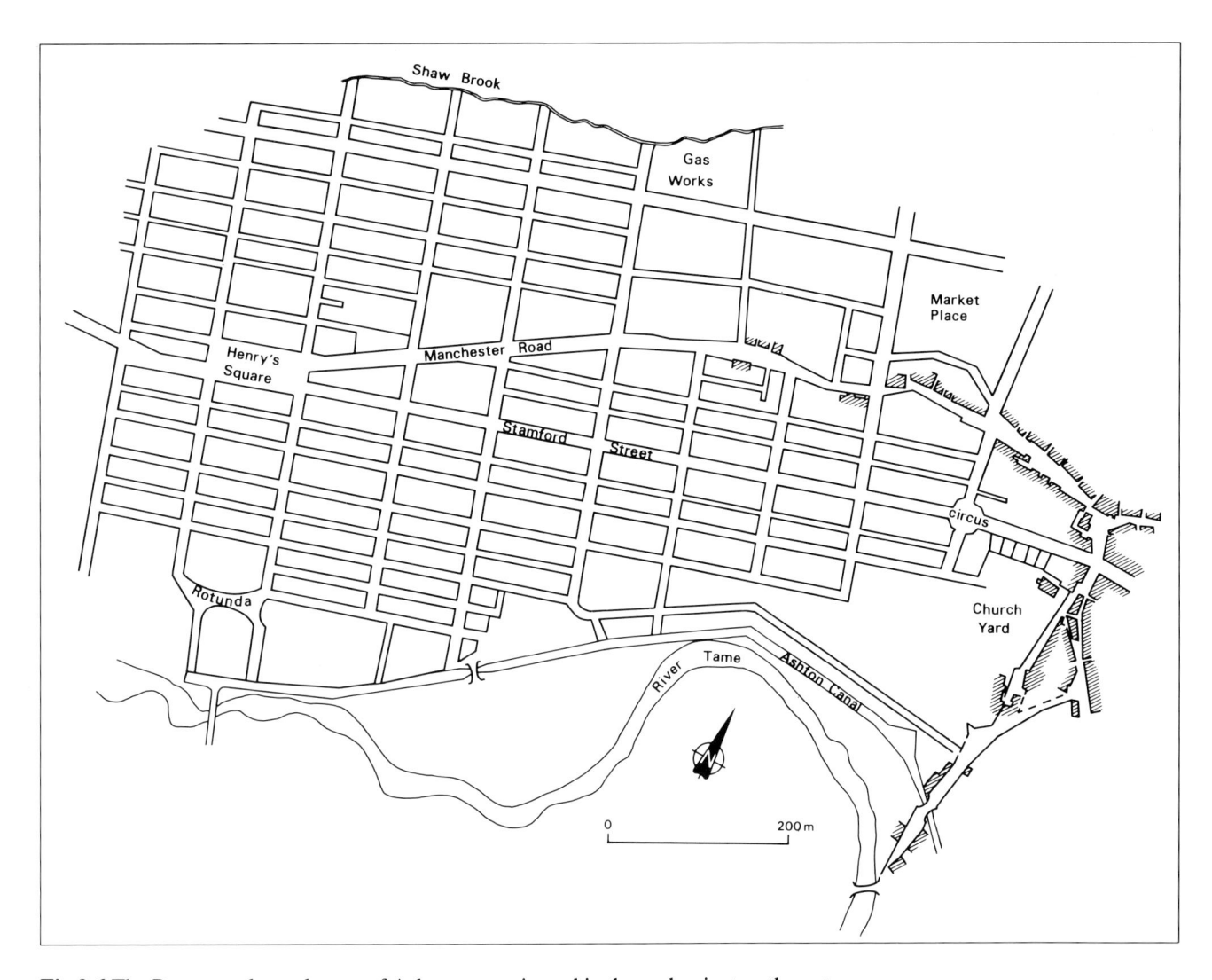

Fig 9.6 The Regency planned town of Ashton as envisaged in the early nineteenth century.
Based on an undated plan in the Cordingley archives (ESRCA 14), probably drawn in the years 1819-20, this shows the proposals for the second phase of the Georgian and Regency planned town, with the streets and squares labelled as on the original plan. Especially notable are the sites of the future gas works and new market which were integral parts of this phase of development.

in scale, so that there was a juxtaposition of social classes, the evidence for which can still be seen at the eastern end of the town around the Circus. At the eastern end of Stamford Street stands a fine double-fronted Georgian town house of the period 1787-1803 (see above). Just round the corner, in Wellington Street, stands a row of five three-storey workers' cottages (Fig 9.7; Plate 9.4). These were originally a six-bay three-storey loomshop also built in 1787-1803, probably by James Harrop and John Taylor (ESRCA 16). Each floor appears to have been completely open, and there were loading doors at the eastern and western ends. In the early nineteenth century the building was converted into cottages by the insertion of simple brick partitions on the ground and first floors. Other small workshops can be found between Stamford Street and Old Street, particularly along Wellington Street and Wood Street, although their precise function is unclear.

The later development of Ashton

During the second half of the nineteenth century there were certain shifts in house type and quality visible in Ashton but also common to all other urban areas of Tameside during this period. Much of the later nineteenth-century domestic development of Ashton was concentrated to the west and east of the Georgian and Regency town and the houses are much more varied in type than their early nineteenth-century predecessors. Semi-detached houses, dwellings with bay windows, and Accrington brick occur for the first time, providing greater distinction in house type, and there is greater use of decoration. Furthermore, the vast majority of this new housing was built by private companies rather than mill-owners (Harrop 1974, 44-6).

The most significant change in this period was the passing of the Ashton-under-Lyne Improvement Act in 1886 which allowed the borough to control many

Chapter 9 Urban Communities

Plate 9.4 Loomshop in Wellington Street, Ashton.
This building was built in the period 1787-1803, probably by James Harrop and John Taylor. The structure was originally a three-storey loomshop, each floor being open to allow the maximum space and light for weaving. The lower two floors were later divided into separate dwellings but the third floor remains open and is the only known surviving example of its kind in Tameside.

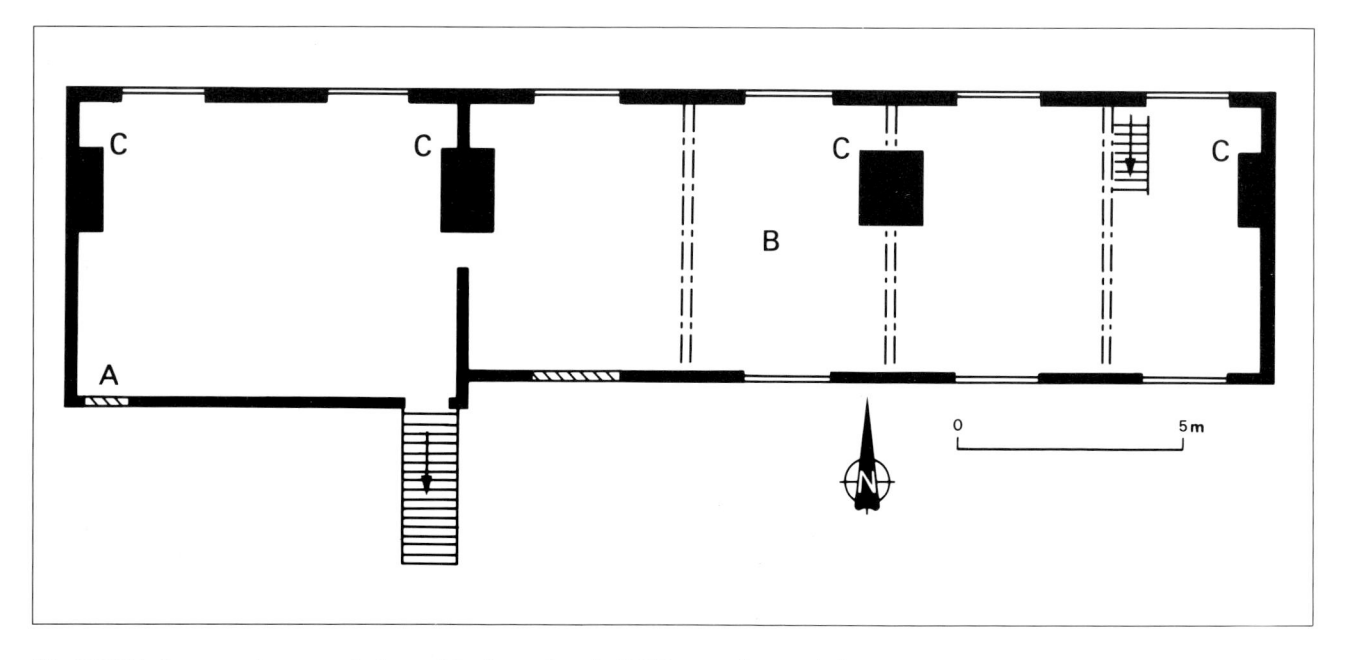

Fig 9.7 Third-storey plan, as existing, of the loomshop in Wellington Street, Ashton.
Key: A – original three-storey access; B – loomshop; C – later brick chimney.

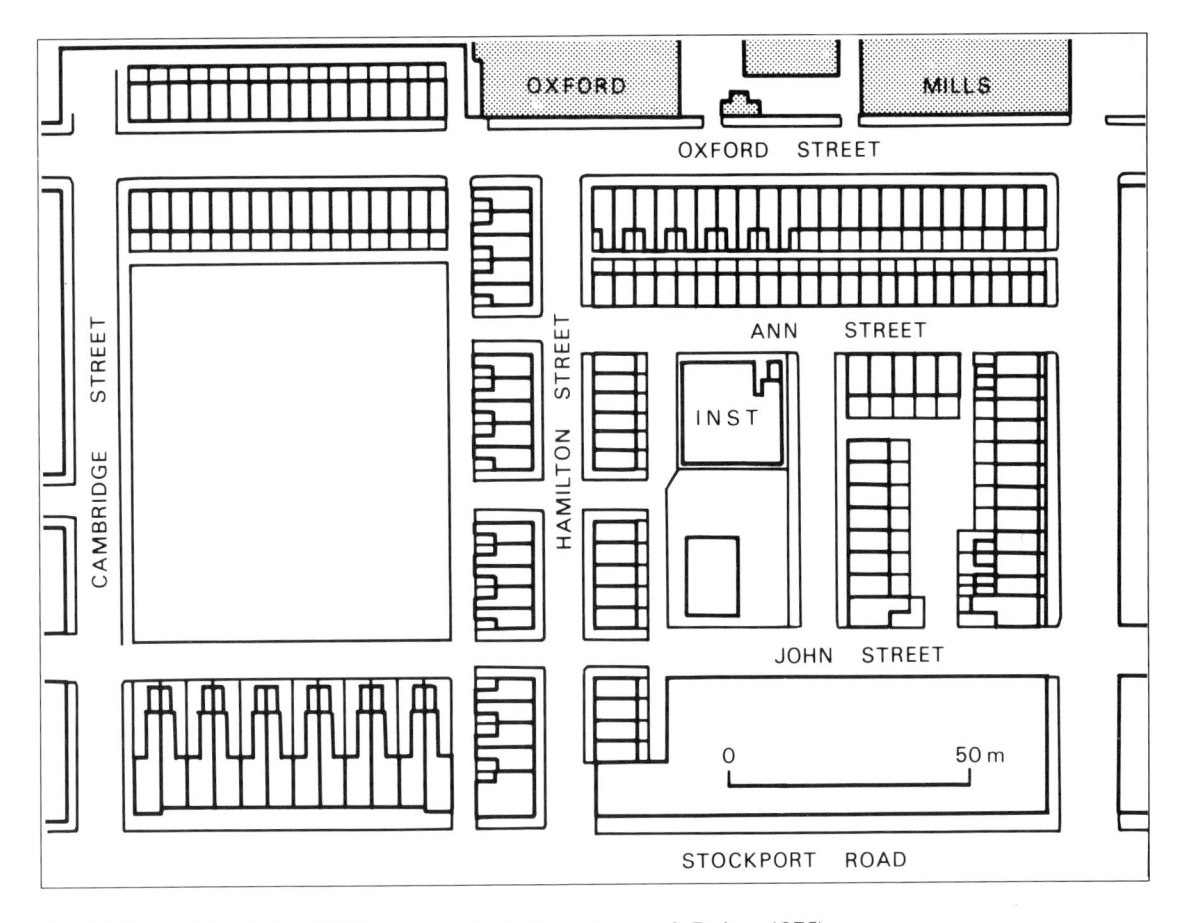

Fig 9.8 Plan of the Oxford Mills community (after Ashmore & Bolton 1975).
This was a small factory colony built by Hugh Mason in the years 1845-71, in Guide Bridge, on the south-west edge of Ashton town. The community not only comprised ranges of terraced houses grouped around the mills but also included an institute, on Ann Street, and a recreation ground and gymnasium on John Street.

aspects of housing, including the minimum heights of rooms, proper drainage of each property and a regular system for the disposal of night-soil (*ibid*, 41). By the end of the century the council were converting all privies into water closets and in 1903 opened a sewage disposal works in Dukinfield (*ibid*, 44).

Smaller-scale developments, such as the construction of Market Avenue in 1847 and, later, of the Stamford and Clarence arcades, were carried out in the commercial town core, while to the north and west of the Georgian and Regency town large public buildings – the market hall, the town hall, the public library and the public baths – were erected. The main building material continued to be brick, although there are some public buildings, such as the town hall, constructed in stone. Even so the unity of the Georgian plan was preserved, thanks to the continued ownership of most of Ashton by the earls of Stamford, their estate being administered by Cordingleys.

Oxford Mills community

This settlement was founded in 1845, following the building of the first of the two Oxford Mills, in Guide Bridge, by Thomas Mason & Sons in 1840 (Ashmore & Bolton 1975, 38). Land for the community was bought in four lots during the years 1845-71 and a total of 150 houses were built, those in the Ann Street and Hamilton Street areas being erected first (*ibid*, 39-40; Fig 9.8). The houses varied considerably in style and were a mixture of long rows of twelve, sixteen or 22 terraces and short rows of four, five or six terraces. All were brick-built and had two storeys.

Reach described the community in 1849, praising Hugh Mason for spending

'£1,000 in drainage, by which the refuse from every house is carried down into the river. The cottages are of two kinds – four- and six-roomed. For the former 3s per week is charged, for the latter 4s 3d per week...I inspected one of the four-roomed class. There was a lobby, and the stairs leading to the bedrooms were nicely carpeted. The front room was furnished strictly as a parlour; but the back one, or kitchen, which opened into a flagged yard, was obviously the ordinary sitting room' (Aspin 1972, 77).

Chapter 9 Urban Communities

When these houses were sold in 1931 the weekly rents were 5s 10d in Ann Street, the smallest dwellings, 7s to 8s 10d in Hamilton Street, 7s 3d to 10s in Bright and Gibson terraces and 11s 6½d to 30s in Trafalgar Square. The 1871 census records that of the 233 men and women living in these streets 205 worked in Oxford Mills and that most were born locally (TLSL Census returns). Buildings were also provided for the leisure and educational needs of the workforce. These included a library, reading room and baths, all housed in the institute opened in 1868 in Ann Street, and a recreation ground and gymnasium, opened in 1870 in John Street (Ashmore & Bolton 1975, 41-2).

Park Bridge ironworking community

Park Bridge is the oldest surviving example in the North-West of an industrial engineering community. The works were founded around 1784, probably by Samuel Lees the elder, on the site of a corn-mill in the Medlock valley (see Chapter 7). The associated community lies immediately north of the site, at the top of the valley, and has two main groups of housing. The earliest is Dean Terrace, a single row of workers' cottages. Dingle Terrace to the east was built in the late nineteenth century and consists of two rows of brick-built workers' cottages. The village institute, at its western end, was built in 1866. Keverlow Farm, at the eastern end of Dean Terrace, was once a public house, while north of the terrace lay St James's church and school, also built in 1866. Dean House, between the housing and the workshops, was the home of the Lees family (Ashmore 1969, 86-7).

9.4 Audenshaw

Besides Ashton town there were a number of small settlements in Ashton parish which saw expansion from the late eighteenth century onwards. These included Hurst, a northern suburb of Ashton which was given its own local board in 1861 and later became an urban district council, and Mossley which although originally part of Ashton parish was not included in the new borough, having instead its own board and later itself becoming a borough. Particularly notable was the division of Audenshaw which later became an urban district council and whose settlement pattern was characterized by a nucleated core, in the ancient hamlet of Audenshaw, rather than by dispersed farmsteads as seen elsewhere in pre-industrial Tameside.

Audenshaw village

Audenshaw village was a nucleated settlement located on a T-junction between the road from Denton to Ashton and the turnpike from Manchester to Ashton. There was a small hamlet here by the seventeenth century (Nevell 1991, 22), but despite the close proximity of both Denton and Ashton this does not appear to have grown significantly during the Industrial Revolution. This may have been because the village was isolated from the mainstream of developments. In 1765 the road from Denton to Ashton via Audenshaw was superseded by a more direct turnpike route between Stockport, Denton and Ashton, while in 1825 the Manchester to Ashton turnpike was diverted northwards across Ashton Moss. The new routes provided faster access to Ashton but left Audenshaw as a rural backwater and ultimately contributed to its demise under the Audenshaw reservoirs in the period 1875-84 (Denton Local History Society 1991, 5-7).

Hooley Hill

Hooley Hill, which became the core of the later Audenshaw UDC, developed along the turnpike route between Stockport, Denton and Ashton where it crossed the road from Audenshaw to Dukinfield (Plate 1.1). The main period of growth was from the 1790s to the 1830s, when a strong hatting industry was established in the village (see Chapter 4). In 1795 Aikin reckoned that there were 238 houses in Audenshaw, most of them in the new settlement known as Quebec, later to become Hooley Hill (Aikin 1795, 229, 233). In 1823 Butterworth described the settlement as 'now a very populous village' and noted that there were over 250 houses here and a population of about 1500. There was a small Wesleyan Methodist chapel, with a school attached, and a New Connexion Methodist chapel. The majority of the buildings were strung along Guide Lane. These were terraced houses, 'all modern brick erections' and occupied by hatters and their families, while the residence of one of the wealthiest and most important hat manufacturers in the locality, Mr Bradbury, was located at the southern end of the village (Butterworth 1823, 86-7).

The severe depression in the felt hatting industry during the 1840s and 1850s appears to have arrested the growth of the village, which warranted little more than a passing reference from Butterworth in 1842 (Butterworth 1842, 125). This stagnation is reflected in the population of the Audenshaw division, which had risen from around 1500 in 1795 to 5374 in 1841, the year the hatting depression struck the area, remaining static for a decade after this date before resuming a slow growth and reaching 7958 in 1891 (*ibid*, 126; Table 2.1). This slow expansion in the latter half of the nineteenth century was concentrated in two areas. The first was around the junction of Guide Lane and

Shepley Road, the second slightly further north, where a series of streets, including Pleasant Street, Bridge Street and Tame Street, developed east of Guide Lane.

9.5 Denton

The modern town of Denton is comprised of two earlier townships, Denton and Haughton. Prior to the eighteenth century there was no significant urban centre innthe district, which was dominated by dispersed farmsteads (Young 1982, 6). However, during the late eighteenth century the development of the felt hatting and coal-mining industries led to the emergence of two significant villages: Denton, whose eighteenth-century core lay around Denton chapel and the junction of Town Lane and Stockport Road, and Haughton Green, an arrangement of houses around a green in the southern part of Haughton township (Young 1982, 1; Aikin 1795, 456).

Denton had the advantage of being at the crossroads of the Stockport to Ashton turnpike route and the Manchester to Hyde and Mottram turnpike, established in 1765 and 1818 respectively. As a result of this, a ribbon development of housing, mainly brick-built terraces, grew along Stockport Road between Town Lane and Hyde Road, and along Hyde Road towards the Tame and the river crossing to Hyde. By the mid-nineteenth century new housing in the township was concentrated in this area, centred on the crossroads although still located only along the two main thoroughfares (LRO DRM 1/37).

The rapid development of Denton and Haughton is reflected in the speed of growth in the population. Booker estimated that in 1774 there were 227 houses and 1212 inhabitants in the two townships, with Haughton having the slightly larger population (Booker 1855, 8, 134). Both townships appear to have matched each other in growth during the first half of the nineteenth century. In 1801 Denton had a population of 1362 to Haughton's 1139, and by 1841 these figures were 3440 and 3319 respectively (Table 2.1).

After the hatting depression of the 1840s and 1850s, Denton was initially the slower of the two townships to recover, but by the 1860s, thanks to the establishment of new mechanized hat factories, had embarked on a period of rapid growth. Haughton, on the other hand, in the late nineteenth century witnessed a decline in its coal-mining industry, as a consequence of which urban development shifted northwards from Haughton Green to Hyde Road and the River Tame crossing, where a number of cotton mills had been set up in the mid-nineteenth century (see Chapter 3). The differing economic fortunes of the two townships were reflected in the growth of their populations; in 1891, the last year in which the townships were assessed separately in the census before being merged to formed Denton UDC in 1894, that of Denton had reached 8666 and that of Haughton 5327 (Table 2.1).

The urban growth of Denton in the late nineteenth and early twentieth centuries was concentrated around the new hat factories. Both Moores' and Wilson's hat factories had associated brick-built terraced housing immediately adjacent to the works, on new streets west of the old town centre, Crown Point, while east of Crown Point terraced housing began to develop both to the north and south of Hyde Road.

Dane Bank hatting community

Although much of the area's urban growth in the nineteenth century was focused on Denton town, there were other small communities which grew independently of the centre. One of the best known of these was the Dane Bank hatting community, which developed on Windmill Lane on the western side of the township. This was a small collection of buildings, ranging from the Woolfendens' hat factory to workers' terraced housing and the factory owners' town houses (Fig 9.9). Although most of the factory and its associated community has been demolished, enough survives to trace the development of the company and the site from its foundation in 1830.

Joseph Woolfenden bought Dane Shot Bank Farm, now known as Dane Bank Farm, on the edge of Denton moor, in 1820 and started making hats in 1830. This was in a small workshop which still stands against the western gable of the farmhouse. Later a large factory was built nearby (see Chapter 4).

During the second half of the nineteenth century terraced houses were built in Joseph Street and Daneshot Street for the hat workers, east of the factory. These were two-storey, brick-built, slate roofed houses, of two-up two-down design. They had rectangular sash windows with stone sills and headers. To the west of the factory there are a set of terraces fronting Windmill Lane which still survive and are of a similar design (Holding 1986, 58, 60).

The community was completed by three large houses built for the Woolfenden family opposite the factory, on the southern side of Windmill Lane (Smith 1966, 6). These are two-storey buildings, with a centrally placed brick-arched doorway flanked by two ground-floor bay windows. Each upper storey has three rectangular sash windows on the front elevation, and below the eaves runs a line of dentillated brickwork (Holding 1986, 59).

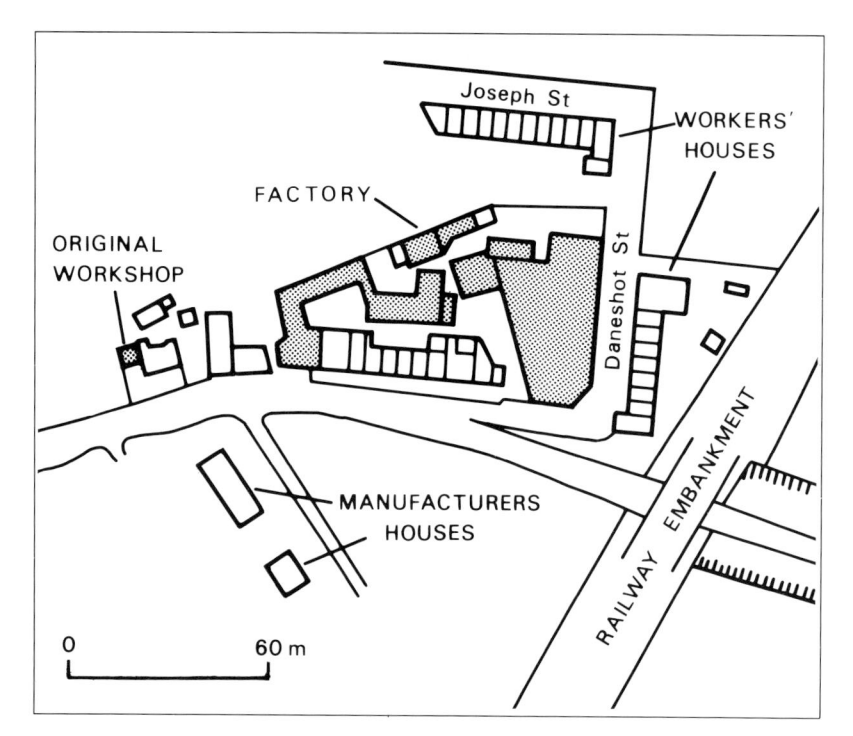

Fig 9.9 Plan of the Dane Bank hatting community (after Smith 1966). This small community was established in the mid-nineteenth century by the Woolfenden family, who owned the hatting factory at the centre of the complex. The family also built, for their own use, three large houses close to the factory but set in extensive grounds.

9.6 Droylsden

For much of the eighteenth century Droylsden, in common with most of Tameside, was a rural community dominated by dispersed farmsteads. By the last quarter of the century a small village, principally made up of a few farmsteads, had developed at the T-junction of Greenside Lane and Market Street, known then as Lane Head. These buildings appear to have been a mixture of stone and brick farmhouses. From 1783 a second urban core developed around the Moravian settlement in Fairfield, some distance south of Lane Head, along Annitt Lane, later Fairfield Road. It was characterized by brick-built two- and three-storey dwellings set around a court and a chapel. The history of this settlement is described below.

Droylsden developed in a series of steps, rather than at a steady pace. The building of the Ashton Canal, and its branch northwards to Fairbottom, may have prompted the establishment in the 1800s of the Droylsden Copperas Works on Edge Lane and the bleach and dyeworks on Greenside Lane, between the canal and Lane Head (see Chapter 3). As a result of these initiatives the population grew from 1552 in 1801 to 2855 in 1821 (Table 2.1). Johnson's survey of the township in 1819 indicates that much of this expansion was related to a ribbon development of housing along Moorside Street east of Greenside Lane, and around the junction of Market Street and Ashton Hill Lane (Speake & Witty 1953, 202).

The population remained roughly stable in the 1820s, the next upsurge coinciding with the introduction of factory-based cotton spinning and weaving in the 1830s, prompting a population increase from 2996 in 1831 to 4933 in 1841 (Table 2.1). The new mills were built along the Ashton Canal and by 1845 comprised four establishments, Edge Lane, Droylsden, Victoria and Fairfield mills. All bar Edge Lane were concentrated immediately west of Market Street, between its junction with Ashton Hill Lane and Greenside Lane, and by 1847 there was a continuous ribbon development of housing between these two junctions (LRO DRM 1/39).

Between 1841 and 1861 the population of the township nearly doubled, to 8798 (Table 2.1). Much of this increase was accounted for by the immigration of Irish workers (Higson 1859, 23-4). New building in the mid-nineteenth century was concentrated around Lane Head, where terraced housing along Baguley Street and Campbell Street was first built in this period, and around Lane End, where a mechanics' institute, a school and a Wesleyan Methodist chapel were built, as well as terraced housing along Durham Street. The Droylsden New Gas Company was also established in the township during the 1850s by a group of local cotton mill-owners (see Chapter 8). Droylsden local board was established in 1858 and in 1894 became Droylsden UDC (Speake & Witty 1953, 195).

After 1861 the population remained stable before increasing by 28% between 1881 and 1901, rising from 8679 to 11,087 (Table 2.1). It was during this period that urban development began to spread to the west and east of Market Street along new roads such as Hart Street, Medlock Street, Oldham Street and Dunkirk Street, with the result that by 1931 there were 3543 houses in the township (*ibid*, 195).

Fairfield Moravian settlement

Between 1783 and 1830 the religious sect which founded the Fairfield Moravian settlement was the largest community in the township, while maintaining an identity distinct from all others in Tameside. The Moravians were a Protestant group who originated in Bohemia in the fifteenth century and first came to Britain in the early eighteenth century from Herrnhut in Saxony (Langton 1956, 59-62). A feature of their system was the establishment of self-sufficient settlements on the pattern of Herrnhut, each living an inner life of its own and supporting itself by its own handicrafts. The first Moravian settlement in Tameside was founded at Chapel Hill in Dukinfield in 1743 (Aikin 1795, 454). When the lease on this land expired in 1783 the community was forced to look elsewhere and in that year purchased an estate of 54 acres on land once forming part of Broad Oak Farm in Droylsden (Mellows 1977, 19-21; Speake & Witty 1953, 133).

The initial Fairfield settlement was completed in 1785 and was equipped with a chapel and brick houses arranged around a central square. Later, schools for both boys and girls were built to the east and west of the square. Perhaps the best early description of the settlement was given by Aikin:

'Fairfield is a new settlement belonging to the Moravians, near four miles from Manchester and within two fields of the Ashton turnpike road. Though established within these twenty years it has the appearance of a little town. There is a large and commodious chapel, with an excellent organ. The ground plot is laid out with great taste and judgement. It forms a large square. The chapel and some large dwelling houses well built of brick form the front. On each side of the chapel is a row of elegant large houses. These, with the chapel, form a large square mass of buildings, round which is a broad paved street, and the whole is flagged round. On the outer side of the street is another row of excellent buildings, which surrounds the whole, except the front; at a short distance from which is a fine row of kitchen gardens, and opposite to the chapel a large burying ground; the whole divided and surrounded with quickset hedges. One of the houses is a convenient inn with stabling, etc, for the accommodation of those who frequent the place' (Aikin 1795, 232).

Some of these buildings still survive, although many have been considerably altered. Amongst the most complete are three houses, nos 31B, 31C and 32 Fairfield Square (Fig 9.10). Although somewhat altered in the late nineteenth century, they retain many original features. The buildings are built in brick and are of two storeys with slate roofs and ridge chimney stacks. The facade of no 32 is the nearest to its original form with a four-panelled door and two three-light casement windows on each floor with stone sills and brick arches.

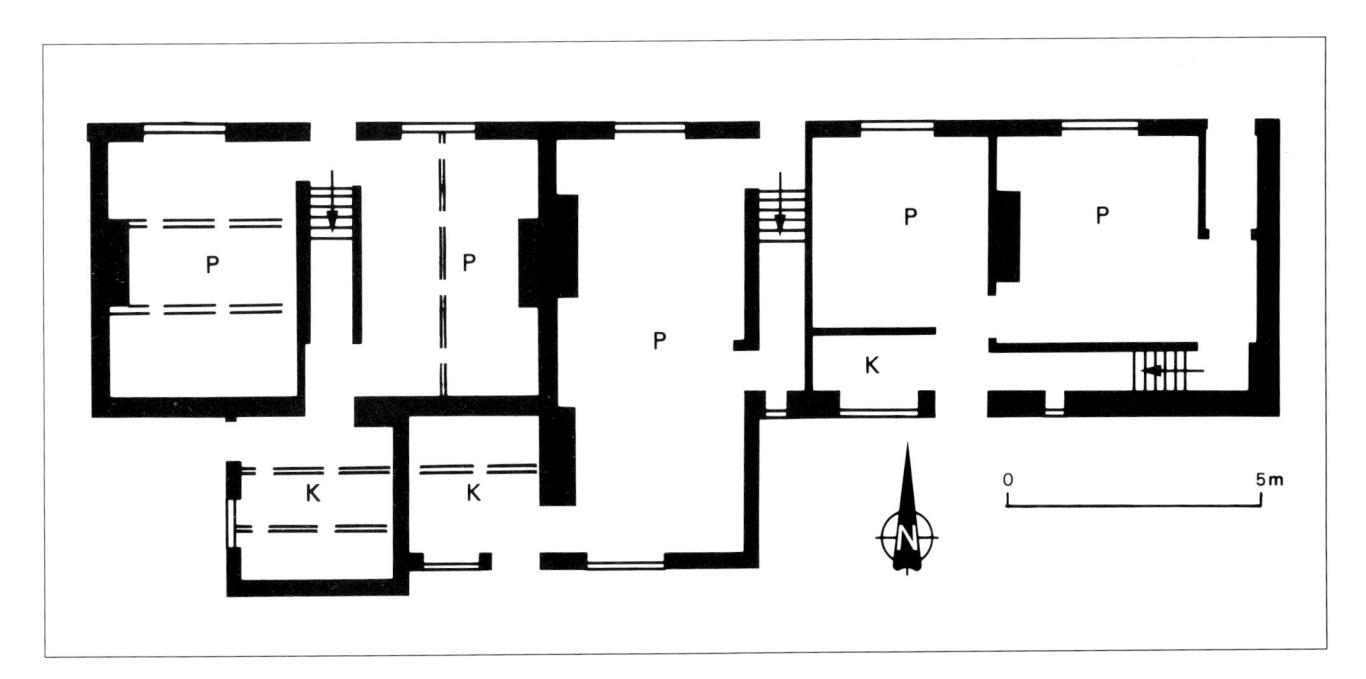

Fig 9.10 Plan of (from left to right) nos 32, 31C and 31B Fairfield Square.
Key: P – parlour; K – kitchen.
These town houses are among the best surviving buildings erected by the Fairfield Moravian community in the late eighteenth century. Although altered in the late nineteenth century, these houses were originally each of two bays with a central staircase and windows to either side.

Chapter 9 Urban Communities

9.7 Dukinfield

The eighteenth-century township

The growth of urban Dukinfield began with the construction of the Circus, the earliest purpose-built workers' community in Tameside. This unusual feature was erected by Sir John Astley sometime between his inheriting the Dukinfield estate in 1759 and his death in 1787 (Ormerod 1882, 818). Prior to this date the township of Dukinfield was essentially rural, being dominated by eleven dispersed farmsteads in 1692 (Nevell 1991, 27, 144). There was, however, a hamlet strung out along Old Road and Town Lane. Its core lay at the junction of Pickford Lane and Town Lane, the Dukinfield estate map of 1692 recording nineteen buildings in this area (TLSL DD 229/1). It was here that Dukinfield Old Chapel was erected in 1707, the area later becoming known as Chapel Hill (Butterworth 1842, 167).

As late as the 1770s, when Burdett carried out the first detailed survey of Cheshire, this area was still the only urban core in the township. However, by 1795 there had been a rapid growth in the settlement, with housing expanding eastwards along Oxford Road towards Stalybridge, and northwards along Town Lane towards the River Tame and Ashton. By this date the Circus lay in the heart of the expanding village, and although the Moravian community, established on Chapel Hill in 1743, had moved in 1783 to Droylsden the buildings relating to their small community were still in use (Aikin 1795, 454).

Dukinfield Circus

The earliest surviving account of the Circus is given by Aikin in 1795:

> 'on the summit above Dukinfield-lodge...he [Sir John Astley] erected a handsome circus of houses for the accommodation of industrious inhabitants, which was filled as soon as finished. The buildings are of brick, and the road divides it into two half circles. From a water engine which he built in the Tame for the use of the lodge, the water is forced up to a reservoir, whence the circus and most of the town is supplied' (Aikin 1795, 453).

This circus was composed of two semi-circular arrangements of brick-built buildings later known as the Half Moon and the Crescent (Plate 9.1). Within each crescent were six pairs of houses. The plan of the eastern half of the circus has been partly recovered by recent excavation (GMAU 1993). Each house was single-bay, double-depth and of three storeys with a staircase immediately behind the front doorway. In a number of houses there was an additional single-storey room to the rear, which may have been used as a workshop. On each storey was a wide brick-arched casement window, with two sixteen-pane lights.

Aikin's comment that the Circus was built for the 'accommodation of industrious inhabitants' can at the moment only be substantiated for the nineteenth century. Pigot's directory of 1841 lists seven tradesmen as resident in the 'Half Moon'. These were George Byrom, plumber and glazier, William Denby, shopkeeper, James Hardman, shopkeeper, John Harrop, plumber and glazier, William Roylance, tin-plate worker, Nancy Spragg, druggist, and Joshua Whittaker, shoemaker (Pigot & Co 1841, 46-9).

The development of the Circus can in part be recovered from the nineteenth- and twentieth-century map evidence. The earliest representation occurs on Greenwood's map of Cheshire in 1819, which shows Old Road as bisecting the Circus. However, by 1829, when Teesdale published a new map of Cheshire, Crescent Road, parallel to and to the west of Old Road, had been built. The construction of this new road appears to have caused the demolition of the northernmost pair of houses in the western half of the Circus and necessitated the rebuilding of the neighbouring pair. Two further pairs of houses were lost in the last quarter of the nineteenth century, when Foundry Street was extended into the centre of the eastern half of the Circus. The site then remained untouched until January 1963 when storm damage to the eastern half precipitated its demolition. The western half followed a few years later. Today the only fragment to survive is the pair of houses in the western half of the Circus at the junction of Chapel Street and Town Lane. Although the facade appears to have been rebuilt in the 1820s, when Crescent Road was constructed, much of the internal fabric probably dates from the eighteenth century.

Nineteenth-century Dukinfield

During the first quarter of the nineteenth century Dukinfield's population grew very rapidly, especially in the area of the Ashton bridge over the River Tame. In 1842 Edwin Butterworth noted that

> 'the transition of Dukinfield from a retired woody agricultural district to a populous town-like manufacturing village, has been wrought in the course of sixty years, owing, in a great measure, to the establishment of cotton manufactories' (Butterworth 1842, 171).

It was also in part due to the proximity of the western half of the township to the growing urban centre of Ashton-under-Lyne (Haynes forthcoming).

Aikin estimated that there were 252 families in the township in 1795, a figure which Butterworth translated as approximately 1134 inhabitants (Aikin 1795, 456; Butterworth 1842, 172). When the first census was taken in 1801 the population had reached 1737, and by 1811 there were 3053 individuals living in 497 houses. The greatest period of growth in the township, however, was between 1821 and 1831 when the population nearly trebled from 5096 to 14,681, further rising to 22,394 in 1841 (Table 2.1). The number of inhabited dwellings grew from 777 in 1821 to 2465 in 1831 and 3982 in 1841 (Butterworth 1842, 172-3). Approximately half of this increase appears to have taken placed in that part of Dukinfield which in 1857 was included within the new borough of Stalybridge, but nevertheless it is clear that the northern half of old Dukinfield was altered almost beyond recognition. Analysis of the land tax returns for the township in the 1820s indicates that the Astley estate was quick to exploit such a rapid growth in population and was at least in part responsible for the more than threefold increase in housing between 1821 and 1831. A good proportion of this new housing was concentrated in a formal development in the north-western area of the township, by the River Tame around the Ashton bridge and the upper end of Town Lane. This was immediately by the heart of the Dukinfield cotton industry at Bridge Eye on the Tame. A roughly square grid-iron of streets was laid out in this area between 1819 and 1824 (Bowman 1960, 329; Greenwood's map of Cheshire 1819). It was defined by the new Wharf Street in the north and King Street in the west, with the eighteenth-century Astley Street in the south and Town Lane in the east finishing the grid. In 1823 James Butterworth noted of this area that

> 'the improving part of Dukinfield, and which promises to be the most extensive and populous, is branching out into streets in every direction along the banks of the Tame, near the bridge leading to Ashton. Very large cotton mills are erected, and others in a state of great forwardness, with numerous warehouses, cottages, shops etc' (Butterworth 1823, 188).

By 1872 this grid had been completely filled and had been extended westwards to the River Tame, while King Street had been extended southwards to join Pickford Lane (OS 6in to 1 mile First Edition, Cheshire sheet IV). Park Road, along the southern bank of the Tame, was built in the 1850s and opened up that area of the township between the Ashton bridge and Stalybridge to industrial and housing development. This area was characterized by brick-built terraced housing but there was also a district of back-to-back housing known, unofficially, as 'Cuckoo Square' (Haynes forthcoming).

This rapid growth led to the establishment of a highways board in the township in 1836 and in 1857 a local board of health was also created. These boards were amalgamated into an urban district council in 1895 and in 1899 the township became a borough (Hickey 1926, 61-2).

The creation of the borough of Stalybridge in 1857 removed a significant proportion of the population of the township, which dropped from 26,418 in 1851 to 15,024 in 1861. However, growth continued, albeit slowly, during the second half of the nineteenth century so that by 1901 the population was 18,929, peaking at 19,509 in 1921 (Table 2.1). During this period the grid-pattern of streets in north-western Dukinfield was filled. Most of the houses along Chapel Street and King Street south of Chapel Street were built in the 1880s and 1890s (Pavasovic 1984, 47). Urban expansion also moved south-west of Pickford Lane and a small separate community grew around Dukinfield Hall, which was converted into workers' housing in the mid-nineteenth century. Overshadowing this community, in the triangle formed by the Peak Forest Canal, the Manchester to Sheffield railway and Globe Lane, were Barn Meadow, Dukinfield Hall, Old Hall and Union mills. By 1930 houses stretched as far south as Boyd's Walk and were advancing down Birch Lane and Cheetham Hill Road. Much of the old eighteenth- and early nineteenth-century core of Dukinfield was demolished in the post-war period and little now remains.

9.8 Hyde

Before the late eighteenth century the modern district of Hyde, encompassing the townships of Hyde, Godley and Newton and the northern part of Werneth, was characterized by dispersed farmsteads. The only substantial centre of population was Gee Cross, also known as Hyde Chapel, a hamlet in the southern part of the modern town. During the early nineteenth century there was a decisive shift in the focus of settlement, away from Gee Cross, northwards to the new town of Hyde, which owes its existence entirely to the establishment of the factory-based cotton industry in this area during the last two decades of the eighteenth century.

Gee Cross

Prior to the Industrial Revolution Gee Cross was a hamlet composed of three seventeenth-century farmsteads, then in the township of Werneth; Gerrards Wood Farm, Gerrards Fold and Geecross Fold (Nevell

1991, 45, 145). During the eighteenth century the domestic spinning and weaving of cotton became widespread in this area and, combined with the construction of the new turnpike road from Stockport to Mottram through Gee Cross, begun in 1765, and a plentiful supply of small, fast flowing streams running down the northern flanks of Werneth Low, led to the rapid growth of the village (Booth 1987, 8). The speed of the development of Gee Cross can be gauged from Aikin's remark that

> 'about twenty-five years ago there was only one house besides; now the place looks like a little town, and forms a continued street for nearly a mile' (Aikin 1795, 450).

Examples of this first wave of cotton-related building, weavers' cottages built of stone with flat-faced mullion windows, can still be seen along Knott Lane at Pole Bank Cottages, and along Mottram Old Road at the northern end of the village (Bann 1976, 14-15; Shortland 1966, 11).

With the growth of water-powered cotton spinning from the 1780s the success of Gee Cross seemed assured and in the years 1780-1800 ten textile sites were established in the neighbourhood of the village. However, in the early nineteenth century, as steam-powered mills were being established elsewhere in the Borough, the village found itself disadvantaged by the absence of a local supply of coal; after the opening in 1804 of Gee Cross Mill, by the Peak Forest Canal, no further mills were built in the area. This might have led to the decline of the settlement, but the directories of the first half of the nineteenth century indicate that by the 1820s, if not earlier, the inhabitants had found an alternative source of employment in the felt hatting industry, which at this date was still largely domestic-based (Table 4.2).

By 1839 the settlement was spread across six streets, the chief ones being Stockport Road and Mottram Old Road, the others comprising the lesser roads of Joel Lane, Higham Lane, Back Bower Lane and Lilly Street (CRO EDT 417). Many of these buildings were large two-storey stone-built terraces, often with a single-storey stone-built hat-planking shop standing separately to the rear or side. Approximately three-quarters of the houses in the village were rented from the Tatton estate.

A study by Booth of the spread of property ownership in Werneth township during the period 1797-1821, using the evidence of the land tax returns and the local poor rates, indicates that Gee Cross had ceased expanding by about 1820. This evidence shows very little growth in the absolute numbers of properties in the township which rose only from 68 to 72 between 1797 and 1821; however, during this same period the number of properties controlled by cotton mill-owners rose significantly, from six in 1797 to nineteen in 1821, suggesting that the mill-owners of the Gee Cross area were acquiring control of existing property, rather than establishing new properties (Booth 1987, 21). This is the reverse of the trend seen in the same period in the major cotton centres of Dukinfield, Hyde and Stalybridge, and may itself be an indication that the cotton industry in the Gee Cross area was not as strong as elsewhere in Tameside. This impression is confirmed by the slow rise in the population of Werneth township between 1801, when it was 1152, and 1811, when it was 1304. Although it rose to 1804 in 1821 and leapt to 3462 in 1831, the majority of this last increase appears to have been accounted for by the growth of Compstall Bridge in the southern part of the township (now in Stockport Metropolitan Borough), rather than of Gee Cross itself (Table 2.1; Thelwall 1972, 1-2).

By the mid-nineteenth century hat making was the dominant industry in Gee Cross. In 1857 34 hat shops were recorded in the village and from the 1860s, as trade revived, new factory-based hat manufacturers were established in the Gee Cross area (see Chapter 4). However, further urban growth was confined to the expansion of the ribbon development along Stockport Road, between Gee Cross and the southern confines of Hyde, so that by the early twentieth century there was a continuous stream of housing between the two centres.

Hyde

The core of modern Hyde, centred on the junction of Market Street and Market Place, owes its origins to the years 1784-95 when the first cotton mills were established on the north-west edge of the later town of Hyde. Aikin states that by 1795 Red Pump Street, that part of modern Market Street between the market and the Peak Forest Canal, was 'a new village lately built by Mr Sidebottom' (Aikin 1795, 450; Butterworth 1827, 295). Nathan Sidebotham was one of the most prominent of the first generation of mill-owners in the Hyde area, establishing his first cotton factory, Kingston Mill, in 1784 on Wilson Brook, near to where it flowed into the River Tame. Red Pump Street ran eastwards away from this mill and was originally composed of a row of ten stone-built cottages (Middleton 1932, 65). The Sidebothams quickly expanded their family business and by 1800 William Sidebotham was running three mills in the Hyde and Haughton area. Hyde owed its long-term success as a town to the presence of local coal deposits and the proximity of the Peak Forest Canal, which enabled the local cotton mill-owners from 1800 onwards to exploit the use of steam power in the industry.

The initial village established by Nathan Sidebotham in the period 1784-95 was quickly enlarged by the Ashton family, who during the 1800s became the most important mill-owning family in the district, and one of the most influential in the Lancashire cotton industry. With the establishment of the steam-powered Greencroft Mill in 1805 and Carrfield Mill in 1817, both in the Flowery Field district of Hyde, the Ashtons needed a local supply of labour and accordingly set about constructing their own community. The Flowery Field community was arranged in eight streets built in the period 1805-41, Bryce, Gain, Mulberry, Nanthrop, Spring Gardens, Throstle Bank, Well Meadow and Whitehart, which still survive (Shortland 1966, 36-9). Thomas Ashton initially erected 300 stone-built terraced cottages of two storeys (Faucher 1844, 105-6). They were originally let at 3s and 3s 6d a week and, according to Leon Faucher,

> 'each house contains upon the ground floor a sitting-room, a kitchen and a back yard and above are two or three bedrooms. The proprietor furnishes, at his own charge, water to the houses, keeps them in good repair, and pays the local rates' (*ibid*, 106).

Ure, writing in the 1830s, noted that the Ashtons had also built 'a handsome school house' and that the workers' cottages were 'more richly furnished than any common work-people's dwellings which I had ever seen before' (Ure 1835, 348). Thomas Ashton's own local residence was the grand Flowery Field House, between Throstle Bank Mill and Carrfield Mill and set in extensive grounds (Shortland 1966, 31).

Alongside Red Pump Street a further row of cottages was built around 1800 on New Street, now Water Street (Middleton 1932, 65). These were also stone-built terraces and although nearly all have been demolished a single example remains on the corner of Water Street and Cross Street. This is a two-storey stone-built house with flat-faced mullion windows and two rooms on each floor.

The rapid expansion of the cotton industry and its workforce in Hyde is reflected in the population growth of the township in the latter half of the eighteenth century and the first half of the nineteenth century. Booth has used the Hyde chapel registers from 1750-1800 to estimate the population of the Hyde area before the first census was taken in 1801. Hyde chapel, as a Presbyterian place of worship, served a wider area than that of the modern town of Hyde, the baptismal entries including families in Manchester, Stockport and other parts of eastern Cheshire. The majority of entries are, nevertheless, from the immediate neighbourhood of Hyde. Booth's research suggested that the population of this area was around 496 in 1751 and remained fairly stable until the 1780s, growing to 1309 by 1793 (Booth 1987, 26-7). While these figures show the general trend of the population in the Hyde area in the late eighteenth century, they probably exceed the actual population of Hyde township which the 1801 census gives as only 1063. The population had trebled by 1821 to 3355, but it was the next two decades which marked the emergence of Hyde as a major urban centre in Tameside, indeed in the North-West. Between the years 1821 and 1841 the population of the township rose threefold to 10,170 (Table 2.1). Most of this population was employed in the cotton industry. In 1844 Faucher supposed that 10,000 people worked in the Hyde factories of the Ashton family alone (Shortland 1966, 36).

This growth is well illustrated by the maps of Greenwood (1819), Teesdale (1828-9), Bryant (1829-31) and the Ordnance Survey 1in to 1 mile First Edition (1841-2). It was during this period, 1819-42, that workers' housing for the cotton industry was built in the area now bounded by Market Street to the north-east and Great Norbury Street to the south-west. By 1832 Cross Street, Milk Street and Port Street (which included the modern Boardman Street) had been laid out and housing built there (CRO QDP 110). The oldest properties around Milk Street were composed of two-storey brick-built terraces, to the rear of which were narrow alleyways running between small high-walled yards with outside privies (Shortland 1966, 74). Croft Street shows examples of the earlier and later Victorian styles of building. Lower and middle Croft Street consist of house types similar to those originally found in Milk Street. These are brick-built terraces fronting directly onto the street. The upper end of the street contains housing of the late Victorian period. Here there are short brick-built terraces set back from the road behind small front gardens, while those at the western end of the street have bay windows and larger gardens. Croft Street now forms one of the best remaining groups of mid- to late nineteenth-century industrial housing in Tameside.

Booth has shown that the main promoters of this planned industrial town were the local mill-owners. His study indicated a rise in the number of houses in the township from around 65 in 1780 to over 1800 in 1846. Significantly by 1846 nearly half of these new properties, 818 houses, were built and owned by local mill-owners; indeed between 1780 and 1821 it was the cotton mill-owners who accounted for nearly all new buildings (Booth 1987, 19). From 1821 onwards it would seem that a large degree of speculative building was taking place, concentrated in the grid-iron development of streets in the area between Great Norbury

Chapter 9 Urban Communities

Plate 9.5 Housing in Hyde town centre.
Much of Hyde's housing stock was built by local mill-owning families such as the Ashtons. Expansion during the mid- and late nineteenth century was concentrated in the area of Great Norbury Street, seen here looking towards St George's church. This is a mixed development with a wide range of house types for differing social groups. On one side of the street are large semi-detached villas for the mill managers and foremen and on the other side smaller terraced housing for local mill operatives.

Street and Market Street. By 1846 the mill-owners of the Hyde area owned 47.5% of the property in Hyde, while the largest non-mill-owning property holder was Edward Hyde Clark, with 1.5% (*ibid*, 29).

The growth in the population of the area, stimulated by the arrival of mechanized hat-making factories in the 1860s and 1870s, led to the creation of the borough of Hyde in 1881 (Middleton 1932, 265). The first reform to local government in Hyde had been the establishment of a highways board in 1836 (*ibid*, 260). This was followed by the founding of a local board of health in 1863, which in 1877 was extended to include Newton (which had been given a local board in 1872), Godley and northern Werneth (*ibid*, 263). In 1881, when the borough of Hyde was established, the population of the area had reached 28,630 of which 6235 were employed in 21 cotton mills and 1623 in 22 hat works. There were also 6740 inhabited houses in the new borough (Table 2.1; Shortland 1966, 25).

The expansion of the town in the second half of the nineteenth century mainly involved the infilling of the grid-iron pattern of streets in the Great Norbury Street and Market Street area (Plate 9.5). By the First World War this area had been completely built upon and new areas, particularly between Hyde and Gee Cross and in the Godley area, were also being built upon. Houses built during the 1920s and 1930s occur in three main areas: between Dowson Road and Stockport Road; the Sheffield Road area of Godley; and the Talbot Road area of Newton. These were characterized by two-storey semi-detached brick-built dwellings (Shortland 1966, 84).

9.9 Longdendale

The modern district of Longdendale has three urban centres, Broadbottom, Hollingworth and Mottram, and their origin, growth and decline in the period 1700-1930 were closely allied to the fate of the local textile industry. In 1717 Bishop Gastrell described the parish of Mottram-in-Longdendale as 'a wild country consisting of Hills and Moors' (CRO P25/8/4). By the late nineteenth century this was an area dominated by textile factories and three sizeable villages, Mottram, Hollingworth and Broadbottom. The first two of these were created urban district councils in 1894, and belated recognition of the close relationship of the three settlements was given in 1936 by the creation of Longdendale UDC, which included not only Mottram and Hollingworth townships but also parts of Matley and Hattersley (Harris 1979, 220-1).

Mottram

Mottram village developed as the medieval centre of western Longdendale and by the early eighteenth century had two main areas. The medieval core was perched on Warhill, where a few houses and farmsteads were strung along the road between St Michael's church and Parsonage Farm (Nevell 1991, 101-2). Few buildings of the pre-industrial period survive in this area, although earthworks of house platforms can still be seen lining the western side of Littlemore Road between the top of Church Brow and Parsonage Farm. The second centre of activity lay at the northern foot of Warhill, where a small group of farmsteads and inns, one of which contained the manorial court rooms, lined Church Brow and Back Lane.

Until the last two decades of the eighteenth century Mottram was a small rural community whose economy was largely based upon agriculture, with handloom weaving providing a secondary source of income. The chief period of growth in the village was during the period 1780-1820, when Mottram was at the heart of cotton spinning and handloom weaving in western Longdendale. During the 1780s and 1790s the Tollemache estate drew up a series of leases for the construction of new houses and other buildings in lower Mottram. These fell into two main groups: firstly, three three-storey stone-built weavers' cottages were built on Ashworth Lane; secondly, workers' housing was built at the bottom of Church Brow and two rows of two-storey stone-built cottages erected along the newly laid alignment of Market Street (CRO DTW 2477/F/12). In this same period two cotton shops, one purpose-built, were established in the village by John Wagstaffe (see Chapter 3).

Aikin in 1795 commented that Mottram

'contains 127 houses, which are for the most part built of a thick flag stone, and covered with a thick, heavy slate, of nearly the same quality, no other covering being able to endure the strong blasts of wind which occasionally occur. Of late, many houses in the skirts of the town are built with brick. About fifty years ago, the houses were few in number, and principally situated on the top of the hill, adjoining the churchyard...It is only of late years that the town has had any considerable increase' (Aikin 1795, 458).

By 1819 Greenwood's map of Cheshire shows that the village had expanded northwards as far as the modern junction of Stalybridge Road with Backmoor. The population of the township had doubled between 1801 and 1821, rising from 948 to 1944, and rising once more in the 1830s to reach 3247 in 1841 (Table 2.1). However, it is apparent that the main era of growth in Mottram village was over by 1821, the rise in population in the 1830s being largely accounted for by the development of Broadbottom. In the middle decades of the century there was some development of houses along Hyde Road, while the later part of the nineteenth century saw a ribbon development of housing along Backmoor and Mottram Road. Despite the establishment of a candle works and a new cotton mill in the town in the 1850s, the population of the township rose only slightly between 1841 and 1861, from 3247 to 3406 (Kelly & Co 1857; Table 2.1).

The development of Mottram is thus substantially different to that seen in most other parts of Tameside. Its initial growth owed its origins to the ready supply of handloom weavers, in an area where textile production can be traced back to the seventeenth century, and to the presence of wealthy yeomen farmers, such as John Wagstaffe, who were willing to invest in the new cotton industry during the 1780s and 1790s. Aikin could comment in 1795 that

'the cotton trade is the principal source of employment to the young people in the town, and the surrounding district' (Aikin 1795, 458).

However, because Mottram had no fast flowing streams and only a limited supply of local coal, the new spinning shops set up in this area quickly became obsolete, and it is noticeable that in the land tax returns for the period 1800-20 the references to cotton shops and weavers in Mottram village cease (CRO QDV2/299). Their place is taken by an increasing number of shopkeepers, a trend reflected in the directory entries for the village from the 1820s onwards, and confirmed by the local tithe award (Table 7.2; CRO EDT 281/2). This evidence suggests that by the mid-nineteenth century Mottram had become a substantial market and dormitory village.

Chapter 9 Urban Communities

Plate 9.6 Weavers' cottages, Summerbottom in Broadbottom, Longdendale.
Built in 1790 by John Swindells of Hodge Mill, these six three-storey dwellings had a loomshop running the full length of the upper floor.

The cotton famine of 1861-5 marked the end of expansion in both Mottram and Broadbottom, the population of the township falling from 3406 in 1861 to 2590 in 1871. Thereafter the population recovered slowly, reaching 3270 in 1891. Mottram was created a local board in 1873 and a UDC in 1894. After 1891, however, its population steadily fell to reach 2636 in 1931, a decline which appears to be directly linked to that of the cotton industry in the township.

Hollingworth

The development of an urban core in the township of Hollingworth appears to have been stimulated by the growth of the textile industry in Longdendale in the late eighteenth century, and further encouraged by its location at the T-junction of the Manchester to Salters Brook turnpike and Woolley Lane leading to Glossop. The original core of Hollingworth was Wednesough Green, a development of three-storey stone-built weavers' cottages, the earliest of which were built in 1772; Burdett's survey of Cheshire, published in 1777, shows that the northern and eastern sides of the Green had also been built upon (J Powell 1977, 11). In the 1790s houses began to spring up around the junction of Woolley Lane and Market Street, then called Treacle Street. At that date Wednesough Green and Treacle Street were still separated by open country so that Aikin could state that

'these two places have of late increased very much, owing to the land's being freehold, and sold for building on. It is chiefly the property of Mr Egerton, of Tatton' (Aikin 1795, 469).

A plan of the Salters Brook turnpike through Mottram and western Hollingworth drawn in 1810 indicates that by that date the houses along Treacle Street had reached the eastern edge of Wednesough Green (Powell Collection). By 1841 ribbon development along Market Street had moved as far east as Manor House near Millbrook, on Hollingworth Brook, and a number of streets had been built to the north and south of the turnpike. These included Canon Street, Spring Street, Wood Street, Green Lane, Gas Street, Moorfield Terrace and Water Lane. Most of these dwellings were stone-built two-storey terraced houses, although in the original core of Treacle Street were two sets of three-storey weavers' cottages, one built in stone, the other in brick (J Powell 1977, 11).

The stone weavers' cottages still survive, although much altered.

This expansion appears to have been achieved at a steady rate, the population of the township rising from 910 in 1801 to 2347 in 1851, around which figure it stayed before rising in the 1870s and 1880s to a peak of 2895 in 1891, only to fall back to 2299 in 1931 (Table 2.1). The rise in population in the 1870s and 1880s is reflected in the construction of new buildings along Market Street (J Powell 1977, 8-9). Hollingworth was created a local board in 1871 and a UDC in 1894. Its revival was short-lived, for when the local cotton industry went into permanent decline so did the population of the township.

Broadbottom

Before the arrival of John Swindells at Hodge Mill on the banks of the Etherow the Broadbottom area was an isolated rural community of dispersed farmsteads. Aikin could remark on the loneliness of the Etherow valley through Broadbottom:

> 'From Whitegate-house is a steep descent of near a mile to Broad-bottom-bridge, which crosses the Mersey, in a most delightful and romantic situation... Below the bridge is Broad-bottom, a house belonging to Mr Bostock, in a very lonely, but pleasing situation, surrounded by fine meadow ground, which is partly encircled by the Mersey' (Aikin 1795, 464-5).

This 'fine meadow ground' was the site of the later Broadbottom Mills (Broad Mills) cotton-spinning and weaving complex.

The genesis of Broadbottom began when Swindells, who had leased Hodge Mill in 1789, was forced to build lodgings for his cotton operatives because of the isolated nature of the district. In 1790 he gained a lease from Lord Tollemache to build six cottages on a 'part of a field...called Summerbottom' (CRO DTW 2477/F/12). Each cottage was stone-built and had three storeys of one bay and double-depth, with a loomshop running the full length of the upper floor (Plate 9.6). These can still be seen today, although between 1841 and 1872 a further four cottages were added to the eastern end (Powell Collection; OS 6in to 1 mile First Edition, Cheshire sheet XI).

The urban core of the community, however, lay a few hundred metres eastward, immediately north of the Broadbottom Mills complex founded by William and George Sidebottom in 1801-2. The earliest workers' houses built by the Sidebottoms were three rows of two-storey stone-built terraced houses, one of twelve and two of fifteen cottages, known as Bottoms Street and Old Street, which are shown on a plan of 1817 (CRO QDP 39). Further expansion occurred in 1827 with the building of the two-storey stone-built terraces known as Lower Market Street and Well Row (Powell Collection). The stone terraces on Market Street and Bank Street were built in the period 1841-7, and the two rows of fifteen and eighteen cottages which comprise New Street were built in 1851. The stone terraces of Hurst Crescent, Travis Terrace and Banton Terrace, on Mottram Road, and Brick Terrace, were all built in the period 1847-72. The Sidebottoms' own residence in the village was Harewood Lodge, which they had built in the early to mid-1820s on the lower slopes of Warhill (Fig 9.11).

Broadbottom's expansion was brought to a halt by the cotton famine of 1861-5, and although two new mills were established in the village in the period 1861-9 further urban development did not occur. The fact that Broadbottom remained part of the Mottram local board and the later Mottram UDC reflects its failure to grow in the post-cotton famine period.

9.10 Mossley

Mossley in the eighteenth century was a scattered farming community with a strong domestic-based woollen industry. The modern town was spread across three counties, Top Mossley being in Ashton township in Lancashire, Micklehurst in the township of Tintwistle in Cheshire, and the remainder forming part of the Quickmere division of Saddleworth township in the West Riding of Yorkshire. The majority of land was owned by the Stamford estate but, unlike in Ashton, this did not play an active part in the early development of the town. As a result of the division of Mossley between three townships, no census returns are given for the town until after its unification under a local board in 1864 but contemporary accounts of the town can be used to give a rough guide to its growth.

The main period of urban development began in the late eighteenth century, when the original focus of settlement was in Top Mossley. In the vicinity of the Market Place can still be found a number of weavers' cottages from this period. These include three-storey stone-built cottages on Church Street and Anthony Street and in the triangle of buildings formed by Market Place, Arundel Street and Waterton Lane. Other buildings of this type can also be seen on Stockport Road and Carrhill Road (Fig 3.7). Aikin described Mossley in 1795 as

> 'a considerable village, with upwards of 100 houses, many of them large and well built, chiefly of stone' (Aikin 1795, 231).

Chapter 9 Urban Communities

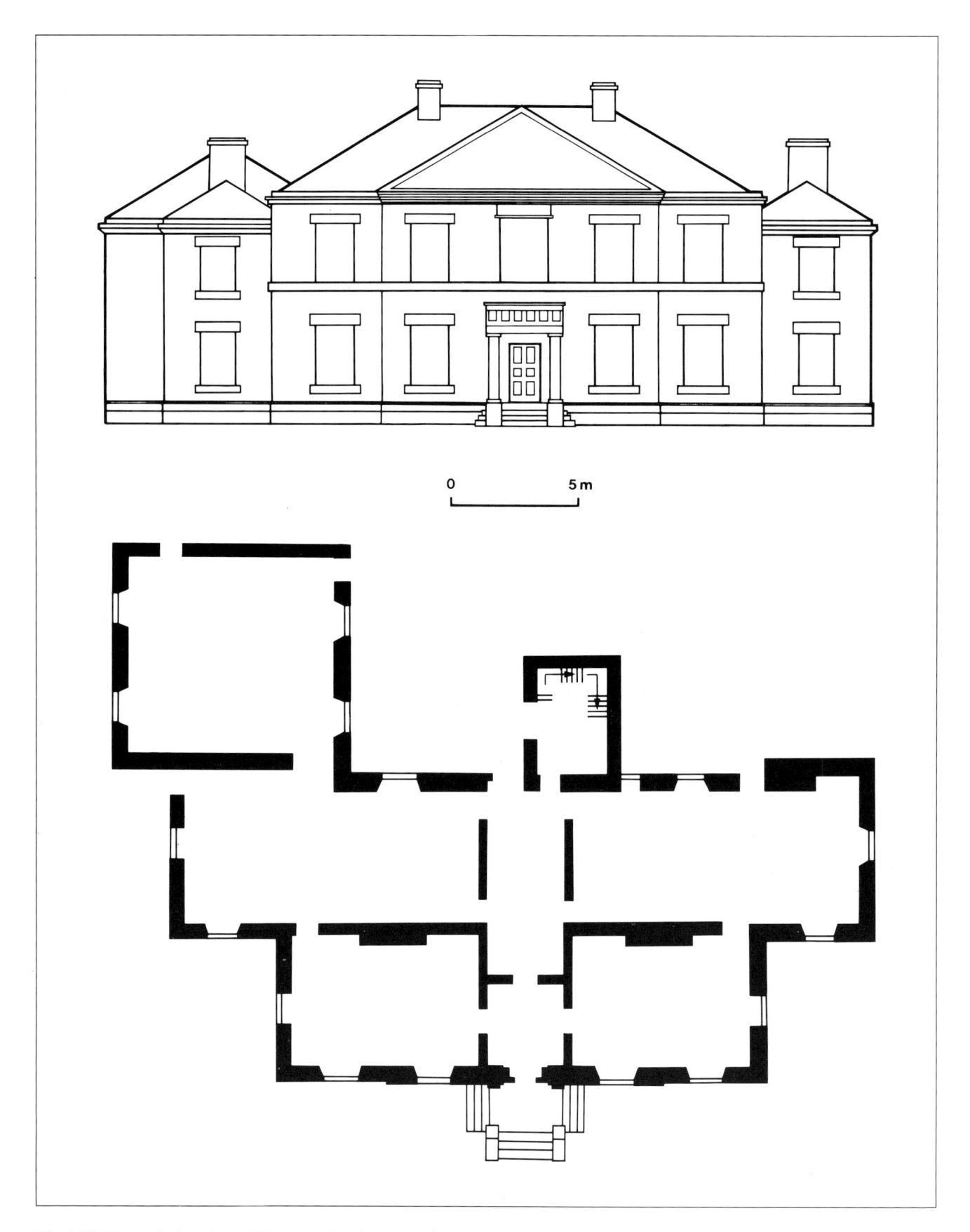

Fig 9.11 Plan and elevation of Harewood Lodge, Broadbottom.
This grand residence, built in the Georgian style, was erected by William and George Sidebottom in the early to mid-1820s on the southern slopes of Warhill. Set in extensive grounds, it overlooked the large complex of Broad Mills, which the brothers had founded in the period 1801-2, although it was separated from the works by the growth of Broadbottom village.

Chapter 9 Urban Communities

There was also a chapel, now St George's church, in the gift of the rector of Ashton and founded in 1755 (Butterworth 1823, 117).

The village continued to expand in the first half of the nineteenth century. Edwin Butterworth estimated that in 1821 there were approximately 300 houses and a population of 1212. At this date woollen manufacture was still the principal occupation of the inhabitants, although Butterworth noted that cotton production was becoming increasingly popular. The number of houses had risen to over 500 in 1841 but Butterworth reckoned that the population was only 1500 (Butterworth 1842, 136). Much of the increase in population in the early nineteenth century could be accounted for by immigration from northern Lancashire and Ireland (Kenworthy 1928, 2). Its rise appears to have been directly linked with the progress of the cotton industry which between 1833 and 1862 saw at least fourteen new cotton mills being built in the area (see Chapter 3).

Butterworth also noted the growth of Brookbottom, in the Quickmere part of Mossley (Butterworth 1842, 136). Much of the new housing of Mossley in the early nineteenth century appears to have been concentrated in this area, and to have been built by local mill-owning families such as the Andrews, Buckleys, Lawtons and Mayalls. There were two centres of urban expansion in this part of Mossley, each of which was focused on a group of cotton mills established in the 1820s and 1830s. Around Brookbottom and Valley mills, immediately north of Top Mossley, grew up a small community of two-storey stone-built terraced houses along Lees Road and Stockport Road. The Rough Town area of Mossley lay on the west bank of the River Tame, by the Carr Hill, Wood End and Roughtown mills. Fine two-storey stone-built terraces of the first half of the nineteenth century can still be seen in this area. In particular Granby Row, a line of eleven cottages on Carrhill Road, and Beatties Buildings, a line of seven cottages east of Roughtown Road, belong to the period prior to 1822 (Barnes *et al* 1983, 101). Another pre-1822 development is Quickwood. Here, at the western end of the seventeenth-century Mossley Manor House, stands a row of seven two-storey, two-bay, single-depth, stone-built workers' cottages, built in three phases spanning the late eighteenth and early nineteenth centuries and encompassed in the ornate garden wall of the adjoining manor house. Further terraces on Carrhill Road east of Granby Row and along Milton Street belong to the period 1822-51 (*ibid*, 123).

An unflattering description of a visit to Mossley was given in the *Ashton Reporter* in 1856:

'We noticed diverse seventeenth-century dwellings with mullioned windows and protecting weather labels. We were led to believe that the inhabitants of the village were advanced in civilisation beyond their brethren generally in the south Lancashire villages ...but scarce could we traverse a dozen or twenty yards without knots of urchins and hobble-te-hoys passing audible but not flattering remarks, of not the most complimentary nature...we resolved never again to visit Mossley without having hired for the day a new policeman' (*Ashton Reporter* 6/11/1856).

Mossley continued to prosper in the mid-nineteenth century, its population reaching 10,000 in the 1860s (Eckersley 1991, 112). Such was the rate of growth by 1860 that the *Saddleworth Reporter* could state that

'the progress of Mossley in wealth and population during the last twenty years has brought it to that state which makes it difficult to determine whether to speak of it as a town or a village' (*Saddleworth Reporter* 10/3/1860).

Mid-nineteenth-century building activity was focused on the line of Arundel Street and Stockport Road (between Top Mossley and Brookbottom) and to the east of the Market Place. In the arm of the junction formed by Arundel Street, Waterton Lane and Earl Street is a courtyard development of fifteen two-storey stone-built terraced houses, with two entrances into the inner courtyard from Waterton Lane. East of the Market Place is a more formal development of houses in a small area of grid-iron streets bounded by George Street, Hanover Street, Mountain Street and Stamford Street. Within this area were a series of courtyard terraced-housing developments. The best preserved lies between Curzon Street and Lorne Street. Here a set of two-storey two-bay workers' cottages have stone facades but Accrington-brick rear elevations. The Stamford estate was responsible for this building development along with other streets in Mossley, including Egmont Street, George Street, Hanover Street, Russell Street and Stamford Road (TLSL DDS 107, 187, 420, 494). The quality of the housing built by the local mill-owners could vary greatly. In 1876, during an outbreak of scarlet fever, the district medical officer severely censured the great mill-owning Mayall family, who at that time ran the largest cotton-spinning company in the world, as well as certain other Mossley mill-owners, for the seriously defective sanitary conditions of much of their housing stock (Eckersley 1991, 101-2).

Late nineteenth-century development was concentrated in the valley on the eastern side of the town in Micklehurst, around the group of mills along Micklehurst and Stayley roads. This is an area of long rows of brick-built terraced housing. The result is a west-east

Chapter 9 Urban Communities

division in the building materials used in the township. The areas west of the Tame which developed largely before the advent of the railways were built in stone, while those areas east of the Tame, which grew after the arrival of the railway (the Micklehurst Loop) in 1885, are largely in brick.

Mossley was created a local board in 1864 and granted municipal status in 1885. By this date the cotton industry of the town had already begun its long decline. The population peaked at 14,162 in 1891 and after that date, despite a shift from cotton production back to woollens, gradually fell to 12,041 by 1931 (Table 2.1).

9.11 Stalybridge

Stalybridge, like Mossley, developed in the Tame valley on either side of the river, and was thus divided between Lancashire and Cheshire. Unlike Mossley, however, the two halves of the town were quickly united under a single board, in 1828 (March 1957, 77). Before the Industrial Revolution Stalybridge was a small hamlet on the Lancashire side of the Tame, strung out along Rassbottom and Market streets. The first bridge at Stayley was probably on the line of the modern bridge over the Tame on Mottram Road and is mentioned as early as the seventeenth century (Nevell 1991, 121).

The earliest description of Stalybridge is by Aikin, in 1795:

'The place is now a very large and extensive village, the houses well built, some of stone, but the greatest part of brick. On an eminence stands an octagon chapel of the church of England, in which is an organ. Part of the village is on the Cheshire side of the Tame, but by far the greatest in Lancashire, in a continued street of half a mile, well paved. The greatest part of this village, as well as the chapel, has been built in the last eighteen years' (Aikin 1795, 230).

The spur for this development was the cotton industry. One of the earliest cotton-spinning mills in Tameside, the Old Soot Poke, was founded here in 1776, the same year in which the chapel was built, and by 1800 there were ten mills working in the area, most of them close to the River Tame (Haynes 1990, 16; see Chapter 3). Initially these mills were located in Stayley because of the fast flowing waters of the Tame and the ready supply of experienced textile workers; as Aikin noted in 1795,

'This place has been famous, for a great length of time, for woollen cloth, dyers and pressers, as well as weavers' (Aikin 1795, 230).

Its continued success was due to the good communications provided by the opening of the Huddersfield Canal in 1797 and by the local supplies of coal from Ashton and Stalybridge itself. Harrop reckons that by 1795 the village contained 220 houses and a population of over 1000 (Harrop 1989, 7).

The rate of growth of Stalybridge continued to accelerate during the first two decades of the nineteenth century, and by 1823 James Butterworth estimated that there were 900 houses, a total population of 5500 and 26 mills, needing a workforce of 9000 operatives (Butterworth 1823, 127);

'This place may now, with great propriety be considered not only as one of the handsomest, but largest of those places called villages, either in Lancashire or Cheshire' (*ibid*, 124).

Remains of the eighteenth- and early nineteenth-century expansion of Stalybridge can still be seen on the northern, Lancashire side of the Tame. Most of the eighteenth-century houses along Rassbottom Street and Market Street have long since been replaced, although several three-storey brick-built houses of the early nineteenth century still survive along the southern side of Market Street. However, slightly further to the east on Cocker Hill can be found a group of stone-built dwellings of this period. The earliest is a small early eighteenth-century farmhouse at the bottom of the hill, but towards the top are a range of stone-built two-storey terrace cottages and three-storey weavers' cottages at Higher Croft (Fig 3.7).

During the 1820s Stalybridge's growth was phenomenal. Edwin Butterworth reckoned that by 1831 the town contained 14,216 people – a nearly threefold increase in eight years – living in 2357 houses (Butterworth 1842, 147). This expansion slowed during the 1830s but, even so, in 1842 Butterworth held that

'Staley-bridge, or, as lately changed to Stalybridge, is one of the largest towns, either in Lancashire or Cheshire, wholly owing its origin to the success which followed the establishment of the cotton manufacture' (*ibid*, 138).

He estimated that there were 32 cotton factories in the vicinity of Stalybridge, 3100 houses and a population of around 21,000 (*ibid*, 148). This and earlier estimates of the town's population may give too high a figure, as the census of 1861 noted only 14,000 individuals in 1851 in the area of the later borough, but the general trends are no doubt correct.

Along with this growth came a demand for self-government, the new town being located in three different parishes. As a result in 1828 the Stalybridge Improvement Act was passed. This fixed the boundaries of the new self-governing town, and established an elected board responsible for law and order, highway maintenance, the cleaning of streets and their lighting by gas, and the provision of new sewers, paving and footways. The act also allowed for the erection of a market (King & King 1989, 28). This led to the construction of the Stalybridge Gas Works in 1829 and the new Market Hall, opened in 1831 (*ibid*, 32). A generation later, in 1857, the town was granted a borough charter.

The rapidity of this growth is indicated by the figures which Butterworth gives for the rate of building in Stalybridge during the 1820s; nearly 800 houses were built in the years 1823-5, and nearly 700 in the period 1827-9. The 1830s saw many more hundreds built (Butterworth 1942, 146). Commenting on the quality of this housing, Butterworth was scathing:

'many of the streets have been rather hastily and imperfectly constructed; numbers of the dwellings are small, and of slight erection; the inmates are too much crowded; and the low situation of a great portion of the town is unfavourable to health, yet many habitations are neatly built and well placed' (Butterworth 1842, 145).

These were sentiments echoed by Engels who visited Stalybridge in 1844 (see above). A survey in 1836 noted that of the 3313 properties examined, 670 were single-room dwellings and 56 cellar dwellings (Butterworth 1842, 147).

Most of this new housing was located to the south of the Tame, particularly in that part of the new police district in Dukinfield known as Castle Hall. A map surveyed by Dawson in 1832, but not published until 1837, shows that the area between the River Tame and High Street had already been built upon, while the grid-iron of streets south of High Street and defined by Forester Street in the west and Hough Hill Road in the east was built during the period 1832-41 (Dawson 1837, map 1; OS 1in to 1mile First Edition). Most of this housing was brick-built two-storey terraces.

After the period of rapid expansion in the 1820s and 1830s the growth of the town appears to have decelerated, no new mills being established in the period 1837-51. The first accurate figures for the level of Stalybridge's population do not occur until 1861, when the census recorded 18,130 people in the municipal borough (Table 2.1). If the estimated figure of 14,000 given by the census of 1861 for the same area in 1851 is correct, in the period 1851-61 the population had increased by a third, perhaps spurred by the establishment of five new cotton mills in the borough during the period 1851-62 (Appendix 1).

The cotton famine of 1861-5, however, was to have a disastrous effect on Stalybridge's population. Haynes has estimated that about 42% of the inhabitants were directly dependent on the cotton industry for employment in the early 1860s (Haynes 1990, 8). In the light of this figure it is perhaps not surprising that Stalybridge was one of the worst affected districts in the North-West and that by 1871 the population had dropped to 15,323.

The late nineteenth century saw the resumption of slow growth in both Stalybridge's cotton industry and its population, which by 1881, at 16,384, had still not recovered its level of 1861. After 1881 the rate of growth is difficult to gauge, since the borough was subsequently extended to include Stayley township. However, between 1891 and 1901 the population of the enlarged borough increased only slightly, from 26,783 to 27,673. Thereafter there was a slow decline to 24,823 by 1931 (Table 2.1; Haynes 1990, 11).

This slow resurgence and subsequent decline is reflected in the small number of areas developed for housing from 1870 onwards. North of the river the Stamford estate built Cambridge Street and Cumberland Street in 1883 and Astley Road in 1897, all to the north of Wakefield Road (TLSL DDS 507, 604). Ribbon development occurred along Mottram Road, and between Copley and Stalybridge along Huddersfield Road. The Stamford estate was also responsible for a new development of terraced brick-built housing between Mottram Old Road and Huddersfield Road. In this area Taylor and Winton streets were built in 1887 and Hawke Street in 1894 (TLSL DDS 212, 627, 634). Outside these areas most new building work concentrated on filling the existing street pattern, and on the replacement of the badly built dwellings of the 1820s and 1830s. As a result, by 1930 the urban area of Stalybridge was little changed to that recorded on the Ordnance Survey 6in to 1 mile First Edition map of the area, surveyed in the years 1870-2.

Chapter 10

Conclusion

'The physical remains of this great period of Lancashire history are now the everyday environment of a large proportion of the county's inhabitants. The great spinning mills and weaving sheds of the textile towns, the pithead gear and slag heaps of collieries, the engineering, chemical, glass and soap works, long terraces of workers' houses, Gothic town halls, churches and chapels erected with money made by Victorian manufacturers, are the familiar features of the urban landscape.'

(Ashmore 1969, 13)

There is a certain irony in the scope of this third volume of *A History and Archaeology of Tameside*, for whilst it covers only 230 years, by far the shortest period studied in the series, it encompasses a vast amount of evidence, many times more than the previous two volumes put together. This immediately raises the problem of how to sift and order such a mountain of material, which includes upstanding building remains, contemporary eyewitness accounts and studies, official records and new types of evidence such as photographic and oral sources. There have been a number of studies of the social and political changes which occurred in Tameside during the late eighteenth and nineteenth centuries, but few which have sought to relate these developments to the physical evidence for the rise and fall of the great industries of this period and their lasting impact on the landscape.

In common with the previous two volumes, this present work is a study of the landscape and people of Tameside, and in particular of the impact of industrialization on what had been a largely rural society in an agriculturally marginal area of the North-West. It is inevitably a subjective survey by one author using those sources best suited to the marrying of the industrial archaeological remains and the documentary material. It is hoped that the resulting work provides a fitting framework for the momentous events which have shaped the modern landscape and society of Tameside over the last three hundred years.

A number of major themes have emerged from this study: the close relationship between population growth and the industrialization of the Borough; the social changes and stresses engendered by these developments; and above all the interdependence of the new industries of the Industrial Revolution in Tameside.

In 1700 the population of Tameside was sparse and, although absolute figures are not available, is unlikely to have exceeded 4000, with Ashton being the chief urban centre, containing around 550 people or about 14% of the total population (Nevell 1991, 103-4). By the time of the first census in 1801 the population of Tameside had risen to about 28,500 (Table 2.1). By 1931 this figure had grown to around 184,500, of whom 28% lived in the municipal borough of Ashton-under-Lyne and 17% in the municipal borough of Hyde. This represented an increase of over 180,000 between 1700 and 1931, or roughly forty-six fold, compared to a ten-fold increase nationally in the same period (Cootes 1982, 179). Ashton town led the way in population growth during the eighteenth century, attracting immigrants from the surrounding countryside as the foundations of the Industrial Revolution were established in the area in the form of domestic spinning and weaving. The full relationship between the establishment of the factory system and the population explosion is perhaps best seen in the area of Hyde chapel, whose population remained stable in the latter half of the eighteenth century, until the establishment in the 1780s of factory-based cotton spinning in Gee Cross and along Red Pump Street, the future core of Hyde town. Between 1780 and 1881, when the borough of Hyde was established, the population of this area leapt from around 500 to 28,630. A similar spectacular leap in population can be seen in Stalybridge although accurate figures for the town's rate of growth before 1851 are difficult to establish.

The industrialization and urbanization of Tameside was rapid. As late as 1795 Aikin could describe the

Chapter 10 Conclusion

Plate 10.1 Georgian shop front, Stamford Street, Ashton.
This original shop front of the period 1787-1803 was built during the early years of the Industrial Revolution when the Georgian town plan was being established and cotton-spinning mills were first being founded in Ashton. This building has witnessed approximately 200 years of change, as Ashton developed from a market centre, through the Georgian planned town, into the industrial heart of Tameside, and finally back to a market centre. The survival of the building provides a tangible link with the past, its history spanning a period of rapid economic and social change in the lives of the people of Tameside.

lower reaches of the River Tame, around Dukinfield and Hyde, as one of the most beautiful locations in the North-West (Aikin 1795, 450-1). Sixty-five years later in 1860 the changes wrought on the countryside were noted by James Garnett, a Lancashire weaver, who commented that in his lifetime in the Hyde and Newton area villages had turned into towns, and that fields were now covered in streets and large factories (Brigg 1982, 97). Inevitably the development of an urban society in such a short span led to the growth of many new social pressures and stresses. In Tameside these were expressed in the campaigns for better working conditions, perhaps best exemplified in the rise of the Trade Unions; in the growth of violence and popular agitation for political reform such as Chartism; and in the growing stratification of society as expressed in the contrast not only between the towering new cotton factories and the humble farmstead, but also between the often appalling housing conditions of the first two generations of factory employees and the homes of the factory owners themselves. With the rapid slow down in population and industrial growth and the development of local government in the Borough during the latter half of the nineteenth century, opportunities arose to relieve these stresses. Since then a century of reform and continued urbanization has swept away

Chapter 10 Conclusion

much of the physical evidence of the Industrial Revolution, but nevertheless many buildings and factories survive to complement the extensive documentary material for this period.

The interdependence of the great industries of Tameside is apparent from the late eighteenth century, although from the establishment of the first cotton factories in the 1770s it was cotton spinning which dominated the industrial history of the Borough. The cotton and coal industries, and to a lesser degree the hatting trade, were dependent for their success on a number of common factors: the existence of a ready-trained workforce; the opportunity to increase production through innovations in technology; and the rise of a growing band of wealthy yeomen farmers who had surplus cash to invest, such as the great mill-owning Ashton family in Hyde, the coal-mining family of Fletcher in Denton, the Lees family who established the Park Bridge ironworks, and in the hatting trade the Woolfendens of Dane Bank. As the textile industry grew so did the supply industries of coal and engineering. These new industries helped to encourage the development of new transport systems in the Borough; turnpikes in the mid-eighteenth century, canals in the late eighteenth century and railways in the mid-nineteenth century. The workforce of the textile industry had to be housed, at first in small purpose-built communities next to the cotton factories, later in an ever increasing urban spread which led to the growth of the gas, water and electricity industries in an effort to improve living conditions.

Between the establishment of the first cotton-spinning mill in the 1770s and the collapse of the textile industry in the 1920s and 1930s perhaps the most important event, socially and economically, was the cotton famine of 1861-5. The short-lived boom which occurred in the years immediately following the famine marked the end of the rapid industrial and population expansion of the early nineteenth century and a transition to the slow down in demographic and industrial growth of the late nineteenth century. Only hatting witnessed unhindered expansion in the late nineteenth and early twentieth centuries.

By the early twentieth century the landscape of Tameside had been exploited for over 9000 years, yet the last two hundred years had seen the greatest development of the area, in terms of population, urban and industrial growth. The Tame valley was now dominated by a chain of factories from Denton to Mossley, and away from the river the lowland areas of the Borough were being increasingly covered by housing and urban spread. Even the upland areas were affected by this dramatic growth in human activity, criss-crossed by walls and circumscribed by new roads and railways. The communities of the Borough had also been radically altered, with the farmstead pushed to the fringes of the landscape and society, leaving the great urban areas of Ashton, Dukinfield, Hyde and Stalybridge to dominate not only the landscape but also people's lives.

Appendix 1
The Textile Sites of Tameside

Introduction

During the research for the third volume of *A History and Archaeology of Tameside* the location of 274 textile sites was established. (A textile site is here defined as a single site containing a building or complex of buildings used solely in the manufacture of textiles or for their warehousing; numerous domestic sites which were also used for the production of textiles, such as weavers' cottages, are not included within this number.) Although in the last two decades several surveys which deal with the textile industry in Tameside have been published or produced, these have been mostly restricted to specific parts of the Borough (Bann 1976; Eckersley 1991; Haynes 1987, 1990 & forthcoming). The recent study by Williams with Farnie (1992) includes a useful summary of the development of the cotton industry in Tameside and a gazetteer of mill sites from all branches of the textile industry in the Borough. However, the latter includes only those mills still standing in 1985-6 and initially identified from map evidence; consequently, at a little over 100, these represent less than half of the textile sites now known from the period *c* 1763-1930 and listed in the following gazetteer. This present list should itself not be seen as definitive, since further research will undoubtedly identify new sites and reveal additional processes in the mills already known.

The gazetteer is primarily designed to be used in conjunction with the tables in Chapter 3 (Tables 3.1-3.7) and the distribution maps in that same chapter showing the location of the textile sites of Tameside (Figs 3.1-3.6 & 3.9). The list is arranged by districts which mostly coincide with the local divisions existing prior to the creation of Tameside in 1974, with the exceptions that Audenshaw is here included within the Ashton-under-Lyne district, and Denton within the Hyde district. Within each district sites are arranged by their National Grid Reference. Where a site has undergone a change of name, all known forms are given. These details are followed by the type of activity on the site and its date range, and each entry is concluded with a summary of the main sources, both published and unpublished. Fuller descriptions of each site, including details of the owners of each mill and a description of any remains, can be found on the Greater Manchester Sites and Monuments Record (GM SMR), held by the Greater Manchester Archaeological Unit at the University of Manchester. The GMAU also holds a copy of the archive of the Greater Manchester Textile Mills Survey, a joint project undertaken by the GMAU and the Royal Commission on the Historic Monuments of England (RCHME), the findings of which are published in summary form in the work by Williams with Farnie (1992). The original archive of that survey is now held in the John Rylands University Library of Manchester. Included within the survey are aerial photographs of a number of Tameside mills and these are identified in the gazetteer below by the prefix SF.

The Gazetteer

Ashton-under-Lyne (including Audenshaw)

1) **Moss Brook Mill**, Audenshaw, SJ 9046 9750
Silk crape *c* 1863-87.
OS Lancashire 6in sheet 105, 1863 revision; Worrall 1887.

2) **Dean Head Mill**, Audenshaw, SJ 9102 9732
Cotton spinning *c* 1793-1863/95.
LRO QDL Sal, Audenshaw 1793. OS Lancashire 6in sheet 105, 1863 revision. Gone by OS 1in 1895 revision.

3) **Slate Lane/York Mills**, Audenshaw, SJ 9102 9755
Cotton spinning and later waste *c* 1909-33.
OS Lancashire 6in sheet 105, 1909 revision; Worrall 1933.

4) **Guide Bridge Mills**, Audenshaw, SJ 9231 9785
Cotton spinning 1876-1937.
GM SMR 3398, photo nos 0951-4, SF 3194 78-81; Haynes 1987, 47; Williams with Farnie 1992, no 983; Worrall 1937.

5) **Fern Mill**, Ashton, SJ 9260 9832
Combined 1856 - post-1933.
GM SMR 3339, photo no 0959, SF 3194 86-94; Haynes 1987, 33; Williams with Farnie 1992, no 976.

6) **Braganza Mill**, Audenshaw, SJ 9262 9664
Cotton spinning 1828-63/95.
LRO QDL Sal, Audenshaw 1828. OS Lancashire 6in sheet 105, 1863 revision. Gone by OS 1in 1895 revision.

7) **Guide Mills**, Ashton, SJ 9262 9761
Cotton spinning 1841/2-1950s.
Ashmore 1982, 79; GM SMR 3391, photo no 0946, SF 3194 82-5; Haynes 1987, 37; Williams with Farnie 1992, no 984.

8) **Ryecroft Mills**, Ashton, SJ 9273 9830
Combined 1832/4-1938.
Ashmore 1982, 78; GM SMR 3340, photo nos 0955-8, 0960, SF 3194 86-94; Haynes 1987, 33; Williams with Farnie 1992, no 1026.

9) **Duncan Street Mills**, Ashton, SJ 9275 9767
Combined 1850-1960s.
GM SMR 3392, photo no 0947, SF 3194 99-102; Haynes 1987, 39; Williams with Farnie 1992, no 974.

10) **Birch Mill**, Ashton, SJ 9290 9770
Cotton spinning 1846-1931.
Ashmore 1982, 79; Haynes 1987, 38; Williams with Farnie 1992, no 954.

Appendix 1 The Textile Sites of Tameside

11) **Ryecroft Mills**, Ashton town, SJ 9290 9840
Cotton spinning 1825-40s. Combined 1840s-1950s.
Haynes 1987, 30.

12) **Shepley Mills**, Audenshaw, SJ 9305 9664
Print works *c* 1777-1937.
Aikin 1795, 456; Graham 1846, 424-5; Worrall 1937.

13) **Oxford Mills**, Ashton, SJ 9306 9796
Cotton spinning 1840-51. Combined 1851-1955.
Ashmore 1982, 78-9; Ashmore & Bolton 1975, 38-9; GM SMR 3395, photo nos 0941-5; Haynes 1987, 37; Williams with Farnie 1992, no 1010.

14) **Bardsley Vale Mill**, Ashton, SD 9314 0133
Combined 1857-91.
GM SMR 3332, photo nos 1016-17, SF 3192 9-13; Haynes 1987, 42.

15) **Bardsley Mills**, Ashton, SD 9315 0130
Cotton spinning *c* 1835-91.
Ashmore 1982, 77; GM SMR 3332, photo no 1016, SF 3192 9-13; Haynes 1987, 35; Williams with Farnie 1992, no 949.

16) **Grosvenor Mill**, Ashton town, SJ 9317 9805
Combined 1853-1950s.
GM SMR 3396, photo nos 0949-50, SF 3194 106-8; Haynes 1987, 40; Williams with Farnie 1992, no 981.

17) **West Mill**, Ashton, SJ 9325 9810
Cotton spinning *c* 1835-47. Combined 1847-83.
Haynes 1987, 36.

18) **Junction Mills**, Ashton, SJ 9325 9845
Cotton spinning 1831/3-37. Combined 1837-1930.
GM SMR 3460, photo no 0970; Haynes 1987, 34-5; Williams with Farnie 1992, nos 994 & 995.

19) **Portland Mills**, Ashton, SJ 9332 9885
Cotton spinning 1824-50; 1874-1903. Combined 1850-74.
GM SMR 3348 & 3554, photo nos 0928-37, SF 4013 17-20; Haynes 1987, 28; Williams with Farnie 1992, nos 957 & 977.

20) **Walk Mill**, Ashton, SJ 9334 9832
Cotton spinning *c* 1836-1908.
Haynes 1987, 36.

21) **Wilshaw Mill**, Ashton, SD 9334 0020
Cotton spinning *c* 1854-88.
Haynes 1987, 40-1.

22) **Rock Mill**, Ashton, SD 9334 0020
Cotton spinning 1891-1960s.
Haynes 1987, 49.

23) **Tudor Mill**, Ashton, SJ 9335 9845
Cotton spinning 1901-60s.
Haynes 1987, 51.

24) **Bridge End Mills**, Spring Grove Terrace, Ashton town, SJ 9338 9825
Cotton spinning *c* 1864-1920s.
Haynes 1987, 45.

25) **Egret Mill**, Ashton town, SJ 9340 9880
Combined 1823 - *c* 1881/4. Weaving *c* 1881/4 - *c* 1887.
Haynes 1987, 25-6.

26) **Bank Mills**, Ashton town, SJ 935 985
Cotton spinning 1823-1937.
Haynes 1987, 24-5.

27) **Flash Hall Mills**, Ashton town, SJ 935 989
Combined *c* 1818 - *c* 1864.
Haynes 1987, 24.

28) **Atlas Mill**, Ashton, SD 9350 0010
Cotton spinning, later artificial fibres, 1898-1990s.
Ashmore 1982, 77; GM SMR 3330, photo nos 0925-7; Haynes 1987, 50; Williams with Farnie 1992, no 945.

29) **Cross Street Mill**, Ashton, SJ 9352 9888
Cotton spinning 1823-55.
Haynes 1987, 25.

30) **Old Street Mill**, Ashton town, SJ 9354 9884
Cotton spinning 1823 - *c* 1878/82.
Haynes 1987, 26.

31) **Good Hope Mill**, Ashton, SJ 9355 9895
Combined 1824-95.
GM SMR 3347 & 3581, photo nos 0931-3; Haynes 1987, 27; Williams with Farnie 1992, no 979.

32) **Stanley Mill**, Ashton town, SJ 9360 9905
Cotton spinning 1823 - *c* 1864. Combined *c* 1864 - *c* 1889.
Haynes 1987, 25.

33) **Bankfield Mill**, Ashton town, SJ 9364 9857
Combined *c* 1820/1-81.
Haynes 1987, 24; Williams with Farnie 1992, no 947.

34) **Cavendish Mill**, Ashton town, SJ 9364 9857
Cotton spinning 1884/5-1934.
Ashmore 1982, 76; GM SMR 3345, photo no 0966; Haynes 1987, 47-8; Williams with Farnie 1992, no 965.

35) **Cavendish Street Mill**, Ashton town, SJ 9367 9871
Combined 1825-77. Cotton spinning 1877-1936.
Haynes 1987, 29.

36) **Gas Street Mill**, Ashton, SJ 9369 9904
Cotton spinning 1817-28/32. Combined 1828/32-1903.
Haynes 1987, 23.

37) **Ashton Old Mill**, Ashton, SJ 9370 9849
Printing 1773-84. Cotton spinning 1784-1892.
Graham 1846, 343; Haynes 1987, 10-11; Nevell 1991, 55-6; Williams with Farnie 1992, no 1009.

38) **Croft Mill**, Ashton town, SJ 9370 9895
Cotton spinning 1815-24/8. Combined 1824/8-97/8.
Haynes 1987, 22.

39) **Albion Mill**, Ashton town, SJ 9371 9865
Cotton spinning 1825-61. Combined 1861-1933.
Haynes 1987, 29.

40) **Charlestown Mill**, Ashton, SJ 9376 9932
Cotton spinning *c* 1800 - *c* 1855.
Haynes 1987, 18.

41) **Wharf Mill**, Ashton, SJ 9377 9875
Combined 1825-50. Cotton spinning 1850-1950s.
GM SMR 3346, photo nos 0967, 0972-7; Haynes 1987, 30; Williams with Farnie 1992, no 1053.

42) **Delamere Street Mill**, Ashton town, SJ 9382 9901
Spinning and doubling *c* 1803 - *c* 1914.
Haynes 1987, 19.

43) **Park Bridge Mill**, Ashton, SD 9392 0240
Cotton spinning 1885-1931.
Haynes 1987, 48.

44) **Lees Street Mill**, Ashton, SJ 9393 9970
Cotton waste and spinning 1864-1932.
GM SMR 3350, photo nos 0922-4, SF 4337 17-21; Haynes 1987, 46; Williams with Farnie 1992, no 998; Worrall 1932.

45) **Kenworthy's Mill**, Stamford Street, Ashton town, SJ 9395 9895
Cotton spinning 1803-30s. Combined 1830s-87/8.
Haynes 1987, 18-19.

46) **Foundry Street Mill**, Ashton town, SJ 9396 9904
Cotton spinning *c* 1794/8 - *c* 1845.
Haynes 1987, 14.

47) **Gladstone Mill**, Ashton, SJ 9399 9878
Combined 1856/61-74/92.
Haynes 1987, 46.

Appendix 1 The Textile Sites of Tameside

48) **Brassey's Mill**, Ashton, SJ 9400 9877
Cotton weaving *c* 1861 - *c* 1871.
Haynes 1987, 46-7.

49) **Oldham's Mill**, Ashton town, SJ 9400 9898
Cotton spinning *c* 1793 - *c* 1869.
Haynes 1987, 13-14.

50) **Grey Street Mill**, Ashton town, SJ 9403 9896
Cotton spinning *c* 1798-1864.
Haynes 1987, 16-17.

51) **Knowles' Mill**, Ashton, SJ 9406 9877
Cotton spinning *c* 1861-78.
Haynes 1987, 43.

52) **Wood and Harrop's Mill**, Ashton town, SJ 9407 9904
Cotton spinning 1793 - *c* 1831.
Haynes 1987, 13.

53) **James Ogden's Mill**, Ashton, SJ 9414 9910
Cotton spinning *c* 1800-6.
Haynes 1987, 17.

54) **Bridge End Mill**, Whitelands, Ashton, SJ 9416 9868
Cotton doubling *c* 1864 - *c* 1885.
Haynes 1987, 45.

55) **Hurst Mount Mill**, Hurst, SJ 9420 9958
Cotton spinning 1802 - *c* 1914.
GM SMR 3373, photo nos 0999-1001, SF 4446 51-4; Haynes 1987, 17-18; Williams with Farnie 1992, no 991.

56) **Minerva Mill**, Ashton, SJ 9425 9845
Cotton spinning 1891-1920s.
Haynes 1987, 48.

57) **Texas Mill**, Ashton, SJ 9430 9845
Cotton spinning, later artificial fibres, 1905-71.
Haynes 1987, 53.

58) **Hurst Brook Mill**, Hurst, SJ 9434 9962
Cotton spinning *c* 1788/9 - *c* 1871.
Graham 1846, 391; Haynes 1987, 11.

59) **Sharp's Shrubbies**, Ashton, SJ 9435 9853
Cotton weaving 1857 - *c* 1896; 1920s-30. Combined *c* 1896-1920s.
GM SMR 3472, photo nos 0816-17, 0820, SF 4013 60-3; Haynes 1987, 42; Williams with Farnie 1992, no 1055.

60) **Ralph Ogden's Mill**, Ashton, *c* SJ 944 994
Cotton spinning *c* 1803 - *c* 1808.
Haynes 1987, 18.

61) **Bengal Mill**, Ashton, SJ 9440 9974
Cotton spinning *c* 1800 - *c* 1822.
Haynes 1987, 17.

62) **Waterside Mills**, Ashton, SJ 9441 9850
Cotton spinning 1863 - *c* 1896; 1920s-50s. Combined *c* 1896-1920s.
GM SMR 3352, photo nos 0356-7, 0815, SF 4013 51; Haynes 1987, 42; Williams with Farnie 1992, no 1048.

63) **Harper Mills**, Ashton, SJ 9445 9915
Cotton spinning 1855-1920s.
GM SMR 3474, photo nos 2565-6, SF 4446 55-9; Haynes 1987, 41; Williams with Farnie 1992, no 985.

64) **Leigh/Tame Valley Thread Mill**, Ashton, SJ 945 985
Cotton spinning 1864/7-1930.
Haynes 1987, 45; Worrall 1930.

65) **Wellington Mills**, Ashton, SJ 9450 9857
Combined 1857-1960s.
GM SMR 3353, photo nos 0818-26, SF 4013 52-5; Haynes 1987, 41; Williams with Farnie 1992, no 1050.

66) **Whitelands Mills**, Ashton, SJ 9455 9840
Combined 1875-1933.
GM SMR 3372, photo nos 0827, 0829-30, SF 4014 13-16; Haynes 1987, 47; Williams with Farnie 1992, no 1054; Worrall 1933.

67) **Curzon/Alger Mill**, Ashton, SJ 9466 9990
Cotton spinning 1899-1942.
Ashmore 1982, 77; GM SMR 3333, photo nos 0978-9, 2555-6, SF 4013 25-8; Haynes 1987, 50; Williams with Farnie 1992, nos 942 & 971.

68) **Cedar Mill**, Ashton, SD 9470 0010
Cotton spinning 1903-70s.
Ashmore 1982, 77; GM SMR 3336, photo nos 2548-54, 2557, SF 4014 54-7; Haynes 1987, 51; Williams with Farnie 1992, no 966.

69) **Hurst Mills**, Hurst Cross, SD 9495 0025
Cotton spinning *c* 1795/6 - *c* 1828. Combined *c* 1828-1931.
Ashmore 1982, 77; GM SMR 3453, photo no 2555; Haynes 1987, 16; Williams with Farnie 1992, no 990.

70) **Currier Slacks Mill**, Ashton, SJ 9497 9890
Cotton spinning *c* 1794 - *c* 1864/8.
Haynes 1987, 15.

71) **Carrs/Whittaker's Mill**, Hurst, SJ 9500 9970
Combined 1847-1930.
Haynes 1987, 39; Worrall 1930.

72) **Carrs/Stamford Commercial Mill**, Ashton, SD 9522 0002
Cotton weaving 1884-1950s.
GM SMR 3335, photo nos 0982-3, SF 3158 54-7; Haynes 1987, 48; Williams with Farnie 1992, nos 963 & 1034.

73) **Cockbrook Mill**, Ashton town, SJ 9523 9879
Cotton spinning early 1790s-1903.
Haynes 1987, 13.

74) **Throstle Nest Mill**, Ashton, SJ 9529 9888
Cotton spinning *c* 1779-1864/92.
Haynes 1987, 10.

75) **Higham Fold Mill**, Ashton, SJ 9530 9895
Cotton spinning early 1790s-1896.
Haynes 1987, 13.

76) **Gibraltar Mill**, Hurst, SD 953 005
Cotton spinning *c* 1794/6-1804.
Haynes 1987, 15-16.

77) **Park Hall Mill**, Ashton, SJ 9547 9918
Cotton spinning *c* 1805 - *c* 1884/92.
Haynes 1987, 19.

78) **Hazelhurst Mill**, Hazelhurst, SD 9596 0084
Cotton spinning early 1790s-1883.
Haynes 1987, 15.

79) **Mellor's Mill**, Hazelhurst, SD 960 012
Cotton spinning 1788/9 - *c* 1822/35.
Haynes 1987, 12.

80) **Tongue Bottom**, Hurst, *c* SD 961 015
Cotton spinning *c* 1788 - *c* 1838.
Haynes 1987, 11-12.

Droylsden

81) **Edge Lane Mill**, Droylsden, SJ 8922 9790
Weaving 1835-72. Cotton spinning 1872 - post-1960.
Speake & Witty 1953, 91, 121, 175-6; OS 1:2500 SJ 8997, 1960 revision.

Appendix 1 The Textile Sites of Tameside

82) **Droylsden Copperas/Springfield Print Works**, Droylsden, SJ 8955 9765
Copperas works, later print works *c* 1800-1933.
GM SMR 3481, photo nos 0912-15, SF 4446 44-6; Speake & Witty 1953, 94, 172-3; Williams with Farnie 1992, no 1031.

83) **Fairfield Dyeing Works**, Droylsden, SJ 8975 9767
Dyeworks *c* 1856-1916.
GM SMR 3482, photo nos 0909-11; Speake & Witty 1953, 93, 179; Williams with Farnie 1992, no 944.

84) **Victoria Mills**, Droylsden, SJ 9006 9804
Combined 1845 - *c* 1922.
GM SMR 3384, photo nos 0917-19, SF 3194 74-7; Speake & Witty 1953, 91; Williams with Farnie 1992, no 1047.

85) **Boys' Boarding Academy**, Fairfield, SJ 9008 9766
Cotton spinning *c* 1790-1803.
Speake & Witty 1953, 139.

86) **Boys' Sunday School**, Fairfield, SJ 9009 9761
Cotton spinning 1790 - *c* 1800.
Speake & Witty 1953, 139.

87) **Angola Mill**, Droylsden, SJ 9014 9795
Weaving 1850-onwards.
GM SMR 3385, photo no 2564, SF 3194 66-73; Speake & Witty 1953, 91-2, 175; Williams with Farnie 1992, no 943.

88) **Nos 21 & 22 Fairfield Square**, Fairfield, SJ 9015 9767
Cotton warehouse *c* 1786 - *c* 1813.
Speake & Witty 1953, 138.

89) **Fairfield Mills**, Droylsden, SJ 9025 9816
Combined 1837-onwards.
GM SMR 3387, photo nos 0920-1, SF 3159 2-6; Speake & Witty 1953, 177-9; Williams with Farnie 1992, no 975.

90) **Droylsden Mills**, Droylsden, SJ 9026 9788
Combined 1839-1927. Rayon manufacture 1927 - post-1953.
GM SMR 3386, photo nos 0901-8, 0916, SF 3194 66-73; Speake & Witty 1953, 91, 175; Williams with Farnie 1992, no 972.

91) **Greenside Lane Dyeworks**, Droylsden, SJ 9037 9825
Bleach and dyeworks *c* 1806 - post-1960.
Higson 1859, 101; Speake & Witty 1953, 35, 70-2, 93, 176; OS 1:2500 SJ 9098, 1960 revision.

92) **John Hammond's Factory**, Droylsden, SJ 9039 9787
Cotton carding and spinning 1790 - *c* 1793.
Higson 1859, 90-1; Speake & Witty 1953, 39-40.

93) **Albion Mill**, Droylsden, SJ 9040 9879
Cotton spinning 1869 - *c* 1953.
Speake & Witty 1953, 92, 180.

94) **Beetle Dyeing and Finishing Works**, Droylsden, SJ 9045 9859
Dyeing works 1863 - post-1953.
GM SMR 3528, photo no 0965, SF 3194 61-5; Speake & Witty 1953, 174; Williams with Farnie 1992, no 953.

95) **Oakfield Mill**, Droylsden, SJ 9052 9890
Cotton spinning 1877-1904. Combined 1904 - post-1953.
Oldham Chronicle 14/4/1877; Speake & Witty 1953, 176-7.

96) **Saxon Mill**, Droylsden, SJ 9057 9877
Cotton spinning 1906 - post-1953.
Ashmore 1982, 91; Haynes 1987, 50; Speake & Witty 1953, 174; Williams with Farnie 1992, no 1027.

97) **Swindell and Booth's Factory**, Droylsden, SJ 9062 9843
Cotton spinning *c* 1785 - *c* 1790.
Higson 1859, 89, 91; Speake & Witty 1953, 87.

98) **Royal Mill**, Droylsden, SJ 9095 9908
Combined 1859-1933.
GM SMR 3586, photo no 0963, SF 3194 53-6; Speake & Witty 1953, 92; Williams with Farnie 1992, no 1025.

99) **Lumb Mill**, Littlemoss, SJ 9110 9942
Combined *c* 1860 - *c* 1950.
Ashmore 1982, 91; Bowman 1950, 136; GM SMR 3505, photo nos 0961-2, SF 3194 49-52; Speake & Witty 1953; Williams with Farnie 1992, no 1002.

Dukinfield

100) **Union Mill**, Dukinfield, SJ 9326 9731
Combined 1850-83.
Haynes forthcoming.

101) **Barn Meadow Mills**, Dukinfield, SJ 9327 9705
Combined 1834-80/4.
GM SMR 3485, photo nos 1002-5, SF 4446 109-11; Haynes forthcoming.

102) **Stanlet Wood Mill**, Dukinfield, SJ 9332 9753
Cotton spinning, later doubling *c* 1861/64-96.
Haynes forthcoming.

103) **Dukinfield Hall/Dog Lane Mill**, Dukinfield, SJ 9335 9711
Cotton spinning 1838-94.
Haynes forthcoming.

104) **Old Hall Mill**, Dukinfield, SJ 9351 9691
Cotton weaving 1864-1931.
Haynes forthcoming; Worrall 1931.

105) **Dukinfield/Aqueduct Mill**, Dukinfield, SJ 9352 9839
Cotton spinning, later doubling 1841 - *c* 1945.
Haynes forthcoming.

106) **Waterside/Alma Mill**, Dukinfield, SJ 9370 9845
Cotton spinning, later reeling and winding *c* 1841 - *c* 1914.
Haynes forthcoming.

107) **St Helena's Mill**, Dukinfield, *c* SJ 938 984
Wool carding *c* 1807 - *c* 1836.
Haynes forthcoming.

108) **Warbrick's Mill**, Dukinfield, SJ 9386 9844
Cotton doubling *c* 1825/6 - *c* 1831.
Haynes forthcoming.

109) **Furnace Mill**, Dukinfield, SJ 9395 9852
Cotton spinning 1792-1876/96. Weaving 1833.
Haynes forthcoming; PP 1834 xx, D1.

110) **Bridge Eye Mills**, Dukinfield, SJ 9400 9864
Cotton spinning 1815 - *c* 1828. Combined *c* 1828 - *c* 1887.
Haynes forthcoming; PP 1834 xx, D1.

111) **St Helens Mill**, Dukinfield, SJ 9408 9850
Cotton spinning 1819-36. Combined 1836-76.
Haynes forthcoming; PP 1834 xx, D1.

112) **Dukinfield New Mill**, Dukinfield, SJ 9410 9860
Cotton spinning 1802 - *c* 1833. Combined *c* 1833-1933.
Haynes forthcoming; PP 1834 xx, D1.

113) **Astley Mill**, Dukinfield, SJ 9420 9696
Cotton spinning and doubling 1883/4-1931.
Haynes forthcoming; Worrall 1931.

114) **Victoria Mill**, Dukinfield, SJ 9422 9672
Cotton spinning 1861 - *c* 1960.
GM SMR 3401, photo no 0831; Haynes forthcoming; Williams with Farnie 1992, no 1045.

Appendix 1 The Textile Sites of Tameside

115) **Chapel Hill Mill**, Dukinfield, SJ 9425 9810
Cotton warehouse 1792 - *c* 1803. Cotton spinning *c* 1803-59/64. Combined 1859/64-74. Weaving 1874-1962.
Haynes forthcoming.

116) **Albert Mill**, Dukinfield, SJ 9428 9658
Cotton spinning 1873/4-1932. Waste 1932 - *c* 1960.
GM SMR 3438, photo no 0834, SF 4446 101-8; Haynes forthcoming; Williams with Farnie 1992, no 940.

117) **Dukinfield Old Mill**, Dukinfield, SJ 9447 9841
Cotton spinning 1792-1955.
Ashmore 1982, 92; GM SMR 3354, photo nos 0813, 0820, SF 4013 64-6; Haynes forthcoming; Williams with Farnie 1992, no 973.

118) **Park Road Mill**, Dukinfield, SJ 9456 9840
Cotton spinning 1892-1965.
GM SMR 3355, photo nos 0809-10, 0812, 0820, SF 4013 64-7; Haynes forthcoming; Williams with Farnie 1992, no 1011.

119) **Queen Mill**, Dukinfield, SJ 9470 9780
Cotton spinning *c* 1900-59.
Ashmore 1982, 92; Haynes forthcoming.

120) **River Mill**, Dukinfield, SJ 9470 9837
Combined 1877-1934.
Ashmore 1982, 92; GM SMR 3356, photo nos 0807, 0811, 0814; Haynes forthcoming; Williams with Farnie 1992, no 1024.

121) **Oxford Road Mills**, Dukinfield, SJ 9476 9780
Cotton spinning 1815 - *c* 1828; 1898-1937. Combined *c* 1828-98.
Haynes forthcoming.

122) **Tameside Mills**, Dukinfield, SJ 9483 9834
Cotton spinning and doubling 1852/4-1937.
GM SMR 3357, photo no 0806, SF 4014 17-20; Haynes forthcoming; Williams with Farnie 1992, no 1038.

123) **Tame Valley/Crescent Mills**, Dukinfield, SJ 9500 9830
Cotton spinning 1853-onwards.
Ashmore 1982, 92; GM SMR 3358, photo nos 0802-5, 0828; Haynes forthcoming; Williams with Farnie 1992, no 1037.

124) **Tower Mill**, Dukinfield, SJ 9510 9820
Cotton spinning 1885-1955.
Ashmore 1982, 92; GM SMR 3359, photo nos 0798-0801; Haynes forthcoming; Williams with Farnie 1992, no 1040.

125) **Sandy Vale Bleach Works**, Dukinfield, SJ 9515 9806
Dye and bleach works *c* 1825 - post-1939.
CRO QDV2/148; Pavasovic 1984, 17; PP 1854-5 xviii, 56; PP 1868-9 xiv, 34.

Hyde (including Denton)

126) **Alpha/Phoenix Mill**, Denton, SJ 9200 9572
Cotton winding 1862-1932.
GM SMR 3410, photo nos 1011-13; Williams with Farnie 1992, no 1012; Worrall 1932.

127) **Moorfield Mill**, Haughton, SJ 9338 9427
Cotton spinning *c* 1840-1933.
Booker 1855, 136; Cronin 1985, 55; Middleton 1936, 159; Worrall 1933.

128) **Haughton Dale/Meadow Factory**, Haughton, SJ 9345 9300
Cotton spinning 1790-1853.
Cronin 1985, 54.

129) **Broomstair Mill**, Denton, SJ 9365 9532
Textile weaving and finishing *c* 1855 - post-1939.
Booker 1855, 136; GM SMR 3492, photo nos 0879-80; Williams with Farnie 1992, no 958; Worrall 1939.

130) **Gibraltar Mill**, Hyde, SJ 9400 9382
Cotton spinning 1791-1825/7. Combined 1825/7-1927.
Bann 1976, 17, 24, 37; CRO QDV2/499; Cronin 1985, 54-5.

131) **Kingston Mills**, Hyde, SJ 9413 9535
Cotton spinning 1784 - *c* 1822. Combined *c* 1822-1927.
Bann 1976, 17, 37; CRO QDV2/231; Cronin 1985, 54-5; GM SMR 3420, photo nos 0881-3, 0886; Williams with Farnie 1992, no 996.

132) **Gee Cross/Apethorn/Linnet New Mill**, Hyde, SJ 9416 9365
Cotton spinning 1804-25/7. Combined 1825/7-1934.
Ashmore 1982, 98-100; Bann 1976, 24, 30, 33, 38; CRO QDV2/499; GM SMR 3443, photo no 0668; Williams with Farnie 1992, no 978.

133) **Throstle Bank Mill**, Hyde, SJ 9420 9560
Combined 1869-onwards.
Ashmore 1982, 100; Bann 1976, 42; GM SMR 3499, photo nos 0876-8; Williams with Farnie 1992, no 1039.

134) **Wharf Mill**, Hyde, SJ 9420 9565
Cotton weaving 1905-76/82.
Ashmore 1982, 99; Bann 1976, 32, 42.

135) **Providence Mill**, Hyde, SJ 9435 9446
Cotton spinning 1867-1933.
Bann 1976, 38; GM SMR 3442, photo nos 0862-4; Williams with Farnie 1992, no 1015; Worrall 1933.

136) **Barnfield Mill**, Hyde, SJ 9436 9492
Cotton spinning and finishing 1853-1930.
Ashmore 1982, 99; Bann 1976, 38; GM SMR 3445, photo no 0861; Williams with Farnie 1992, no 951; Worrall 1930.

137) **Birch Mill**, Hyde, SJ 9437 9504
Combined 1838-86.
Bann 1976, 24, 30.

138) **Millwood Mill**, Hyde, SJ 9438 9491
Combined 1854-1938.
Ashmore 1982, 99; Bann 1976, 30, 38; GM SMR 3441, photo nos 0859-60; Williams with Farnie 1992, no 951.

139) **Birchfield Mill**, Hyde, SJ 9450 9497
Cotton winsey 1864 - *c* 1910.
Bann 1976, 49.

140) **Greencroft Mill**, Hyde, SJ 9455 9506
Combined 1805-1938.
Ashmore 1982, 99; Bann 1976, 38; GM SMR 3429, photo nos 0854-8; Williams with Farnie 1992, no 980; Worrall 1938.

141) **Doctor's Factory**, Werneth, SJ 9465 9346
Cotton spinning 1780/90-1823.
Bann 1976, 17, 19.

142) **Greenfield Mill**, Hyde, SJ 9468 9488
Cotton spinning 1792-1822. Combined 1822 - *c* 1887/1910.
Bann 1976, 23; PP 1834 xx, D1, 61 no 44.

143) **Carrfield Mill**, Hyde, SJ 9470 9540
Cotton spinning 1817 - *c* 1821. Combined *c* 1821-onwards.
Ashmore 1982, 100; Bann 1976, 24, 42; CRO QDV2/231; GM SMR 3455, photo nos 0835-7; PP 1834 xx, D1, 57 no 41; Williams with Farnie 1992, no 961.

144) **Bayleyfield Mills**, Hyde, SJ 9470 9558
Combined 1824-onwards.
Ashmore 1982, 100; Bann 1976, 42; GM SMR 3430, photo nos 0835-7; PP 1834 xx, D1, 57 no 41; Williams with Farnie 1992, no 952.

145) **Longmeadow Mill**, Hyde, SJ 9480 9500
Cotton spinning 1818-22; 1873/87 - *c* 1896. Combined 1822-73/87.
Bann 1976, 24, 30; PP 1834 xx, D1, 59 no 43.

Appendix 1 The Textile Sites of Tameside

146) **Gerrard's Mill**, Gee Cross, SJ 9484 9339
Cotton spinning *c* 1795-1831/42.
Bann 1976, 24; CRO QDV2/499; Bryant's map of Cheshire 1829-31; OS First Edition 1in 1842.

147) **Johnson Brook Mill**, Hyde, SJ 9500 9652
Cotton spinning 1872-1974.
Bann 1976, 27, 42; GM SMR 3436, photo nos 0865-70, SF 4446 89-92.

148) **Hyde Mill**, Hyde, SJ 9510 9650
Cotton spinning 1906-59/64.
Ashmore 1982, 100; Bann 1976, 33, 38, 41; GM SMR 3436, photo nos 0865-70, SF 4446 89-92; Williams with Farnie 1992, no 993.

149) **Newton Bank Print Works**, Newton, SJ 9515 9520
Print works 1812-1982/6.
Ashmore 1982, 99; Bann 1976, 24, 42; CRO QDV2/313; GM SMR 3433, photo nos 0841-3; PP 1868-9 xiv, 38; Williams with Farnie 1992, no 1005.

150) **Marler's Mill**, Hyde, SJ 9521 9600
Combined *c* 1822-86.
Bann 1976, 30; CRO QDV2/313.

151) **Spring Bank Mills**, Hyde, SJ 9530 9430
Cotton spinning 1864-1906.
Ashmore 1982, 99; Bann 1976, 27.

152) **Slack Mills**, Hyde, SJ 9536 9454
Cotton spinning *c* 1793-1819. Combined 1819-1959.
Ashmore 1982, 99; Bann 1976, 32, 41; CRO QDV2/231; GM SMR 3440, photo nos 0848-53; PP 1834 xx, D1, 58 no 42; Williams with Farnie 1992, no 1028.

153) **Newton Moor Mills**, Newton, SJ 9537 9608
Cotton spinning *c* 1802 - *c* 1810. Combined *c* 1810-1964.
Ashmore 1982, 98; Bann 1976, 42; GM SMR 3435, photo nos 0871-5, SF 4446 100; PP 1834 xx, D1, 55 no 40; Williams with Farnie 1992, no 1006.

154) **Boston Mill No 1**, Hyde, SJ 9545 9516
Cotton spinning 1798 - *c* 1827. Combined *c* 1827-87.
Bann 1976, 17, 30.

155) **Boston Mill No 2**, Hyde, SJ 9550 9508
Combined 1836-87.
Bann 1976, 24, 30.

156) **Flash Brook Mill**, Gee Cross, SJ 9553 9349
Cotton spinning 1789-1841.
Bann 1976, 18-19; CRO QDV2/499; GM SMR 3446, photo nos 0891-7.

157) **Highbank Mill**, Hyde, SJ 9555 9516
Combined *c* 1872-1937.
Bann 1976, 30; Worrall 1937.

158) **Clough Gate Mill**, Hyde, SJ 9556 9377
Cotton spinning *c* 1800-19/29.
Bann 1976, 49; Greenwood's map of Cheshire 1819; Teesdale's map of Cheshire 1828-9.

159) **High Street Mills**, Godley, SJ 9558 9522
Combined 1834-1931.
Bann 1976, 24, 30, 38; Worrall 1931.

160) **Godley Mill**, Godley, SJ 9560 9539
Cotton spinning 1783 - *c* 1821. Combined *c* 1821-86.
Bann 1976, 17, 30; CRO QDV2/174; PP 1834 xx, D1.

161) **Bone Mill**, Godley, SJ 9580 9505
Cotton spinning *c* 1819-72/87.
CRO QDP 110; Worrall 1887.

162) **Lees Factory/Middle Mill**, Newton, SJ 9608 9635
Cotton spinning *c* 1811 - *c* 1891.
Bann 1976, 30; CRO QDV2/313.

163) **Lees Street Mill**, Newton, SJ 9612 9628
Cotton spinning *c* 1829/31 - *c* 1891
Bann 1976, 30; Bryant's map of Cheshire 1829-31.

164) **Shaw Hall Mill**, Hyde, SJ 9658 9630
Cotton spinning 1832-87.
Bann 1976, 24; Worrall 1887.

Longdendale

165) **Lowe's Factory**, Broadbottom, SJ 9873 9411
Cotton spinning *c* 1794 - *c* 1820.
Aikin 1795, 457; CRO QDV2/299; GMCRO M95 Chapman Papers Box 13.

166) **West End Mill**, Broadbottom, SJ 9877 9381
Cotton spinning, later waste *c* 1869 - *c* 1914.
GM SMR 3447, photo nos 0887-9, SF 4538 70-4; Kelly & Co 1914; Slater 1869; Williams with Farnie 1992, no 1052.

167) **Moss/Wharf/Hodge Mill**, Broadbottom, SJ 9880 9332
Cotton spinning 1796 - *c* 1879.
CRO DTW 2477/F/12; CRO QDV2/299; Slater 1879.

168) **Mottram Old/Roe Cross Mill**, Mottram, SJ 9889 9596
Wool *c* 1781-1828. Cotton waste *c* 1828 - *c* 1874.
GM SMR 3412; Morris & Co 1874; Teesdale's map of Cheshire 1828-9.

169) **Hodge Print Works**, Broadbottom, SJ 9897 9359
Wool finishing *c* 1763-89. Cotton spinning 1789-1805. Bleaching 1805-26. Bleaching and printing 1826-1913.
Graham 1846, 388; Nevell forthcoming; Powell 1988.

170) **Spout Green Mill**, Roe Cross, *c* SJ 990 962
Cotton spinning *c* 1887-1909/14.
Kelly & Co 1914; Worrall 1887.

171) **Wagstaffe's Factory**, Mottram, SJ 9929 9556
Cotton spinning 1786 - *c* 1813.
CRO DTW 2477/B/10; CRO EDT 281/1; CRO QDV2/299.

172) **Dry Mill**, Mottram, SJ 9930 9556
Cotton spinning *c* 1796 - *c* 1813.
CRO DTW 2477/F/12; CRO EDT 281/1 & 2; CRO QDV2/299.

173) **Victoria/Albert/Roughfield Mill**, Mottram, SJ 9930 9575
Cotton spinning 1852 - *c* 1869.
Slater 1869; Whellan & Co 1852.

174) **Broadbottom/Broad Mills**, Broadbottom, SJ 995 934
Cotton spinning 1802-34. Combined 1834-1938.
Arrowsmith 1992; Ashmore 1982, 85.

175) **Limefield Mill**, Broadbottom, SJ 9970 9353
Combined 1861-1990s.
Ashmore 1982, 85; GM SMR 3535, photo no 0890, SF 4538 66-9; Powell Collection; Williams with Farnie 1992, no 999.

176) **Albion Mill**, Hollingworth, SK 0016 9610
Cotton spinning 1794-1960s.
Ashmore 1982, 97; CRO QDV2/217.

177) **Dog Kennel Mill**, Thorncliffe Vale, Hollingworth, SK 0041 9658
Cotton spinning *c* 1786 - *c* 1823.
CRO QDV2/217; GMCRO M95 Chapman Papers Box 13.

178) **Cardwell's Factory/Arrowscroft Mill**, Hollingworth, SK 0062 9612
Cotton spinning *c* 1795-1972.
Ashmore 1982, 97; CRO QDV2/217; GM SMR 3525, photo nos 1024-7; Williams with Farnie 1992, no 988.

Appendix 1 The Textile Sites of Tameside

179) **Bent Mill**, Hollingworth, SK 0068 9661
Engraving mill *c* 1861 - *c* 1914.
GM SMR 3463; Kelly & Co 1914; Slater 1861.

180) **Mersey Mills**, Hollingworth, SK 0100 9595
Combined 1859-1939.
GM SMR 3523, photo nos 1020-3; Hanmer & Winterbottom 1991, 130; Williams with Farnie 1992, no 1003; Worrall 1939.

181) **Millbrook Mills**, Hollingworth, SK 0106 9675
Cotton spinning 1789-1882.
CRO QDV2/217; Hanmer & Winterbottom 1991, 111; PP 1834 xx, D1, 87 no 65.

182) **Hollingworth Bleach and Print Works**, Hollingworth, SK 0110 9610
Print works *c* 1790 - *c* 1970.
Aikin 1795; Ashmore 1982, 97; CRO QDV2/217; GM SMR 3522 & 3524, photo nos 1018-23; Graham 1846, 389; Powell Collection; Williams with Farnie 1992, nos 1000 & 1021.

Mossley

183) **Hopkins Farm**, Mossley, SD 9654 0029
Print works 1803 - pre-1823.
Graham 1846, 381.

184) **Smeath Meadows/Waterton Mill**, Brookbottom, SD 9685 0255
Cotton spinning 1813 - post-1954.
Kenworthy 1928, 14; *Manchester Mercury* 3/5/1813.

185) **Brookbottom Mill No 1**, Brookbottom, SD 9694 0264
Cotton spinning 1824/5 - post-1954.
Barnes 1980, 8; Eckersley 1991, 82; GM SMR 3326, photo no 0728, SF 4104 1-6; Williams with Farnie 1992, no 1029; OS 1:2500 sheet SD 9802, 1954 revision.

186) **Brookbottom Mill No 2**, Brookbottom, SD 9695 0264
Cotton spinning 1833/5 - post-1954.
Barnes 1980, 8; GM SMR 3326, photo no 0728, SF 4104 1-6; Williams with Farnie 1992, no 1029; OS 1:2500 sheet SD 9802, 1954 revision.

187) **Hart/Valley Mills**, Brookbottom, SD 9695 0275
Cotton spinning 1819/21-90s.
Barnes 1980, 8; GM SMR 3328, photo no 0730; Williams with Farnie 1992, no 1043.

188) **Albion Mill**, Mossley, SD 9712 0250
Cotton spinning 1837-1938.
Mr I Haynes pers comm; Pigot & Co 1841; Slater 1843; Worrall 1938.

189) **Westhill Mill**, Mossley, SD 9722 0252
Cotton spinning 1900-31.
Williams with Farnie 1992, 28; Worrall 1931.

190) **Weir Mill**, Mossley, SD 9728 0096
Cotton spinning 1845-1935.
GM SMR 3338, photo nos 0992-3, SF 4104 44-9; Williams with Farnie 1992, no 1049; Worrall 1935.

191) **Scout/New Scout Mill**, Mossley, SD 9732 0120
?Fulling *c* 1777. Cotton spinning pre-1793-1935.
Aikin 1795, 231; Eckersley 1991, 25; Kenworthy 1928, 12, 14, 16; Worrall 1935; Burdett's map of Cheshire 1777.

192) **Britannia Old Mill**, Mossley, SD 9737 0214
Cotton spinning 1849-1931.
Eckersley 1991, 12, 24; Worrall 1931.

193) **Black Rock Mill**, Mossley, SD 9740 0059
Wool *c* 1781 - *c* 1810. Cotton spinning *c* 1810-76.
Eckersley 1991, 25.

194) **Longlands Mill**, Mossley, SD 9744 0205
Cotton spinning 1871-1931.
Eckersley 1991, 63; GM SMR 3306, photo nos 0714-15; Williams with Farnie 1992, no 1001; Worrall 1931.

195) **Britannia New Mill**, Mossley, SD 9744 0214
Cotton spinning 1858-onwards.
Eckersley 1991, 19; GM SMR 3307, photo no 0716, SF 4104 25-8; Williams with Farnie 1992, no 956.

196) **River Mill**, Mossley, SD 9748 0190
Cotton spinning *c* 1848-1938.
Eckersley 1991, 66; GM SMR 3304, photo nos 0705-6, SF 4104 42-3; Williams with Farnie 1992, no 1023; Worrall 1938.

197) **Albert Mill**, Mossley, SD 9750 0167
Cotton spinning 1860/1 - *c* 1960.
Eckersley 1991, 40.

198) **Border/Mossley Brow Mill**, Mossley, SD 9751 0241
Cotton spinning 1873/4-1933. Wool combing and warehouse 1933-86.
Dupont-Lhotelain 1982, 13; GM SMR 3309, photo no 0691.

199) **Victoria Mills**, Mossley, SD 9754 0216
Cotton weaving *c* 1853 - *c* 1930. Wool *c* 1930-38.
Eckersley 1991, 81; GM SMR 3308, photo no 0717, SF 4104 25-28; Williams with Farnie 1992, no 1046; Worrall 1938.

200) **South End Mills**, Micklehurst, SD 9755 0179
Cotton spinning 1859/62-1930.
Eckersley 1991, 19; Worrall 1930.

201) **Queen Street Mills**, Mossley, SD 9755 0210
Cotton spinning, later cotton waste 1844/5-onwards.
Eckersley 1991, 81; GM SMR 3305, photo no 0713, SF 4104 25-34; Williams with Farnie 1992, no 1017.

202) **Bottoms Old Mill**, Mossley, SD 9758 0205
Fulling mill *c* 1777 - *c* 1807. Cotton spinning *c* 1807-1931.
Ashmore 1982, 117; Kenworthy 1928, 16; Worrall 1931; Burdett's map of Cheshire 1777.

203) **Milton Mills**, Mossley, SD 9761 0248
Wool carding and spinning 1891/2-onwards.
Ashmore 1982, 118; Dupont-Lhotelain 1982, 13, 28; GM SMR 3310, photo no 0689, SF 4104 20-4; Williams with Farnie 1992, no 1004.

204) **Creswell/Carr Hill Mill**, Mossley, SD 9761 0260
Woollen scribbling 1793-1818. Combined cotton 1818-1933. Wool 1933-onwards.
Aikin 1795, 456; Ashmore 1982, 117-18; Barnes 1980, 8; Barnes *et al* 1983, 101; Dupont Lhotelain 1982, 39; GM SMR 3311, photo no 0690, SF 4104 16-19; Kenworthy 1928, 12-13; Pigot & Co 1841; Williams with Farnie 1992, no 962.

205) **Croft Mill**, Mossley, SD 9765 0202
Cotton spinning *c* 1838 - *c* 1960.
Ashmore 1982, 117; Pigot & Co 1841.

206) **Bottoms New/Bankside Mill**, Micklehurst, SD 9768 0152
Wool *c* 1829/31 - post-1872.
CRO QDV2/427; OS First Edition 6in Cheshire sheet III, surveyed 1872.

207) **Quickwood/Woodend Mill**, Mossley, SD 9769 0262
Cotton spinning 1848-50. Combined 1850-1960.
Ashmore 1982, 118; Barnes 1980, 8; GM SMR 3312, photo nos 0682-8; Williams with Farnie 1992, no 1056.

208) **New Hollins/Victoria Mill**, Micklehurst, SD 9777 0194
Cotton spinning *c* 1829/31-1933. Wool 1933-61.
Dupont-Lhotelain 1982, 13, 32.

Appendix 1 The Textile Sites of Tameside

209) **Albert/Brunswick Mill**, Mossley, SD 9779 0182
Cotton spinning *c* 1853-1933. Wool 1933-90.
Ashmore 1982, 117; Dupont-Lhotelain 1982, 13, 38; Eckersley 1991, 85; GM SMR 3315, photo nos 0707-8, SF 4104 35-8; Williams with Farnie 1992, nos 941 & 959.

210) **Stamford Mill**, Mossley, SD 9785 0275
Cotton spinning 1860/1-1960.
Barnes 1980, 7-8.

211) **Andrew/Roughtown Mill**, Mossley, SD 9788 0292
Fulling 1765-1871. Cotton spinning 1805-1960.
Barnes 1980, 7-8; Kenworthy 1928, 5, 12-13.

212) **Platt's Mill**, Micklehurst, SD 9802 0299
?Wool *c* 1796 - *c* 1829.
CRO QDV2/427.

213) **Springbank Mill**, Micklehurst, SD 9805 0186
Wool *c* 1887-onwards.
Worrall 1887.

214) **Oldham Stair/Hollins Mill**, Micklehurst, SD 9805 0195.
Wool *c* 1795 - *c* 1874; 1898-1938. Cotton spinning *c* 1874-98.
Ashmore 1982, 117; GM SMR 3318, photo nos 0709-11; Williams with Farnie 1992, no 989; Worrall 1938.

215) **Bank Mill**, Micklehurst, SD 9806 0326
Combined 1862 - post-1954.
GM SMR 3301, photo no 2547, SF 4104 7-12; Williams with Farnie 1992, no 946; OS 1:2500 sheet SD 9803, 1954 revision.

216) **Spring/Una Mill**, Micklehurst, SD 9810 0344
Cotton spinning 1861/2-1929.
Mr I Haynes pers comm; Worrall 1929.

217) **Union Mill**, Micklehurst, SD 9812 0330
Combined 1862/3 - post-1954.
GM SMR 3302, photo nos 0646, 0679-81, SF 4104 7-12; Williams with Farnie 1992, no 1041; OS 1:2500 sheet SD 9803, 1954 revision.

218) **Doctor Mill**, Micklehurst, SD 9816 0202
Wool 1797 - *c* 1896.
Ashmore 1982, 117; Kenworthy 1928, 5; TLSL DD 241/2.

219) **Castle Clough Mill**, Micklehurst, SD 9820 0160
Wool *c* 1795 - *c* 1896.
Ashmore 1982, 117.

220) **Squire Mills**, Micklehurst, SD 9830 0203
Wool *c* 1819 - post-1954.
Ashmore 1982, 117; GM SMR 3320, photo nos 0719-23; Williams with Farnie 1992, no 1032; OS 1:2500 sheet SD 9802, 1954 revision.

221) **Greaves/Vale Mills**, Micklehurst, SD 9838 0202
Wool 1792-1834. Cotton spinning 1834 - *c* 1841. Wool *c* 1841 - post-1954.
Ashmore 1982, 117; CRO QDV2/427; GM SMR 3321, photo nos 0724-7, SF 4538 3-5; Kenworthy 1928, 5; Pigot & Co 1841; PP 1834 xx, D1, 20 no 12; Williams with Farnie 1992, no 1042; OS 1:2500 sheet SD 9802, 1954 revision.

222) **Brick Mill**, SD 9847 0204
Wool 1804-1930.
Kenworthy 1928, 5; Worrall 1930.

223) **Castle Mill**, Micklehurst, SD 9852 0156
Wool *c* 1795 - *c* 1872.
Ashmore 1982, 117.

224) **Clough Mill**, Micklehurst, SD 9860 0204
Wool 1778-1931.
Ashmore 1982, 117; Kenworthy 1928, 5; TLSL DD 241/2; Worrall 1931.

225) **Carr Mill**, Micklehurst, SD 9878 0118
Cotton spinning 1799 - *c* 1841. Wool *c* 1841 - *c* 1909.
Ashmore 1982, 117; *Manchester Mercury* 22/10/1799; Pigot & Co 1841.

226) **Buckton Vale Print Works**, Mossley, SD 9905 0095
Wool *c* 1777 - *c* 1800. Cotton spinning *c* 1800 - *c* 1826. Dye and print works *c* 1826-1980s.
Aikin 1795, 456; Ashmore 1982, 117; CRO QDV2/427; GM SMR 3527, photo nos 0944-98, SF 4104 50-4; Graham 1846, 358; Kenworthy 1928, 7; Williams with Farnie 1992, no 960; Burdett's map of Cheshire 1777.

Stalybridge

227) **Premier Mill**, Stalybridge, SJ 9517 9827
Combined 1906-82.
GM SMR 3361 photo nos 0751, 2561-2, SF 4014 1-4; Haynes 1990, 38-9; Williams with Farnie 1992, no 1014.

228) **Ray Mill**, Stalybridge, SJ 9522 9833
Cotton spinning 1907-82.
GM SMR 3360, photo nos 0757-60, SF 4014 1 & 9; Haynes 1990, 38-9; Williams with Farnie 1992, nos 1018 & 1019.

229) **Clarence Mill**, Stalybridge, SJ 9526 9847
Combined 1862-1960.
GM SMR 3371, photo nos 0791-7, SF 3158 59-61; Haynes 1990, 35-6; Williams with Farnie 1992, no 968.

230) **Victor Mill**, Stalybridge, SJ 9528 9818
Cotton spinning 1903-82.
Ashmore 1982, 138; GM SMR 3362, photo nos 0745-50, 0752-6, SF 4014 5-8; Haynes 1990, 38-9; Williams with Farnie 1992, no 1044.

231) **Phoenix Mill**, Stalybridge, SJ 9543 9814
Cotton spinning *c* 1869 - *c* 1876.
GM SMR 3536, photo nos 0743-4; Haynes 1990, 36; Williams with Farnie 1992, no 1013.

232) **Aqueduct Mills**, Stalybridge, SJ 9544 9816
Cotton spinning, later artificial fibre 1823/4 - *c* 1984.
Ashmore 1982, 138; Haynes 1990, 29-30.

233) **Robinson Street Mill**, Stalybridge, SJ 9550 9812
Cotton spinning 1823/4-1920s.
Haynes 1990, 30.

234) **Hollins Mill**, Stalybridge, SJ 9553 9795
Cotton spinning 1826-82.
Haynes 1990, 31.

235) **Castle Mill**, Stalybridge, SJ 9560 9829
Cotton spinning 1891 - *c* 1930.
Haynes 1990, 37-8.

236) **Bayley Street Mill**, Stalybridge, SJ 9570 9840
Combined *c* 1836-1903/6.
Haynes 1990, 33.

237) **Bridge Street Mills**, Stalybridge, SJ 9577 9823
Cotton spinning 1815 - *c* 1953.
Ashmore 1982, 138; Haynes 1990, 28.

238) **Stalybridge Mill**, Stalybridge, SJ 9582 9840
Cotton spinning 1881-1966.
Haynes 1990, 36-7; *Textile Recorder* i, no 7, 1883, 156-8.

239) **Kershaw Wood Mill**, Stalybridge, SJ 9584 9857
Combined 1837-78.
Haynes 1990, 33-4.

240) **Quarry Street Mills**, Stalybridge, SJ 9585 9805
Combined 1834 - *c* 1957.
GM SMR 3402, photo nos 0737-9, SF 4014 21-4; Haynes 1990, 32-3; Williams with Farnie 1992, no 1016.

241) **Bayley's Mill**, Stalybridge, SJ 9590 9824
Cotton spinning 1812-24. Combined 1824-1903/6.
Haynes 1990, 28.

242) **Johnson Side Mill**, Stalybridge, SJ 9590 9842
Cotton spinning 1854/5-70s.
GM SMR 3367, SF 4014 25-8; Haynes 1990, 19-21.

243) **Lilley's Mill**, Stalybridge, c SJ 959 990
Wool c 1790 - c 1802. Cotton spinning c 1802-7.
Haynes 1990, 27-8.

244) **Rassbottom Mill**, Stalybridge, SJ 9591 9845
Cotton spinning 1795/7 - c 1825. Combined c 1825 - c 1933.
GM SMR 3367, SF 4014 25-8; Haynes 1990, 19-21; Williams with Farnie 1992, no 958.

245) **Wareing's Mill**, Stalybridge, SJ 9595 9836
Cotton spinning c 1821-1900/3.
Haynes 1990, 29.

246) **Harrop Street Mills**, Stalybridge, SJ 9604 9853
Cotton spinning 1823-83.
GM SMR 3470, photo nos 0740-2, SF 4446 84-7; Haynes 1990, 20-1; Williams with Farnie 1992, no 986.

247) **The 'Old Soot Poke'**, Stalybridge, SJ 9604 9867
Cotton spinning 1776 - c 1816.
Haynes 1990, 16.

248) **Grosvenor Street Mills**, Stalybridge, SJ 9605 9830
Cotton spinning 1805-24/5. Combined 1824/5-1955.
GM SMR 3370, photo nos 0669-74; Haynes 1990, 25-6; Williams with Farnie 1992, no 982.

249) **The 'Hen-cote'**, Stalybridge, SJ 9606 9852
Cotton spinning c 1800 - c 1819.
CRO QDV2/393; Haynes 1990, 18.

250) **Garside's Mill**, Stalybridge, SJ 9609 9868
Cotton spinning c 1798-1826.
Haynes 1990, 21-2.

251) **Water Street Mill**, Stalybridge, SJ 9614 9855
Cotton spinning 1797 - c 1870s.
Haynes 1990, 21.

252) **Bayley's/Hope Mill**, Stalybridge, SJ 9614 9863
Cotton spinning c 1800 - c 1857.
Haynes 1990, 22.

253) **Queen Street Mill**, Stalybridge, SJ 9614 9867
Cotton spinning 1803-81.
Haynes 1990, 23.

254) **Castle Street Mill (Hall's)**, Stalybridge, SJ 9619 9849
Cotton spinning 1815-83.
Haynes 1990, 28-9.

255) **Adsheads' Mill**, Stalybridge, SJ 9620 9854
Cotton spinning c 1795 - c 1818.
Haynes 1990, 18-19.

256) **King Street Mill**, Stalybridge, SJ 9624 9865
Cotton spinning c 1800-70s.
Haynes 1990, 22.

257) **Castle Street Mills**, Stalybridge, SJ 9625 9855
Cotton spinning 1805-1961.
Ashmore 1982, 137-8; GM SMR 3368, photo nos 0675-8, SF 4014 29-32; Haynes 1990, 27; Williams with Farnie 1992, no 964.

258) **Stalybridge Woollen/Corn Mill**, Stalybridge, SJ 9665 9855
Wool c 1800 - c 1821/5.
GM SMR 3588, photo nos 2558-60; Haynes 1990, 17-18.

259) **Stokes Mills**, Stalybridge, SJ 9673 9867
Combined c 1825 - c 1966.
GM SMR 3382, photo nos 0772-4, SF 4014 37-40; Williams with Farnie 1992, no 1036.

260) **Higher Mill**, Stalybridge, SJ 9675 9885
Wool c 1775-1827. Cotton spinning 1803-73.
GM SMR 3476, photo nos 0775-6, SF 4014 45; Haynes 1990, 22-3; Williams with Farnie 1992, no 987.

261) **Bankwood/Cheethams Mill**, Stalybridge, SJ 9680 9822
Combined 1831-1935.
GM SMR 3383, photo nos 0735-6, SF 3159 1; Haynes 1990, 32; Williams with Farnie 1992, nos 948 & 967.

262) **Albion Mills**, Stalybridge, SJ 9685 9858
Cotton spinning 1824 - c 1940.
Haynes 1990, 30-1.

263) **Riverside Mill**, Stalybridge, SJ 9685 9890
Weaving 1883-89; 1930s - c 1962. Cotton spinning 1889-1930s.
Haynes 1990, 37-8.

264) **Staley New Mills**, Stalybridge, SJ 9705 9850
Cotton spinning 1824-96.
Ashmore 1982, 137; Haynes 1990, 31.

265) **River Meadow Mills**, Stalybridge, SJ 9708 9930
Combined 1851 - c 1935.
GM SMR 3377, photo nos 0778-81, SF 4014 58-61; Haynes 1990, 34-5; Williams with Farnie 1992, no 1022.

266) **North End Mill**, Stalybridge, SJ 9710 9920
Combined 1851-1930.
Haynes 1990, 34-5.

267) **Copley Mills**, Stalybridge, SJ 9725 9880
Cotton spinning 1827-1974.
Ashmore 1982, 137; GM SMR 3379, photo nos 0732-4, SF 4014 46-9; Haynes 1990, 31-2; Williams with Farnie 1992, no 970.

268) **Heyrod Mill/Hartshead Print Works**, Stalybridge, SJ 9726 9964
Cotton spinning c 1786-1848. Print works 1848 - c 1920.
Aikin 1795, 456; Haynes 1990, 17; Yates's map of Lancashire 1786.

269) **Valley Mill**, Stalybridge, SJ 9750 9691
Wool c 1790 - c 1840. Cotton spinning c 1840-72/96.
Haynes 1990, 34.

270) **Spring Grove Mill**, Stalybridge, SJ 9757 9992
Cotton spinning 1818-68. Wool 1868-1969.
GM SMR 3337, photo nos 0785-90, SF 4014 56-7; Haynes 1990, 29; Williams with Farnie 1992, no 1030.

271) **Staley Mill**, Stalybridge, SJ 9780 9955
Cotton spinning 1803 - c 1837. Combined c 1837-1969.
Ashmore 1982, 137; GM SMR 3375, photo no 0779, SF 4014 62-5; Haynes 1990, 23-4; Williams with Farnie 1992, no 1033.

272) **New Mill/Oakwood**, Stalybridge, SJ 9785 9970
Cotton spinning 1851-1961.
Ashmore 1982, 137; GM SMR 3376, photo nos 0776-84, SF 4014 58-61; Haynes 1990, 35; Williams with Farnie 1992, no 1008.

273) **Crows i' th' Wood Mill**, Stalybridge, SD 9789 0070
Wool c 1795 - c 1872.
CRO QDV2/393; OS First Edition 6in Cheshire sheet III, surveyed 1872.

274) **Staley/Howard's/Castle Hall Mill**, Stalybridge, SJ 9794 9943
Cotton spinning 1805-96. Wool 1896-1962.
Haynes 1990, 24-5; Nevell 1991, 56.

Appendix 2
The Earl of Stamford Records in the Cordingley Archives, Ashton-under-Lyne: Part 2, the Maps

Since 1819 the stewardship of the earl of Stamford's Cheshire and Lancashire estates has been held by the firm of estate agents and surveyors Cordingleys. On the death of the widow of the seventh earl in 1950 the Stamford estates were divided between Mrs Eileen Bissel and Lord Deramore. Cordingleys in Ashton-under-Lyne currently hold the documentary material for the Stamford estates in Lancashire, specifically for Ashton-under-Lyne, on behalf of Lord Deramore. A list of the medieval documents still held by Cordingleys has already been published (Nevell 1991, 131-2; ESRCA 1-13). Most of the Stamford estate maps held by Cordingleys were transferred to the Tameside Local Studies Library a few years ago. However, a small number of large-scale plans, covering the period 1741-1832, are still held by Cordingleys. These form the subject of this appendix. The catalogue numbers used in the text are a continuation of those published in 1991. Copies of all of these maps, except ESRCA 15, 17 and 18, are now held in the Tameside Local Studies Library, Stalybridge. All enquiries should be directed in the first instance to the Local Studies Librarian.

ESRCA 14
'plan/of the/ASHTON DEMESNE/shewing its/BOUNDARIES/as copied from a plan/drawn in 1742 by I. HUSSEY/and the Streets ETc as now/laid out by/JOEL HAWKYARD'
Size 65cm x 45cm. Scale in yards. Parchment with a cloth edging. Hand coloured. Not dated but probably *c* 1819-20.

ESRCA 15
'A/PLAN/of/Ashton underline/Belonging to/the Right Honourable/Mary COUNTESS OF STAMFORD/Survey'd and Plan'd/By T. Tinker 1765'
Size 300cm x 176cm. Scale in yards. Parchment on a cloth backing. Hand coloured. Covers the whole of the ancient parish of Ashton-under-Lyne.

ESRCA 16
'A PLAN/of Lands in Ashton underline in the County of Lancaster Belonging to/The Rt Honble Earl of STAMFORD/Taken by Wm Wright and laid out in order for Building upon by J. Sidebottam, Manchr/April 1787'
Size 101cm x 54cm. Scale in yards. Parchment on a cloth backing. Hand coloured.

ESRCA 17
'PLAN/OF/DEMESNE LAND/laid out for building upon/at ASHTON UNDERLYNE/in the County Palatine/of/LANCASTER/BELONGING TO THE RT HONBLE/THE/EARL OF STAMFORD AND WARRINGTON/by/Joel Hawkyard, Ashton Underlyne. 1820'
Size 195 cm x 135cm. Scale in yards. Parchment on a cloth backing. Hand coloured in green and red. Covers the area from St Peter's church (shown) in the west to Delamere St in the east, and from the Ashton Canal in the south to Shaw Brook in the north.

ESRCA 18
Copy of ESRCA 17 with the same date, title and details.

ESRCA 19
'PLAN/OF PART OF THE/DEMESNE LAND/AT/Ashton Underlyne/BELONGING TO THE RT HONBLE THE EARL OF/STAMFORD and WARRINGTON/By Joel Hawkyard Land Surveyor/Ashton Underlyne/JanY 22nd 1822'
Size 127cm x 75cm. Scale in yards. Hand coloured. Parchment on a cloth backing.

ESRCA 20
'PLAN OF LANDS laid out for BUILDING UPON/lying contiguous to the TOWN of/ASHTON Underlyne/by Joel Hawkyard Ashton underlyne March 1828'
Size 111cm x 74cm. Scale in yards. Hand coloured in green, blue and red. Parchment on a cloth backing with red cloth binding.

ESRCA 21
Copy of ESRCA 19 with the same title, size and design except not dated and inscribed 'Designed and Drawn by Joel Hawkyard'.

ESRCA 22
'PLAN of Building Land in ASHTON UNDERLYNE/By Joel Hawkyard Land Surveyor Octr 1829'
Size 82cm x 65cm. Scale in yards. Hand coloured. Parchment on a cloth backing with green cloth edging.

ESRCA 23
'PLAN/of/PREMISES, and LAND/laid out for building upon/at/ASHTON UNDER LYNE/By Joel Hawkyard 1832'
Size 83cm x 64cm. Scale in yards. Hand coloured. Parchment on a cloth backing with green cloth edging.

Glossary

Aggregative analysis - a method of studying the population of a parish by plotting over time the trends in baptisms, marriages and burials from the parish registers.

Bason - early name for a kettle, a large container used for boiling water and sulphuric acid in the planking process of hat making.

Bay - in a building the distance between roof trusses or load-bearing walls.

Beam engine - first developed by Boulton and Watt in 1781 and subsequently advanced through various improvements, this remained the common form of steam engine in use in textile mills until its gradual replacement by the horizontal engine from the 1870s onwards. The centrally pivoted beam was connected at one end to a piston and at the other to a crankshaft and flywheel, the rotary motion of which was transmitted via gears, shafting and belts to drive the machines used in the textile manufacturing process.

Borough - pre-1835 a chartered town with its own court, the charter usually being given by the crown. In 1835 the Municipal Corporations Act allowed the creation by Parliament of new self-governing boroughs, with elected councils, in the new industrial towns.

Boss - an ornamental block usually set at the junction of two or more ribs, or members, in a vaulted ceiling.

Bowkhouse - a bleaching house.

Broad canal - a canal with locks capable of taking boats and barges with beams, or widths, of up to fifteen feet.

Carding - the process of disentangling and straightening fibres in preparation for spinning. Carding was initially carried out by hand but in the late eighteenth century was mechanized, the fibres being fed over a rotating drum fitted with spikes.

Circus - a circular arrangement of buildings, often taking the form of two crescents or four quadrants.

Clerestory - the upper stage of the main walls of a church above the aisle roofs, pierced by windows.

Clothier - an individual specializing in the production and sale of cloth.

Colliery - a mining complex run by one company.

Combined firm - a textile firm which both spun and wove fabric, in Tameside usually cotton; also known as an integrated firm.

Copperas - sulphate of iron, also known as green vitriol, used in the textile industry during the dyeing process.

Cotton famine - the name given to the years 1861-5 during which the supply of raw cotton from the United States of America to Great Britain was cut off as a result of the American Civil War. The Lancashire textile region was heavily reliant on American cotton and as a consequence output and employment in the industry were severely reduced, with some mills working short-time and others being forced into temporary or permanent closure.

Count - a measure of thickness of yarn.

Court leet - the judicial court of a manor.

Double-depth - a structure two rooms deep.

Doubling mill - a cotton mill which specialized in spinning a strong yarn with two or more threads.

Engraving mill - a mill specializing in the manufacture of engraved printing rollers used in the printing of textiles.

Entablature - in a beam engine the cross piece, set between the engine house walls, which carries the beam.

Factory system - a means of mechanized manufacture of goods, typically textiles, which necessitated the concentration of the workforce in a single building or complex.

Friendly societies - local welfare organizations which for a weekly subscription provided members with cash benefits in times of need, such as allowances for sickness, a pension in old age and a lump sum to aid with funeral expenses.

Fulling - the shrinking and thickening of wetted woollen cloth as part of the finishing process of its manufacture. Fulling was initially carried out by walking on the cloth, but as early as the medieval period fulling mills, often water-powered, were introduced in which the cloth was repeatedly struck by wooden hammers, or stocks. Fulling mills represent the earliest stage in the mechanization of textile manufacture.

Fustian - a type of cloth made using a linen warp and a cotton weft. Fustians were a staple product of the Lancashire textile district from the seventeenth century onwards and provided the foundations for the establishment of the factory-based cotton industry in the late eighteenth century.

Gritstone - another name for Millstone Grit deposits, a type of Carboniferous rock.

Hammer-beam roof - a roof construction in which the principal rafters are supported by an arrangement of a short, braced horizontal beam and a vertical post.

High farming - a term used to describe those farms in the mid-nineteenth century on which heavy investment in new machinery, buildings and labour took place.

Glossary

Horizontal engine - a steam engine in which the piston is set in a horizontal plane and is directly linked via a connecting rod to the crankshaft and flywheel. From the 1870s horizontal engines began to replace beam engines as the main power source in textile mills.

Horse-gin - in the coal-mining industry, a hoisting machine turned by a horse.

Hundred - an administrative subdivision of a county. Their origins lie in the late Anglo-Saxon period.

Inverted compound engine - a form of vertical engine, introduced in the 1880s and capable of generating high powers, of up to 2000hp.

Jacquard loom - a loom capable of weaving complex checks and fabrics by using a card punched with holes, wrapped around a cylinder, as a guide for a set of needles; these deflected hooks into the path of a rising knife to lift a number of warp threads. Named after the French inventor Joseph Marie Jacquard who first demonstrated the machine in 1801.

Joint-stock limited liability company - a limited liability company, the capital of which is divided into small units or shares owned by more than one firm or individual.

Laithe house - a range of farm buildings under one roof with a domestic dwelling at one end and a combined barn and stable or cow house at the other end, with no internal communication between the two suites of buildings.

Leat - the artificial channel dug from a river or reservoir to supply water to a water-wheel.

Limited liability company - a company in which the shareholders are not personally liable for any losses.

Lives - a term used to describe a lease covering the life of a tenant, often including his or her descendants down to the third generation, usually relating to agricultural land and property.

Local board - a unit of local government created in the nineteenth century to oversee specific subjects such as highways, sanitation and policing in those townships without municipal borough status. The representatives of the boards were elected. They were replaced in 1894 by urban and rural district councils.

Manor - a medieval territorial and administrative unit held by a lord.

Mule - the name given to the machine invented in 1779 by Samuel Crompton which combined the bare spindle spinning of the jenny with the drafting rollers of the water frame.

Mullion - the vertical post subdividing a window into lights.

Murphy Riots - name given to the anti-Catholic riots of 1867 in many midland and northern English towns engendered by the anti-Catholic speeches of William Murphy and others.

Narrow boat - canal barges with a six feet beam and usually 70 feet in length.

Narrow canal - a canal with locks only seven feet wide, and thus capable of taking only narrow boats.

Newcomen engine - developed in 1705-6 and also known as the atmospheric engine, this used a simple piston to raise and lower a pivoting beam. The engines lacked the rotary motion which enabled later beam engines to drive industrial machinery but their vertical motion was put to a common use in pumping water from mine workings.

Nucleated settlement - a settlement in which the main group of buildings forms a concentrated mass, usually around a focal point such as a church or market place.

Parish - a township or group of townships possessing its own church and vicar.

Plug Riots - name given to the textile strikes of 1842 when workers, striking in support of the People's Charter, pulled the plugs out of the boilers in their local mills.

Pugging machine - a machine used to mix clay in brick and tile manufacture.

Putting out - a system by which a master clothier would employ textile spinners and weavers working at home, sometimes in rows of cottages built by the employer.

Quarter Sessions - the law court of a hundred, meeting four times a year.

Rectified photography - a technique for drawing buildings from photographs using known fixed points to create a grid from which the elevation can be reconstructed.

Ring spinning - the ring spinning machine was developed in America in 1828 and involved a continuous process which normally produced a strong but lean yarn. It only became popular in Britain towards the end of the nineteenth century.

Rope-drive - a form of power transmission system in textile mills which from the 1870s began to replace the earlier upright shaft system. A grooved flywheel carried a series of continuous heavy ropes providing a separate power system to the line shafting on each floor of a mill.

Scribbling mill - a type of early water-powered woollen mill specializing in the cleaning and disentangling of woollen fibres, the equivalent of the carding process in the cotton industry.

Scutcher - a machine for removing impurities from the raw cotton.

Shippon - a cow house where cattle are tethered during winter and which is also used for milking.

Single-depth - a building one room deep.

Single-unit firms - a firm which owns only one site.

Sites and Monuments Record - a list of archaeological sites, finds, and historic buildings within a county. Usually held and updated by a county archaeologist.

Spindleage - the number of spinning spindles contained by a cotton mill, thus defining its spinning capacity.

Spinning jenny - a hand-powered machine for the multiple spinning of cotton designed by Hargreaves in 1764.

Taking-in door - an exterior upper-storey door in an industrial or agricultural building used for loading and unloading raw material, produce or goods, usually via a hoist.

Tithe - the tenth part of a person's income which was taken towards the upkeep of the incumbent of the local parish church.

Township - a medieval division of a parish.

Transept - the transverse arms of a cruciform, or cross-shaped, church.

Undercroft - a vaulted room, sometimes underground, below an upper room such as a church or chapel.

Upcast - the ventilation shaft in a mine used for drawing foul air from the underground workings.

Upright shaft - in a textile mill, the vertical shaft, or column, which carried the rotary power of an engine; on each floor of the mill gears transferred this power to horizontal line shafting, suspended from the ceiling, from which in turn belts drove individual machines. From the 1870s such upright shafts were superseded by rope-drives.

Urban district - the smallest unit of local government in urban areas, created under the Local Government Act of 1894.

Vestry - the governing body of a parish.

Wakes - a celebration in honour of a holy day, often accompanied by fairs and markets.

Warp - in weaving the threads running lengthways across a piece of fabric.

Warping mill - a type of early cotton mill which concentrated on the spinning of cotton threads for warping.

Water frame - a cotton-spinning machine designed by Richard Arkwright in 1769, powered by water and capable of running many dozens of spindles.

Weft - in weaving the threads running horizontally across the fabric.

Sources

Primary Sources

British Gas Archives, Partington (BGA)

DNGC Droylsden Gas Company records, 1857-69.

HGCBM Hyde Gas Company records.

Cheshire Record Office (CRO)

D73 Will of Sir William Dukinfield Daniel, 8/12/1756.

DAR/I/16 Werneth manor court book, 1588-1658.

DDX 67/7 Deeds, Werneth township.

DDX 87/2 Hollingworth moor, access to, 1638.

DTW 2343/F/16 Mottram estate, steward's accounts for 1826.

DTW 2477/A/1 Tintwistle estate accounts.

DTW 2477/B/10 Mottram estate survey and valuation, 1799.

DTW 2477/B/12 Mottram estate survey and valuation, 1813.

DTW 2477/B/13 Mottram estate survey and valuation, 1826.

DTW 2477/F/12 Mottram estate, steward's accounts and deeds for 1771-99.

EDP 198/10 Mottram parish records.

EDT 143/1 & 2 Tithe map and apportionment for Dukinfield, 1845.

EDT 217/1 & 2 Tithe map and apportionment for Hyde, 1839.

EDT 281/1 & 2 Tithe map and apportionment for Mottram, 1847.

EDT 292/1 & 2 Tithe map and apportionment for Newton, 1845.

EDT 417/1 & 2 Tithe map and apportionment for Werneth, 1839.

MF41/1-9 Mottram-in-Longdendale parish registers.

P25 Mottram-in-Longdendale parish bundle.

QDP 39 Plan of a proposed Road from the Turnpike Road at or near Mottram Toll-bar to Broadbottom Bridge, 1817.

QDP 67 1/2 Plan of the proposed Turnpike Road from Ridgehill within Hartshead, Ashton-underlyne in the County of Lancaster to Hole House within Saddleworth, West Riding of the County of York, 1825.

QDP 67 B2/5 Plan of the Proposed Diversions, Branches and Extensions of the Manchester and Saltersbrook Turnpike Road, 1825.

QDP 110 Plan of the Intended Turnpike Road from Hyde to Mottram Both in the County of Chester, 1832.

QDV2/148 Dukinfield land tax returns 1780-1831.

QDV2/174 Godley land tax returns 1781-1831.

QDV2/204 Hattersley land tax returns 1780-1831.

QDV2/217 Hollingworth land tax returns 1780-1831.

QDV2/231 Hyde land tax returns 1780-1831.

QDV2/285 Matley land tax returns 1780-1831.

QDV2/299 Mottram land tax returns 1780-1831.

QDV2/313 Newton land tax returns 1781-1831.

QDV2/393 Stayley land tax returns 1780-1831.

QDV2/427 Tintwistle (Mickelhurst division) land tax returns 1780-1831.

QDV2/499 Werneth land tax returns 1780-1831.

WS Wills and inventories.

Directories

Bagshaw S, 1850, *History, gazetteer and directory of the county of Chester*.

Baines E, 1825, *History, directory, and gazetteer of the County Palatine of Lancaster*, vol 2.

Bancks G, 1800, *Manchester and Salford directory*.

Dean R & W & Co, 1808, *Manchester and Salford directory for 1808 and 1809*.

Dean R & W & Co, 1811, *Manchester and Salford directory*.

Holme E, 1788, *A directory for the towns of Manchester and Salford*.

Kelly & Co, 1857, *Post Office directory of Cheshire*.

Kelly & Co, 1901, *Kelly's directory of Lancashire*.

Kelly & Co, 1902, *Kelly's directory of Cheshire*.

Kelly & Co, 1914, *Kelly's directory of Cheshire*.

Kelly & Co, 1934, *Kelly's directory of Cheshire*.

Morris & Co, 1874, *Commercial directory and gazetteer of Cheshire with Stalybridge*.

Pigot J & Dean R & W, 1821-2, *New directory of Manchester and Salford*.

Pigot J & Sons, 1832, *General and classified directory of Manchester*.

Pigot J & Sons, 1834, *National commercial directory for the counties of Chester, Cumberland, Durham, Lancaster.*

Pigot J & Co, 1841, *Royal national and commercial directory.*

Scholes J, 1797, *Manchester and Salford directory,* 2nd edition.

Slater I, 1843, *A directory of Manchester and Salford and the townships contiguous.*

Slater I, 1861, *Royal national commercial directory of Manchester and Liverpool.*

Slater I, 1869, *Royal national commercial directory.*

Slater I, 1871-2, *General and classified directory and street register of Manchester and Salford.*

Slater I, 1874, *Royal national commercial directory.*

Slater I, 1877, *Royal national commercial directory of Manchester and Salford.*

Slater I, 1879, *Royal national commercial directory of Lancashire, and the manufacturing district around Manchester.*

Slater I, 1892, *Royal national commercial directory of Lancashire and the manufacturing district around Manchester.*

Wardle M & Pratt, 1816, *The commercial directory of Manchester.*

Whellan W & Co, 1852, *A new alphabetical and classified directory of Manchester and Salford.*

Worrall J, 1882-1930, *The Cotton Spinners' and Manufacturers' Directory and Engineers' and Machine Makers' Advertiser.*

Worrall J, 1931-70, *The Lancashire Textile Industry.*

The Earl of Stamford Records in the Cordingley Archives, Ashton-under-Lyne

ESRCA 14-23 (see Appendix 2).

Greater Manchester Archaeological Unit

GM SMR Greater Manchester Sites and Monuments Record.

Greater Manchester County Record Office (GMCRO)

M95 Chapman Papers Box 13 Hattersley court book and suite rolls.

John Rylands University Library of Manchester

Dunham Massey MSS, Accession 27/3/92 Box 6, Stamford estate survey, 1704.

Dunham Massey MSS, Accession 8/5/92 Box 4/1, Stamford estate survey, 1702.

Lancashire Record Office (LRO)

DDHu 12/32 & 33 Leases referring to mines in Denton in 1788-9, Hulton family papers.

DDHu 32/3 & 4 Letters referring to the Beat Bank branch of the Ashton Canal, Hulton family papers.

DDRe 6/7 Fairbottom Coal Company.

DDX 326 Ellis Fletcher collection.

DDX 614/19 Fairbottom Coal Company dividends.

DRM 1/37 Tithe map and apportionment for Denton, 1849.

DRM 1/39 Tithe map and apportionment for Droylsden, 1847.

DRM 1/50 Tithe map and apportionment for Haughton, 1845.

QDL Sal Land tax returns for Salford Hundred.

QSP Quarter sessions papers.

WCW Wills and inventories.

Newspapers

Ashton Reporter, 6/11/1856, 1/8/1857, 13/12/1864, 23/9/1865, 5/4/1913. Tameside Local Studies Library.

Ashton Standard, 24/7/1858. Tameside Local Studies Library.

Colliery Guardian, 5/8/1892. Salford Mining Museum.

Hatters Gazette, 15/4/1925. Oldham Local Studies Centre.

Manchester Guardian, 18/3/1837, 13/4/1842. Manchester Central Library.

Manchester Mercury, 22/10/1799, 3/5/1813. Manchester Central Library.

North Cheshire Herald, 29/3/1873, 8/11/1873, 5/3/1910. Tameside Local Studies Library.

Oldham Chronicle, 14/4/1877. Oldham Local Studies Centre.

Penny Magazine, January 1841. Stockport Local Heritage Library.

Saddleworth Reporter, 10/3/1860. Oldham Local Studies Centre.

Stockport Advertiser 16/9/1853. Stockport Local Heritage Library.

Textile Recorder i, no 7, 1883; xxvi, no 304, 1908. Manchester Central Library.

Parliamentary Papers

1834, volume xix, *Reports from Commissioners: 1834. Factories Inquiry: 167. Supplementary Report from Commissioners Part 1.*

Sources

1834, volume xx, *Reports from Commissioners: 1834. Factories Inquiry: 167. Supplementary Report from Commissioners Part 2.*

1835, volume xiii, 'Report from Select Committee on hand-loom weavers' petitions; with the minutes of evidence, and index', *Reports from Committees: 1835. Session 19 February - 10 September 1835*, 1-440.

1854-5, volume xviii, 'Bleaching Works', *Reports from Commissioners: 1854-55. Session 12 December 1854 - 14 August 1855*, 5-152.

1868-9, volume xiv, 'Print Works Act and Bleaching and Dyeing Works Acts', *Reports from Commissioners: 1868-9. Session 10 December 1868 - 11 August 1869*, 777-896.

Powell Collection (Private collection of Mrs Joyce Powell)

Mottram rate books, 1858-9.

Plan of Hollingworth Hall Farm, 1951.

Plan of the Salters Brook turnpike road in Mottram town, 1810.

Plan of the Several Roads in the Township of Hollingworth, drawn in 1810.

Receipts and bills for Joseph Booth's shop, 43-43a Market Street, Broadbottom, 1846-79 (217 documents).

Sale catalogue for the Hollingworth Old Hall and Thorncliffe estates, 1890.

Sale catalogue for the Tatton estate in Werneth, 1857.

Sale catalogue for part of the Tollemache estate in Mottram, 1841.

Sale catalogue for the Tollemache estate in Mottram, 1919.

St Michael's Parish Church, Ashton-under-Lyne

Plan of the Salters Brook Turnpike Trust, *c* 1799-1803.

Tameside Local Studies Library, Stalybridge (TLSL)

An Act for the diversion of the Manchester to Salters Brook Turnpike Trust, 1825.

DD 1/1/1-37 Day books of Hyde John Clarke, 1819-57.

DD 1/1/38-41 Diaries of John Clarke, 1842-5.

DD 1/1/42-84 Day books of John Clarke, 1860-1902.

DD 2/93 Haughton Colliery coal dispute, 1852.

DD 13/17/11 Documents referring to Boulton Sidings, Dukinfield.

DD 13/22/2 Articles and pictures on local worthies.

DD 60 Ashton Moss Colliery Company.

DD 73/4 The Wheatsheaf: Ashton-under-Lyne Co-operative Society. 19 vols. July 1912-October 1918.

DD 83 Denton Colliery Company Ltd Statement of Affairs 1929-31.

DD 112/1 Abstract of title to foundries and other properties in Dukinfield.

DD 153/1 Withdrawals book of Droylsden Co-operative Society, June 1901-November 1909.

DD 174/5 Ashton Working Men's Co-operative Society Ltd, certificate of studentship, Hilda Crane, 1914.

DD 216/1 Receipt stubs for gas bills for the Hyde Gas Company, 1862-3.

DD 227/1 *Lightning – the Popular & Business Review of Electricity*, 1897.

DD 229/1 Dukinfield estate map, 1692.

DD 241/2 Radcliffe family papers.

DD 246 Records of Mossley Co-operative Society 1859-1958.

DD 250 Records of Stalybridge Good Intent Industrial Co-operative Society (founded 1859) & Hyde Equitable Co-operative Society (founded 1862).

DD 268 Material relating to Waterloo Co-operative Society, 1866-1947.

DD 269 Material relating to Higher Hurst Co-operative Society, 1864-1955.

DD 270 Material relating to Hurst Brook Co-operative Society, 1890-1929.

DD 271 Material relating to Ashton-under-Lyne Co-operative Society, 1870-1977.

DDG 2/2/2 Documents referring to proposed purchase of Hyde Gas Company's undertakings by Hyde borough in the early 1880s.

DDG 2/2/3 Documents referring to proposed purchase of Hyde Gas Company's undertakings by the Hyde borough in the early 1890s.

DDG 2/2/17 Statement of gas made and sold by the Hyde Gas Company, 1857-1879.

DDG 6/21 Hyde Gas Company papers relating to a special order to acquire the undertakings of Dukinfield and Denton, 1920-37.

DDL Lees family papers (Park Bridge ironworks).

DDS 107 Section of part of Russell Street, Mossley, April 1872.

DDS 187 Plan of George Street, Mossley, May 1880.

DDS 188 Bayleyfield Colliery.

DDS 212 Section and plan of proposed Hawke Street, Stalybridge, 1894.

Sources

DDS 248 Plan of the proposed shippon at Knott Lanes, Ashton, July 1922.

DDS 302 Plan of proposed shippon of John Slater of Holehouse Farm, Micklehurst, January 1902.

DDS 319 Plan of proposed stable at Lower Fold, Alt Hill, November 1897.

DDS 349 Plan of proposed stable at Lilly Lanes, Hartshead, on J Ogden's farm, 1914.

DDS 354 Proposed shippon at Roe Cross, Matley, 1914.

DDS 355 Proposed dairy, Higher Harpley Farm, Stalybridge, 1914.

DDS 356 Proposed shippon and mixing room at Mossley Cross, 1907.

DDS 357 Proposed shippon at the Fold, Stayley, July 1911.

DDS 411 Plan of dairy erected at Fields Farm, June 1914.

DDS 420 Plan and sections of houses along Stamford Road and Hanover Street, Mossley.

DDS 494 Section of Egmont Street, Mossley.

DDS 507 Plan and section of Cambridge and Cumberland streets, Stalybridge, 1883.

DDS 604 Plan of proposed Astley Road, Stalybridge, 1897.

DDS 627 Plan of proposed Taylor Street, Stalybridge.

DDS 634 Plan of proposed Winton Street, Stalybridge.

DDS 776 Hyde Green Farm, Stayley, plan showing new fittings in shippon and repairs to roof of farmhouse, *c* 1900.

DDS 838 Map of Hattersley near Mottram, showing freehold land and names of owners of plots in the area, mid-nineteenth century.

DDS 908 Proposed shippon at Flax Fields, Stayley, 1908.

DDS 932 Plan of proposed farm building at Kershaw Hey Farm, near Mossley, 1913, and proposed shippon and dairy.

DDS 953 Plan of proposed farmhouse at Knott Lanes of Herbert Walker, 1915.

DDS 1055 Plan of plots and owners of land around Ashton Moss, *c* 1831-46.

DDS 1082 Plan of proposed shippon at Hazelhurst near Hurst.

DDS 1095 Plan of proposed farmhouse at Denton Lane, Audenshaw, of Samuel Clayton, 1914.

DDS 1113 Plan of proposed farmhouse, Williamson Lane, Droylsden, 1895.

DDS 1233 Plan of proposed stable in the farm of David Parnell, Luzley, 1913.

DDS 1280 Plan of proposed farmhouse at Timperley, Ashton-under-Lyne, 1908.

DDS 1307 Plan of proposed farmhouse at Hartshead Green, 1909.

DDS 1476 Plan of repairs to shippon and dairy in the occupation of J W Webb, Audenshaw, 1907.

DDS 1529 Plans of proposed farmhouse and dairy at Stayley Hall, 1912.

DDS 1603 Ashton Moss tenancies in 1933, scale 1:2500.

DDS 1616 Plan of Ashton Moss tenancies in 1900, scale 1:2500.

DDS 2076 Broad Oak Colliery railway branch line, 1847.

DDTR 3/1 OAHET Tramways Order, 1883.

DDTR 3/4 & 6 Correspondence between Denton local board and City of London Contract Corporation re OAHET Tramways Order and proposed tramways in Denton.

DDTR 3/19 Documents relating to the purchase of the tramways of OAHET Ltd by Ashton and Hyde corporations and Denton and Audenshaw UDCs, 1914-19.

DDTR 5/1 Tramways Order re Hyde Corporation Tramways, 1901.

DDTR 7/1/7 Tramways and Electric Traction. Proposals for consideration at a conference of Denton and Gorton district councils held at Gorton, June 1898.

DDTR 7/1/10 Documents relating to the Manchester Carriageway & Tramways Company in Tameside, 1896-1901.

DDTR 12 Records relating to the South East Lancashire Electricity District.

DD/WW/2 Documents relating to Hyde Joint Waterworks Undertaking.

DD/WW/86 An Act allowing for the building of the Swineshaw reservoirs, 1864.

MF Census returns, 1841-71.

MF 83 Rayner Stephens, sermons and speeches, 1839.

TTM 1 Copy book of mortgages of the tolls of the Manchester to Salters Brook Turnpike Trust, 1794-1857.

TTM 964 Conveyance relating to the auction of the Manchester to Salters Brook Turnpike Trust, 19th November 1884.

TTM 965 Manchester to Salters Brook Turnpike Trust annual income and expenditure statements, 1874-84.

TTM 1188/1-2 Correspondence relating to proposals to repeal the Manchester, Hyde and Mottram Turnpike Act, 1858-77.

Tameside MBC (Council Offices, Wellington Road, Ashton-under-Lyne)

Broad Saw Mill deeds.

Sources

Secondary Sources

Aikin J, 1795, *A Description of the Country Thirty to Forty Miles round Manchester*. London.

Aldcroft D H, 1974, *Studies in British Transport History 1870-1970*. London, David & Charles.

Armstrong J, 1989, 'Transport and Trade', *in* Pope (ed), 96-133.

Arrowsmith P, 1992, 'Broad Mills, Broadbottom. A 19th Century Cotton Mill in the Etherow Valley', *Archaeology North-West* 4, 23-7.

Ashmore O, 1969, *The Industrial Archaeology of Lancashire*. London, David & Charles.

Ashmore O, 1974, 'The Industrial Archaeology of Ashton', *in* Harrop & Rose (eds), 86-107.

Ashmore O, 1975, *The Industrial Archaeology of Stockport*. University of Manchester Dept of Extra Mural Studies.

Ashmore O, 1982, *The Industrial Archaeology of North-West England*. Manchester University Press.

Ashmore O & Bolton T, 1975, 'Hugh Mason and the Oxford Mills Community, Ashton-under-Lyne', *Transactions of the Lancashire and Cheshire Antiquarian Society* 78, 38-50.

Ashton Brothers & Co Ltd, 1961, *Making For a New Age at Ashtons*. Hyde.

Ashton-under-Lyne Corporation Manual, 1912-13, Ashton-under-Lyne.

Ashworth W, 1954, *The Genesis of Modern British Town Planning: A Study in Economic and Social History of the Nineteenth and Twentieth Centuries*. London, Routledge & Kegan Paul.

Aspin C (ed), 1972, *Manchester and the Textile Districts in 1849 by Angus Bethune Reach*. Helmshore Local History Society.

Baines E, 1836, *History of the County Palatine and Duchy of Lancaster*, 3 vols. London.

Bairstow M, 1986, *The Sheffield Ashton Under Lyne & Manchester Railway. The Woodhead Line*. Pudsey, Martin Bairstow.

Bairstow M, 1990, *The Leeds Huddersfield and Manchester Railway. The Standedge Line*, 2nd edition. Halifax, Martin Bairstow.

Bann J E, 1976, *The Changing Distribution of the Cotton Industry in Hyde*. Unpublished BA dissertation, Newcastle-upon-Tyne University. Copy in Tameside Local Studies Library.

Barnes B, 1979, 'The Early Cotton Industry in Saddleworth. Part 1', *Saddleworth Historical Society Bulletin* 9, 45-52.

Barnes B, 1980, 'The Early Cotton Industry in Saddleworth. Part 3', *Saddleworth Historical Society Bulletin* 10, 7-15.

Barnes B, 1983, 'Early Woollen Mills in a Pennine Parish, Saddleworth, and the Upper Tame Valley', *Saddleworth Historical Society Bulletin* 13, 24-56.

Barnes B, Buckley P M, Hunt J M & Petford A J, 1983, *Saddleworth Surveyed. Selected Maps of the Township 1625-1851*. Saddleworth Historical Society.

Benson A P, 1983, *Textile Machines*. Shire Publications Ltd.

Binfield J C G, 1988, 'The dynamic of grandeur: Albion Church, Ashton-under-Lyne', *Transactions of the Lancashire and Cheshire Antiquarian Society* 85, 173-92.

Booker Rev J, 1855, 'A History of the Ancient Chapel of Denton in Manchester Parish' *in* W Langton (ed), *Cheshire Miscellanies*. Chetham Society, vol 37.

Booth P N, 1987, *The Effect of the Growth of the Cotton Industry on the Growth and Patterns of Settlement in South-east Manchester*. Unpublished BA dissertation, University College of Wales, Aberystwyth. Copy in Tameside Local Studies Library.

Bott O, 1986, 'Cornmill Sites in Cheshire 1066-1850, Part 6, Mills Recorded 1701-1850', *Cheshire History* 17, 27-33.

Bowman W M, 1950, *Five Thousand Acres of Old Ashton. The History of the Limehurst Rural District*. (Republished 1990; Leeds, MTD Rigg Publications.)

Bowman W M, 1960, *England in Ashton-under-Lyne*. Ashton-under-Lyne Corporation.

Brierley H (ed), 1928, *The Parish Registers of Ashton-under-Lyne, 1594-1720*. Lancashire Parish Register Society, vol 65.

Brigg M (ed), 1982, *The Journals of a Lancashire Weaver. 1856-60, 1860-64, 1872-75*. Record Society of Lancashire and Cheshire, vol 122.

Brunskill R W, 1987, *Traditional Farm Buildings of Britain*. London, Victor Gollanz Ltd.

Butterworth E, 1842, *An Historical Account of the Towns of Ashton-under-Lyne, Stalybridge and Dukinfield*. Ashton-under-Lyne.

Butterworth J, 1823, *History and description of the Town and Parish of Ashton-under-Lyne in the county of Lancaster and the village of Dukinfield in the county of Chester*. Ashton-under-Lyne.

Butterworth J, 1827, *History and description of the towns and parishes of Stockport, Ashton-under-Lyne, Mottram-long-den-dale and Glossop*. Oldham.

Caffrey H C, 1985, 'Hatting in Denton', *in* Lock (ed), 27-39.

Cassidy J, 1974, 'A Guide to Stamford Park', *in* Harrop & Rose (eds), 50-9.

Census 1871, *Census of England and Wales 1871. Population Tables...Volume 1, Counties*. HMSO, 1872.

Census 1891, *Census of England and Wales 1891. Area, House, and Population. Volume II*. HMSO, 1893.

Census 1901, *Census of England and Wales 1901. Summary Tables*. HMSO, 1903.

Census 1911, *Census of England and Wales 1911. Summary Tables*. HMSO, 1915.

Census 1921, *Census of England and Wales 1921. General Report with Appendices*. HMSO, 1927.

Census 1931, *Census of England and Wales 1931. Preliminary Report*. HMSO, 1931.

Chadwick E (ed), *The Report on the Sanitary Conditions of the Labouring Population (1842)*. HMSO.

Chadwick W, not dated (c 1870), *Reminiscences of Mottram*. (Republished 1972; Longdendale Amenity Society.)

Cherry G E, 1972, *Urban Change and Planning. A History of Urban Development in Britain since 1750*. Henley-on-Thames, G T Foulis & Co Ltd.

Church R with Hall A & Kanefsky J, 1986, *The History of the British Coal Industry. Volume 3: 1830-1913. Victorian Pre-eminence*. Oxford University Press.

Cootes R J, 1982, *Britain since 1700*, 2nd edition. London, Longman.

Cordingley E J, 1986, *The Effect of the Industrial Revolution upon Ashton-under-Lyne, in the Deramore Family's Lancashire Estates, and the Management of the Estate*. Unpublished BSc dissertation, Newcastle-upon-Tyne Polytechnic.

Cotton N, 1977, *Popular Movements in Ashton-under-Lyne and Stalybridge before 1832*. Unpublished MLitt thesis, University of Birmingham Faculty of Arts. Copy in Tameside Local Studies Library.

Coulthart J R, 1844, *Report on the Sanitary Conditions of the Town of Ashton-under-Lyne*. HMSO.

Cronin J, 1985, 'Victorian Haughton. A picture of Denton's twin town in 1851 from the Census Records', *in* Lock (ed), 40-57.

Cronin P & Yearsley C, 1985, 'Coal Mining in Denton and Haughton', *in* Lock (ed), 58-69.

Davies S, 1960, *The Agricultural History of Cheshire 1750-1850*. Chetham Society, 3rd series, vol 10.

Dawson R, 1837, *Plans of Municipal Boroughs of England and Wales; showing their boundaries and divisions into wards*. HMSO.

Denton Local History Society, 1991, *Kingswater. The Story of Debdale Vale*. Denton, Two Trees Press Ltd.

Dickinson J, 1855, 'Statistics of the Collieries of Lancashire, Cheshire, and North Wales', *Memoirs of the Literary and Philosophical Society of Manchester*, 2nd series 12, 71-107.

DoE 1987, *Department of the Environment, List of Buildings of Special Architectural or Historical Interest. Borough of Tameside, Greater Manchester*. Department of the Environment.

Down P, Duckett F, King H & Whitbread M, 1989, *150th Anniversary St Peters Stalybridge 1839-1989*. Oldham.

Dupont-Lhotelain H (ed), 1982, *The Story of the Mossley Wool and Spinning Co Ltd on the Occasion of its Golden Anniversary, 1932-82*. Mossley Wool and Spinning Co Ltd.

Earwaker J P, 1880, *East Cheshire Past and Present*, vol 2. London.

Eckersley T P, 1991, *The Growth of the Cotton Industry in Mossley with Special Reference to the Mayalls*. Unpublished MA thesis, Manchester Polytechnic Dept of Economics and Economic History. Copy in Tameside Local Studies Library.

Engels F, 1845, *The Condition of the Working Class in England, 1845*. (Republished 1982; London, Granada.)

Farnie D A, 1979, *The English Cotton Industry and the World Market 1815-1896*. Oxford University Press.

Farnie D A, 1990a, 'John Worrall of Oldham, Directory-Publisher to Lancashire and to the World, 1868-1970', *Manchester Region History Review* 4, 30-5.

Farnie D A, 1990b, 'The textile machine-making industry and the world market 1870-1960', *Business History* 32, 150-70.

Farnie D A & Yonekawa S, 1988, 'The Emergence of the Large Firm in the Cotton Spinning Industries of the World, 1883-1938', *Textile History* 19, 171-210.

Farrer W & Brownbill J (eds), 1908, *The Victoria History of the County of Lancaster*, vol 2. London, Constable & Co.

Faucher M L, 1844, *Manchester in 1844. Its present condition and future prospects. Translated from the French with copious notes appended by a member of the Manchester Athenaeum*. Manchester.

Fitton R S (ed), 1965, *The Family Economy of the Working Classes in the Cotton Industry 1784-1833, by Frances Collier*. Chetham Society, 3rd series, vol 12.

Fleischmann R K, 1973, *Conditions of life among the Cotton Workers of south eastern Lancashire during the Industrial Revolution*. Unpublished PhD thesis, State University of New York at Buffalo. Copy in Tameside Local Studies Library.

Fletcher T W, 1961, 'Lancashire Livestock Farming during the Great Depression', *Agricultural History Review* 9, 17-42.

Flinn M W with Stoker D, 1984, *The History of the British Coal Industry. Volume 2, 1700-1830: The Industrial Revolution*. Oxford University Press.

Garnett W J, 1849, 'Farming of Lancashire', *Journal of the Royal Agricultural Society of England* 10, 1-51.

Sources

Giles C & Goodall I H, 1992, *Yorkshire Textile Mills. The Buildings of the Yorkshire Textile Industry 1770-1930.* HMSO.

Giles P M, 1959, 'The Felt-hatting industry, c. 1500-1850, with special reference to Lancashire and Cheshire', *Transactions of the Lancashire and Cheshire Antiquarian Society* 69, 104-32.

Glover W, 1884, *History of Ashton-under-Lyne and the surrounding district.* Ashton-under-Lyne.

GMAU, 1993, *Fishpond Yard, Dukinfield, Excavation Report.* Unpublished report, Greater Manchester Archaeological Unit.

Gordon A, 1896, *Historical account of Dukinfield Old Chapel and its School.* Manchester, Hyde and London.

Gow J J, 1974, 'Leisure in Ashton-under-Lyne, 1855', *in* Harrop & Rose (eds), 76-85.

Graham J, 1846, *History of printworks in the Manchester District, 1760-1846.* Original ms in Manchester Central Library, Local Studies Unit.

Gurr D & Hunt J (eds), 1985, *The Cotton Mills of Oldham.* Oldham Leisure Services.

Hadfield C & Biddle G, 1970, *The Canals of North West England.* Newton Abbot, David & Charles.

Hall R G, 1991, *Work, class and politics in Ashton-under-Lyne, 1830-1860.* Unpublished PhD thesis, Vanderbilt University, Nashville, Tennessee. Copy in Tameside Local Studies Library.

Hanmer J & Winterbottom D, 1991, *The Book of Glossop.* Buckingham, Barracuda Books Ltd.

Harley J B, 1968, *A map of the County of Lancashire, 1786. By William Yates.* Historical Society of Lancashire and Cheshire.

Harley J B & Laxton P (eds), 1974, *A Survey of the County Palatine of Chester by P P Burdett 1777.* Historical Society of Lancashire and Cheshire, Occasional Series, vol 1.

Harris B E (ed), 1979, *The Victoria History of the County of Chester*, vol 2. University of London Institute of Historical Research.

Harrop S, 1974, 'Nineteenth Century Housing in Ashton', *in* Harrop & Rose (eds), 29-49.

Harrop S, 1989, 'Why was Stalybridge First? The Cultural Background to the Town's Industrial Growth', *in* Lock (ed), 6-26.

Harrop S A & Rose E A (eds), 1974, *Victorian Ashton.* Tameside Libraries and Arts Committee.

Haynes I, 1987, *Cotton in Ashton.* The Libraries and Arts Committee, Tameside Metropolitan Borough Council.

Haynes I, 1990, *Stalybridge Cotton Mills.* Radcliffe, Neil Richardson.

Haynes I, forthcoming, *Dukinfield Cotton Mills.* Radcliffe, Neil Richardson.

Hellowell F, 1966, *The Felt Hatting Industry with Special Reference to its Rise in Denton, Lancashire.* Unpublished dissertation, Edge Hill College of Education. Copy in Tameside Local Studies Library.

Hennessey R A S, 1972, *The Electric Revolution.* London, Oriel Press.

Hey J, 1979, *Higher Hurst. The growth and development of an industrial community in Lancashire in the nineteenth century.* Unpublished Local History Certificate essay, University of Manchester Dept of Extra Mural Studies.

Hey D, 1984a, 'The North-West Midlands: Derbyshire, Staffordshire, Cheshire and Shropshire', *in* Thirsk (ed), 129-58.

Hey D, 1984b, 'Yorkshire and Lancashire', *in* Thirsk (ed), 59-86.

Hickey J E, 1926, *Dukinfield Past and Present.* (Republished 1992; Leeds, MTD Rigg Publications.)

Higson J, 1859, *Historical and Descriptive Notices of Droylsden Past and Present.* Manchester.

Hill S, 1907, *Bygone Stalybridge.* (Republished 1987; Leeds, MTD Rigg Publications.)

Hodson H, 1978, *Cheshire, 1660-1780: Restoration to Industrial Revolution.* A History of Cheshire vol 9. Cheshire Community Council.

Holding T, 1986, *An Archaeological Survey of the Hatting Industry in Denton, Manchester.* Unpublished ms. Copy in Tameside Local Studies Library.

Holland J, 1969, *Parkbridge: An Historical Ironworks.* Unpublished ms. Copy in Tameside Local Studies Library.

Holt G U, 1978, *A Regional History of the Railways of Great Britain. Volume X. The North West.* London, David & Charles.

Holt J, 1795, *General View of the Agriculture of the County of Lancaster, with Observations on the Means of its Improvement.* (Republished 1969; London, David & Charles Reprints.)

Hyde W G S, 1978, *Greater Manchester Transport Review.* Mossley, Transport Publishing Co.

Hyde W G S, 1980, *A History of Public Transport in Ashton-under-Lyne.* Mossley, Manchester Transport Museum Society.

James L, 1983, *A Chronology of the Construction of Britain's Railways 1778-1855.* London, Ian Allen Ltd.

Jones C, 1989, 'Coal, gas, and electricity', *in* Pope (ed), 68-95.

Jones S G, 1987, 'Work, Leisure and the Political Economy of the Cotton Districts Between the Wars', *Textile History* 18, 33-58.

Jones S G, 1989, 'Recreational and Cultural Provision in Hyde between the Wars', *in* Lock (ed), 131-47.

Keaveney E & Brown D L, 1974, *A History of the Ashton-under-Lyne Canal*. Manchester, Peak Forest Canal Society.

Kenworthy F, 1928, *The Industrial Development of Mossley, Lancashire*. Unpublished BA dissertation, University of Manchester Dept of History. Copy in Tameside Local Studies Library.

Kenworthy F, 1929, *Industrial Development of Ashton-under-Lyne. 1780-1850*. Unpublished MA thesis, University of Manchester Dept of History. Copy in Tameside Local Studies Library.

King H & King D, 1989, 'Stalybridge – a New Town', *in* Lock (ed), 27-34.

Lamb B, 1968, *A Report and Survey of John Hall & Son (Dukinfield) Ltd 1792-1967*. Manchester Region Industrial Archaeology Society. Unpublished ms. Copy in Tameside Local Studies Library.

Langton, E, 1956, *History of the Moravian Church. The Story of the First International Protestant Church*. London, Allen & Unwin Ltd.

Lawton K W, 1989, 'Ashton-under-Lyne, Stalybridge, and Dukinfield (District) Waterworks. Part 1. The Legislation and Works Prior to 1907', *Saddleworth Historical Society Bulletin* 19, 2-11.

Lewis J, 1868, 'The Agricultural Returns of 1866 and 1867', *Journal of the Royal Agricultural Society of England*, 2nd series 4, 214-47.

Lewis J P, 1965, *Building Cycles and Britain's Growth*. London, Macmillan.

Lock A, 1981a, *Ashton in Old Photographs*. The Libraries and Arts Committee, Tameside Metropolitan Borough.

Lock A, 1981b, *Hyde in Old Photographs*. The Libraries and Arts Committee, Tameside Metropolitan Borough.

Lock A, 1982, *Droylsden in Old Photographs*. The Libraries and Arts Committee, Tameside Metropolitan Borough.

Lock A, 1983, *Mossley in Old Photographs*. The Libraries and Arts Committee, Tameside Metropolitan Borough.

Lock A (ed), 1985, *Looking Back at Denton*. The Libraries and Arts Committee, Tameside Metropolitan Borough.

Lock A (ed), 1986, *Looking Back at Hyde*. The Libraries and Arts Committee, Tameside Metropolitan Borough.

Lock A (ed), 1989, *Looking Back at Stalybridge*. The Libraries and Arts Committee, Tameside Metropolitan Borough.

Mackenzie J C, 1965, 'The composition and nutritional value of diets in Manchester and Dukinfield in 1841', *Transactions of the Lancashire and Cheshire Antiquarian Society* 72 (for 1962), 123-40.

Maddock G, 1986, 'The Apethorn Lane Murder and its Background' *in* Lock (ed), 6-29.

Magee R, 1989, *A Directory of Ashton Pubs and their Licensees*. Radcliffe, Neil Richardson.

Manchester Statistical Society, 1838, *Report of a Committee of the Manchester Statistical Society on the Condition of the Working Classes in an Extensive Manufacturing District in 1834, 1835, and 1836*. Manchester.

March J W (ed), 1957, *Stalybridge, Cheshire. Centenary Souvenir 1857-1957*. Stalybridge Corporation.

Marsh M, 1985, 'Shopping in Denton in the early years of the Twentieth Century', *in* Lock (ed), 70-82.

Marshall J, 1981, *Forgotten Railways: North-West England*. London, David & Charles.

Mellows F M, 1977, *A Short History of Fairfield Moravian Church*. Bradford, The Puritan Press.

Middleton T, 1932, *The History of Hyde and its neighbourhood*. Hyde.

Middleton T, 1936, *The History of Denton and Haughton*. Hyde.

Mines Department, 1928, *Catalogue of Plans of Abandoned Mines*, vol 1 (Lancashire etc). HMSO.

Mines Report, 1873, *Mines Department, Inspectors' reports on Collieries*. HMSO.

Mines Report, 1886, *Mines Department, Inspectors' reports on Collieries*. HMSO.

Mines Report, 1887, *Mines Department, Inspectors' reports on Collieries*. HMSO.

Mingay G E, 1986, *The Transformation of Britain*. London, Routledge & Kegan Paul.

Mingay G E (ed), 1989, *The Agrarian History of England and Wales. Volume VI. 1750-1850*. Cambridge University Press.

Mitchell B R with Deane P, 1971, *Abstract of British Historical Studies*, 2nd edition. University of Cambridge Department of Applied Economics, monograph no 17. Cambridge University Press.

Moore J, 1971, *The Demographic History of a Town. Ashton-under-Lyne, Agricultural 1597, Industrial 1840*. Unpublished BSc dissertation, University of Salford. Copy in Tameside Local Studies Library.

Morris D, 1992, *Stalybridge Corn Mill – Historical Development*. Unpublished ms.

Mossley Municipal Borough, 1935, *Mossley Jubilee Souvenir, 1885-1935*.

Mui H C & Mui L H, 1989, *Shops and Shopkeeping in Eighteenth Century England*. London and Montreal, Routledge.

Musson A E, 1973, 'Engineering', *in* Smith (ed), 55-61.

Sources

Nevell M D, 1991, *Tameside 1066-1700*. Tameside Metropolitan Borough Council with the Greater Manchester Archaeological Unit.

Nevell M D, 1992, *Tameside Before 1066*. Tameside Metropolitan Borough Council with the Greater Manchester Archaeological Unit.

Nevell M D, forthcoming, 'The Hodge Print Works, Broadbottom', *Archaeology North-West* 6.

Newton S, 1970, *Coal mining: Dukinfield's dead industry*. Unpublished ms. Copy in Tameside Local Studies Library.

Oldham & Son Ltd, 1949, *Oldham, Equipment for the Hat Manufactory Industry*. Catalogue. Copy in Tameside Local Studies Library.

Ormerod G, 1882, *The History of the County Palatine and City of Chester* (revised and enlarged by T Helsby), vol 3. London.

Owen D, 1977, *Canals to Manchester*. Manchester University Press.

Paget-Tomlinson E, 1993, *The Illustrated History of Canal and River Navigations*. Sheffield, Sheffield Academic Press.

Palin W, 1845, 'The Farming of Cheshire', *Journal of the Royal Agricultural Society of England* 5, 57-111.

Parry W A, 1908, *History of Hurst and Neighbourhood with Illustrations*. Ashton-under-Lyne.

Pavasovic M, 1984, *No mean city. A History of Dukinfield*. Swinton, Neil Richardson.

Pawson E, 1977, *Transport and Economy: The Turnpike Roads of Eighteenth Century Britain*. London, Academic Press.

Perry P J (ed), 1973, *British Agriculture 1875-1914*. London, Methuen & Co Ltd.

Perry P J, 1974, *British Farming in the Great Depression 1870-1914*. Newton Abbot, David & Charles.

Petford A J, 1987, 'The Process of Enclosure in Saddleworth, 1625-1834', *Transactions of the Lancashire and Cheshire Antiquarian Society* 84, 78-117.

Pope R (ed), 1989, *Atlas of British Social and Economic History since c.1700*. London, Routledge.

Porter S, 1990, *Exploring Local History: Sources for Local Historians*. London, Batsford.

Powell J, 1976, *The Parish of Mottram-in-Longdendale, 1570-1680*. Unpublished Local History Certificate dissertation, University of Manchester Dept of Extra Mural Studies.

Powell J, 1977, *Longdendale in Retrospect*. Oldham, Longdendale Amenity Society.

Powell J, 1988, *The Hodge Print Works*. Unpublished ms.

Powell M, 1977, *Nineteenth Century Census Enumeration Schedules and their Use to the Geographer*. Unpublished Geography Long Essay, Mottram College of Higher Education. Copy in Tameside Local Studies Library.

Preece G, 1981, *Coalmining. A Handbook to the History of Coalmining Gallery, Salford Museum of Mining*. City of Salford Cultural Services.

Preece G, 1985, *Coalmining in Salford. A Photographic Record*. City of Salford Cultural Services.

Preece G, 1989, 'The Art Collections of the Cheetham Family and the Encouragement of Cultural Provision in Stalybridge', *in* Lock (ed), 104-119.

Quayle T, 1988, *Reservoirs in the Hills*. North West Water.

Richardson J, 1986, *The Local Historian's Encyclopedia*, 2nd edition. Hertford, Historical Publications.

Riden P, 1987, *Record Sources for Local History*. London, Batsford.

Ridgway M, 1988, *The Hyde Lane Colliery disaster, Hyde, 1889. A case study on health and safety in the mines during the latter part of the nineteenth century*. Unpublished BA dissertation, Manchester Polytechnic Faculty of Humanities, Law and Social Sciences. Copy in Tameside Local Studies Library.

Rose A G, 1957, 'The Plug Riots of 1842 in Lancashire and Cheshire', *Transactions of the Lancashire and Cheshire Antiquarian Society* 67, 75-112.

Rose E A, 1974, 'Ashton Churches and Chapels', *in* Harrop & Rose (eds), 60-76.

Rose E A (ed), 1985, *A Stalybridge Scrapbook*. Stalybridge Historical Society.

Rothwell W, 1850, *Report of the Agriculture of the County of Lancaster*. London.

Scard G, 1981, *Squire and Tenant: Rural Life in Cheshire, 1760-1900. A History of Cheshire*, vol 10. Cheshire Community Council.

Scola R, 1992, *Feeding the Victorian City. The Food Supply of Manchester 1770-1870*. Manchester University Press.

Shortland A, 1966, *The Effect of the Cotton Industry and Changing Industrial Structure on the Development of Hyde*. Unpublished ms. Copy in Tameside Local Studies Library.

Smith D M, 1966, 'The Hatting Industry in Denton, Lancashire', *Industrial Archaeology* 3, 1-7.

Smith J H (ed), 1973, *The Great Human Exploit. Historic Industries of the North West*. University of Manchester Dept of Extra Mural Studies.

Smith J H, 1980, *The development of the English felt and silk hat trades 1500-1912*, 2 vols. Unpublished PhD thesis, University of Manchester Dept of History.

Speake R & Witty F R, 1953, *A History of Droylsden*. Stockport, Cloister Press Ltd.

Spence N A, 1989, 'Joseph Rayner Stephens - He Hath Done What He Could', *in* Lock (ed), 35-48.

Stott I, 1983, *Townhall buildings in Tameside*. Unpublished Post-graduate thesis, University of Manchester Dept of Architecture and Planning.

Supple B, 1987, *The History of the British Coal Industry. Volume 4, 1913-1946: The Political Economy of Decline*. Oxford University Press.

Taylor C M, 1992, *An examination of Chartist activity in Stalybridge, Ashton-under-Lyne and Hyde, 1838-1848*. Unpublished PhD thesis, University of York Dept of History. Copy in Tameside Local Studies Library.

Thelwall R E, 1972, *The Andrews and Compstall their Village*. Cheshire County Council Libraries and Museums, and Marple Antiquarian Society.

Thirsk J (ed), 1984, *The Agrarian History of England and Wales. Volume V, 1640-1750. Part 1. Regional Farming Systems*. Cambridge University Press.

Thompson J, 1907, *Ashton-under-Lyne Working Men's Co-operative Society Ltd Jubilee Souvenir Book 1857-1907*. Ashton-under-Lyne.

Trotter F M, 1954, 'The Lancashire Coalfield', *in* A Truman (ed), *The Coalfields of Great Britain*, 199-218. London, Edward Arnold Publishers Ltd.

Ure A, 1835, *Cotton Manufacture of Great Britain systematically investigated*. London.

Walton J K, 1987, *Lancashire: A Social History 1558-1939*. Manchester University Press.

Ward J T, 1958, 'Revolutionary Tory: the life of Joseph Rayner Stephens of Ashton-under-Lyne (1805-1879)', *Transactions of the Lancashire and Cheshire Antiquarian Society* 68, 93-116.

Ward J T, 1966, 'The factory movement in Lancashire', *Transactions of the Lancashire and Cheshire Antiquarian Society* 75-6 (for 1965-6), 186-210.

Whetham E H, (ed), 1978, *The Agrarian History of England and Wales. Volume VIII. 1914-39*. Cambridge University Press.

Wild M T, 1970, 'The Saddleworth Parish Registers as a Source for the History of the West Riding Textile Industry during the Eighteenth Century', *Textile History 1* (for 1968-70), 214-32.

Wilkins-Jones C, 1978, *Tameside. An outline history of those parts of Lancashire and Cheshire now in Tameside Metropolitan Borough*. Tameside Metropolitan Borough Libraries & Arts.

Wilkins-Jones C, 1979, *Stalybridge in Old Photographs*. The Libraries and Arts Committee, Tameside Metropolitan Borough Council.

Williams C M (ed), 1991, *Guide to the Cheshire Record Office (and Chester Diocesan Record Office)*. Cheshire County Council.

Williams M with Farnie D A, 1992, *Cotton Mills in Greater Manchester*. Preston, Carnegie Publishing Ltd.

Wilson J F, 1991, *Lighting the Town. A Study of Management in the North-West Gas Industry 1805-1880*. London, Paul Chapman Publishing Ltd.

Young J, 1982, *Some aspects of the history of Denton and Haughton, Lancashire, prior to the eighteenth century*. Unpublished Local History Certificate dissertation, University of Manchester Dept of Extra Mural Studies.

Young J, 1985, 'Denton and Haughton in Tudor and Stuart Times', *in* Lock (ed), 14-26.

Index

Adamson, Hatchett & Acrow, engineers	110
Adamson, Joseph & Co, engineers	110
Adshead family, mill-owners	55-6, 133
Alma Iron Works	110
Alt Edge	11, 83, 89, 101, 108
Alt Hill	83
Altrincham	93, 122
Andrew, John, of Mossley, mill-owner	50, 165
Andrews, Giles and Mark, of Mossley, mill-owners	50
Angel Inn, Mottram	81

Ashton
Albion Church	143
Ann St	151-2
barracks	20
baths	23, 142
Bentinck St	147-8
Boodle St	99
Booth St	147-8
bridge	156-7
Cavendish St	147-8
Chester Square	131
Clarence Arcade	151
corn-mill	36, 145
court leet	13, 16
Crickety Lane	102, 137, 146
Currier Slacks Lane	102
Delamere St	5, 147-8
District Infirmary	22-3
George St	148
Grey St	147
Hamilton St	151-2
Henry Square	142, 147
Infirmary	144
Katherine St	86, 110, 147-8
local board	14, 19, 24
Manchester Rd	121, 142, 146
Margaret St	147-8
Market Avenue	148, 151
Market Hall	113
Market Place	15, 144, 147
mill-building syndicate	33, 38, 40, 64
Mill Lane	110, 146, 148
municipal borough	4, 7, 11, 13-15, 18, 21-4, 26, 35-7, 39, 57, 64, 66, 76, 110-11, 113-14, 118, 120, 127-32, 135-6, 142, 144-6, 149, 168, 170
New Wharf	119, 125, 147
Old Court House	16
Old Square	141, 146, 148
Old St	5, 137, 146-9
Old Wharf	111, 121
parish	4, 5, 10-11, 16, 39, 58, 83, 92, 98, 108, 152
Park Parade Bridge	129
poor law union	16
Portland Place	147-8
Portland St	129, 147-8
Razzles public house	146
St Michael's Parish Church	2, 5, 71, 141-2
St Michael's Square	16
Scotland St	5, 147
Stamford Arcade	75, 151
Stamford St	36, 75, 141, 146-9, 169
Stile Barn Rd	147
town	5-9, 11, 25, 28, 31, 33, 35-6, 40-1, 50, 55, 63, 72, 75, 82-3, 86, 89, 92-3, 98-103, 108, 110, 112-13, 117, 121, 137-41, 145-7, 152, 155-7, 163, 166
town hall	143-4
Town Lane	146-7
Trafalgar Square	147, 152
vestry	13
Warrington St	146-8
Waterworks Company	17, 132
Welbeck St	147-8
Wellington St	35, 149, 151

see also Collieries, Co-operative Societies, Gas Companies, Hugh Mason, Textile Sites

Ashton Canal	36, 39-41, 63, 65, 93, 98-9, 102-3, 109-10, 119, 122, 124-5, 154
Ashton Canal Warehouse	6-7, 13, 125
Ashton family, of Hyde, mill-owners	22, 25-6, 31, 44-5, 104-5, 110, 132-3, 140, 142, 145, 159, 170
Ashton Moss	86-7, 121, 127-8, 152

see also Collieries

Ashworth Lane, Mottram	46, 140
Astley Cheetham Public Library, Stalybridge	18
Astley family, lords of Dukinfield	26, 41, 96, 104, 130-1, 137, 156-7

Audenshaw
division	4, 10, 40, 66, 72, 82, 89, 93, 107, 111, 113, 120-1, 144
local board	17, 130
reservoirs	132, 152
Saxon's Lane End	121
UDC	11, 13, 17, 28, 35, 152

Barn Meadow Iron Works	110
Bateman & Sherratt, mine-owners	104
Bayley, James, mill-owner	56
Beat Bank Canal	99, 103, 122
Bellhouse, David, builder	113, 125
Bertenshaw family, hatters	70
Bevan's Works, iron makers	110
Bickerton, Henry Neild, engineer	110
Bolden, George & Co, mill-owners	43
Booth, Isaac, of Hyde, mill-owner	134
Booth, Joseph, of Broadbottom, grocer	115-17
Bostock, John	62-3, 116, 163
Boston, Ashton-under-Lyne	136
Braddock family, mine-owners	105
Bridge End ironworks	110
Brierley, Thomas, dyeworks-owner	41
British Electric Traction Company	130

Broadbottom
Benton Terrace	163
Brick Terrace	163
Lower Market St/Market St	115-16, 163
New St	163
Old St	163

Index

Travis Terrace	163
village	4, 6-7, 13, 57, 62, 107, 114-15, 117, 121, 127, 140, 161-2
Well Row	163

see also *Joseph Booth, Collieries, Co-operative Societies, Crescent Row, Summerbottom, Textile Sites*

Broad Oak Farm, Droylsden	155
Brookbottom, Mossley	50, 165-6
Brown, Thomas, mill-owner	55
Brundret, James, dyeworks-owner	39
Buckley, Abel, mill-owner	142-3
Buckley, Edmund, mill-owner	39-40
Buckley, Nathaniel, mill-owner	150
Buckley, Robert, mill-owner	52-3, 165
Buckley family, of Stalybridge, mill-owners and corn-millers	145
Byrom, Joseph & Sons, mill-owners	40
Calico Printers Association Ltd	57-8
Canals see *Ashton, Huddersfield, Peak Forest*	
Car Brook, Micklehurst	48, 50
Cardwell, Thomas, mill-owner	61, 105
Carr Farm	105
Castle Iron Works	110
Chadwick, Edward, mill-owner	36
Chadwick, John, mill-owner	36, 43
Chamber Hills	144
Chapman, John	93
Charlestown, Ashton	136, 138, 147
Cheetham, George, mill-owner	57, 133, 142, 145
Cheetham Park, Stalybridge	18, 45
Cheshire	2, 4-6, 20, 26, 48, 74, 80, 85-7, 89, 91, 93-4, 100, 120, 129, 145, 156, 159, 163, 166
Chew Valley, Saddleworth	132
Clarke family, of Hyde	85, 97-8, 159-60
Clegg, Samuel, gas engineer	132-3
Clementson, Edward and John, mill-owners	63
Cock Brook	36, 145
Cocke, Samuel, inn keeper	46
Collieries	
Ashton Moss Colliery	98, 101-2
Astley Deep Pit	104-5
Bayleyfield Colliery	104-5
Broadcar Colliery	102
Broad Oak Colliery	99, 102
Broomstair Colliery	102, 105
Chamber Colliery Company	103
Chapel Colliery	104-5
Daisyfield Colliery	104
Denton Colliery	3, 98-104
Dewsnap Colliery, Dukinfield	99, 104-5
Dog Lane Colliery	104
Dunkirk Coal Company	104
Dunkirk Colliery, Dukinfield	104
Dunkirk Colliery, Newton	104
Ellis Pit, Denton	101
Fairbottom Coal Company	98-9, 102
Fairbottom Colliery	9, 102, 109
Flowery Field Colliery	104
Glass House Fold Colliery, Haughton	102, 104
Hague/Hague Carr Colliery	97, 99, 105
Haughton Colliery	100, 102, 104
Hulme's Pit	98, 101
Hurst Knowl Colliery	102
Hyde Lane Colliery	99, 102, 104-5
Kingston Colliery, Hyde	101, 105
Ladder Pit, Denton	101
Leylands Colliery, Broadbottom	106-7
Lorsdfield Colliery	99
Mottram Colliery	99, 105
Muslin Street Colliery, Newton	104
New Heys Pit	102
Newton Wood Colliery	100, 104
Peacock Colliery	104
Rabbit Hole/Back Lane Colliery	104
Rocher New pit	98-9, 102
Rocher Old pit	98
Town Lane Colliery	104
Victoria Colliery, Dukinfield	104
Victoria Pit, Denton	104
Compstall Bridge	158
Co-operative Societies	114-15
Copley	167
Courtaulds	64
Cowley, Mr, mill-owner	39
Crescent Row, Broadbottom	58
Crows i' th' Wood	55
Cryer, Eli, ironworker	110
Dane Bank Farm	68-9, 153
Dane Bank hatting community, Denton	66, 140, 142, 153, 170

see also *J Woolfenden & Sons, under Hat Manufacturers*

Davies, Robert, mill-owner	41
Deanhead Farm	120
Dean House, Park Bridge	142, 152
Denton	
Annan St	67, 74, 76
Bright St	77, 140
Chapel	153
Crown Point	71, 121, 153
Heaton St	74, 76-7
Law St	74
local board	13, 16-17, 128, 133, 136, 153
Market Place	113
Taylor Lane	70
township	4, 7, 16, 43-4, 66-9, 73-4, 76, 96-100, 102-4, 110-13, 122, 140, 142, 152-3, 170
Two Trees Lane	102
UDC	11, 17, 28, 76, 130, 153
Wilton St	77-8, 140
Windmill Lane	153

see also *Collieries, Co-operative Societies, Dane Bank, Gas Companies, Hat Manufacturers, Textile Sites*

Doveholes limestone quarries	122, 124
Droylsden	
Bull's Head Inn	39
Copperas Works	39-40, 154
Edge Lane	154
Fairfield Rd	154
Greenside Lane	154
Lane Head	154
local board	16-17, 154
Market St	154
township	4, 16, 28, 31, 33, 66, 72-3, 92-3, 110-11, 113, 125, 127, 154
UDC	11, 13, 17, 39, 135, 154

see also *Co-operative Societies, Fairfield Moravian settlement, Gas Companies, Textile Sites*

Dukinfield	
bridge	41, 122

Index

Chapel Hill	155-6
Circus	132, 137, 156
Cuckoo Square	157
Fishpond Yard	132
Globe Lane	130, 157
hall	157
King St	140, 157
library	18
local board	13, 16, 36, 128, 133, 136
Moravian settlement	41, 155-6
municipal borough	4, 11, 14, 17-18, 130, 144, 170
New Chapel	132
Old Chapel	142, 148, 156
park	18, 145
town hall	143-5, 151
Town Lane	156-7
township	7, 10, 16, 19, 21, 26-7, 33, 35, 66, 76, 92, 96, 99-100, 104-5, 108, 110-13, 118, 122, 127, 129, 131-2, 142, 152, 156-7, 167, 169
Wharf St	157

see also Astley family, Co-operative Societies, Gas Companies, Textile Sites

Dukinfield family *see Astley family*

Dysart, earl of	26, 95
Egerton family, of Tatton	3, 26, 72, 87-8, 90-1
Etchells, Matthew, mill-owner	55
Etherow, River	45, 58, 61-2, 129, 162-3
Fairbottom	
Bobs	98
canal branch	109, 122, 124, 129
hamlet	91, 101, 154

see also Collieries

Fairfield	
Boys' Academy	39
Boys' Sunday School	39
Locks	125
Moravian settlement	39, 120, 127, 142, 154-5
Square	155
Faulkner, Matthew, mill-owner	55
Fernihough & Sons, iron makers	110
Fletcher family, mine-owners	102-4, 170
Flowery Field community	24, 44, 140, 159
Garforth, W & J, iron makers	110
Garside, John, mine-owner	104
Gas Companies	17, 133-4, 154, 167
Gee Cross	
Back Bower Lane	158
Fold	157
Grapes Inn	73
Joel Lane	68, 73, 158
Knott Lane	44, 158
Mottram Old Rd	44, 73, 158
Pole Bank Cottages	158
Stockport Rd	73, 158
village	9, 43-4, 66, 72, 74, 76, 132, 140, 142, 157-8, 160, 168

see also Textile Sites

Gerrards Brook	44
Gerrards Farm	44, 157
Glossop	
brook	43
township	45, 48, 118, 127, 130-1, 162

see also Textile Sites

Glyco Metal Co Ltd	111
Godley	
Green	86-7
reservoir	132
township	11, 16, 27, 43, 72, 77, 81, 86, 121, 127-8, 157, 160
Goodier, George, mill-owner	26
Gorton UDC	129-30, 136
Greenfield, Saddleworth	127, 132
Greenside Farm, Droylsden	39
Greenside Lane Farm, Droylsden	39
Guide Bridge	36, 41, 120, 127-8, 130, 140, 151
Hague, The	97-8, 100, 105
Hague Farm	26, 95, 105
Hall, Edward, mill-owner	55
Hall, John & Son, brick and tile makers	108, 112
Hammond, John, mill-owner	39
Hardy's Farm	103
Harewood Lodge	142
Harrison, Mr, of Stalybridge, mill-owner	133
Harrop, John, mill-owner	36
Harrop, Joseph, mill-owner	26
Hartshead	10, 35, 83, 89, 102, 112
Hat Manufacturers	
Ashworth's, of Denton, hatters	72
Associated British Hat Manufacturers	77
Bentley, John, Robert and Andrew, of Denton	72
James Bevan & Co Ltd	74
Bond's, of Denton	72
Mr Bradbury	152
Bromley & Peacock, of Denton	71
William Brown & Sons Ltd	74
Carlton Company	75
John Cheetham & Sons Ltd	74, 110
Cook, Smith & Co	74
Denton Hat Company	75
James Higinbotham & Sons	74, 79
Joseph Howe & Sons	67, 74, 76-7
J Moores & Sons	68, 74, 77, 153
Thornley & Booth Ltd	74-5
Joseph Wilson & Sons Ltd	77-9, 153
J Woolfenden & Sons	66, 153, 170

see also Dane Bank hatting community

Hattersley	
civil parish	11, 17, 130, 161
manorial court	13
township	4, 13, 16, 27, 66, 81-3, 89, 92-3, 121, 130
Haughton	
Green	70, 77, 88, 104, 153
local board	17
St Anne's Church	143
township	11, 13, 16, 43-4, 72-4, 100, 102, 104-5, 153, 158
Union St	73

see also Collieries, Textile Sites

Hawkyard, Joel, surveyor	147
Hazelhurst	35, 83, 100, 140
Heap family, farmers	83
Heaps, William, mill-owner	50
Heaton Norris	60, 103, 125, 127
Heginbottom, James, mill-owner	40
Heyrod	121
Hibbert family, of Hyde, mill-owners	134
Hillend estate, Mottram	26, 46, 95
Hilton, John, mine-owner	104
Hindley, Ignatius, mill-owner	39

196

Index

Hodge Cottage, Broadbottom	58-9
Hodge Hall, Broadbottom	58-9
Hollingworth	
brook	45, 162
local board	17
Manor House	162
Market St	162-3
moor	87
Moorfield Terrace	162
township	4, 6-7, 16, 26-7, 45-6, 61-2, 71, 73-4, 91, 105, 114, 117, 161-2
UDC	11, 17, 130, 162-3

see also Co-operative Societies, Textile Sites

Hollingworth Hall Farm	81, 88
Hollingworth Old Hall	89, 92
Hollinwood, Oldham	36, 39, 40, 122, 124
Hooley Hill	
Guide Lane	71-2, 152-3
Quebec	72, 152
village	69, 71-2, 152

see also Hat Manufacturers

Howard, Daniel, mill-owner	56
Huddersfield	121-2, 127
Huddersfield Canal	5, 50, 55, 119, 122, 124-5, 145, 166
Hulton family	98, 103
Hurst	
brook	36
local board	16-17
village	58, 75, 83, 98, 100, 130, 132, 152
UDC	11, 17, 35

see also Collieries, Co-operative Societies, Textile Sites, John Whittaker,

Hurst Clough, Mottram	105
Hyde	
Clarendon Place	79
Cooper St	74
George St	74
Great Norbury St	159
Hall	85, 88, 98
highway board	16-17, 24, 132, 136
Johnson Brook	110
Joint Waterworks Undertaking	132
Market Place	113, 158
Market St	158-60
Milk St	159
Mount St	79
municipal borough	4, 11, 14-15, 17-18, 26, 43, 45, 66, 130, 134, 168
park	18, 145
Stockport Rd	160
Thomas St	79
township	6, 7, 9, 11, 20-1, 26-8, 31, 33, 41, 44, 55, 69, 72, 74, 76, 85, 88, 92, 96, 98, 100, 102, 104-5, 108, 110-14, 117-18, 121-2, 127-9, 132-4, 137, 140, 142, 153, 157-8, 161, 169
Water St	74, 159

see also Collieries, Co-operative Societies, Gas Companies, Hat Manufacturers, Red Pump St, Textile Sites

Hyde, Abel, mill-owner	26
Hyde chapel	9, 142, 157, 159, 168
Hyde Hall, Denton	87
Hyde, Werneth and Newton Waterworks Company	132
Irish immigration	21, 27, 165
Kenworthy family	102, 143
Kershaw, Charles, mill-owner	140
Kershaw, Hugh, mill-owner	50, 55
Kershaw, Ralph and James, mill-owners	140
Knott Hill Reservoir, Ashton	132
Knott Lanes division	8, 10
Koch, C V, mill-owner	43
Lancashire	2, 4-6, 20, 31-3, 36, 45, 48, 53, 74, 80, 84, 86, 89, 91, 93, 96-7, 100, 120, 126, 137, 163, 166, 168
Latex Engineering Co	111
Leech, John, of Stalybridge, mill-owner	133
Leeds	41, 117, 123, 127
Lees, Joseph, mill-owner	26
Lees, Robert, mill-owner	41
Lees & Booth, mine-owners	102
Lees Factory, Newton	44
Lees family, ironworkers	108-10, 129, 142, 152, 170

see also Park Bridge

Leigh & Bradbury, mine-owners	102, 105
Leylands Farm	107
Limehurst rural district	11
Littlemoss	11, 35, 83, 89

see also New Row

Liverpool	25, 52, 123, 126
London	66-7, 73-4, 86, 121, 127, 133, 147
Longdendale	
estate	105
lordship of	93
UDC	11, 17, 113, 161
valley	28, 31, 33, 40, 45, 48, 60-1, 85-7, 93-5, 105, 112, 114-15, 120, 127, 133
Lowe, Joseph, mill-owner	39
Luzley	83
Macclesfield	
hundred	85-6, 91
town	90, 147
Mallalieu, Joseph, mill-owner	39
Manchester	
Belle Vue	25
Carriage & Tramways Company	17, 130
city	1, 11, 13-14, 18-20, 35, 39-41, 44, 57-8, 67, 69-72, 86, 89, 95-6, 99, 102, 108, 110, 112-13, 117-19, 120-3, 125-7, 129-35, 142, 147, 153, 155, 159
Eye Hospital	22
Infirmary	22
Regiment	20
Manchester & Salford Waterworks Company	132
Manchester to Salters Brook Turnpike	5, 40, 119, 121, 147, 162
Manor Farm	88
Marsland, Samuel, mill-owner	26
Mason, Hugh, mill-owner	18, 23-5, 140, 142-3, 151

see also Ashton baths, Oxford Mills community

Matley	
civil parish	11, 13, 17, 130, 161
township	16, 27, 83, 89, 92, 121
Matley, Samuel, print works owner	58-60, 107
Mayall family, mill-owners of Mossley	22-4, 33, 50, 52-3, 129, 142, 165-6
McDouall, Dr Paul Murray, Chartist campaigner	19, 20, 22
Medlock Valley	102, 109, 129, 152
Micklehurst	
division	10, 48, 50, 93-4, 163, 166
railway loop	127-9, 166

see also Car and Tum Brooks

Index

Millbrook	56, 62, 162
Miller, Mr, mill-owner	39
Moorgate Farm, Stalybridge	83
Moravian settlement *see Dukinfield, Fairfield*	
Moss, Edward, of Mottram, farmer	88, 95
Moss, Edward, mill-owner	58
Mossley	
Anthony St	140, 163
Arundel St	163, 165
Back Percy St	140
Beatties Buildings	165
Carrhill Rd	140, 163
Curzon St	140, 165
Granby Row	165
local board	10, 17, 22-3, 25, 28, 132, 163
Manor House	165
Market Place	163, 165
municipal borough	4, 11, 13, 15, 17, 53, 130, 133, 170
Old Market Place	140
Stockport Lane	163, 165
village	6-7, 31, 33, 35, 40-1, 48, 50, 63, 82-3, 85-7, 112-14, 121, 127-8, 140, 142, 152, 165-6
Waterton Lane	163, 165
see also Co-operative Societies, Textile Sites	
Mottram	
Back Lane	60-1, 161
Backmoor	97, 120, 161
local board	17, 162
Lower Market Place	74
Hillend Lane	121
manorial court	131
Market/Mottram St	60-1, 161
parish	8, 45, 71, 80
St Michael's Parish Church	2, 161
Tollemache estate	86, 89-90
township	4, 7, 13, 16, 26-7, 45-6, 58, 60-1, 66, 71, 73-4, 81, 85, 87-9, 92, 94-6, 98-100, 105, 112-14, 116-18, 120-1, 140, 153, 158, 161
village	5-6, 9, 82, 161
UDC	11, 17, 130, 162-3
see also Ashworth Lane, Collieries, Hillend estate, The Mudd, Old Post Office Farm, Textile Sites	
Mudd, The, Mottram	46, 105
Nalty, Mr, mill-owner	39
Nash, John, print works owner	36
National Gas Engine Co Ltd	110
New Row weaving community, Littlemoss	35
Newton	
Hall	88
Heath/Moor	44, 84, 98, 104, 136
local board	17
Lodge	145
Muslin St	44
Talbot Rd	160
township	11, 13, 16, 26, 43-5, 81, 85, 96, 100, 104-5, 110, 118, 127, 132, 157, 160, 169
see also Collieries, Textile Sites	
Newton, John, mine-owner	104
Newton House/Line Edge Reservoir	132
Old Clockhouse Farm, Droylsden	39
Oldham	11, 14, 50, 66, 98, 103, 121-2, 127, 129, 132, 134, 154
Oldham, J & Son Ltd, hat machine makers	110
Oldham, John, of Hyde, hatter	74
Oldham, Ashton & Hyde Electric Tramway Company	130, 135
Oldham family, of Mottram, hatters	71
Old Post Office Farm	60
Ollerenshaw, James, of Ashton, hatter	75
Ollerenshaw, Samuel, mill-owner	40
Orrell, John, mill-owner	55
Oxford Mills community	18, 24-5, 142, 151-2
Park Bridge	
Dean Terrace	152
Dingle Terrace	152
ironworking community	98, 108, 110, 122, 128-9, 142, 152
St James' church	152
Park Bridge ironworks	3, 109, 170
Park Hall Reservoir, Ashton	132
Parsonage Farm, Mottram	46, 105, 161
Peak Forest Canal	41, 43, 99, 110, 112, 124-5, 157-8
Perrin's, of Hyde, hat machine makers	69, 110
Phillips, Thomas, print works owner	36
Phoenix Iron Works	110
Pitt and Nelson public house, Ashton	25, 148
Platt, Robert, mill-owner	25
Platt, Thomas, mill-owner	50
Pole Bank Hall	142
Portland Basin	7, 113, 119, 122, 125
Portland Place	125
Quick/Quickmere	6, 10, 48, 92-3, 163, 165
Quick moor	86-7
Railway Companies	
Great Central	127, 130
see also Manchester, Sheffield & Lincolnshire	
Great Grimsby & Sheffield	127
Huddersfield & Manchester	124, 127
Lancashire & Yorkshire	57, 99, 117, 126
Leeds, Dewsbury & Manchester	127
London, Midland & Scottish	124
London & North Eastern	127
London & North Western	52, 57, 9, 103, 124, 126, 128-9
Manchester & Leeds	127
Manchester, Sheffield & Lincolnshire	57, 110, 127-8, 134, 157
see also Great Central	
Midland Railway Company	53, 128
Oldham, Ashton-under-Lyne & Guide Bridge	102, 109, 127, 129-30
Sheffield, Ashton-under-Lyne & Manchester	99, 117, 118, 124, 126-7
Sheffield & Lincolnshire Junction	127
Ralph Fold	43
Redfern, John & Sons	22, 63
Red Pump St, Hyde	9, 44, 158, 168
Reyner, Alfred, of Ashton, mill-owner	143
Rhodes Farm, Werneth	81
Ridgehill, Ashton	50, 83, 121
Robinson, Samuel, mill-owner	18
Rochdale Canal	112, 122
Rocher Vale	98
see also Collieries	
Roe Cross Farm	88
Rothwell, Peter, miner	104
Roughtown, Mossley	50, 165
Ryecroft Hall, Ashton	142

Index

Saddleworth	
parish	6, 10, 48, 50, 55, 83, 92, 163
township	6, 10, 121, 127, 130, 132
Sandiford, James, mill-owner	41
Schofield, John, mill-owner	63
Scholefield, James and Susan, millers	58
Shaw, Thomas, mine-owner	102, 104
Sheffield	11, 41, 121, 123, 129
Shepley Hall	36
Sheppard, William, mill-owner	45
Sidebotham family, of Hyde, mill-owners	44, 143, 158
Sidebottom, J, surveyor	147
Sidebottom family, of Longdendale, mill-owners	45-6, 48, 62-3, 140-2, 163
Sinderland Hall Farm	93
Smallshaw	131
Somers, J D, iron makers	110
Stalybridge	
Castle Hall	167
Cocker Hill	166
corn-mill	145-6
High St	167
library	142
local board	8, 10, 13, 19-21, 25, 28, 127
Market Hall	113, 167
Market St	166
Melbourne St	125
Mottram Rd	146, 166, 167
municipal borough	4, 11, 13, 15, 18, 33, 36, 43, 50, 53, 56, 64, 66, 76, 110, 114, 118, 128-9, 132-3, 135-6, 140, 145, 157-8, 167, 170
St Peter's Church	142
town hall	130
village	6-7, 30-1, 40-1, 55, 57, 72, 82-3, 92, 99, 104-5, 112-13, 117, 120-2, 125, 142, 147, 156, 167
Wakefield Rd	121, 167
see also Co-operative Societies, Gas Companies, Textile Sites	
Stalybridge, Hyde, Mossley & Dukinfield Tramways & Electricity Board (SHMD)	17, 64, 130-1, 135
Stamford, earls of	26, 92-3, 102, 144, 151
Stamford Arms public house, Ashton	25
Stamford estate	3-4, 81-2, 86, 89, 92-3, 98, 136, 147, 166-7
Stamford Park, Ashton	18, 145
Standedge	50, 121-2, 126-9
Stanfield, Richard, mill-owner	63
Stayley	
corn-mill	145
Hall	88
township	10-11, 13, 26-7, 45, 55, 81, 83, 85, 89, 92-3, 121
Stephens, Joseph Rayner, social reformer	19-20
Stockport	14, 19, 44, 57, 66-7, 69, 72-4, 103, 110, 117, 121-2, 127-8, 130, 147, 152-3, 158-9
Stott, Sidney, mill architect	64
Summerbottom weavers' cottages, Broadbottom	58, 163
Swindells, John, mill-owner	39, 58, 107, 162-3
Swindell's Fold, Godley	85
Swineshaw Brook	55
Swineshaw Valley	132
Swire, Samuel, mine-owner	102
Tame	
river	28, 31, 36, 41, 43-4, 48, 50, 52, 55, 88, 97-8, 101-2, 104, 110, 119, 125, 127-8, 131, 135, 145, 147, 153, 156-8, 165-7, 169
valley	41, 103, 122, 166, 170
Tatton estates in Tameside see Egerton family, Werneth	
Taylor Lang & Co, iron makers	110
Textile Sites	
Adsheads' Mill, Stalybridge	55
Albert Mill, Dukinfield	43
Albert Mill, Mossley	53, 63
Albion Mill, Droylsden	40
Albion Mill, Mossley	53
Albion Mills, Stalybridge	55
Alpha/Phoenix Mill, Denton	44
Andrew/Roughtown Mill, Mossley	50, 165
Angola Mill, Droylsden	40
Aqueduct Mill, Stalybridge	56
Arrowscroft Mill, Hollingworth	105
Astley Mill, Dukinfield	43
Atlas Mill, Ashton	38
Bankfield Mill, Ashton	22, 37, 63
Bankwood/Cheethams Mill, Stalybridge	57, 142
Barn Meadow Mills, Dukinfield	43, 157
Bayleyfield Mills, Hyde	44
Bent Mill, Hollingworth	48, 162-3
Black Rock Mill, Mossley	50
Border/Mossley Brow Mill, Mossley	53, 63
Boston Mill No 1, Hyde	44, 74, 134
Bottoms New/Bankside Mill, Mossley	50
Bottoms Old Mill, Mossley	52
Brassey's Mill, Ashton	37
Brick Mill, Mossley	50
Bridge Eye Mills, Dukinfield	43
Britannia Mill, Mossley	23, 52, 129
Broadbottom/Broad Mills	7, 29, 46, 61-3, 142, 162-3
Brunswick Mill, Mossley	52, 63
Buckton Vale Print Works, Mossley	30
Carr Mill, Mossley	50, 53
Carrfield Mill, Hyde	44, 159
Carrs/Whittaker's Mill, Ashton	37, 57
Castle Clough Mill, Mossley	50
Castle Mill, Stalybridge	57
Cavendish Mill, Ashton	37, 63, 65
Cedar Mill, Ashton	9, 38
Chapel Hill Mill, Dukinfield	41, 43
Clarence Mill, Stalybridge	57
Clough Mill, Mossley	50
Copley Mills, Stalybridge	56-7
Creswell/Carr Hill Mill, Mossley	53, 165
Croft Mill, Ashton	36
Croft Mill, Mossley	53
Crows i' th' Wood Mill, Stalybridge	56
Curzon/Alger Mill, Ashton	38
Doctor Mill, Mossley	50
Doctor's Factory, Gee Cross	44
Dog Kennel Mill, Hollingworth	45
Droylsden Copperas/Springfield Print Works	40
Droylsden Mills	40, 154
Dry Mill, Mottram	60-1
Dukinfield/Aqueduct Mill	157
Dukinfield Hall/Dog Lane Mill	43
Dukinfield Old Mill	41
Edge Lane Mill, Droylsden	32, 40
Fairfield cotton warehouse	39
Fairfield Dyeworks	40
Fairfield Mills	40, 154
Flash Brook Mill, Werneth	44
Flash Hall Mills, Ashton	36
Furnace Mill, Dukinfield	41

Index

Gee Cross/Apethorn/Linnet New Mill, Hyde	44, 158
Gerrards Mill	44
Godley Mill	44
Good Hope Mill, Ashton	57
Greencroft Mill, Hyde	44, 159
Greenfield Mill, Hyde	44, 79
Greenside Lane Dyeworks, Droylsden	39
Grosvenor Street Mills, Stalybridge	133
Hammond's Factory, Droylsden	39
Harper Mills, Ashton	36
Hart/Valley Mill, Mossley	50, 165
Heyrod Mill/Hartshead Print Works, Stalybridge	55, 57
Higher Mill, Stalybridge	55-6
Hodge Print Works	7, 30, 45, 48, 57-9, 107, 162-3
Hyde Mill	45
Johnson Brook Mill, Hyde	44
Kingston Mills, Hyde	44, 158
Lilley's Mill, Stalybridge	56
Limefield Mill, Broadbottom	163
Longlands Mills, Mossley	52-3
Lowe's Factory, Mottram	60-1
Lumb Mill, Droylsden	40
Mersey Mills, Hollingworth	162-3
Millbrook Mills, Hollingworth	45-6, 141
Milton Mills, Mossley	63
Minerva Mill, Ashton	38
New Hollins/Victoria Mill, Mossley	50
Old Hall Mill, Dukinfield	43
Oldham Stair/Hollins Mill, Mossley	50, 53
Old Soot Poke Mill, Stalybridge	30, 55, 166
Park Hall Mill, Ashton	36
Park Road Mill, Dukinfield	43
Phoenix Mill, Stalybridge	57
Platt's Mill, Mossley	50
Premier Mill, Stalybridge	33, 56-7, 64
Queen Mill, Dukinfield	43
Queen Street Mill, Mossley	50, 52-3
Quickwood/Woodend Mill, Mossley	52, 165
Ray Mill, Stalybridge	33, 57, 64
River Mill, Dukinfield	43
River Mill, Mossley	52
Riverside Mill, Stalybridge	57
Robinson Street Mill, Stalybridge	56-7
Rock Mill, Ashton	38
Roughtown Mill *see Andrew Mill*	
Royal Mill, Droylsden	40
St Helena's Mill, Dukinfield	40
Sandy Vale Bleach Works, Dukinfield	41, 43
Saxon Mill, Droylsden	40
Scout/New Scout Mill, Mossley	50, 52
Slack Mills, Hyde	44-5
Smeath Meadows/Waterton Mill, Mossley	50
South End Mills, Mossley	52
Spout Green Mill, Mottram	48, 102
Springbank Mill, Mossley	53
Spring Grove Mill, Stalybridge	57
Staley/Howard's/Castle Hall Mill, Stalybridge	57
Staley New Mills, Stalybridge	56, 133
Stalybridge Mill	57
Stalybridge Woollen/Corn Mill	6, 56
Stamford Mill, Mossley	53
Tameside Mills, Dukinfield	43
Tame Valley/Crescent Mills, Dukinfield	43
Texas Mill, Ashton	38
Throstle Bank Mill, Hyde	159
Throstle Nest, Ashton	36
Tower Mill, Dukinfield	43
Tudor Mill, Ashton	38
Union Mill, Dukinfield	43, 157
Victor Mill, Stalybridge	33, 57, 64
Victoria Mill, Dukinfield	40, 43
Victoria Mills, Droylsden	154
Victoria Mills, Mossley	53
Wagstaffe's Factory, Mottram	6, 60-1
Wareing's Mill, Stalybridge	56
Waterside/Alma Mill, Dukinfield	43
Water Street Mill, Stalybridge	31, 55
West End Mill, Broadbottom	48, 162
Westhill Mill, Mossley	53
Wharf Mill, Hyde	44
Whittaker's Mill *see Carrs Mill*	
Thorncliffe Hall estate	48, 89
Thornley, William, mine-owner	105
Tintwistle	5, 10, 16, 88, 91-5, 121, 130
Tollemache family	3, 26, 58, 88, 92-5, 105, 107, 162-3
Tombottom Reservoir, Ashton	132
Torkington Farm	103
Tum Brook, Micklehurst	48, 50
Uppermill	50, 121-2
Victoria Boiler Iron Works	110
Wadsworth & Co Ltd, textile machine manufacturers	110
Wagstaffe, J G & Co, ironworkers	110
Wagstaffe, John, farmer and mill-owner	46, 56, 60-1, 161
Wainwright, George, mill-owner	43
Walker, Ashworth & Linney, of Denton, hatters	74
Walker, Thomas and William, of Denton, silk hatters	73
Walker Fold	43
Wareing, J & W, mill-owners	56
Warhill, Mottram	87, 97, 105, 142, 161
Waterside Iron Works	110
Wednesough Green, Hollingworth	46, 74, 162
Werneth	
Egertons of Tatton, estate of	68, 90-2, 158
Low	44, 87, 89
township	10-11, 13, 43, 72, 80-1, 86, 89, 91, 122, 132, 157, 160
see also Textile Sites	
Wheatsheaf public house, Ashton	23
Whitehall, Mossley,	142
Whittaker, John, mill-owner	23-4, 102
Wilbraham family	93
Wild, William, mine-owner	104
Wilkinson, James, mill-owner	56
Wilson Brook	44, 158
Wilton & Co, hat machine makers	69, 110
Wood, Edward, of Ashton, hatter	75
Wood, John, mill-owner	36
Woodhead	120, 123, 126-7
Woolley & Hampson, mine-owners	104-5
Wright, William, surveyor	147
Wych, Richard, mill-owner	44
Yorkshire	48, 86, 93, 117, 126, 163